Contemporary Pakistani Fiction in English

Looking at a wide selection of Pakistani novels in English, this book explores how literary texts imaginatively probe the past, convey the present, and project a future in terms that facilitate a sense of collective belonging. The novels discussed cover a range of historical movements and developments, including pre-20th century Islamic history, the 1947 partition, the 1971 Pakistani war, the Zia years, and post-9/11 Pakistan, as well as pervasive themes, including ethnonationalist tensions, the zamindari system, and conspiracy thinking.

The book offers a range of representations of how and whether collective belonging takes shape, and illustrates how the Pakistani novel in English, often overshadowed by the proliferation of the Indian novel in English, complements Pakistani multi-lingual literary imaginaries by presenting alternatives to standard versions of history and by highlighting the issues English-language literary production brings to the fore in a broader Pakistani context. It goes on to look at the literary devices and themes used to portray idea, nation and state as a foundation for collective belonging. The book illustrates the distinct contributions the Pakistani novel in English makes to the larger fields of postcolonial and South Asian literary and cultural studies.

Cara Cilano is Professor of English at the University of North Carolina Wilmington, USA. She is the author of *National Identities in Pakistan: The 1971 war in contemporary Pakistani fiction* (Routledge 2010).

Routledge contemporary South Asia series

Contemporary Pakistani Fiction in English

Idea, nation, state

Cara N. Cilano

Routledge
Taylor & Francis Group

LONDON AND NEW YORK

First published 2013
by Routledge
2 Park Square, Milton Park, Abingdon, Oxon OX14 4RN

Simultaneously published in the USA and Canada
by Routledge
711 Third Avenue, New York, NY 10017

Routledge is an imprint of the Taylor & Francis Group, an informa business

British Library Cataloguing in Publication Data
A catalogue record for this book is available from the British Library

Library of Congress Cataloging in Publication Data
Cilano, Cara.
Contemporary Pakistani fiction in English: idea, nation, state / Cara N. Cilano.
  p. cm. – (Routledge contemporary South Asia series; 67)
Includes bibliographical references and index.
1. Pakistani fiction (English)–History and criticism. 2. Group identity–Pakistan.
I. Title.
PR9540.4C55 2013
823'.920995491–dc23   2012039543

ISBN: 978-0-415-68276-3 (hbk)
ISBN: 978-0-203-55224-7 (ebk)

Typeset in Times New Roman
by Deer Park Productions

MIX
Paper from
responsible sources
FSC   FSC® C013056
www.fsc.org

Printed and bound in Great Britain by
TJ International Ltd, Padstow, Cornwall

to Lee,
friend and inspiration

Contents

Acknowledgments

Many people lent me their time or helped me make time to see this project to publication. Students from several courses over the past few years worked with me to think through a number of the novels I discuss here. Participants at more than one South Asia Conference in Madison, WI, gave my ideas a fair hearing and provided invaluable feedback. I'm honored to work with Dorothea Schaefter and Jillian Morrison at Routledge, who have both been supportive and encouraging. My semester at Swansea University allowed me the opportunity to write for long periods in the most conducive environment. This book will always bring me back to Mumbles.

I am also grateful to the people who allowed my life over the past two years to be about more than this book. My parents, Marc and Sheri, Lisa, Chris and Heidi, Todd: they all reminded me that I am a daughter and sister, too. Sammy, Sofia, and Benjamin (and Max) filled those few days away from research and writing with laughter and lots of fun.

With good humor and generosity, Lee has been my touchstone for years and years. I'm just trying to keep up.

Introduction

Idea, Nation, State

Spoiler alert: this book concludes with an argument advocating the end of
national identities. This argument, developed through an analysis of Kamila
Shamsie's 2009 novel *Burnt Shadows*, doesn't lobby for cosmopolitanism or
hyphenated identities. Instead, the argument concentrates on the novel's protagonist, Hiroko Tanaka, a Japanese woman who survives the US bombing of
Nagasaki and, subsequently, also lives through the 1947 partition of India and
Pakistan, Islamization under Zia, the Afghan War, and 9/11. Appalled by the lure
of collective mythologies, the expense of national belonging, and the brutalities
committed by states to uphold these myths and insure security, Hiroko insists on
a "human" identity that takes shape through the recognition of historical experience as an equalizing force, suggesting along the way that historical narratives
can bear meaning outside of national confines.

At first glance, my analysis of *Burnt Shadows* appears to have led me far
afield from the titular focus of *Contemporary Pakistani Fiction in English: Idea,
Nation, State*. After some consideration, however, this reading of *Burnt Shadows*
illustrates one of the ways literary narratives can operate in a broader field of
representation: as an imaginative alternative to dominant forms of identification.
Thus, similar to Ayesha Jalal's call for "a study of the past through rigorous
investigative methods of critical inquiry" that would cultivate a "[c]ritical awareness of Pakistan's present problems…and help create the political will…to chart
a future" ("Past" 9, 20), *Contemporary Pakistani Fiction in English* explores how
literary texts imaginatively probe the past, convey the present, and project a
future in terms that facilitate a sense of collective belonging. The three terms
listed in my subtitle—idea, nation, and state—motivate these explorations, as
they attract or repel the attachments necessary to formulate a collective identity
or sense of belonging to Pakistan. The literary texts I discuss offer a range of
representations of how and whether this collective belonging takes shape. That is,
these literary analyses do not forward a single definition of Pakistaniness nor
construct a theoretical model that applies across the more than two dozen fictions
examined here. Instead, they offer readings that conjure a myriad of possibilities,
creating a spectrum that runs from a reinforcement of dominant modes of belonging to a reinvention of the terms of collective attachments. This variety, then,
challenges assumptions about Pakistan's "failure" as an idea or a nation or a state.

In their avoidance of such assumptions, these analyses contribute to Naveeda Khan's against the grain reading of the discursive framing of Pakistan as a "failure," which allows her to identify how "failure" can invite a recognition of the state's constructedness, can present an "opportunity to dream of alternative modes of association," and/or can prompt a consideration of "the threats and possibilities of the realm of foreignness within the nation-state as within the self" (1–2).

Before detailing my methodology, I want to specify how my analyses conceptualize idea, nation, and state. In the Pakistani context, these three terms interrelate; the boundaries between them blur. For the sake of clarity, however, I want to untangle these concepts momentarily. For my purposes, the idea of Pakistan holds a very specific historical meaning through its reference to the version of Muslim nationalism promoted by the Muslim League in the final years of British rule in South Asia. The "two-nation" theory, an argument that India's Muslims represent a unique and separate community, rests at the base of this idea (Jalal, "Past" 10). As the League negotiated with the All-India National Congress and the British through the 1930s and 1940s, "community" became "nation" (hinting at one way the line between the concepts of idea and nation blurs). Farzana Shaikh asserts that the views expounded by various Muslim League luminaries, especially Muhammad Iqbal and Muhammad Ali Jinnah, facilitated this shift as they built upon the foundations of nineteenth-century reformers, such as Sayyid Ahmad Khan (29–40).[1] The idea of Pakistan, according to Shaikh, proved enticing for some because of its promise to provide a "homeland" for India's Muslims and, for others, to provide a safe haven for Islam (34–7): "the idea of a 'homeland' exercised, as it still does, a powerful hold on the Pakistani imagination" (38).[2] As an abstraction, the idea of Pakistan draws a deep affective attachment, which helps account for the frequency with which the idea and its primary proponent—Jinnah—are mythologized as Pakistan's origin and founder, respectively. Portraits of Jinnah appear several times throughout the fictions analyzed here, including in Daniyal Mueenuddin's *In Other Rooms, Other Wonders*, Mohammed Hanif's *A Case of Exploding Mangoes*, and HM Naqvi's *Home Boy*, working metonymically to remind characters and readers alike of the power of these myths.

Beneath the abstraction's haze, however, lies a more contentious history. Jalal points out that, while "Indian Muslims shared a common religious identity, [they] were hardly united in their politics, which were more often defined by class, regional and ideological affiliations" ("Past" 10). These divergent politics force a recognition that, as Naveeda Khan states, "the demand for Pakistan did not arrive on the crest of widespread support but on a patchwork of agreements and horse trading amongst Muslim elites…" (6). There was neither political consensus nor "any mandate for [Pakistan's] creation" (Naveeda Khan 6). Mehr Nigar Masroor's *Shadows of Time* and Mumtaz Shah Nawaz's *The Heart Divided* animate these reservations and ambivalences through their characters' political (un)involvement in the Muslim League or the Congress. Beyond these political differences, one could also qualify the extent to which religious identities were shared, as hindsight testifies to the vast differences in Islamic practices across what became the geographical expanse of Pakistan. Many of these fictions, including all the volumes in Tariq Ali's Islam Quintet and Uzma Aslam Khan's *The Geometry of God*, value these differences, thus challenging any universal definition of "Muslim" or "Islam." Jalal recognizes these diverse practices as one of the "contradictions" that remain unresolved as Muslim nationalism achieved territorialization, leaving the nation of Pakistan "struggl[ing] to define an identity that is both Islamic and national" ("Past" 11). These "historical facts" do not "corroborate" official Pakistani nationalism (Jalal, "Past" 10) and, as a result, call attention to instances when the idea of Pakistan is idealized and mythologized.

The differences between how the idea of Pakistan is mythologized, on the one hand, and the circumstances that surround the idea's genesis and deployment, on the other, complicate the transition from idea to nation that occurred in 1947. Partition's genocidal violence, for instance, sullies any triumphalism over having achieved independence. This violence strained the two new nations' bureaucratic resources, as well as their populations' humanity. Further, as Vazira Fazila-Yacoobali Zamindar argues, "[T]he bureaucratic violence of drawing political boundaries and nationalizing identities" (2) protracted the lethal violence of 1947, creating a "long Partition" that "unsettles [the] national closure" (7) usually associated with the achievement of nationhood. Ali Sethi's *The Wish Maker*, Sorayya Y. Khan's *Five Queen's Road*, and Maniza Naqvi's *A Matter of Detail* represent this bureaucratic violence through characters who inhabited the Muslim majority areas of northwest India before the 1947 partition and, thus, experience a curious displacement of identity afterward despite never having left "home." Zamindar's emphasis on how the state's actions at the time of partition—i.e., the drawing of boundaries and the documentation of citizens—impact the consolidation of the nation shows how all three concepts work in concert or at cross purposes and, thus, always influence how citizens envision their connection to any of the terms individually. As an illustration of the interrelations between idea, nation, and state, the complications accompanying the attainment of independence in August 1947 also point toward an array of possible sites for affective attachment or repellence.

The "nation" of Pakistan represents, in part, the territorialization of the idea and also the articulation through official nationalist discourses of what it means to be Pakistani. The term's usage here refers both to these historical developments and to collective social formations grounded in Pakistan that may run counter to official nationalist discourses. As is well known, the British partitioned both Punjab and Bengal, creating a cleaved nation separated by one thousand miles of enemy territory. Initially comprised of five provinces—Punjab, Sindh, Balochistan, the Northwest Frontier Province, and Bengal—Pakistan as a territorialized entity embodied an irony: under British rule, these geographical areas were predominantly Muslim and, not coincidentally, not all strongholds for the Muslim League. The Indian Muslims, called muhajirs, who did migrate to the newly created Pakistan came from Muslim minority areas that remained a part of India. Pakistan's topographic and demographic realities vex any attempt to address Etienne Balibar's question regarding how individuals are "nationalized, or in other words, socialized in the dominant form of national belonging" (346–7). Nationalist discourses certainly forward this socialization process but do not guarantee it. One of the unique aspects of the creation of the nation of Pakistan is that the political party that dominated the negotiations for independence, the Muslim League, automatically assumed leadership in the new nation. As a result, the League's version of Muslim nationalism became Pakistan's prevailing nationalism. This discursive continuity provides both the origin and the telos necessary for the construction of a national identity, for, as Balibar asserts, "[p]roject and destiny are the two symmetrical figures of the illusion of national identity" (338). Representations of unity through a shared Muslim identity carried over from Muslim to Pakistani nationalism, as did the privileging of Urdu over the regional languages. Yet, according to Jalal, "Despite a well-orchestrated official nationalism, Pakistan ever since its creation has been searching for moorings somewhere in the twilight zone between myth and history" ("Past" 9). Part of the disjuncture between myth and history derives from the fact that, as I note above, religious practices varied, and the Pakistani government has had no great success in defining "Islam" nor its relation to national identities or to the state. Further, the imposition of Urdu, a non-territorialized language, created friction between the center and the provinces almost immediately. These factors prompt Amina Yaqin to conclude that, as a nation, Pakistan "is different from that…integrated 'Imagined Community,' as theorized by Benedict Anderson, [which] com[es] together through a common language and the rise of a homogenizing print capitalism" (115). Along what lines, then, does integration into a shared national belonging take place in Pakistan? According to Balibar, "the question of the nation form…is, at bottom, the question of knowing in what historical conditions it is possible to institute such a thing" (345). To refine this point somewhat, understanding the possibility of integration (not homogenization) is a question of knowing how narratives, including literary ones, represent the historical conditions surrounding "such a thing."

Official nationalism and alternative constructs of the nation encourage integration through a variety of affective attachments. Several aspects of Muslim nationalism, including its emphasis on a homeland, retain their appeal as Pakistani nationalism re-articulates them. Muhajir identities manifest most explicitly the pull exerted by the hope of a homeland. According to Shaikh, the homeland idea "bears all the hallmarks of a modern restatement of the Prophetic migration, complete with the sacrifices and sufferings endured by a beleaguered community forced to abandon their hearth and home" (38). Steeped in religious connotations, muhajir identities often come across as the most "true" definition of Pakistaniness. Shamsie's *Burnt Shadows* incorporates the power of the muhajir mythology to illustrate how its characters' establish a sense of belonging to Pakistan. In contrast to these visions of an ideal or true definition of national belonging, other articulations of the nation reflect a greater sensitivity to the linguistic, cultural, religious, and social diversities in the areas that comprise Pakistan. Mohsin Hamid's *The Reluctant Fundamentalist* and Shamsie's *Kartography* both cast a vision of a democratic Pakistan that draws on the strength that can come from difference, while Bapsi Sidhwa's *Cracking India* represents minority existence within the new nation's borders. Between the one and the many, competing claims of belonging emerge, for instance, in the form of a "sons of the soil" argument, a position that often draws from a long colonial history. Nadeem Aslam's *Seasons of the Rainbird* and Moni Mohsin's *The End of Innocence* feature characters whose identities take shape largely due to connections to the land that long pre-date the creation of Pakistan, thereby introducing a different definition of the nation. Other monied—but not necessarily landed—interests similarly make aggressive claims to belonging, testifying to the significant chasm between the privileged and the poor in Pakistan. Hamid's *Moth Smoke*, Adam Zameenzad's *The 13th House*, and Shahbano Bilgrami's *Without Dreams* craft such a class-focused vision from both sides of the divide. In all of its forms, the nation continues to resonate, but, significantly, not all alternatives to Pakistani nationalism bend toward greater inclusiveness. Imaginative retellings of the Pakistani nation, then, rely upon an assortment of political and ideological perspectives, perhaps substantiating Naveeda Khan's assessment that the state has not "successfully naturalis[ed]" a "single vision" of the nation (14).

Both theoretically and in the specific case of Pakistan, connections exist between the nation and the state. Take Naveeda Khan's assertion regarding the state's lack of success in "naturalising" a single vision of the nation, for instance. Her point speaks to how state institutions and functions can concretize the nation's abstraction by supporting citizens and facilitating day-to-day existence. The inverse also applies, and here's where Naveeda Khan's argument gestures: the state can also undermine the nation through its inability to cultivate and sustain civil society. According to Kamran Asdar Ali, such fissures between state and nation have arisen somewhat ironically in Pakistan, for, as much as the Muslim League "sought to transcend divisions among Muslims through the symbol of the emergent state and the formation of the moral sovereign, the diversity of people's lives and the particularistic cultural experiences remained in perpetual tension to this order" ("Progressives" 3). Ali's assessment of the Pakistani context reflects a broader theoretical point about the relationship between states and nations. In an effort to approach the interrelations between the two concepts, Philip Abrams uses the terms "state-system" and "state-idea." "State-system" refers to the "internal and external relations of political and governmental institutions" (Abrams 75) and, thus, includes the military, the civil service, and other bureaucratic entities. "State-idea" refers to the representations that legitimate the state's rule and role through encouraging collective identification in the nation (75).[3] This process of legitimation through representation (discursive not electoral) serves a key role in bridging state and nation. Matthew Hart and Jim Hansen emphasize how "legitimation can...be accomplished by using language and culture to provide a conceptual and emotional unity between state and people..." (506). Literature and other forms of artistic production can promote collective identifications, moving the idea of the nation away from traditional notions of consanguinity and soil and toward "organiz[ation] under a single government" (Hart and Hansen 505). In this way, culture can help bind nation and state just as much as it can stand in opposition to one or both. At base, culture helps "manufacture... consent" (Hart 1066), be it to the state's power, the nation's emotional appeal, and/or an alternative affectively attractive formation.

Within this context of legitimation through cultural production, *Contemporary Pakistani Fiction in English* specifies its interest in the state through an exploration of the "everyday state," which is a concept that encompasses the "function[s] of the state in everyday life, where it [is] actually lived by ordinary people..." (Sherman, Gould, and Ansari 2). As literary genres, novels and short fiction lend a distinct perspective to the state's functions on-the-ground, as these forms' very development signals a turn away from the epic's grand sweep toward the more ordinary, mundane, and individually focused. To remark upon the genres' particular characteristics is not, however, to privilege them as unmediated reflections of actual life. Rather, as James Wood holds, "fiction is both artifice and verisimilitude" (xiii), a combination achieved as the fiction "inherits" the "language of the world" and "turn[s] it into novelistic style" through literary devices and a variety of processes, such as the selection of detail (35). Thus, while governing practices, specific laws, and bureaucratic institutions matter, my analyses pay more attention to how fiction imagines the experience of these practices, laws, and institutions. In this way, the "everyday state" advances what John Marx describes as a "more diverse sense of the state [, which in turn] suggests a different notion of state power than that associated with the rule of law" (606). The benefit of a focus on the "everyday state," in Naveeda Khan's view, is that it "yields a differentiated milieu, a complex range of unexpected turn of events [sic] leading to different outcomes" (22). Novels such as Khushwant Singh's *Train to Pakistan*, Saad Ashraf's *The Postmaster*, and Durdana Soomro and Ghazala Hameed's *Bengal Raag*, for example, all attest to the positive contributions of the state to their characters' formulations of collective belonging, while Shamsie's *Broken Verses* and Bina Shah's *The 786 Cybercafé* highlight the state's corruption and, thus, its repellent features. These differing representations illustrate David Gilmartin's claim regarding how a focus on the everyday brings to light the tensions between the idealized nation and the realities of the state, which "makes social (and one might extend this to say, political) life possible" ("Living" 523). Nadeem Aslam's *The Wasted Vigil*, as its title suggests, concentrates on these tensions between the ideal and the real through its decades-spanning representations of US–Pakistan–Afghanistan relations, illuminating the tragic disillusionment that can follow from the irreconcilability of nation, state, and affective attachment. My analyses' attention to the "everyday state," then, helps concretize the abstractions of both the idea of Pakistan and the nation as sites of collective belonging.

Another term in my title—English—also merits elaboration. For several decades now, the use of English in postcolonial settings around the world has garnered much commentary. Ngũgĩ wa Thiong'o's 1986 essay "The Language of African Literature" argues that literature written in English by Africans can't be considered "African Literature," for "African literature can only be written in the African languages, that is, the languages of the African peasantry and working class, the major alliance of classes in each of our nationalisms and the agency for the coming inevitable revolutionary break with neo-colonialism" (163). With a clear viewpoint on literature's role in politics, Ngũgĩ denies "Afro-European" literature agency and authenticity; instead, this category of literature expands colonial traditions, becoming British or French literature. In his infamous introduction to *Mirrorwork: 50 Years of Indian Writing in English, 1947–1997*, Salman Rushdie counters the impulse behind Ngũgĩ's denial, arguing that, while some perceive Indian writing in English as a "postcolonial anomaly," the "bastard child of Empire" (x), the language used in this category of literary production has, like Urdu, "become an Indian language" (xi). Admittedly, Rushdie's assessment that "'Indo-Anglian' literature represents perhaps the most valuable contribution India has yet made to the world of books" provoked a backlash (viii). Nevertheless, his historicization of English language literary production beggars charges of inauthenticity.[4] Commentators in Pakistan rehearse many of the same points in their debates over the place of English in the country's cultural productions. Replicating the denial argument, Ashfaq Ali Khan claims, "For over a hundred years English has been the instrument of foreign exploitation in this country" (2). By turns, AA Khan continues, English makes the Pakistani a "slave" of the British, while it also "put[s] a wall" between English and non-English speaking Pakistanis (3).[5] AA Khan appears to historicize English's presence in South Asia, but he does so only to deride the language as a colonial holdover, a trend Muneeza Shamsie identifies as a force that marginalizes English language literary production (xi). Many others also contest the charge of inauthenticity AA Khan levies. Alamgir Hashmi, for instance, holds that English in Pakistan has "outstripped its colonial origins" ("Pakistani" 50), while Claire Chambers points out that, for many writers who went through English-medium schools in Pakistan or elsewhere, English is "their strongest language" (122). In the context of Pakistan's multi-lingual population, Ankhi Mukherjee claims that English-language literature "put[s] in place new structures of difference" (280), necessitating a continual critical re-evaluation of relations between center and periphery, a process that would recognize the legitimacy and encompass all of Pakistan's languages.

With *Contemporary Pakistani Fiction in English*, I contribute to this ongoing discussion over the place of English language literary production in Pakistan. Rather than simply planting my flag in the ground of "outstripped colonial origins," I want to explore what's at stake in recognizing English language literature as belonging to a multi-lingual Pakistani literary tradition. What "diversity" signifies is central to this exploration. Aamir Mufti identifies a false dichotomy involving the place of English language literary production in the "institution of world literature":

> On the one hand, Anglophone literary expression, the end product of an epochal historical process of assimilation, is packaged in the world literary system…as an instance of pure diversity; on the other, Indian languages, especially the nationalized forms of Urdu and Hindi, stake their claim to authentic national expression against the alien presence of English. In fact neither end of this polarity can do the work it is marshaled to do within the globalizing cultural logics of the late-capitalist world.
>
> (492)

Mufti's skepticism over the insufficiency of these polarities derives from how the tensions between these types of literary production emerged in the first place. Orientalism, that vast discursive system stemming from the long history of the colonial encounter, Mufti contends, "made possible…the appearance of the latter group of languages [i.e. Urdu and Hindi] and textual traditions for the first time within the structures and terms of the former [i.e. English]" (493). The projects associated with colonialism and the discourses contributing to Orientalism manufacture the field that connects English, Urdu, and Hindi literary production, which Mufti calls "the plane of equivalence that is literature" (493). This production of a common location—which isn't to say that these literatures are equally positioned—illustrates how "'diversity' itself—national, religious, civilizational, continental—is a colonial and Orientalist problematic…" (Mufti 493). Mufti's argument deflates claims to authenticity, indeed, discredits the "authentic" as a category, by highlighting the opposition's conditions of emergence. The promotion of Urdu and Hindi, in Mufti's example, as the proper and suitable "nationalized forms" for literary production in Pakistan and India, gathers its potency through the encounter with English, not outside or independent of it. "Diversity," then, is less coincidental variety and more historical product, rife with power dynamics and competing impulses.

Any recognition of English language literature as part of Pakistan's multilingual traditions must, then, account for this historical production and its attendant power dynamics. There's no gainsaying the English language's association with privilege in Pakistan, nor with the reality that publishing in English grants a considerably larger reading public for writers. Both of these points speak to the power dynamics associated with English in Pakistan. With respect to identity, though, the conversation changes somewhat. Mufti's point about "diversity," embodied in the putatively polar opposition of English vs. Urdu and Hindi, necessitates identifying the historical parameters within which definitions of Pakistaniness take shape, since Urdu is the language or "national form" bonded to this national identity. Amina Yaqin argues that this "national form" needs to align with official Pakistani nationalist ideologies:

> [F]or the Urdu intellectual cultural vision to be in accord with the ideological nation, it ought to portray the Pakistani "self" as different, "Othering" the

national self from the rival neighbor India and imagining a unique cultural heritage.

(118)

Yaqin's point stretches back to the appeal the idea of Pakistan possesses: that India's Muslims represent a unique community turned nation. To maintain and justify this uniqueness, Yaqin contends, requires a self-propelled "Othering" vis-à-vis India. No sameness can exist. But, as Yaqin observes, sameness does exist across the border, both in terms of the Muslims who became Indians and the use of Urdu in India both before and after partition (118–19). Ambivalence results from the tensions between ideological dictates and historical realities (Yaqin 119). As the vitriol of anti-English arguments indicate, sharing this language with non-Pakistanis, including Indians, represents a similar ideological challenge to nationalist discourses: how to differentiate or Other the Pakistani "self" from other English speakers so as to bolster Pakistan's uniqueness and its founding mythologies? In other words, to admit the legitimacy of English language literary production, indeed of Pakistan's entire non-Urdu literary production, requires a reckoning with the "realm of foreignness within the nation as within the self," to borrow Naveeda Khan's words again (2). Such a reckoning bears no foregone conclusions, as the literary analyses that follow attest, but it does foreground the ambivalence Yaqin identifies. And that ambivalence helps make plain how power works in the articulation of identities and the assignment of affective resonance.

Contemporary Pakistani Fiction in English joins Tariq Rahman's 1991 *A History of Pakistani Literature in English* as the only book-length studies on this topic. Called "encyclopedic" by Claire Chambers (123), Rahman's contribution constructs a chronological history interspersed with chapters devoted to Ahmed Ali, Zulfikar Ghose, and Bapsi Sidhwa, along with additional chapters focused on genres other than fiction. Expansive and indispensible as a resource, Rahman's book also situates Pakistani English language literature in the context of other Third World literatures, finding the former less responsive to history and not as political as its African and Caribbean counterparts, for example (*History* 224, 228). Rahman works with a "loose rather than strict[,] cultural rather than political" definition of "Pakistani" (*History* 11), allowing him to consider Ali's association with the All-India Progressive Writers Association (*History* 31), Ghose's diasporic "alienation and deracination" (*History* 89), and Sidhwa's representations of the Pakistani Parsi community (*History* 125). While acknowledging a liberal tendency throughout, Rahman nonetheless expresses some disappointment at the English language tradition's general lack of direct engagement with the major events of Pakistani history, finding fault in writers' failure to fictionalize Jinnah, the Ayub era, the 1965 and 1971 wars, and Zia's military regime (*History* 225–7).

Far from exhaustive, my own contribution maintains a strong interest in history but diverges from Rahman's project in how it envisions the connection between historical events and literary narratives. In each chapter, I center a major historical event or development. My literary analyses all share three primary concerns: how the literary texts represent the event or development; how the literary treatment of this event or development informs the fictions' portrayal of idea, nation, and/or state as a suitable foundation for collective belonging; and what literary devices or themes the fictions use to articulate their affective attachments to shared identifications. Chapter 1 focuses on the 1947 partition in Khushwant Singh's 1956 *Train to Pakistan*, Mumtaz Shah Nawaz's 1957 *The Heart Divided*, Bapsi Sidhwa's 1988/1991 *Cracking India*, Mehr Nigar Masroor's 1987 *Shadows of Time*, Sorayya Y. Khan's 2009 *Five Queen's Road*, and Saad Ashraf's 2004 *The Postmaster*. No single vision of affective attachment emerges from these novels taken as a whole. Rather, the point is to recognize the multiple forms of belonging these fictions promote: some, like Singh's novel, highlight the necessity of the state, while others, like Masroor's, decry its totalitarianism. Indeed, all the chapters are similarly inconsistent, which is to say, the analyses argue for a ranging understanding of Pakistani identities rather than impose a single argument or definition as a gold standard. Chapter 1 is, however, somewhat anomalous, as I identify a different literary device or theme in my exploration of each fiction that I then tie to a subsequent chapter; the remaining chapters are unified by a focus on either device or theme.

In my analysis of *Train to Pakistan*, I concentrate on how Singh's portrayal of region—the Punjab—through his conjuration of the fictional village, Mano Majra, illustrates the interworkings of regional practices, bureaucratic structures, and political agendas. These interworkings facilitate the transition from idea to nation. Shah Nawaz's novel presents a gendered redefinition of the "good Muslim" through its representation of political activism in the Muslim League, thereby optimistically forecasting a more inclusive notion of the Pakistani nation. Sidhwa's narrator, Lenny, occupies center stage in my analysis of her novel. Narrating as both a child and an adult, Lenny's voice calls into question the conventions through which we recognize memory as memory, and, as a result, destabilizes the myths enshrouding the idea of Pakistan. Masroor's *Shadows of Time* thematizes syncretism—political, religious, cultural, social—and imagines a definition of the Pakistani nation that would value the composite over the pure. S. Khan's novel presents an ironic depiction of migrancy by showcasing the disorientation of a Hindu man who refuses to leave Lahore or the house that lends the novel its title. This character's out-of-placeness serves as a foil for the state-sponsored ways other characters solidify their claims of belonging. State functions also make an appearance in Ashraf's *The Postmaster* under the guise of the Posts and Telegraphs Department of the Civil Service of Pakistan. The novel appears to wax nostalgic for British bureaucracy and the order it lent, but, under the surface of this Raj nostalgia is a frustrated optimism for what the nation of Pakistan, assisted by an efficient state, could be.

Chapter two centers on the 1971 civil war that resulted in the creation of Bangladesh. My analyses of Moni Mohsin's 2006 *The End of Innocence*, Durdana Soomro and Ghazala Hameed's 2006 *Bengal Raag*, and Shahbano Bilgrami's 2007 *Without Dreams* all focus on the figure of the child, thus tying this chapter to my discussion of Sidhwa's novel. The child characters, who in some cases also act as narrator, gauge, with varying outcomes, how vulnerable they and other characters are to the violence of the state, made manifest in the war. Chapter three looks at how contemporary fiction represents Islamic cultures before the creation of Pakistan. Tied thematically to Masroor's novel, Tariq Ali's Islam Quintet, which was started in 1992 with the publication of *Shadows of the Pomegranate Tree* and concluded in 2010 with *Night of the Golden Butterfly*, uses syncretism, especially the tolerance it entails, to call into question whether an inclusive definition of the Pakistani nation can even be articulated in the absence of self-generated (that is, bottom-up rather than top-down) representations and interpretations. Chapter four extends this concern with Islam through a focus on Zia's Pakistan (1977–1988). Like Shah Nawaz's novel, the fictions discussed here—Uzma Aslam Khan's 2009 *The Geometry of God*, Ali Sethi's 2009 *The Wish Maker*, Kamila Shamsie's 2005 *Broken Verses*, and Mohammed Hanif's 2008 *A Case of Exploding Mangoes*—all challenge the dominant definition of the "good Muslim," derived at this historical juncture by Zia's Islamization scheme, along significantly gendered, indeed outright queer, lines. Collectively, these fictions re-imagine a more inclusive nation.

Chapters five and six look at historical developments rather than events, per se. Featuring a slate of Karachi novels—Kamila Shamsie's 2004 *Kartography*, Bina Shah's 2004 *The 786 Cybercafé*, Adam Zameenzad's 1989 *The 13th House*, and Maniza Naqvi's 2008 *A Matter of Detail*—Chapter five foregrounds the idea of mobility and its relation to nostalgia, thus connecting to Ashraf's *The Postmaster*. Premised on the idea drawn from mobility studies that identities take shape through interactions with place, these analyses investigate how Karachi's breakneck changes induce and prevent, alternately, a nostalgic stuckness that either inhibits or facilitates affective attachments to city and to nation. Chapter six extends Singh's regional focus through its representation of the zamindari system in both rural and urban Punjab. Nadeem Aslam's 1993 *Season of the Rainbirds*, Daniyal Mueenuddin's 2009 *In Other Rooms, Other Wonders*, and Mohsin Hamid's 2000 *Moth Smoke* all figure the zamindari class as a state-like actor, demanding affective attachment through long-standing claims to land and wealth that pre-date Pakistan. These three novels use gossip thematically and structurally to represent the consolidation of zamindari power at certain times, as well as its vulnerability at others. Chapter seven concentrates on post-9/11 fictions: Nadeem Aslam's 2008 *The Wasted Vigil*, Mohsin Hamid's 2007 *The Reluctant Fundamentalist*, Kamila Shamsie's 2009 *Burnt Shadows*, and HM Naqvi's 2009 *Home Boy*. Linked via the theme of migrancy to S. Khan's *Five Queen's Road*, these novels unsettle conventional migrant tropes by stressing its brutality. By drawing attention to how brutal cross-cultural and international encounters can be, the fictions discussed here concretize the abstractions attending "war on terror" discourses, and variously assert revised definitions of the nation or attempt to reach beyond that concept's definitional parameters.

Part I
Idea to nation

1   1947

Many framings of Pakistan's historical emergence borrow birth metaphors. Historian Ian Talbot, for instance, comments, "Pakistan's birth was a difficult one which involved the immense suffering of thousands of its citizens" (*Pakistan* 95). Working this metaphor hard, Talbot identifies Great Britain as a "midwife" and India as Pakistan's "elder sibling" (*Pakistan* 95). Political Scientist Philip Oldenburg similarly uses familial language to link these subcontinental neighbors, naming India and Pakistan "fraternal twins" (1). This rhetorical tendency extends beyond scholarly treatments of the 1947 partition that drew international borders between India and the two wings of Pakistan. Jawaharlal Nehru, for instance, proclaims in his "Tryst with Destiny" speech delivered as India gained its independence, "Before the birth of freedom, we have endured all the pains of labour and our hearts are heavy with the memory of this sorrow" ("Tryst"). For his part, Muhammad Ali Jinnah avoids the language of birthing but retains an idea of inevitability. In Jinnah's Presidential Address to the Constituent Assembly, delivered on 11 August 1947, he declares that the partition of Punjab and Bengal "had to take place" ("Constituent Assembly" 17). All of these framings share a tendency to naturalize the creation of Pakistan (and India). Presenting the transition from the idea to the nation of Pakistan as unavoidable implies the inescapability of the violence attending the mass migration in both directions across the newly created borders, a peculiar specter of death hovering over the new-born nation. At the same time, this air of the inexorable also neatly reinforces certain historiographical proclivities that mythologize the Muslim League and Jinnah, as well as position the territorialization of the idea of Pakistan as the sole intent of League politics from the start.[1]

In spite of this naturalizing language, several prominent historiographical interventions attempt a counter-reading of these persistent national myths.[2] While debates over why partition happened and what Jinnah's and the League's intentions were have for decades swung scholarly opinion away from Jinnah's unproblematized apotheosis, other scholars, including Vazira Fazila-Yacoobali Zamindar, explore "*what* happened at Partition" rather than continuing to focus intently on "*why* Partition happened" (244; emphasis in original). This shift in impulse entails, in part, a move toward the qualitative aspects of this historical moment and its aftermath. Farzana Shaikh announces just such a purpose in the opening of *Making Sense of Pakistan*: "This book—a *work of interpretation* rather than historical research*—addresses the political, economic and strategic implications of Pakistan's uncertain national identity" (1; emphasis added). Shaikh's declared intent to interpret rather than to amass historical research is an attempt, in my view, to identify the ways in which a variety of discourses re-present or endow with meaning events from Pakistan's past. In effect, we can understand Shaikh's approach, to think of it in terms of Zamindar's "*what*," as a tracing of how certain meanings reverberate through arenas such as politics, economics, culture, and so on.

Jill Didur undertakes this type of project in her analyses of partition literature, critiquing the impulse to treat this literature as "'documenting' rather than re-presenting the violence" of partition ("Fragments" 5). The ways in which partition literature narrates "subjectivity, agency, nationalism, and history," Didur continues, deserve attention ("Fragments" 5). Thus, Zamindar's "*what*" also directs our critical gaze toward what structures and devices literature uses, for example, to make partition experiences legible or meaningful. With this emphasis on structures and devices, Didur's critical position aligns with David Gilmartin's interest in deflating the once-popular scholarly view that

> Pakistan's distinctive origins made it different and special, the product of a historical moment that in some ways transcended the structures of power and everyday life that shaped the territories that in fact came to comprise the country.
>
> ("Living the Tensions" 522)

The adoption of the view Gilmartin troubles would result in a false conception of a harmonious Pakistani national unity, a condition the nation hasn't enjoyed or achieved at any point in its history. In place of this exceptionalism, Gilmartin emphasizes "the tensions between ideals and realities [as] ultimately constitutive of both community and self" ("Living the Tensions" 523). Gilmartin sees these tensions, arising from ethnic, linguistic, religious, economic, political, and social differences, to name only a few, as points of negotiation rather than pitfalls that necessarily lead to all-out conflict ("Living the Tensions" 523–4). Weighing the "*what*" over the "*why*" accommodates a variety of views on what aspects of Pakistan's past, present, and future resonate. Literature, while not a privileged discourse that provides untrammelled access to "human" experience, does none-theless imagine an array of meanings that correspond to actual events, sometimes reinforcing and other times challenging received narratives.

The six novels I take up in this chapter—Khushwant Singh's 1956 *Train to Pakistan*, Mumtaz Shah Nawaz's 1957 *The Heart Divided*, Bapsi Sidhwa's 1988/1991 *Cracking India*, Mehr Nigar Masroor's 1987 *Shadows of Time*, Sorayya Y. Khan's 2009 *Five Queen's Road*, and Saad Ashraf's 2004 *The Postmaster*—all animate the "*what*" of partition by focusing on the tensions between, for instance, national dictates and regional loyalties; idealized visions of independence and the familiar venalities of bureaucratic life; and rigid definitions of "Muslim" and the varied lived experiences of this identity. As I mention in the introduction, the structure of this chapter on the 1947 partition is anomalous compared to the rest of the book. All of my analyses begin with the question of how the literature represents the affective resonance of Pakistan as idea, nation, and/or state. But, whereas my literary analyses in the rest of the chapters focus on a central theme or device shared across the fiction and situate that theme or device in each chapter's specific historical event or development, here I use each partition novel to introduce a theme or device that will be of primary concern in a subsequent chapter. Also, rather than foreground an overarching historical context here before launching into my analyses, as I do in the chapters that follow, I have incorporated the details pertinent to each novel individually.

In my analysis of Singh's *Train to Pakistan*, I consider how the tensions emerging as local practices, bureaucratic structures, and political agendas interact to inflect attitudes toward the transition from colony to nation, a shift made urgent and dangerous as partition's violence manifests in Mano Majra, the novel's setting. Singh's concentration on setting encourages a regionally sensitive analysis, which I take up again and in greater detail in Chapter six. Shah Nawaz's *The Heart Divided* stresses a gendered political conversion, I argue, to expand how the elite discourses of the League posit an idea of "Muslim" that precludes broad identification. The novel's use of gender to re-define "Muslim" highlights many of the same dynamics found in the analyses I conduct in Chapter four on Zia's Islamization. I concentrate on the metafictional elements of the narrator's role in Bapsi Sidhwa's *Cracking India* to contend that the novel subtly re-constructs a recognizable "memory," for instance, to examine the narrative implications of privileging such a discourse in the context of historical trauma. This section's spotlight on Lenny, Sidhwa's child narrator, ties my analysis of *Cracking India* to those in Chapter two, wherein the novels about 1971 all also feature the figure of the child prominently. *Shadows of Time*, Masroor's sweeping novel, uses its vast geographical and historical span, I maintain, to promote a syncretic idea of the subcontinent's history and various national identities. Syncretism is prominent, too, in Chapter three, which looks at Tariq Ali's fictive renderings of Islam, pre-partition. S. Khan's *Five Queen's Road* engages with partition's displacement of minorities by, ironically, focusing on characters who remain in place. The novel's depiction of the disorientation that results because of mass movement troubles all the characters' claims to belonging, even if some enjoy state support. Chapter seven, on post-9/11 novels, similarly focuses on migrancy as a thematic that inflects the ability to belong. Ashraf's *The Postmaster* rounds out this chapter on partition fiction with its critical portrayal of nostalgia. Rather than a pure indulgence in "raj nostalgia," this novel uses nostalgia not to hold onto the past but to push for a future that better matches the potential laden in the idea of Pakistan. This sense of nostalgia as a hope for the future also emerges in Chapter five, which focuses on Karachi novels.

Khushwant Singh's 1956 novel *Train to Pakistan* offers a region-specific representation of the 1947 partition through its focus on Mano Majra, a fictional Punjabi town, situated mere miles from the new national border.[3] To view this novel as a regional approach to an international event matters because such a geographically precise portrayal of this historical moment allows readers to see the challenges both Pakistan and India faced in the first years of their existence as they set about consolidating new unified national identities. These challenges include the negotiation of regional, bureaucratic, and political priorities, practices, and loyalties, themselves interwoven in complicated ways. This novel illustrates how, at the intersection of the bureaucratic and the regional, for instance, the transition from colony to nation occurred smoothly. At other intersections, including between the political and the regional, however, tensions between a unifying national vision and the intransigence of local priorities obstruct the transition from colony to nation. Less a novel that captures the "human" aspects of this historical trauma, *Train to Pakistan* represents, instead, the unremarkable "successes" of British colonization, thoroughly indigenized, as well as the anxieties over the "failure" of national consolidation, brought to light via conflicting ideologies. From within this complicated mixing of the local, bureaucratic, and political, the novel suggests that the new national projects both Pakistan and India undertake in 1947 bear the potential to succeed and to fail simultaneously.

Train to Pakistan opens in August 1947, a moment on the verge of partition and monsoon season. The rainy season is late, which causes residents throughout the Punjab to claim that "God was punishing them for their sins" (Singh 1). As if in affirmation of that fear, the communal violence that accompanies the mass migration of Muslims traveling west and Hindus and Sikhs traveling east soon engulfs the entire region. At the same time, Mano Majra serves as the site of a murder-burglary, attempted communist activities, and "ghost train" way-station. All these events occur almost simultaneously, a coincidental timeline that works in the fiction as a key aspect of the plan conjured by the district's magistrate, Hukum Chand, to save Mano Majra from erupting into communal violence of its own. This plan involves first arresting on false pretenses Mano Majra's notorious budmash, Juggut Singh (Jugga), and the newly arrived communist worker, Iqbal, for the murder of Lala Ram Lal, Mano Majra's Hindu moneylender, and then releasing them in the hopes that one or the other will be able to avert a planned attack on a Muslim-filled train heading to Pakistan. Hukum Chand's plan does succeed in that the train passes through Mano Majra unmolested, but its safe passage comes at the cost of Jugga's life, sacrificed, the novel encourages the reader to believe, for the love of a Muslim girl, Nooran. Thus, love prevails, in a sense; Jugga emerges as the most manly and heroic, while both Hukum Chand's and Iqbal's characters betray some indignity in that neither the bureaucrat nor the political activist possesses the courage necessary to sacrifice himself directly.[4] Following this narrative trajectory, many of the received interpretations of *Train to Pakistan* reveal a shared investment in identifying the novel's (in)abilities to convey universals of human experience, such as the nobility or venality of the individual in times of crises (Jugga as noble, Iqbal and Hukum Chand as less so), and the triumph of heteronormative love over the violence of communal politics (Daiya 62).

The novel's regional focus demonstrates why Mano Majra and its inhabitants only appear to be punished by God and/or to be isolated and insulated from the historical events surrounding partition. The novel's opening paragraphs report in the past tense on the violent responses to partition taking place throughout the subcontinent during the summer of 1947. This detached narratorial overview concludes by honing in on Mano Majra, calling it one of the remaining "oases of peace...lost in the remote reaches of the [Punjabi] frontier" (Singh 2). Framed as an apparent paradise, Mano Majra first appears in the novel as outside of time, one of "a scatter of little villages," that has not been incorporated into any entity larger than itself (Singh 2). Such a presentation of setting prompts several critics to view Mano Majra as "guardedly utopian" (Morey, *Fictions* 168), "sleepy" (Gopal 71), edenic (Girdhari 82), idyllic (Harrington 300), and as "an unsustainable image of national harmony" (Crane 182). Compounding the village's putative isolation, the novel's opening also suggests that Mano Majra is outside of the current politics that go to create history. In the third paragraph, the novel switches to present tense verbs as it describes Mano Majra's topography, making sure to mention the location of the railway station. The following paragraph features yet another shift in verb tense to the present perfect: "Mano Majra has always been known for its railway station" (Singh 3). This use of the present perfect suggests the continuation of the past into the present, augmenting Peter Morey's claim that, while the shift to the present tense "conjures a sense of immediacy," placing the reading in the moment of the summer of 1947, the elaborated description of Mano Majra maintains a "quality of timelessness which gives...the village an air of unreality" (*Fiction* 170). If taken at face value, this presentation of Mano Majra as isolated from politics and history allows the village to function, until the first "ghost train" from Pakistan arrives, as an idealized site of human relations and actions wherein the heroism and romance Jugga embodies emerges as the novel's point. Indeed, the arrival of the "ghost train" marks the village's fall, the moment it goes from pre- to post-lapsarian.

Yet, this image of Mano Majra as pure in its isolation and, later, fallen falters well before the first "ghost train," that is, before any consideration of the specific historical moment of partition occupies the narrative foreground. This competing though subtle representation of Mano Majra as indeed "in" time matters because it recontextualizes the cultural work the novel as a whole does, allowing readers to see the story emerge from a set of dynamics informed by regional, bureaucratic, and political concerns rather than a transparent testimony of the "human" experience of partition. Mano Majra bears many regional specificities, including its particular social stratifications that overlap to some extent with communal identities and other distinctions brought to the fore by outsider characters such as Iqbal. Despite explicitly naming Mano Majra an "oas[i]s of peace," for instance, the detached narration of the early paragraphs also suggests the village's tensions in its description of the center of town, comprised of "three brick buildings": Lala Ram Lal's house and both the Sikh and Muslim places of worship (Singh 2). The narrative voice first describes Lala Ram Lal as the "moneylender" and then, several sentences later, as being the "only Hindu family" (2). This ordering recasts the position of his house next to the two houses of worship, inserting an economic identity alongside religious ones. Similarly, the narrative voice describes the relations between the village's other inhabitants within an economic system: "The Sikhs own all the land around the village; the Muslims are tenants and share the tilling with the owners" (Singh 2). Morey sees these indications of the village's social and economic stratification as hints that "this society carries within it the seeds of its own destruction" (*Fiction* 171). And, indeed, the subinspector of police, a representative of bureaucracy, suspects that the Sikhs' economic dominance helps maintain the purported "peace" of Mano Majra:

> "Every morning and evening the muezzin calls for prayer in the heart of a village like Mano Majra. You ask the Sikhs why they allow it and they answer that the Muslims are their brothers. I am sure they are getting money from them."
>
> (Singh 20)

The subinspector's comment suggests that economic considerations underwrite the putative harmoniousness, the fraternity, of Mano Majra's Sikhs and Muslims. This economic stratification marks one aspect of Mano Majra's regional identity, while it also stabilizes and contextualizes "communal" relations.

The stability of economic stratification does not, however, guarantee village accord. Even in its purported pre-lapsarian state, Mano Majra bears tensions between villagers. On the night of Lala Ram Lal's murder, which takes place before the arrival of the first "ghost train," Jugga keeps an assignation with Nooran, daughter of Mano Majra's imam. On his way out the door, his mother reminds him that the police have prohibited him from leaving Mano Majra after dark (Singh 11). She warns, "'Enemies will see you. They will report you. They will send you back to jail'" (Singh 11). And, when Jugga finally returns to his house after the murder, which had initially kept him from returning to the village, the narrative voice makes plain that "[t]he neighbors had been vigilant and the police were informed immediately" (Singh 55). Thus, Jugga draws his neighbors' suspicion to the point that they inform on him. This distrust hampers the idealization of Mano Majra, intra- or inter-communally. Rather than the isolated and insulated hamlet in the Punjabi frontier, then, Mano Majra emerges as a location with a distinct regional identity cross-hatched by broader forces, especially economic ones, that place the village very squarely in a particular geographical position and historical moment.

Yet, this distrust Mano Majrans bear for Jugga runs against the "Punjabi code," as espoused by Meet Singh, the bhai of the Sikh temple. Since prevailing gossip casts suspicion on Jugga for Lala Ram Lal's murder, Meet Singh appears to Iqbal, an outsider, to be concerned not that "Jugga had committed murder but that his hands were soiled with the blood of a fellow villager" (Singh 41). Such loyalties "baffle" Iqbal, who, according to the narrative voice, has an "anglicized way of looking at things," a view resulting from his urban preferences and England-returned status (Singh 41). For his part, Iqbal cannot understand how living by the "Punjabi code" makes one a "*nar admi*—a he-man who had defied authority (magistrates and police) and religion (oath on scripture) but proved true to friendship" (Singh 41). Iqbal's interactions with the native Mano Majrans foreground another distinct characteristic of the village's regional identity, this so-called Punjabi code. What's striking about this code is its definition in contravention of both bureaucracy and religion. Thus, much as the topography of the village inserts economic identities into the midst of religious ones, the village's shared "code of morals," in Iqbal's words, does not square entirely or neatly with communal identities. At the same time, the village's regional distinctions set it apart from the existing structures of the state, which, given that the novel is set during the summer of 1947, includes both the British colonial and the new Pakistani and Indian national states. These intra-village dynamics challenge the narrative voice's characterization of Mano Majra as an "oas[i]s of peace" and create a more "realistic" sense of the village as a stratified location with distinct region-specific features that strike outsiders, such as Iqbal, as odd.

Further, Iqbal's bafflement over the "Punjabi code" gives the lie to any notion that the characters share a common view of the partition. A conversation involving Iqbal, Meet Singh, Banta Singh, the village lambardar, and Imam Baksh, who is identified only as "the Muslim," serves to lay out the differences between Iqbal's view, on the one hand, and those of these leading figures of Mano Majra, on the other. Following upon the Imam's question—"'What is all this about Pakistan and Hindustan?'"—the lambardar inserts, "'we live in this little village and know nothing....Babuji [Iqbal], tell us, why did the English leave?'" (Singh 47). Both characters' questions give the impression that the villagers have little awareness of the larger political events of the day. Yet, their reaction to Iqbal's anti-colonial argument suggests that the villagers possess an awareness that already shapes their views of current events. As Iqbal attempts to convince his interlocutors of the necessity of British withdrawal, for instance, the narrative voice, rather dryly, claims, "Iqbal's thesis did not cut much ice" (Singh 48). Instead, Banta Singh and Imam Baksh collectively parse Iqbal's choices of phrase:

Iqbal tried to take the offensive. "Why, don't you people want to be free? Do you want to remain slaves all your lives?"

After a long silence the lambardar answered: "Freedom must be a good thing. But what will we get out of it? Educated people like you, Babu Sahib, will get the jobs the English had. Will we get more lands or more buffaloes?"

"No," the Muslim said. "Freedom is for the educated people who fought for it. We were slaves of the English, now we will be slaves of the educated Indians—or the Pakistanis."

(Singh 48)

Banta Singh and Imam Baksh's shared assessment of independence refuses the pieties of nationalist unity and, in their stead, identifies intra-national inequities that are, in their shared view, likely to dog both the new Pakistani and Indian nations.

The change from colony to nation, from this perspective, amounts to little for those who are not of the elite, educated, and presumably urban class. Against this elevated social and political position, the lambardar and the Imam present a unified front, one in line with the "Punjabi code" but that, nonetheless, polishes over the stratifications that exist between them as Sikhs/landowners and Muslims/tenants. The varying perspectives between the lambardar and the Imam, on the one hand, and Iqbal, on the other, provide just one example of how the differences constituting Mano Majra affect views of the new nations' viability or promise.

In addition to its regional particularities and how they shape the villagers' views of independence, the trains' regulating functions also shape Mano Majra's historicity and, in turn, the novel's representation of the emergence of both Pakistan and India. Readers' introduction to Mano Majra requires attention to the role the railway plays in the village's identity, which is also a way to understand how bureaucratized the village is. The narrative voice makes clear that "Mano Majra has always been known for its railway station" (Singh 3). And, while it is the two "ghost trains" that cause such trauma in the village and the passenger train filled with Mano Majra's and Chundunnugger's Muslims that gives the novel its title, the goods and mail trains enliven and regulate Mano Majra's daily life:

> The only regular customers [at the station] are the goods trains. Although Mano Majra seldom has any goods to send or receive, its station sidings are usually occupied by long rows of wagons… Before daybreak, the mail train rushes through on its way to Lahore, and as it approaches the bridge, the driver invariably blows two long blasts of the whistle. In an instant, all Mano Majra comes awake.
>
> (Singh 4)

The day ends as the final goods train "steams in" (Singh 5). As this mention of the trains' regularity suggests, Mano Majra is not so much engaged with large-scale trade with other locations throughout the subcontinent's northwest region as it is connected, even structured by, the relations the trains represent. The architectural functions the railway serves in Mano Majra's identity locate the village as already a part of the larger state apparatus, even as state power shifts from British to Indian and Pakistani hands. That is, given that the goods and mail trains—rather than the express that "do[es] not stop at all" or the "slow passenger trains" of which there are "only two"—order the village's life, Mano Majra takes shape from its location in a larger systems of exchange and control, be they informational or commercial (Singh 3–4). The novel's focus on trains at this historical juncture shows how, in Gyan Prakash's terms, the railways, as a form of technology introduced by colonial rulers and appropriated by postcolonial ones, "forged a link between space and state" (Prakash 160). In addition to being people movers and, later in the novel, death on rails, some of the trains in Singh's novels—in fact, by the narrative voice's count, most of the trains—represent the firm and continuing control of the state and its functionaries, the bureaucratic civil services.

My interest in the trains as examples of the postcolonial state apparatus augments analyses that figure the trains as related to communal identities. Peter Morey and Ralph Crane each focus on how the trains insert colonial history and its consequences, such as the indigenization of colonial technologies and the communal tensions that resulted from attempts to homogenize Indians via nationalist projects, into the novel (Morey 169; Crane 181).[5] Similarly, Marian Aguiar concentrates on the passenger trains in Singh's novel, arguing that they "render in symbolic form shifting local and national identities" (75). This shift occurs as the railway cars themselves become social spaces violently "communally coded" during the partition riots, a violence that "wak[ens the village] to its national identity" (Aguiar 76). However, looking at the trains from a bureaucratic point of view allows one to trace lines of continuity rather than division or rupture or violent awakenings through the historical events of 1947. As Philip Oldenburg illustrates, while, as with so much else, the Indian Civil Service needed to be divided at the time of partition (36), the bureaucratic entities that resulted acted as "two ships of state [that] stabilized remarkably quickly" (38).[6] The extra-textual reality of the state apparatus's stabilizing effect immediately after partition recontextualizes the representation of the bureaucracy in *Train to Pakistan*: whereas, solely at the level of plot, one might read Hukum Chand, "magistrate and deputy commissioner of the district" (Singh 18), as a dissolute drunk (Singh 95), a lecherous nihilist (Singh 87), and a manipulative coward (Singh 99), for instance, his standing as representative of a stabilizing bureaucracy introduces another position from which to view the emergence of the two new nations.

Indeed, the novel links the railway to the village's position in the broader colonial and now national bureaucracies. Just as Mano Majra has "always been known for its railway station" (Singh 3), "[i]n bureaucratic circles Mano Majra has some importance because of an officers' rest house just north of the railway bridge" (Singh 16). Hukum Chand arrives at this rest house early in the novel, and, from there, stage manages the bureaucracy's response to the "ghost trains" and the plan to ambush the train to Pakistan that unfolds in the novel's conclusion (Singh 18). That the narrative voice introduces Hukum Chand as "corpulent" and points out that his "style of smoking betrayed his lower-middle-class origin" hint at a rather sardonic view of the bureaucracy in general, namely, that it facilitates the class mobility and comfort of the socially undistinguished. This light mockery emerges again as Hukum Chand tells the subinspector that he doesn't "'mind your taking whatever you do take, within reason of course—everyone one does that—only be careful'" (Singh 20). The magistrate, as the embodiment of law and order, willingly overlooks and, the suggestion is, even accepts bribes, indicating a troubling kink in the system. Hukum Chand's willingness to tolerate corruption connects to his larger political philosophy, which he presents to the subinspector as apolitical: "'Your principle should be to see everything and say nothing. The world changes so rapidly that if you want to get on you cannot afford to align yourself with any person or point of view'" (Singh 20). While, on the one hand,

Hukum Chand's advice reeks of the self-interest that rationalizes corruption in the first place, on the other hand, it also represents a mindset that values the stability characteristic of a properly functioning bureaucracy: no matter who is in political power, the bureaucrats must attend to the day-to-day state functions.

The attention to the quotidian that Hukum Chand's advice appears to advocate arguably enables Jugga's heroism at the novel's conclusion, thus providing an understanding of a bureaucratic view on independence. As the Muslims of Mano Majra and Chundunnugger prepare to depart from a local refugee camp via a train for Pakistan at the novel's close, Hukum Chand and the subinspector strategize how to safeguard the train's passage through Mano Majra, where a group of Sikhs plan to ambush the train at the bridge over the Sutleg. Distracted by his own concern for Begum Haseena, a young Muslim courtesan, Hukum Chand initially fails to reckon the seriousness of the situation. He asks whether the subinspector has informed the camp's commander about the planned ambush. The subinspector replies, "'[I]f your honor can use influence with these mobs, I can tell the camp commander the plans to ambush the train and persuade him not to go.'" Immediately after this comment, the narrative voice editorializes: "The subinspector was hitting below the belt" (Singh 158). The delivery of the subinspector's dialogue and this narratorial commentary highlights the differences between a politician's and a bureaucrat's role. The politician would use rousing rhetoric to stoke or discourage "mobs" for whatever political end, while the bureaucrat must seek other means to guarantee an ongoing semblance of order. Such a jaded view of the vaunted rhetoric of politicized persuasion emerges explicitly when, through a narrative perspective that privileges Hukum Chand's view, the novel satirizes Nehru's famous formulation that independence marks India's "'tryst with destiny,'" sarcastically calling the rhetoric a "fine speech" (Singh 176). Instead, in Hukum Chand's eyes, the bureaucrat's work involves neither emotion nor morals:

> The right and wrong of his instructions [to release Lala Ram Lal's murderers and set his plan to save the Muslims in motion] did not weigh too heavily on him. He was a magistrate, not a missionary. It was the day-to-day problems to which he had to find answers. He had no need to equate them to some unknown absolute standard. There were not many "oughts" in his life. There were just the "is"'s.
>
> (Singh 100)

The bureaucrat's objective is communally unmotivated, politically disinterested, and structurally impersonal; that, at the novel's close, it "saves" a trainload of Muslims through stage-managing Jugga's heroic sacrifice suggests a dedication to maintaining order and state control more than a commitment to regional, political, or ideological ideals. The novel's representation of bureaucratic structures thus heralds the new nations' success.

This impersonal stance also characterizes the political (rather than the regional or bureaucratic) commentary on the creation of Pakistan and India or, at least, how the novel frames a communist political view. Iqbal's inabilities to carry out his "social work" with any measure of success constitutes less a failure on his part and more a commentary on how the Communist Party was operating in coordination with and in opposition with the Congress and the Muslim League throughout the 1940s. According to Kamran Asdar Ali's account of communist party organization just before and after partition, the Communist Party of India vacillated on the Pakistan question, at first supporting the demand and, later, recanting that view ("Communists" 507). At issue for the Communist Party of India and, by 1948, the Communist Party of Pakistan was the fact that elites comprised the two dominant parties in the decolonization process (Ali, "Communists" 511). Nonetheless, the Communist Party of Pakistan did align with the Muslim League for a time in 1946 in order to defeat the Union Party in the Punjab (Ali 510). In Ali's view, this unexpected coalition was "an attempt to radically transform the relationship between a future state and the masses" (510). Iqbal's opinions on the shortcomings of rural activism mirror this top-down political strategy to achieve ideological ends. Fully aware that he can do nothing to quell communal violence in Mano Majra, Iqbal thinks:

> It was fatuous to suggest that the bourgeois revolution could be turned into a proletarian one. The stage had not arrived. The proletariat was indifferent to political freedom for Hindustan or Pakistan, except when it could be given an economic significance like grabbing land by killing an owner who was of a different religious denomination. All that could be done was to divert the kill-and-grab instinct from communal channels and turn it against the propertied class.
>
> (Singh 50)

Iqbal's cynicism inhibits his ability to connect with the villagers, but it also appears to mirror the actual efforts of the Communist Party workers in the subcontinent throughout the latter half of the 1940s. Ultimately, as Ali continues, the Communist Party of Pakistan viewed partition as a "historical mistake," seeing the dissection of India as a "way-station that needed to be passed to arrive at 'real' emancipation" (521). Although in the novel Iqbal insists that he's aligned with the Communist Party of India, the extent to which his views on the creation of India and Pakistan mirror those of the CPP offers a critical view of the ideological viability and desirability of the two new nations. That the last readers know of Iqbal are his alcohol-saturated nihilisms suggests, in turn, that the novel itself casts a wary eye on his views (Singh 169–72).

If Khushwant Singh's *Train to Pakistan* is male-centered, then Mumtaz Shah Nawaz's *The Heart Divided* presents a female-centered counterpoint. Indeed, on the surface, the two novels, published within a year of each other—1956 and 1957, respectively—appear to hold significantly different concerns. Where *Train to Pakistan*, for instance, focuses on a small Punjabi village, *The Heart Divided* centers mostly on the large Punjabi city of Lahore. Yet, in both novels, the interplay between the rural and the urban plays an important role in framing how characters view the idea and the reality of Pakistan. As I have already discussed, this rural-urban interplay emerges most explicitly in Iqbal's impatience with the "Punjabi code" as it's represented in Singh's novel. Shah Nawaz's novel implies this interplay as it locates Lahore's slums as the needful site for direct political action. Indeed, over the course of the novel, both central protagonists, the sisters Sughra and Zohra, commit themselves to assisting the disenfranchised women and laborers who, in the sisters' shared view, are the most deserving beneficiaries of the promise of social justice that the idea of Pakistan holds. Such commitments represent the sisters' political radicalization, as well as the extra-fictional radicalization of the Muslim League itself, but, in the novel, this radicalization nonetheless helps maintain the conservative privilege the sisters enjoy as daughters of an important landowning family. In other words, despite its visions of an Islamic socialist utopia, *The Heart Divided* does not approach critically one of the fundamental power structures in extra-fictional Pakistan that creates inequities in the first place: namely, the Sheikh family's rural landholdings.[7] The sisters' radicalization, then, relies upon the family's social and economic status, positions secured via their zamindar identity.

In effect, then, *The Heart Divided* chronicles the radicalization of nationalist politics and of gender politics, but within limits. Priyamvada Gopal's analysis of the novel's treatment of politics also concentrates on nationalism and gender, arguing that Shah Nawaz's success lies in presenting an unbiased and pluralistic view of the period (1930s to just before partition) (Gopal 73–4). Gopal highlights how *The Heart Divided* uses a gendered script—that of the "asana, or romance"— to portray the illusory unity behind nationalist projects (73). Tariq Rahman makes much the same claim as he argues that Shah Nawaz "tells the reader that honest Muslims and Hindus could be both for and against [the two-nations theory], a fact endorsed by very few writers in Pakistan" (*History* 25). My argument, at its most general, contends that *The Heart Divided* does lean toward the League, though with some ambivalence. More specifically, the novel, whose opening is a retrospective on 1930, parallels the radicalization of Zohra's and Sughra's gender and nationalist politics with the radicalization of the Muslim League's anti-Congress and anti-colonial politics. The sisters move from indirect to direct political participation, both in terms of their gendered roles and their nationalist politics. This move mirrors the extent to which, extra-fictionally, the League's broader nationalist claims to be representative of India's Muslims worked alongside, perhaps even appropriated (albeit temporarily), progressive, even socialist, politics that very much resemble those eventually adopted by Sughra and Zohra. These politics' radical natures and even their parallel paths extend only to a point, however. While the novel concludes with the entire Sheikh family backing the League and the demand for Pakistan, it does so by reconciling Sughra to her zamindar husband and marrying Zohra to her socialist love with the blessings of her father. Sughra's return to the patriarchal fold and Zohra's reception of its beneficence point to a broader narrative reluctance to acknowledge how, politically speaking, tactics trump ideals. *The Heart Divided* is thoroughly political in that it very explicitly takes shape through its immediate historical context, and, as readers removed by more than seven decades from that time, we can also see how the novel attempts to put forth a vision of the nation based upon its own investments in the idea of Pakistan.

The Sheikh family, a prominent fixture in the Punjab as a whole given their "ancestral lands" in Multan and their mansion, Nishat Manzil, in Lahore, occupies the center of Shah Nawaz's fiction. At first, Sughra and Zohra, two young purdah ladies, appear set to follow different paths, as the novel's early chapters focus on Sughra's marriage to her cousin and her preparations for the move to Multan. For her part, Zohra eagerly partakes of the educational opportunities available to her in Lahore and due to her father's liberal ways. Their England-returned brother, Habib, plays an important role through the novel's first half as his love connection with Mohini, Zohra's politically active Hindu friend, allegorizes the impossibility of Congress-League political unity. Mohini's death, occurring just before the historically significant 1937 elections, marks an important shift in the Sheikh family's involvement with nationalist politics in general and League politics more specifically. Subsequent to Mohini's death, both Sughra and Zohra are decidedly out of purdah and, gradually, more directly involved in nationalist politics. Sughra, an exile in Lahore from an unhappy marriage, devotes herself to election canvassing, charity work, and Muslim separatism. Zohra, an exile in Amritsar from a still-too-traditional family intent on arranging her marriage, builds a career in teaching and labor activism. The narrative takes care to punctuate the sisters' growing political participation with references to actual historical events, such as the 1937 elections and the 1940 meeting of the League in Lahore. Such roadmarks encourage a paralleling if not a correlating of Zohra's and Sughra's politics to those of the League, and, indeed, by the novel's conclusion, the two sisters' membership to the party endorses such a reading. Yet, once again, the sisters appear set to follow different tracks, as Sughra looks with "radiant eyes" to Pakistan's future (Shah Nawaz 451) and Zohra harbors a measure of reticence (449).[8]

Although the novel opens at some undetermined point in the future, its action begins in 1930, when, as Zohra reflects, "the change in her life began" (Shah Nawaz 1). Initially, the "change" to which Zohra refers appears to be wholly gendered in nature, as the novel's first event features Zohra venturing out with two girlfriends, Surrayya and Lakshmi. Zohra's friendship with Surrayya causes Mehr, Zohra's mother, some concern, as Surrayya's family "had cast off the veil and went to shops and restaurants with their faces uncovered" (Shah Nawaz 2). As it signals the first instance of narrative and, indeed, generational tension, Zohra's excursion with her non-purdah friends establishes the "conservative" end of the spectrum as far as the Sheikh family's gender politics are concerned. And, although Zohra dares to venture out on this occasion without her burqah, her father ultimately rationalizes the acceptability of her transgression by saying, "'You shouldn't have gone out without your burqah, but it doesn't really matter, since no one recognized you'" (Shah Nawaz 17). Zohra's literal unrecognizability safeguards her own and, more importantly, her family's honor, but, at the same time, this incident serves as the thin edge of the wedge that Zohra uses to hasten her coming out of purdah.

At a figurative level, though, Zohra's unrecognizability establishes another starting point for Zohra and for Sughra, too: that of their indirect political participation. If Surrayya represents progressive Muslim womanhood, then Zohra's other friend Mohini represents progressive Indian womanhood more generally through her direct involvement with the Congress's anti-colonial politics. Certainly, Mohini's direct participation in Indian nationalism serves as the counterpoint and foil to Zohra's indirect participation. Mohini comes from a family very much committed to the Congress's cause, a commitment to which her father's and her sister's incarceration at the novel's opening attest. Quite early on, Mohini is also jailed, a testament to her own political convictions (Shah Nawaz 33). In order to publicize her political victimization, Mohini calls upon Zohra by secretly sending the latter a letter penned in prison. Mohini's letter closes with, "Please get the statement [of her arrest and imprisonment] to the papers for the sake of—Your loving, Mohini" (Shah Nawaz 50). Zohra enlists Surrayya's help—thus braiding together progressive Muslim with progressive Indian womanhood—and "[t]he next day Mohini's statement was featured by all the nationalist newspapers: but how it got into the press was a great mystery which no one could solve" (Shah Nawaz 51). This episode highlights not the ineffectiveness but perhaps the inefficiency of indirect political participation and points toward how, for women outside of purdah (Surrayya) and committed to public—rather than domestic—causes (Mohini), actions can have meaningful effects.[9]

Zohra's nascent political awareness, facilitated by her friendship with Mohini, highlights her family's own temporary disengagement with politics at the novel's earliest narrative point, namely, 1930. *The Heart Divided*, as David Willmer has argued, illustrates how "[t]he political awakening of Muslim women seemed to be inextricably linked to the struggle for a separate Muslim state in India" (574).[10] When Mohini comes to Nishat Manzil to sell salt in support of Gandhi's 1930 Salt March, Jamaluddin, Zohra's father, hesitates to pay an amount equal to his wealth; haltingly, he tells Mohini, "'It's not the money that I hesitate to give, but…you see, Mohini, we are not in this'" (Shah Nawaz 25). Jamaluddin uses the same words when he admonishes Zohra for taking part in a nationalist meeting at her college: "'I think I made it clear to you the day Mohini came to sell salt that we were not in this'" (Shah Nawaz 40). At both junctures, Jamaluddin offers anti-Congress sentiments as reasons for not being politically involved as he was during the Khilafat movement in 1919. Extra-fictionally, 1930 was a significant year for politically-minded Indian Muslims for, in his presidential address to the All-India Muslim League, Muhammad Iqbal first articulated the idea of a separate Muslim state. However, the Muslim League itself was not yet the party that would eventually contest the Congress's political dominance in the subcontinent. Although Jinnah had been involved with the League since 1913, he was not the party's luminary until 1934, when he returned to India from his 1932 self-imposed exile in London (Mahmood 15). The precision of these dates matters as they help justify the fictional apathy of Jamaluddin and many of the other Punjabi Muslims in Shah Nawaz's novel. Further, the extra-fictional latency of League politics at this historical juncture corresponds to the gradual manifestation of Zohra's own—and eventually her family's, too—direct participation in nationalist politics.

Alongside Zohra's growing interest in Congress politics, the novel posits the two sisters as following different gender scripts. Much of the early narrative is devoted to Sughra's wedding—the preparations, the gifts, the ceremonies—and her stifled misgivings about her marriage: "This was the last night of her girlhood and joy and pain, eagerness and apprehension mingled in her heart" (85). Yet, before her marriage and throughout the narrative, Sughra quashes her doubts by subscribing to ideals:

> She looked up once again at the crescent moon with its accompanying star and a joy that was almost like a pain welled up within her. She would live up to her ideal of Muslim womanhood. A dutiful daughter, a loving wife and devoted mother. That is what she wanted to be.
>
> (Shah Nawaz 7)

Even while Sughra lives the disillusionment of her marriage and her life in Multan, she takes comfort in viewing "[t]he moon...sinking slowly towards the west, dragging with it, its accompanying star" (Shah Nawaz 115). The recurrence of the (crescent) moon and star, the image of Islam, connects Sughra to the idea(l) of Pakistan, later made manifest in the nation's flag. Still in purdah, Sughra represents a more traditional definition of Muslim womanhood in the early 1930s. Zohra, on the other hand, "awakens" in just the manner Willmer describes. She chafes at certain traditions, especially purdah, during the same period as Sughra commits herself to the dominant ideal of Muslim womanhood. While Sughra transitions from bride to wife to mother, Zohra steps farther outside of the constraints of purdah. Within the span of just over one year, for example, Zohra unofficially leaves purdah behind, readily securing her father's permission to compete in an intercollegiate debate tournament when, the year prior, he'd refused (Shah Nawaz 69). Indeed, when Sughra voices her objection to Zohra's participation in the tournament, the younger sister responds, "'[N]early eighteen months and things have changed so much. I'm not exactly in purdah now, you know'" (Shah Nawaz 223). Pointedly, the topic of the debate is "'Women's place is in the home and she should not take part in politics,'" and Zohra's speech opposes the claim (Shah Nawaz 224). Though the narrative voice does not provide the text of Zohra's speech, it does feature Zohra's feelings as she delivers her views: "She had felt deeply upon this subject, and now, all the frustrations and longings of a girl behind the purdah, aching to take a citizen's part in the happenings of the world, were poured forth in a voice so full of feeling that all who heard her were visibly affected" (Shah Nawaz 226). Zohra desires to act as a citizen, a subject position no less idealized than Sughra's notion of Muslim womanhood, but, at the same time, Zohra's argument inextricably and radically connects gender and nationalist politics.

The ideological distance between the two sisters' gender and nationalist politics closes as they both adopt a decidedly socialist approach to their work, an approach that each character connects to the League's rather than the Congress's agenda. Conveniently, given the novel's tendency to correlate narrative developments with extra-fictional historical ones, Mohini dies in 1935, a moment on the cusp of a series of elections that hobbled League politics throughout much of northern India.[11] The chapter that begins immediately after Mohini dies opens with "election fever" (Shah Nawaz 230). After repeatedly presenting the Sheikh family as "not in" politics in the first half of the novel, the narrative voice now states that "[s]ome of the better-educated families of Lahore were staunch Muslim Leaguers and among them the Sheikh family was prominent" (Shah Nawaz 231). The sisters' paths cross, politically-speaking, only after Mohini's death, which, as I mention above, is the novel's first sign that Hindu–Muslim unity will not work. Reading Mohini's death in this way matters because it also foreshadows Zohra's own political reconsiderations, which culminate in her leaving the Congress and joining the League. Similarly, Sughra's political trajectory redirects itself as she comes out of purdah and undertakes active involvement in League-related social causes.

The novel is careful to align Sughra with the League consistently; indeed, her loyalty only intensifies and never falters: "although she sympathized with all that Congress had done for the freedom of India, she instinctively turned to the Muslim League for guidance" (Shah Nawaz 260). To gain a measure of solace after the death of her son, who dies just before the 1937 elections, Sughra turns to political work in the shape of community health initiatives in the slums of Lahore. In response to Sughra's uncertainty over whether she has anything to contribute to such initiatives, Rajindar the radical exhorts, "'What can you do? Heavens! Child, do you live in this world or out of it? Can you not look around you? Have you not been into the city and seen the squalor, the sickness and the suffering of tens of thousands of people?'" (Shah Nawaz 255).[12] Rajindar's remonstration prompts Sughra to see that, previously, "[p]olitics for her had consisted mainly of a few books, newspaper reports and talks with members of her family and her friends" (Shah Nawaz 260). Indeed, Sughra reflects on how "her sheltered life had not only been free of want, but [it] had also kept her ignorant of the want of others" (Shah Nawaz 260). Thanks to Rajindar's prodding, Sughra now sees the "great and urgent social problems that confronted the country" (Shah Nawaz 260), and she rather quickly comes out of purdah and devotes herself to the city's neediest women and children. These unfortunate people allow Sughra to align the "freedom that she most longed for"—that of communal self-determination—with "a freedom whereby poverty, disease and ignorance could be abolished forever" (Shah Nawaz 260, 261). In a very direct way, then, Sughra's dedication to political participation connects gender and nationalist politics and bestows upon them a particular socialist bent, all under the League's banner.

Zohra's politics also take a socialist turn and, eventually, fall under the auspices of the League as well. Arrived at via a circuitous route leading to the workers' unions in Amritsar, Zohra's socialist leanings are, in part, an extension of her anti-colonial politics. In the thick of WWII, and thus years after Sughra's own socialist awakening, Zohra sees how many wealthy industrialists throughout India begin to voice their sympathies for the Japanese, a prophylactic measure meant to insure their fortunes should Japan enter India (Shah Nawaz 416). Disgusted over the upper class's willingness to accept fascism, she dedicates herself to securing India's freedom through promoting democracy, and she finds the "same feeling among her friends in the trade unions" (Shah Nawaz 417). As Zohra becomes more enmeshed in labor strikes, she also risks arrest, so Sughra travels to Amritsar to lend support. Facing a lathi-charge, Zohra suddenly sees her sister approach with "a Congress woman followed by over a hundred women" (Shah Nawaz 431). Successful at protecting Zohra and the other demonstrators, Sughra makes a speech:

> All honest people, no matter to what political party they belong, sympathize with you [laborers], and support your just demands,…We Muslim League among them, for we know that you are the sinews of our nation. Unless you support us freedom cannot be ours, as long as you live in want and fear there can be no prosperity.
>
> (Shah Nawaz 431)

These words carefully link the League's politics to socialist concerns. As Sughra continues, she distinguishes the "true" Leaguers from the ministers currently in power, whom she derides as Unionists (Shah Nawaz 432). The speech ends as Sughra quotes Iqbal (Shah Nawaz 432). Pointedly, this episode occurs after the sisters attend the 1940 League session in Lahore, a moment at which Zohra ambivalently recognizes the League's ascendency: "…she saw the fading of her dream, the dream of Hindu-Muslim unity in an India free and whole. But she also saw in these very eyes [in the faces around her] the dawn of a new ideal…" (Shah Nawaz 390). The cumulative effect of what Zohra witnesses at the Lahore session, her involvement with the workers, and her sister's speech arguably sways Zohra to switch her affiliation from the Congress to the League, though not without some reluctance. Zohra tells Sughra that she "'would be out of place'" in the League, to which Sughra responds, "'Nonsense, the doors of the League are open to all. It's a national organization. People of all ideas are there, socialists and democrats, fascists and communists, maulvis and modern men'" (Shah Nawaz 442). Not long after this exchange, Zohra announces her intention of joining the League, a move that allows the two sisters' political affiliations to converge. Their mutual allegiance to the League casts the party as progressive both in terms of gender politics and socialist concerns.

The extra-fictional historical roadmarks of the sisters' respective radicalizations—the election of 1937 for Sughra and the intensification of WWII in the early 1940s for Zohra—similarly chart the League's own radicalization. Indeed, the League had to transform itself to become the "national organization" open to all-comers that Sughra describes. Yet, while the novel marks the change in the League's agenda from what was perceived as an elite movement to a mass one, it doesn't account for the transformation process that historically and fictionally resulted in a party receptive enough to the laundry list of political ideologies Sughra mentions. Historically, the League's transformation followed on the heels of its trouncing by the Congress in the 1937 elections. After the election, the Congress launched Muslim Mass Contact Programme in the United Provinces and, according to Venkat Dhulipala, sought to appeal to Muslims economically, for, as Nehru argued, communalism was "essentially a 'conflict between upper middle class Hindus and Muslims for jobs and power under the new constitution'" (quoted in Dhulipala 608–9).[13] Thus, the Congress's pitch was socialist in tone and aimed at Muslim peasants and workers. As Dhulipala continues, such an economic approach to political affiliation "involved a significant challenge to existing ideas of Muslim community with its own distinctive culture or politics" (610). The Congress's forwarding of a socialist agenda in its attempts to recruit Muslims downplayed the communal differences, holding that the idea of Muslim culture and, hence, Muslim politics as promoted by the League was in fact "the culture of feudal elites, a microscopic minority who claimed descent from the Arabs" (Dhulipala 610). In Dhulipala's reading of the Congress's campaign in the Upper Provinces, the League's own tilt left came about to "meet the Congress challenge" (614). The League "borrowed several leaves from the Congress book" (Dhulipala 614–15) in order to offer Muslims in the United Provinces "a vision of Islamic socialism"(Dhulipala 617) that framed the League as "no less radical or anti-imperialist than the Congress" (Dhulipala 615). Extra-fictionally, the League's transformation proves successful, as the Congress's recruiting campaign halts in 1938 (Dhulipala 620). *The Heart Divided* also represents the League's transformation as a success given Sughra's unproblematized integration of her League loyalties and her socialist tendencies. Zohra herself proclaims, "'[T]he League, which was once the organization of the nawabs and landlords and the rich few only, has grown by leaps and bounds and today no one can deny that it's a people's organization" (Shah Nawaz 448). Yet, the novel does not mention, much less illustrate, how the League's changes relate to the Congress's actions. Indeed, the only acknowledgement that Sughra can make of the Congress's political merits is to praise Hindu thriftiness, a virtue that testifies to the sacrifices Hindus are willing to make to achieve independence (Shah Nawaz 316).

The absence of mention in the novel of the Congress's influence on the League's radicalization, a turn toward socialism crucial to both Sughra's and Zohra's commitment to League politics, stands out for several reasons. First, the novel is given to "purely historical narration," as Rahman phrases it (*History* 25), a tendency that allows the narrative voice to provide in significant detail the minutiae of nationalist political developments for the roughly fifteen years the novel covers. Second, as Dhulipala has it, the Congress's challenge to the League's definition of "Muslim" culture and politics as elitist in its purported purity rather strikingly describes the Sheikh family's pride in their own heritage. Sughra and Zohra's grandfather, for instance, "prided himself on the pure Arab blood of his family." And the wing of the family into which Sughra marries was "a proud and arrogant lot, who traced their descent through hundreds of years to Arab sheikhs who came to India with the early Muslim conquerors"

(Shah Nawaz 4). Sughra's own ideals of Muslim womanhood take shape from these larger claims of Arab purity: "She would be true to her heritage, she, who was a proud daughter of a proud race" (Shah Nawaz 7). Later, in reference to their landholdings in Multan, the family is referred to as "feudal," a designation that suggests that the Sheikh family enjoys not only the privilege of their claims to Arab purity but also the regionally-specific privileges accorded to Punjabi land-owners (Shah Nawaz 126). Such an accounting of privilege resonates with Sughra's political awakening wherein she acknowledges how her own lack of want prevented her from seeing others' misfortune. Zohra is forced to make a similar recognition of privilege due to the chidings of her love interest, Ahmad, political radical and son of her father's former clerk. Upon their first meeting as adults, Ahmad teases Zohra: "'[I]t's all very well for children to play together, but a head clerk's son is not quite the company for the daughter of a rich land-holder!'" (Shah Nawaz 393). Later Ahmad calls Zohra a "'spoilt little girl'" and tells her that "she seldom take[s] the trouble to make [her]self agreeable, and sometimes [she] can be inconsiderate and…and even nasty'" (Shah Nawaz 395, 406). While at first Zohra resists acknowledging the truth of Ahmad's claims, she does so implicitly as he offers such an assessment so as to support his view that she "'could never be a poor man's wife'" (Shah Nawaz 407). By the novel's end, the two are engaged. The sisters' respective political radicalizations allow them to see their own privilege, yet the narrative falls short of exploring fully the foundations of that privilege by having Sughra's and Zohra's socialist activities centered solely on the urban poor and factory workers. Without a full examination of privilege, the novel's vision of the idealized Muslim, especially of idealized Muslim womanhood, stays put as if apolitical.

The dissonance between, on the one hand, the sisters' socialist ideals and the home they find within the radicalized League and, on the other, the unexamined privilege of their landowning heritage marks the limit of the novel's vision of Pakistan. At its conclusion, *The Heart Divided* deploys the recurring image of the crescent moon and star immediately after it hints at partition violence through the figure of Vijay, Mohini's younger brother and, hence, a Congress Hindu living in Lahore:

> [Vijay] pointed as if into the distance and his eyes were haunted. "Look, it comes, nearer and near it comes…the separation and the shadow…the darkest hour…and the rift between us becomes a chasm…and the chasm a sea…a sea of blood and tears…of tears and blood."
>
> (Shah Nawaz 450)

While Habib and his wife, as well as Zohra and Ahmad, look to each other for strength after witnessing Vijay's display, Sughra "left her chair and walked rapidly away, like one in a dream." She looks out the window and sees "high up on the horizon the crescent moon with its accompanying star sailing in a sea of pale green…" As her glance lowers, she also sees the sunset, "a flood of crimson," which causes Sughra to shudder (Shah Nawaz 450). Nonetheless, her vision prompts her to return to Multan and her husband so that, together, they can move "triumphantly" "'[t]owards Pakistan!'" in Mansor's words (Shah Nawaz 451). The adverb "triumphantly," which the narrative voice uses to modify Mansur's directional declarative, suggests that the blood and tears in Vijay's vision may be worth the achievement of Pakistan or, as the novel frames it, Muslim self-determination. Willmer reads this ending as an indication of the novel's optimism over the League's appropriation of gender politics within Muslim nationalist politics, as the movement toward Pakistan will allow Sughra and Mansur to "resolve the contradictions of modernity and tradition together in a shared social space" (587). While certainly the novel's conclusion marks a consolidation, it may well be a conservative, paternalistic one wherein Sughra and Mansur take their positions as Sheikh and Begum of a vast estate. The distance Sughra creates between herself and her siblings after Vijay's display further signals her departure and, perhaps, the novel's from the more transgressive politics and couplings represented by Habib's and Zohra's choices.

For literary scholars, the 1988/1991 publication of Bapsi Sidhwa's *Cracking India* inaugurates what Rosemary Marangoly George calls "Partition Studies," a cross-disciplinary field of inquiry interested in the historiography of the 1947 partition from below.[14] Certainly, *Cracking India* shares much with *Train to Pakistan* and *The Heart Divided*, including what can be read as a tense juxtaposition of the rural and the urban and distinctly gendered concerns. With its later publication date, however, *Cracking India* inflects the critical conversation differently. From 40+ years on, *Cracking India* draws from and participates in/ challenges the discursive mythologizing of the 1947 partition in a different manner than do Singh's and Shah Nawaz's novels. The latter similarly rely upon other representations of anti-colonial activities, League and Congress politics, and partition violence, but, at their moments of production, these novels were not also laden with decades of historical debate and revision.[15] Most scholars frame Sidhwa's novel as contributing to these mythologizing discourses in terms of gender, given that one of the major plotlines involves, first, the adoration of a Hindu Ayah by an intercommunal passel of men and, then, her abduction by a Muslim male mob as communal tensions erupt after the partition.[16] This critical discussion focused on gender in the novel splits along issues of feminist agency, voice, and coalition-building, with Lenny's, the narrator's, class-based (upper middle) and religious (Parsee) identities heavily influencing interpretations.[17]

Indeed, in the scholarly conversation about Sidhwa's novel, Lenny's position is crucial for two primary reasons. First, some scholars cast Lenny's age—she goes from four to eight years old in the novel's 1944–1948 time span—as endowing the narrative voice with objectivity and truthfulness (Mann 72–3), as highlighting the absurdity of communal violence (Rahman, *History* 132–3; Kabir 182), and as producing a developmental narrative (Rastegar 23) that "normalizes" violent communal factions (Sen 79). The other reason scholars focus so intently on Lenny's narrative voice is that it is divided between her child's perspective and her adult one located in an unidentified future. Some commentators view the relationship between Lenny's child and adult narrative voices as "intrusive"

(Gopal 75) or "jarring" (Hai 393). Others consider the differently aged voices as signaling the novel's interest in portraying the fictional Parsee community's complicity in partition (Kabir 182) or as allowing for "very poignant percep-tions of the emotional turbulence of the times" (Ray 132). Jill Didur moves the conversation about Lenny's narrative voice(s) beyond the novel's events to a consideration of the analytical problematic these differently aged perspectives create. "Lenny's naïve narrative perspective," a quality highlighted by the inser-tion of her adult views, contends Didur, "dramatizes the way the tension between text and context opens up a space for interpretation—rather than the search for Truth—in literary representations of 'everyday' history" (*Unsettling* 72). Didur's argument situates *Cracking India*, specifically, and partition literature, generally, as types of discourse that function culturally as representations, just as historical, sociological, and anthropological ones do, rather than as narratives of truth or as purveyors of other humanistic values.

I want to extend Didur's point on *Cracking India*'s status as a cultural product through a focus on the differently aged narrative voices. More specifically, I highlight the novel's insertion of metafictional elements in these voices, which have yielded no critical commentary, to examine how the novel's portrayals of childhood and memory, for example, appear recognizable even while the combi-nation of narrative voices asks readers to question these appearances. Appearances are, in fact, an important point of the novel's metafictional intervention, as they inject a skepticism over how the novel represents the political proclamations and postures of the era. My analysis of Sidhwa's novel will, thus, speak to the novel's relation to the myths of partition discourse, especially those surrounding Jinnah and the Muslim League. The points I raise stand in tension with critiques that would present *Cracking India* as an eye-witness account of partition violence (because of its autobiographical aspects) or as giving voice to silenced memories or as providing the human side of the events that sterile histories leave out.

Cracking India covers four years, from 1944–1948, of its narrator's early life and includes commentary from an adult Lenny, presumably speaking from some point in the 1980s. Lenny initially appears as a precocious child eager to hold on to her polio-related disability in order to retain the attention she receives from the adults around her. Indeed, the attraction and reception of attention, especially of a sexualized variety, seems to be of central concern to the child, as she devotes much time to chronicling the Hindu Ayah's finest attributes and her own sexual curiosity. The narrative voice also records, as if through the milky, naïve lens of a child, the growing political tensions of the era, and it's in compiling these records that the recognition of the differently aged narrative voices becomes so important. Violence erupts across Lahore, and a Muslim male mob, led by one of Ayah's admirers, abducts her. During these terrifying times, Lenny cedes the pole position, allowing Ranna, a village boy and relative of her family's cook, to share his story of the violence in rural Punjab. While Lenny does explicitly incorporate at least two moments of extreme violence—she witnesses the torture of a Hindu man and sees a child's corpse wielded like a trophy by a Sikh mob—her views on the violence deal more with the absences of neighbors, the tensions between her parents, and the overall change in her daily circumstances what with Ayah's loss and the changes in Lahore itself.

Any examination of how the differently aged narrative voices in *Cracking India* operate needs to take into account their metafictional connections. The novel's most explicit metafictional moments occur when Lenny calls attention to Oldhusband, Godmother's spouse, who is otherwise irrelevant to the novel's plotlines. In a scene when Lenny tells Godmother, Slavesister, and their brother-in-law, Dr Mody, about her Sikh neighbor's departure for India, Oldhusband asserts himself in an effort to stunt the others' lamentations, prompting the child Lenny to note, "I have never seen Oldhusband so awesome—not even when he thundered Longfellow at me" (Sidhwa 180). This episode also motivates the adult Lenny to comment, "Oldhusband has been hauled through this book, zombielike, in his cane-bottomed chair...He has been dragged, disgruntled, from the earliest pages to sit mute on the drive...Now that he's had his say, he can peaceably pass away..." (Sidhwa 180–1). Such commentary by the adult Lenny adds another dimension to the relationship between the narrator's voices, as it explicitly points out the very construction of the story: Oldhusband has been "hauled through this book," "dragged...from the earliest pages." The narrator's selectivity—that is, her deliberate decisions about what to include where—directs attention to how the (re)presentation of the characters, events, etc., are designed to create an effect, to be, at once, recognizable as memory, for instance, while also indicating an awareness that the narrative is following the conventions that allow readers to recognize representations as such.

The other very explicit metafictional moment occurs once again in reference to Oldhusband. In the company of the same cast of characters—Godmother, Slavesister, Dr. Mody, and, now also, Adi—Lenny mentions that Oldhusband is in their midst, but then checks herself, an indication of the blurring of the two narrators' voices:

> Oldhusband? He's still inhabiting the pages?
> Clearly, he has not, as I'd thought, passed away.
> Let him stay, as we all stay, in Godmother's talcum-powdered and intrusive wake.
>
> (Sidhwa 249)

Illustrative of the humor that pervades the novel, this passage pokes fun at the narrator's ingenuousness. Here, the metafictional self-awareness challenges the realist convention that would endow the narrator with an ability to know or to control fully the story she's telling.[18] Further, as it pertains to the novel's plot, this metafictional moment also grants insight into how Lenny's voice constructs idealized alternatives, figured—somewhat ironically given the narrator's own admission of lack of control—throughout the story as Godmother's infinite reach and knowledge. In a sense, then, this passage shows how the novel may indulge in the fantasy of rectification, that is, Godmother's ability to "save" Ayah, while also unsettling its possibility.

Much as the narrative voices' metafictional dimensions make recognizable the omniscience of the narrator only to undercut it, they also prompt a reconsideration of what appear to be Lenny's memories. In one of the scenes during which the young Lenny witnesses/partakes in the dynamics between her parents, for example, the adult Lenny concludes the episode with what appears to be a recollection of this scene's consequences: "As the years advance, my sense of inadequacy and unworth advances" (Sidhwa 88). The chapter closes two sentences later with the adult Lenny wondering, "Is that when I learned to tell tales?" Narratorial insertions such as this one complement countless others in which the adult Lenny mentions the passage of time (Sidhwa 125, 171) or when she uses past tense verbs (Sidhwa 44, 96, 264). While it's possible to read all of these instances as part of the exchange between the differently aged narrative voices, that is, as a function of memory, when placed in the context of the novel's metafictional elements, these deployments of what appear as genuine memory can just as plausibly be read as enactments or constructions of what appear to readers as memory.

With respect to the above-cited scene, Lenny's self-examination of the origins of her story-telling talents prompts curiosity over her purpose in representing her parents' relationship as she does. There are many similar scenes wherein Lenny's mother comes off as infantilized or manipulative, and her father as possibly abusive and unfaithful. Is this a way of framing gender dynamics within a specific class or religious group? Can the parents' relationship be a way of outlining Lenny's understanding of the intersections between gender and power? Does the relationship speak to the permeability between the public and private spheres? Does the parents' marriage, with all its troubles, offset the idealization of Godmother's omnipotence; that is, does it act as a foil for Lenny's conjuring of idealized alternatives? In a broader context—that of partition literature—this metafictional reading of Lenny's memories asks readers to assess the value of "eyewitness accounts," of how autobiographical readings endow narratives with authenticity, for example. Such a reading also helps readers trace the conventions partition literature may rely upon, including the use of "memory," so that it can be recognized as a "true" survivor's narrative or as a necessary supplement to the impersonality of historical accounts.

If, as I am suggesting, the metafictional narrative voices deploy and undercut conventions so that readers can ponder why events appear where and how they do in the novel, then Lenny's historical references and presentation of political matters may similarly indicate that a critical distance exists between how these references and matters appear and what purposes these appearances conventionally serve. Both historically and fictionally, the Parsee community in pre-partition India values its political neutrality, a collective characteristic Colonel Bharucha, the community's leader and Lenny's pediatrician, trumpets: "'Don't forget, we are to run with the hounds and hunt with the hare'" (Sidhwa 46). One vociferous member of Colonel Bharucha's audience responds in kind with, "'No one knows which way the wind will blow…. And the Parsees might find themselves championing the wrong side if they don't look before they leap!'" (Sidhwa 46) and

"'[W]e have to move with the times'" (Sidhwa 48). The community's turn to cliché as part of its political rhetoric suggests conventionality in surfeit. As it deploys this predictable script, Lenny's chronicle of the Parsee community's meeting can serve to reinforce the stereotypical/mythologized view of Parsees as politically neutral (or adept), to be sure.[19] At the same time, as Didur argues, the meeting's proceedings "echo British parliamentary rhetoric and illustrate the extent to which the dominant community identity [of the Parsees] has been assimilated with the cultural values and assumptions of the colonizer" (*Unsettling* 77). Yet, given the humorous conclusion to this episode—the audience dissolves into laughter over Hindu and Muslim jokes (Sidhwa 49), which signals a critical distance between the groups wherein the possibility for humor resides—the clichés' very obviousness points toward the narrative's awareness of political posturing, that is, of the distance between the appearance of loyalty or conviction and the ends this appearance serves. In the novel, the Parsee community's interest is in political expediency not ideological fervor, and the metafictional tendencies of the narrative voices suggest the possibility that political stances of all sorts may well be functioning in the same manner.

Such a skepticism of the novel's political and historical representations needs also to be brought to bear on Lenny's presentation of the other characters' political pronouncements and of actual historical figures, such as Gandhi and Jinnah. As some critics have commented, for instance, Lenny's childhood voice presents characters getting their historical references wrong. In the same scene as above, Colonel Bharucha has Gandhi's salt march taking place in 1945 rather than in 1930 (Sidhwa 44). Similarly inaccurate, Lenny's own voice misrepresents how and why Kashmir ended up in India, claiming simply that Nehru's own Kashmiri heritage automatically means that the British would reward the region to him (Sidhwa 169). In Didur's view, such inaccuracies "foreground the narrator's subjective construction of history" (*Unsettling* 172). Certainly, Lenny reveals again and again that she is a motivated and not a disinterested narrator.

At the same time, however, these historical inaccuracies take on additional significance in the context of other characters' political views. At a particularly tense dinner party hosted by Lenny's parents, for instance, the political rhetoric serves a premonitory function. To the British Inspector General of Police's comment that he would celebrate Gandhi's death if the leader weren't such a "'wily Banya [who] is expert on fasting unto death without dying,'" Lenny's Sikh neighbor roars, "'You will not celebrate! You know why? Because rivers of blood will flow in our gutters!'" (Sidhwa 71). The Inspector General responds sarcastically to the Sikh neighbor, making clear that communal violence will surely erupt if the British leave India, to which the neighbor presents a (false) unity among Indians, claiming, "'Hindu, Muslim, Sikh: we all want the same thing! We want independence!'" (Sidhwa 71). The neighbor's "rivers of blood" phrase unmistakably invokes Enoch Powell's infamous 1968 "Rivers of Blood" anti-immigration speech. This anachronistic rendering of British–Indian relations, complete with the Inspector General's (willful) misreading of the Sikh neighbor's meaning, makes the narrative's anticipation of partition violence too knowing. That is, the anachronism locates that violence as part of a post-colonial pattern, one premised on the colonial project's racist legacies that would have the likes of Powell label non-white immigration to Britain "evil" and that would prescribe failure as inherent to postcolonial nationhood. To sketch out such a pattern also calls into question the absolute authenticity of political convictions and actions, as patterns suggest some degree of circumscription and determinism. Moreover, patterns point to emplotment, a narratological function that creates the contexts and meanings of an event. Thus, the novel's historical inaccuracies—the misdated Salt March and the misrepresented awarding of Kashmir—go beyond the narrator's subjective historical investments to show, as well, narrative's signifying ones. Following this line of thought, the Colonel's placement of the Salt March in 1945 and his audience's disparagement of it as a tactic reframe the Quit India movement from one of nationalist commitment to a quest for power, which is precisely what the Colonel concludes (Sidhwa 44–5). Similarly, Lenny's reductive and inaccurate representation of the Kashmir issue allows for the construction of a narrative of victimhood: the British always did like Nehru better. Given that Kashmir remains a volatile region and issue in the context of contemporary India–Pakistan relations, the construction of a victim's narrative clearly has its political uses. All these examples show how the narrative plotting of events affects what the events mean. Thus, Lenny's presentation of the Parsee community's views of Gandhi, for instance, is more than an indication of how that community might have seen Congress nationalism; it is also an illustration of how framing Gandhi's non-violent resistance as privileged or futile contributes to the community's political perspective.

These functions of narrative positioning, highlighted by the narrative voices' metafictional tendencies, call into question where exactly the differently aged narrators stand on the question of the authenticity of nationalist fervor. The high point of communal zeal turned rabid comes when the Muslim male mob descends upon Lenny's house in search of Ayah. Lenny describes this mob, led by Ice-candy-man, as "[c]alculating men, whose ideals and passions have cooled to ice" (Sidhwa 190). On the ground, the Pakistan Movement has failed, in Lenny's estimation, as these "calculating men" act without genuine political or ideological principle. Ice-candy-man's mutations highlight the mob's dangerous disingenuousness. He inhabits at least five different identities—ice-candy seller, birdman, Sufi mystic, poet, and fakir—and speaks three languages, Urdu, English, and Punjabi. This mutability allows Lenny to present the Ice-candy-man as omnipresent: he "moves out of the darkness" after the servants harass Hari in Lenny's yard (126–7); Lenny "sense[s] his presence" as she sits with Ayah and Masseur, another suitor (130); he "prowls" and "lurks" and "follows [Lenny and Ayah] everywhere" (189) until he "disappears across the Wagah border into India" just as Ayah does (Sidhwa 289). Cast as part shape-shifter, part stalker, Ice-candy-man, the most ardent Muslim nationalist in the novel, represents this put-on political fervor as threateningly pervasive and increasingly violent. Further, since Ice-candy-man appears to be motivated as much by jealousy as by indignation over the violence committed against Muslims (Sidhwa 166), his commitment to the Pakistan movement seems qualified at best. Ice-candy-man represents the possibility of communal rabidity at its most extreme.

In her representation of the violent extremes reached by nationalism gone awry, Lenny makes obvious how communal politics readily devolve into barbarous actions far removed from ideals, such as a homeland for India's Muslims that would, at the same time, provide shelter for its own minorities. Her exposure of communalism's basest actions should also inform any reading of her more positive representations of political ideals apparently unsullied. In other words, if one of the purposes served by Lenny's narration of the mob's violent actions is to show how far they are from the League's proclaimed values, then her laudatory representations of Jinnah, for instance, also need to be examined for the purposes they serve. During the dinner party at which the Inspector General and the Sikh neighbor trade barbs, the former portrays Jinnah as having "'the backing of seventy million Muslims!'" and, thus, deserving of the Congress's and the British's serious attention (Sidhwa 71). Such a portrayal of Jinnah as the "sole spokesman," to use Ayesha Jalal's game changing title, endorses a particular slant on the history and politics of this era, overlooking, for instance, not only how the League and the Congress both recruited Indian Muslims' votes but also how other Muslim political organizations vied with the League for a place at the table. Lenny's report of the Inspector General's words, thus, reinscribes a master narrative of the League's political dominance. Later in the novel, Lenny's mother shows her a picture of Jinnah's wife, a Parsee, which prompts Lenny to reflect, "Her daring to no account. Her defiance humbled. Her energy extinguished. Only her image in the photograph and her innocence—remain intact" (Sidhwa 170–1). Ambreen Hai argues that Lenny's inclusion of these reflections on Jinnah's wife "rupture[s] the Muslim nationalist amnesia that idolizes Jinnah but erases his cross-ethnic alliance" (389). Hai's reading of this moment's pathos logically leads to a measured skepticism over the conclusion of this scene. Immediately after Lenny mourns Mrs Jinnah's loss, she wonders,

> But didn't Jinnah, too, die of a broken heart? And today, forty years later, in films of Gandhi's and Mountbatten's lives, in books by British and Indian scholars, Jinnah, who for a decade was known as "Ambassador of Hindu–Muslim Unity," is caricatured, and portrayed as a monster.
>
> (Sidhwa 171)

As this section signals the passage of time, the ability to distinguish at what age Lenny spoke of Mrs Jinnah becomes harder to gauge. At the same time, the criticism she voices over the representations of Jinnah in decades' worth of media and historical accounts constitutes another metafictional moment, emphasizing how the relations between the differently aged narrative voices are not only a way to narrativize memory. This metafictional moment calls Lenny's own representation of both Jinnah and his wife into question. If forty years' worth of history and media can misrepresent Jinnah in Lenny's mind, cannot her own representation perpetrate the same biases but in reverse? The attention the adult Lenny draws to other representations of Jinnah requires that readers maintain a critical distance from what appears to be her own narrative's endorsement of Pakistan's dominant mythology of the man.

Thus, the point is not to decipher how much or why Lenny backs Jinnah but to view the narratives she questions and constructs about him as granting specified meanings to him. Such meanings are different only in degree not kind from the nationalist rabidities of which Lenny accuses the mob that abducts Ayah. To factor in the narrative voice's metafictional aspects shifts how other scholars view the novel's political leanings. With respect to the novel's portrayal of Jinnah, for instance, scholars have commented that Lenny appears to recuperate his image from what she perceives to be its denigration at the hands of pro-Congress and even pro-Hindu discourses. Harveen Mann states that Lenny's portrayal of Jinnah shows "a man truly committed to secular freedom in Pakistan..." (74). And, in an interview with David Montenegro, Sidhwa herself bemoaned how

> Ghandi [sic] totally Hinduized the whole partition movement. This excluded the Muslims there. He brought religion into the Congress Party. And Jinah [sic], who was one of the founders of the party, found he had to edge away from it because it was changing into a Hindu party.
>
> (532)[20]

As an illustration of my point about how narrative emplotment works to influence perspective, Sidhwa rehearses the Muslim League's dominant narrative with respect to its schism with the Congress: the latter was a Hindu party in secular clothing. To call the repetition of this view of the League's stance a rehearsal is not to dismiss it outright; rather, the point is to identify how this aspect of the League's narrative sticks and resonates emotionally decades after the partition.

The analysis that I'm forwarding here has the potential to reframe how readers understand Ayah's dropping out of the narrative and Ranna's dropping in at nearly the same moment. Many of the scholarly treatments of Sidhwa's novel focus on gender, as I've already noted, and the dividing line between these treatments has to do with how successfully *Cracking India* constructs a feminist consciousness. For those who see the novel as failing in this respect, one of the downfalls is the novel's refusal/inability to narrate what happens to Ayah.[21] And some critics view the direct incorporation of Ranna's story as "gratuitous" (Gopal 75–6) or "awkward" (Hai 402). Asha Sen connects the two, arguing that the inclusion of Ranna's story shows that Ayah cannot tell her own (74). To this discussion, I add the following consideration: if Ranna's narrative is included *at the expense* of Ayah's, might this trade-off signal/mirror the dominant conventions of partition history, especially given the novel's metafictional tendencies? In other words, perhaps the recognition of Ayah's narrative/narratorial absence is the point.

Mehr Nigar Masroor's 1987 novel *Shadows of Time* expands the scope of partition literature through both its historical and geographical spans. While all the novels I have already discussed are focused on the Punjab exclusively,

Masroor's novel opens in Calcutta and, later, shifts locations between this site, Delhi, and Lahore. Further, *Shadows of Time* provides a fuller historical chronology than any of the other partition novels discussed as it stretches out over approximately one hundred years. The novel's temporal range and geographical expansiveness allow the narrative to explore political and ideological stances premised upon syncretism in contrast to those endorsing a virulent purity (no matter its basis) as Indians come into an anti-colonial "national consciousness" that eventually develops into a Pakistani nationalism overwritten by Islamization and corruption. *Shadows of Time* thus takes on the good, the bad, and the ugly in both anti-colonial and Pakistani nationalisms. A melodramatic mode serves to heighten the stakes of characters' views and actions while also launching affective appeals to readers that underscore the perceived righteousness of select characters' perspectives. With respect to anti-colonial nationalisms, the novel plays out the tensions between syncretistic and communal politics through personal relationships, including the by now quite familiar trope of inter-communal romance, and across familial generations. These domestic contexts provide much fodder for the narrative's melodramatic tendencies, as romance leads to infidelities and illegitimate children whose "true" identities would wreak havoc on claims of purity. At the same time, the novel's examination of anti-colonial nationalisms also contributes to the construction of the nationalist mythos surrounding Jinnah. As a means of examining the failings of Pakistani nationalism, the novel offers a metacommentary on the function of artistic production in post-partition Pakistan with a focus on Maheen, a Muslim character who becomes a Pakistani and who devotes herself over the next four decades to fostering the arts in Lahore. Maheen's story is itself suffused with melodrama, and her position as a member of the first generation of young people to come of age in the new nation of Pakistan invites a reading of her story's melodramatic tendencies as a marked disillusionment with how that nation failed to fulfill its promise. Combined, the nationalist preoccupations in *Shadows of Time* articulate the artist's bind as Pakistan goes from idea to nation, demonstrating the difficulties involved as art forwards (a certain definition of) Muslim nationalism and then criticizes the nation it achieves.

Melodrama as a popular literary mode must be attuned to the historical and cultural specificities of its moments of production in order to appeal to audiences. As Peter Brooks points out, an unassailable notion of the "good" serves as a fundamental convention of melodrama and needs to be offset by "overt villainy" (11–12). Such "moral polarization" works alongside "the indulgence of strong emotionalism;…extreme states of being, situation, actions; …inflated and extravagant expression, [and] breathtaking peripety" or moments of crisis (Brooks 11–12). *Shadows of Time* contains all these elements, which, at times, makes of the novel a soap opera.[22] But, when these elements bring the political tensions and crises of pre- and post-partition India and Pakistan to the fore, they also call upon melodrama's penchant for "hyperbole and excess" (Cole 303), as well as its sentimentality (J. Smith 5), to consolidate a view of the degree to which the realities of the nation of Pakistan tarnish the idea of Pakistan. The novel's advocacy of a syncretic view of subcontinental histories, cultures, and identities represents the narrative's broadest "good." Personal motives, communal politics, and nationalist ideologies that fetishize purity stand in as syncretism's polarized opposite. The transubstantiation of the idea of Pakistan into the Pakistani nation marks a pivotal moment in the use of melodramatic elements in *Shadows of Time*, as this historical moment, in the novel's imaginary, also involves the shift from a version of Muslim nationalism that embraces syncretism to an orthodox Pakistani nationalism that denies such impure roots. In other words, during the novel's pre-partition era, its melodramatic heroes, including the Hindu Manilal, whom Jagdev Singh labels a "votary of a composite culture untainted by the prejudices of a besmirched past" (255), and the Muslim Farhan, uphold syncretism as a political ideal. The fictional Jinnah presented in this narrative stands in as the manifestation of this ideal. As a melodrama, Masroor's novel "articulates the shared values of the collective," a generic characteristic that Jeffrey Mason argues involves the author and the audience (214–15). And, as Mason further contends, these shared values "becom[e] part of the myth-making apparatus of [the collective's] culture, offering metaphorical and even allegorical action that conveys a world view" (214–15). In this sense, the pre-partition sections of *Shadows of Time* reinforce the pervasive and dominant extra-fictional mythology surrounding Jinnah. Yet, as a novel invested in chronicling Pakistani history, Masroor's narrative also traces the nation's failure to live up to the ideals, including secularity, diversity (through the protection of minorities if not linguistically), and equality, that Jinnah espoused. The novel broaches the representation of this failure through Maheen's struggles to cultivate an artistic environment in post-partition Lahore, wherein artistic production can once again draw from Pakistan's syncretic past without fear of censure or censor.

As I hint above, *Shadows of Time* sprawls over a century of subcontinental history, opening in 1884 and concluding at some point in Zia's Pakistan of the 1980s. Readers are first introduced to three friends—Sisir, Manilal, and Keshab— whose personal and professional lives, as well as their political convictions, allow for the incorporation of scores of other characters across religious communities, generations, and locations. Of these three, Manilal represents the most ideologically unassailable, as he holds "enlightened" political views about Hindu–Muslim unity via a syncretistic understanding of subcontinental political and cultural history. As time ticks by, locations change, and generations pass, other select characters, including Surinder (Manilal's protégé), Farhan, and Maheen (Farhan's daughter), also occupy positions clearly marked by narratorial favor even though their shortcomings are more evident than Manilal's. Despite their flaws, these characters often possess the most clear-sighted politics, i.e. a politics based on syncretism rather than purity, or offer the most insightful critiques of their own historical moments, thereby operating as the narrative's ideological and emotional centers. Such touchstones are important to the narrative's use of melodramatic elements, for this generic mode requires an identifiable "good" with which the audience can identify and empathize. Thus, these characters' political and ideological convictions guide the reader toward their inverse, as well. So, while there are plenty of villainous characters who are vengeful and duplicitous, the novel casts various political and ideological viewpoints as the actual counterpoints to the "good" represented by characters such as Manilal, Farhan, and Maheen. In this way, *Shadows of Time* complicates the so-called "lowbrow" genre of melodrama, using the genre's characteristic heightened emotional appeals to consolidate a liberal political and ideological perspective. From this angle, the novel's use of melodrama speaks to its fictional concern, framed most explicitly in Maheen's subplot, with the place of artistic production in national contexts.

From the start, the narrative endorses an anti-colonial stance that, nonetheless, incorporates "national" identities defined by historical contingencies. The novel's first scene features a discussion involving three friends, Sisir, Manilal, and Keshab, all successful Indian Hindus living in Calcutta. Distinctly anti-colonial in tone, the men's conversation revolves around the Raj's discriminatory practices, especially its revocation of the Ilbert Bill, "which would have allowed Indian magistrates to try European subjects" (Masroor 1). The men are indignant over the British's presumed superiority even while the narrative voice points out that the three friends, all "educated Bengalis," "were wearing the clothes of the ruling English, seated on cane chairs, sipping brandy and soda in complete imitation of the white man's dusk ritual" (Masroor 2). At first glance, there may appear to be a sharp irony operating in this scene of discontent, yet, as the story develops from these men's lives, the irony softens. In its place, the narrative implies that the national identities that are taking shape throughout the novel's temporal span must account for the historical production of identities, especially when they are articulated through the emergence of a national consciousness, which, at this moment in the novel, refers to a united India. Indeed, Sisir, Manilal, and Keshab's anglophilia is merely one manifestation of syncretic identities that the novel advocates. This syncretism bears some complexity in that it allows for anti-colonial sentiment and action even while it acknowledges the acceptance and acceptability of anglophilic norms, for example.[23] Moreover, by advocating syncretism at the historical moment of the novel's opening, the narrative can then present all Indians, regardless of creed, as coming into national consciousness together. As Manilal declares, "'Bengal has now produced enough men conversant with western philosophy, we must also grasp the secret of their power and use it for a national awakening'" (Masroor 3). The extra-fictional historical referent here is, of course, the emergence of the All-India Congress Party, which was founded in 1885. The party's establishment represents the culmination, in the novel's imaginary, of Hindu–Muslim unity, a consolidated anti-colonial front that, according to another character, the British "'dare not allow…to happen again'" (Masroor 24). Thus, the novel's first reference to an emerging national consciousness relies upon a recognition of particular ways in which British power benefits the Indians and a call for a unified—and not divided—representation of the Indian nation.

Just as the novel opens with this positive representation of anglophilia, it also puts a similar emphasis on cultural integration between Hindus and Muslims. Manilal's family, for instance, has a "long association with the mughals. Over centuries a synthesis had taken place between brahmin thought and the Muslim ideas espoused by the ruling mughals" (Masroor 2). Traversing thirty years and the distance from Calcutta to Delhi, the novel picks up this theme of positive syncretism again as it introduces another key character, Farhan, who serves as the educated Muslim counterpoint, though a generation younger, to the three educated Hindus featured at the novel's opening. As a boy, Farhan learned from his mother that "Muslim civilization" in Delhi represented the "finest synthesis [because] Mughal palaces blended with the minarets of mosques which pierced the sky above; while temples below celebrated Shiva's lingam, soft bosomed domes, broad parapets, high fortress walls were legacies of the past..." (Masroor 135). The very topography of place signals the subcontinent's shared history, a characteristic Lahore also manifests: "Lahore derived its name from Leh, son of Ramchandra, the hero of the Ramayana" (Masroor 185). History sediments the city, layering Muslim, Sikh, and British influences—many of them architectural—on top of the "ancient Hindu kingdom" (Masroor 185). Bengal similarly bears the traces of this cultural syncretism, a point Manilal concedes regarding Bengali lyrics that "'do echo shades of Islamic teaching that man represents the highest value'" (Masroor 51). These examples, which the novel places in far-flung locations and at distant temporalities, link a national political consciousness to cultural production, including architecture and literature, through an emphasis on a historically-produced syncretism.

In sharp contrast are the political, ideological, and cultural stances bent on purity and fundamentalisms. Intermittently throughout the novel, the third person narrative voice lays out the historical setting in great detail both to orient the reader to the present circumstances operating at a given plot juncture and to provide the background of the characters' actions and attitudes. As *Shadows of Time* unspools its stories taking place during the 1910s, it connects the advent of WWI with Gandhi's rise to prominence in Indian nationalist politics. Citing Gandhi's claim that "'Politics cannot be divorced from religion,'" the narrative voice recounts the emergence of the Khilafat movement, with particular emphasis on how the Ali brothers link their politics to Gandhi's. As Muhammad Ali proclaims, "'Gandhi alone can be our man'" (Masroor 136). While, from one angle, the Khilafat movement could be viewed as Hindu–Muslim cooperation,[24] several of Masroor's characters, including Farhan's influential uncle, view this inter-communal political solidarity skeptically. Instead, they commit themselves to Jinnah, who pushed for the Lucknow Pact, "which brought about an agreement on the mode and percentage of Muslim representation in the provincial and central legislatures" (Masroor 137). The establishment of separate electorates signifies, as the narrative voice explains, "a very different stance to Muhammad Ali's fervour for Turkey. Instead of demagogy and airy fairy talk on ideals, a practical, pragmatic solution was being worked out to enable the Muslims of India to live in harmony with the larger community—the Hindus" (Masroor 137). Political commitments based on religion appear here as "airy fairy talk," likely to amount to no significant gains that would further the cause of legislative independence from the British.

To underscore the necessary binary, the novel pushes religiously-based political commitment to the point of fanaticism and terrorism, made manifest in Manilal's wife and son, Kauna and Amlok, thereby contrasting Manilal's own centered and privileged perspective. Despite her liberal education and her apparent intellectual "match" with Manilal, Kauna feels a void that can only be filled by performing fanatical pujas to Kali. As the novel presents it, Kauna's religious outlet is a dangerous form of Hindu revivalism promising, according to the pundits in whom Kauna trusts, "'[d]eliverance from those who destroyed your religion and your ways, and the hope of revenge'" (Masroor 27). Kauna initiates her and Manilal's son, Amlok, into this form of worship, and the narrative voice makes it clear that this initiation into fanatical religion leads to his commitment to fanatical politics. By the time of the first partition of Bengal in 1905, for instance, Amlok espouses militant anti-colonialism at a large gathering in Calcutta: "'[W]e must be prepared for great sacrifices...Let not Bengal be afraid to give its own blood for the Bengali motherland'" (Masroor 76). Falling immediately upon the heels of Amlok's speech, the narrative voice comments, "Kauna had done her work well. Blood, sacrifice and violence were the themes of Amlok's speech" (Masroor 76). Amlok soon moves from incendiary words to incendiary actions, for, as the narrative voice puts it, "[f]rom the assassin's dagger to the terrorist's bomb and pistol the step was a short one" (Masroor 94). Arrested and charged for terrorist activities, Amlok is executed but not before Manilal disavows all his son comes to represent:

> "[Y]ou cur, you have betrayed the cause I have brought you up for, which was the freedom of India, not a paltry meaningless vengeance against a few individuals. You have destroyed our family honour, by becoming a murderer, you have cast a horrendous shadow on our religion, which after centuries was being acclaimed as man's noblest expression of thought. You are no son of mine."
>
> (Masroor 108)

Manilal's rejection of Amlok bears great melodramatic appeal: a father disowns a son; family honor is tarnished; vengeance indulged; murders committed. At the same time, however, Manilal conveys a grander principle, the freedom of India achieved through rational political discourse. In fact, though a Hindu, Manilal admires Jinnah, claiming that the latter "'represented the saner, thinking element amongst the Muslims...I know today the whole of India is hailing the new mahatma, but has anyone stopped to think what this mahatma really stands for?'" (Masroor 153). By linking Kauna and Amlok's religious devotion to Kali to extreme and violent pro-Hindu politics, the novel establishes a causal connection between religious fervor and inflexible communal politics. Further, through the emotionally charged domestic drama—the betrayal of a venerated and unsuspecting husband and father by his "primitive" wife and son—this episode also launches an affective appeal to readers that invites them to empathize with the righteousness of Manilal's stance (Masroor 107).

A similar binary that presents the syncretic as good and the fundamentalist as evil appears in the subplot involving Maheen. She and her friend Nishat spectate at a parade celebrating Pakistan's independence, yet both young women feel sad. They "tur[n] away from the festive crowds," and the narrative voice figures their marginalization by likening Maheen and Nishat to

> fossils left on a shore after the sea has moved away, these two clung to that piece of land where the waters of time had left them, destined to change their shapes and hues, compressed by the thrust of new piles of sand and rock which would lie upon them layer upon layer.
>
> (Masroor 328)

This metaphor converts the young women into the very syncretism they value. Yet, by fossilizing them and rendering them partially passive—"the waters of time had left them"—this image also suggests that their efforts to build a life that accords with their ideals will be ineffective. Indeed, as fossils, their views are of the past. Maheen's political marginalization compounds her familial isolation, making her a particularly sympathetic character no matter how flawed. Farhan, her father, has always been absent due to his ongoing love affair with Sarla, a Hindu woman who remains in Delhi after partition. His paternal failures dent his otherwise admirable qualities and keep Maheen from any intimate bond with her father despite their shared political views. Nuzhat, Maheen's mother, eventually begins an affair of her own, and Maheen witnesses one of the illicit couple's romantic interludes (Masroor 342). As a result, Maheen comes to the conclusion that tradition is hypocrisy; significantly, her mother's affair (and not her father's) "had at that impressionable age destroyed the edifice of social values for [Maheen], the moral codes her elders professed to live by..." (Masroor 342). Maheen's rejection of her mother constitutes, on another level, a rejection of the purported purity of tradition, which is synonymous with fundamentalism. On a personal level, it motivates her to marry without her family's knowledge or permission, a match that leaves her unfulfilled and, soon enough, a young widow. These experiences combine to position Maheen as well outside the mainstays of the Pakistani nation, both publicly and privately.

Almost automatically, then, readers encounter Maheen's artistic endeavors as similarly marginal and oppositional. Maheen undertakes her endeavors in 1956, the year Pakistan finally received a constitution and the year it declared itself an Islamic Republic. These historical developments prompt the narrative voice to comment that Pakistan, "the homeland required for the Muslims of India to live and grow in, had picked up the horrendous burden of history, the chequered and disfigured past of Islam and the questionable aspect of a republic" (Masroor 386). "Chequered and disfigured" suggest that the Islam invoked in Pakistan's first constitution stands beside the novel's commentary on the manipulated versions of the religion the ulema lit upon during the Khilafat movement. These two adjectives also highlight the constructedness of what is otherwise presented as the unmediated truths of religion. In this context, Maheen pursues dance as it manifested itself throughout subcontinental history. Her aim is to "creat[e] a new idiom of dance, a Pakistani idiom, which would be secular and related to the life of the people of this land, and could reflect its history in dynamic rhythms" (Masroor 386–7). Not surprisingly given the position from which she begins, Maheen and other artists in Lahore encounter resistance under Ayub's and, later, Yahya's regimes. Pointedly, the narrative voice describes how these artists "kept striving individually and in separate groups. Whatever encouragement they received was of their own making" (Masroor 400). This fictional version of Ayub's government would support artistic production if "no revolutionary ideas were floated in any medium—drama, dance, painting or poetry" (Masoor 400). Maheen's artistic impulses derive their inspiration from the ground up, suggesting that a Pakistani artistic idiom would reflect the diversity of lifeways brought together in the territorialization of the idea of Pakistan. However, such a freeplay of diversity, which would encompass ethnic, linguistic, and religious mulitiplicities, would destabilize the purported unity of Pakistani nationalist identity, defined and implemented from the top down.

In *Shadows of Time*, Maheen and the other Lahori artists can find no place for themselves in what passes for "culture" in the nation of Pakistan. The fictional Zia's seizure of power reduces Maheen to despair: "'Inquiry of the mind, is deplored...Books, music, aesthetics—all have been banished" (Masroor 418). Declaring that the Islamists have "'taken away [her] present,'" Maheen continues to resist the pressure to "purify" her artistic expression:

> "I was the proudest of the vanquished and the free 'cos I had inherited the blending of Muslim and Hindu India. That synthesis spelt out in marble, enunciated in ghazal and measured by the pakhawaj breaking into two to become a *tabla Jori* was my inheritance...I could subscribe to two homelands...because I had measured my dance steps to a hundred different rhythms of the tabla. But when they tell me I cannot dance because it is a sin and I must not vote because it is un-Islamic, and I am only half a human being because I am a woman, then I know something is very wrong."
>
> (Masroor 425–6)

Because Maheen insists on celebrating art forms derived from centuries of subcontinental contact and history, the Pakistani government deems her art not just politically but also morally unacceptable. By casting Maheen's artistic philosophy and expression as unacceptable in its representation of Zia's Pakistan, the narrative traces how far official nationalist discourses have departed from the more inclusive and democratic emphases syncretic anti-colonial nationalisms valued. And, at the level of character, this image of a despondent Maheen garners readerly sympathy, for, in the end, she appears to belong nowhere.

Indeed, *Shadows of Time* does end darkly. The novel's conclusion recounts Maheen's suicide, an action she takes after being diagnosed as terminal with cancer. She plunges into the Indus River, and the note she leaves behind explains that her wish is "'to mingle for ever with the soil and sun [she] love[s] so much'"

(Masroor 437). Maheen embraces syncretism even in defeat. Her sad end marks the ending of a pattern in the novel, as all of its "heroes" meet sad, disappointed, or bitter ends. Manilal, for instance, ends in disillusionment in 1928, declaring, "'I felt strange this morning as if I had two souls with one body, one half of me was Muslim and the other Hindu...Is there truly no hope left? Are we really caught in as Tagore says—the pollutions of the past?'" (Masroor 181). In 1965, Farhan, the fervent League supporter, makes a pilgrimage to Ajmer, India, prompted by the news that his son with Sarla, his Hindu lover, was killed by the Pakistanis in that year's war. Farhan dies, clinging to the idea that he will leave Ajmer to seek out Sarla and his Indian grandchildren. The notion of uniting with his family with Sarla, who have been unknown to him precisely because his affair with Sarla was intercommunal, stirs within Farhan "a new joy, an urgent desire... His grandchildren, the new beginnings of life, of hope, of joy! ...and then, in that moment of longing, finality clutched his throat, reached out to stifle his lungs and silently choked his breath" (Masroor 411). The narrative voice frames all three of these deaths as tragic, ratcheting up the emotional effect and upending the standard melodramatic conclusion that has good triumphing over evil. Indeed, the emotional reverberations emanating from these heroes' wasted ends risk "drowning out the kind of political critique" their stories offer (Cole 304). And, yet, these endings may indicate, in James Smith's understanding of melodrama, "simply alternative formulations of the same conflict, opposite extremes of the same melodramatic spectrum" (9). In that way, Manilal's, Farhan's, and Maheen's lonely and disappointed deaths may serve as invitations to readers to see their political and artistic struggles as ongoing.

Train to Pakistan and *Cracking India* attempted to represent the migration—forced or voluntary—that resulted from the realities of partition in 1947, and *The Heart Divided* hinted at the furious violence of these mass movements of people at its conclusion through the uncanny appearance of Vijay, Mohini's younger brother, at the Sheikh's home in Lahore just as Pakistan is born. Sorayya Khan's 2009 novel, *Five Queen's Road*, remains focused on the Punjab, specifically Lahore, but this novel diverges from the pack through its portrayal of a Hindu man, Dina Lal, who refuses to leave for India. One of the novel's major issues, then, is the place of minorities in the nascent Pakistan. The house whose address gives the novel its name grounds Dina Lal's rationalizations for staying while also providing the basis for other characters, most especially Amir Shah, Dina Lal's Muslim tenant, to articulate their own claims to belonging to the new nation; the house, in a sense, becomes a microcosm of the tensions between majority and minority interests. Yet, the narrative counteracts the characters' every reason or claim, suggesting that the legitimacy of belonging may indeed be a product of historical contingencies.

John Smithson, an Englishman and the "Chief of the North West Railways," commissions the house at Five Queen's Road to very precise specifications (S. Khan 17). So fine is the house that Dina Lal, its eventual owner, wonders "what [it was] about the island left behind that made this strange breed of Englishman insist on green grass while all around the parched ground [was] made of nothing but dust..." (S. Khan 17). This first intimation of the house's out-of-place-ness colors each character's connection to the house, Lahore, and Pakistan. As the novel's constant, the house at Five Queen's Road tethers characters' identities even as it deteriorates over the forty years covered by the storylines. At the earlier narrative plane, which begins in July 1947 and continues through to 1952, Smithson sells the house to Dina Lal, himself wealthy from vast real estate holdings, and the novel presents Dina Lal's motivations for purchasing the house as somewhat perverse, even fueled by vengeance: "*Soon you will be far, far away, Johnny, in your own country—nothing but an island!—and I will live in your house any damn way I please*" (S. Khan 23; emphasis in original). Ownership of Five Queen's Road represents to Dina Lal the power to claim his own country and to determine his own future. Almost immediately, however, Dina Lal recognizes his inability to claim Pakistan unconditionally, as his wife, Janoo, brings home from her daily trips to temples reports of violence against Hindus and Sikhs. As insurance against violation, Dina Lal converts to Islam and hatches a plan to partition the house, and then he invites Amir Shah, a Muslim magistrate, to live in its newly closed off front rooms. Yet, Amir Shah's presence cannot prevent Dina Lal's adult sons from migrating to India, nor can it protect Janoo from abduction at the hands of an unidentified group of Muslim men shortly thereafter. The novel's other primary narrative plane, which begins in August 1957 and continues intermittently through June 1961, revolves primarily around the arrival of Amir Shah's Dutch daughter-in-law Irene at Five Queen's Road. Irene, married to Amir Shah's son, Javid, rounds out the family, which also includes Amir Shah's daughter, Rubina, her husband, and later her own daughter. Relations between tenant and landlord remain rancorous in this later historical plane, and squatters of various types now occupy the once grand gardens surrounding Five Queen's Road. At the later end of this narrative plane, Dina Lal dies, and Amir Shah discovers how his landlord's life was, in effect, a chronicle of Pakistan's early years. Despite what appears to be a turn inward to the domestic, Irene's presence and the topographical changes at the house insert (sometimes subtly) into the novel the broader historical concerns, including Ayub Khan's military coup, the reconstruction of Europe after WWII, and the ascendency of American power, of the late 1950s and early 1960s. The novel closes with an epilogue set in the 1980s. Javid and Irene prevail upon Amir Shah to leave Five Queen's Road, though not Lahore, and the old house is demolished.

The time span covered by the two narrative planes offers a long enough view of Pakistan's early national challenges to outline the change in the status of minorities in Pakistan (and India). Muhammad Ali Jinnah articulated an idealized view of minorities' place in Pakistan in a speech he delivered upon his election as President of the Constituent Assembly in 1947:

> We are starting in the days when there is no discrimination, no distinction between one community and another, no discrimination between one caste or

creed and another. We are starting with this fundamental principle that we are all citizens and equal citizens of one State.

(17)[25]

One hears echoes of Jinnah's proclamations of equality in the "Agreement between India and Pakistan on Minorities" issued jointly by Jawaharlal Nehru and Liaquat Ali Khan in 1950: "Both Governments wish to emphasize that the allegiance and loyalty of the minorities is to the State of which they are citizens, and that it is to the Government of their own State that they look for the redress of their grievances" (344). The difference between these two official statements regarding the status of minorities in Pakistan (and India) is the shift from Jinnah's implicit promise of freedom no matter identity and Nehru and Khan's similarly implicit acknowledgment that "grievances" obstruct minorities' abilities to exercise the freedoms of citizenship in these newly independent countries. The change in minority status apparent in the comparison of these two statements surely reflects a recognition of the realities of mass migration and partition violence.

Partition's displacements and carnage tested the two new nations in several ways, investing the figure of the refugee with literary significance.[26] Gandhi viewed one of these tests as a moral one. According to Alok Bhalla, Gandhi advised Indian Sikhs that their "salvation demanded that the Muslims who had fled [India] or had been forced out of their homes had to be invited back so that they could re-inhabit the places they left behind" ("Moral Action" 111). Offering counsel in kind to Pakistani Muslims, Gandhi reportedly recommended that "if Pakistan wanted to be a *pak* (pure) state then it must take a pledge that it will invite every Hindu and Sikh who had been forced out back to their old homes [in Pakistan] and ensure their safety" (Bhalla, "Moral Action" 111). Gandhi's statements stake communal honor on the migrant's ability to return.[27] Both nations responded to the possibility of refugees returning bureaucratically via ordinances and provisions for evacuee property. Significantly, however, these bureaucratic measures quickly took stock of the reality that evacuees were not likely to return. According to Joseph Schechtman, for instance, in early September 1947, both nations figured that minority evacuation would be temporary and, thus, agreed upon the "unconditional and automatic restoration of property to returning refugee-owners" (407). However, by later that very month, as Schechtman continues, the respective governments instituted policies based upon the "reduced...likelihood of the evacuees' [sic] ultimately recovering their property" (407). Subsequently, each nation concerned itself with the rehabilitation of refugees who crossed into their respective nations rather than out of them (Schechtman 410). The distance between partition's moral and bureaucratic tests of Pakistan (and India) manifests itself in the expectation of return and serves as a stock feature in much partition literature.[28] The Muslims of Mano Majra, for instance, ask the Sikh neighbors to safeguard their property, a promise the Sikhs cannot fulfill thanks to Malli and his gang (Singh 139). Similarly, in *Cracking*

India, Lenny's parents promise to take care of the possessions of their Sikh and Hindu neighbors even as their properties are soon enough occupied by others. In this sense, the minorities remain in Pakistan via their very absence, and their return, which would signal their legitimate belonging, becomes a fetish.[29]

Dina Lal's residence at Five Queen's Road thus confronts these extra-fictional calls for moral remediation and bureaucratic measures, as well as historiographic, ethnographic, and literary mainstays in the study of partition. As a minority still resident in Lahore after the creation of Pakistan, Dina Lal as a character gauges both belonging and displacement. In other words, Dina Lal's attempt to fix his identity through owning Five Queen's Road, arguably a colonial legacy, marks the novel's most immediate power balance. As Dina Lal's motivations for buying Five Queen's Road already indicate, the first power inequity he seeks to right through staying on in Lahore is distinctly anti-colonial. Conceding his own complicity, for "[h]e had profited from the railway lines expanding across his village land," Dina Lal nonetheless has "had enough" by the time 1947 rolls around; Radcliffe's cartographic "etchings" spur Dina Lal to "teach [the British] a lesson. On this side of the lines" in Pakistan (S. Khan 15). Indeed, this opportunity to own as fine a house as the one at Five Queen's Road causes Dina Lal to feel as if he himself were viceroy: from the house's rooftop, "the city spread out like a map beneath him, he had pretended that his life, already full, was only beginning. Like the country, *land of the pure*, just born" (S. Khan 25; emphasis in original). Insofar as Dina Lal feels anti-colonial sentiments, the narrative suggests, he can also enjoy the sense that he is a part of a larger collective, the Pakistan Movement. His invocation of Pakistan as "*land of the pure*" is here distinctly without religious connotation and, instead, appears to derive its power from how aptly it describes the success of achieving Pakistan from an anti-colonial perspective.

Dina Lal's reasons for feeling as though he belongs barely hold up, though, as his adult sons plead with him to leave for India. Tempers flare, and Dina Lal shouts,

> "*This* is our country.' Because the moment got away from him, he added what was, he later acknowledged to Janoo [his wife], a bit of melodrama, "Right here, we have tilled the earth."
>
> Before he could continue, Ram Charan [the older son] interrupted him and laughingly remarked, "You don't work the fields. We're not farmers."
>
> (S. Khan 45; emphasis in original)

The disingenuousness of Dina Lal's romantic self-framing as a "son of the soil"—not (only) Ram Charan's laughter—makes a mockery of his reason even while it rehearses the cant rhetoric of nationalist belonging.[30] But even Dina Lal's sincerely felt attachments to Lahore and the actions they motivate are not enough to secure his belonging there. As the violence mounts, his sons depart in July 1947. Their departure prompts Dina Lal to partition Five Queen's Road and to invite Amir Shah to take up residence; in Dina Lal's reasoning, Amir Shah's presence, along with his own conversion to Islam, would construct a protective barrier around the house. These acts constitute "whatever was necessary to claim [Lahore] back" (S. Khan 52) and signal the dissipation of Dina Lal's sense of having begun a new life in the land of the pure. Within months of Amir Shah's occupancy, however, Janoo is abducted by unidentified men (S. Khan 85). That Amir Shah's presence did nothing to deter this act of violence leads Dina Lal to the conclusion that Amir Shah "had failed in his obligation to protect him and his wife" (S. Khan 91). In the prevailing gender and communal economy of this historical moment, Janoo's abduction tarnishes both men's honor: Dina Lal cannot protect his wife, and Amir Shah, the Pakistani Muslim, cannot protect these members of a minority community. Moreover, Janoo's abduction also represents how limited—if not nonexistent—Dina Lal's agency is. He goes from feeling as though he could claim belonging to Pakistan via ownership of Five Queen's Road to recognizing "[t]he truth was [that] he was left behind" (S. Khan 96). In the trajectory of Dina Lal's life, laid out along the ten plus years of the novel's two primary narrative planes, the power balance shifts from privileging his anti-colonial yet landed identity to enfeebling it due to his religious one.

Amir Shah's claim to belonging also destabilizes over the course of the novel's two narrative planes, though in a less overt fashion than Dina Lal's. From the first chapter, set in August 1957, Amir Shah emerges as the authoritative center of the novel. The plot opens with Amir Shah reading a telegram intended for his son, Javid, telling him of Irene's impending arrival (S. Khan 2). Javid, summoned by his father, "sometimes felt himself still a child" in his father's presence despite being a married and America-returned man (S. Khan 2). Amir Shah's effect on his children, for Rubina holds her father with similar reverence, establishes the older man as the family's anchor and, seemingly, as a reliable center for the novel's otherwise detached narrative perspective. Indeed, in the novel's first unnamed reference to Dina Lal, readers learn that "Amir Shah wasted as little energy as he could on a person [Dina Lal] who had made it his mission to rob him of his peace and property alike" (S. Khan 11). This initial presentation of Dina Lal, made early in the novel but ten years into his and Amir Shah's acquaintance, invites the conclusion that Amir Shah is the proprietor of Five Queen's Road, and legitimately so, as it is Dina Lal who seeks "to rob" his "peace." Although the novel makes Dina Lal's ownership of the house clear when it introduces the earlier narrative plane in the next chapter, Amir Shah's claims of ownership in the later plane promote confusion in the reader and in Irene, too, who must repeatedly ask Javid to clarify the house's history.

These competing ownership claims operate to challenge the legitimacy of Dina Lal's presence, to be sure, but they also work to undermine Amir Shah's seemingly inviolate legitimacy as a Pakistani Muslim as well. After one particularly vicious flare up of the tensions between the two men, for instance, Amir Shah

had launched formal court proceedings to evict Dina Lal from Five Queen's Road. Amir Shah put to his use the Evacuee Property Commission rules and regulations designed to compensate people for property left on the other side of the border during Partition eleven years earlier.

(S. Khan 72)

Amir Shah's "use" of this bureaucratic measure indicates how significantly these rules and regulations have changed since their inception. As I mentioned above, initially both the Pakistani and Indian governments meant to protect the property of refugees *leaving* a place, but Amir Shah's intentions show that they now operate to administer property for the benefit of those *entering* a place. While this scene is the first time the novel has Amir Shah mention claiming property, his actions take place in the novel's later narrative plane, January 1958, to be exact. He invokes the Evacuee Property Commission at several temporally earlier moments, however. As early as 1948, for instance, in response to Rubina's suggestion that they find another place to live since Five Queen's Road "'isn't really our house anyway,'" Amir Shah says, "'You've heard of the Evacuee Property Commission regulations? If I wanted, I could file papers and have part of this house allocated to us to compensate for the land we left behind'" (S. Khan 100). Unquelled, Rubina questions her father: "'Left behind? ...But we've lived in Lahore for years'" (S. Khan 100). Amir Shah's efforts to justify the legitimacy of his recourse to the Commission's regulations, which include his recitation of the fact that they came from Amritsar and were due some compensation "under the laws of Pakistan," come off as disingenuous as did Dina Lal's claim of being a tiller of the soil and, thus, legitimately belonging. The righteousness of his claims further diminishes when he shares his family's history with Irene, explaining that they "had been lucky. By the grace of God, he explained, they were already in Lahore [by August 1947], and had been for years" (S. Khan 114). In this light, Amir Shah's turn to the bureaucratic "justice" available to him as a migrant Pakistani Muslim—and barred to Dina Lal as a native Pakistani Hindu—smacks of corruption.[31] Thus, even if Amir Shah's house in Amritsar was "'[n]ot quite so big,'" his efforts to secure ownership of Five Queen's Road and, by extension, his belonging in Lahore illustrate the shifting of other power balances: a Muslim migrant goes, somewhat dishonestly, from being less to more fortunate under the auspices of Pakistani law and at the minority's expense. Amir Shah's ties to Pakistan, facilitated felicitously as they are through the state, also actually prevent Dina Lal's. *Five Queen's Road* suggests that the Pakistani state discourages the affective attachments of minorities.

With a publication date of 2004, Saad Ashraf's novel, *The Postmaster*, like Sorayya Khan's 2009 *Five Queen's Road*, helps further conventionalize several tropes common to earlier partition fictions while it also expands the boundaries of this subcategory of Pakistani literature. As with many of the other examples of partition literature I have already discussed, *The Postmaster* features an intercommunal love affair between a Muslim man and a Hindu woman. And, similar to *Shadows of Time*, Ashraf's novel covers a lot of ground, starting in Delhi and moving around the north and west of British India until finally ending in Lahore. Additionally, these two novels both figure their key protagonists as disillusioned and frustrated at the time of their deaths. *The Postmaster* shares with *Five Queen's Road* a post-partition interest in the administration of evacuee property in Pakistan, as well as a marked detachment from the escalating political and violent tensions preceding and following from partition itself. That is, both of these recently published novels forego fully or overtly politicizing their characters by not having them directly involved with anti-colonial nationalisms, as the earlier novels do. But—and this is yet another similarity between S. Khan's and Ashraf's novels—both fictions feature main characters who work for the government, S. Khan's Amir Shah in law and Ashraf's main characters, as the novel's title suggests, in the postal service.

Indeed, through Ghulam Rasool, Ashraf's primary protagonist, *The Postmaster* ostensibly flirts with pro-British loyalties, a possible reading made manifest through Ghulam Rasool's trenchant nostalgia for the orderly systems and authority of British India. His dismissal of Pakistan as an amplified get-rich-quick-scheme in a nation's form further compounds this interpretive possibility. Ghulam Rasool's nostalgia, however, is for an ideological center that holds. Indeed, the narrative critiques the racist aspects of British rule while maintaining its more beneficial aspects. The postal system itself represents one of these beneficial aspects insofar as it metaphorizes the centralization of British colonial authority and identity. In other words, the postal system's centralizing functions provide, in part, something to believe in. In contrast, Ghulam Rasool views Pakistan as sorely lacking in this respect. The implication here is that the center upon which Pakistan was founded proved flimsy and without centripetal force.

The Postmaster opens in 1880 and tracks the ascension of Ghulam Nabi in the Indian Posts and Telegraphs Department of the British Raj. Enamored of his government post because it "offered stability and prospects of advancement and, more than that, the respect and awe of his countrymen" (1), Ghulam Nabi is soon promoted and transferred from his native Punjab to Delhi. Here he takes a second wife, Noorani Begum, and starts his life over as if the new city offers him a blank slate. This marriage produces three children, a boy and two girls, and after Ghulam Nabi's early death, Noorani relies on her own resourcefulness to raise her children herself. The novel quickly traverses decades and shifts focus onto Ghulam Rasool, Noorani's son, and his many triumphs, including his academic achievements and his own eventual rise in the Indian Posts and Telegraphs Department. Imbued with his parents' anglophilia, which includes the maxims: "[b]e loyal to the British because loyalty pays" and "[t]he British are the most intelligent race in the world," Ghulam Rasool reaches even higher heights than did his father (Ashraf 17). Further, Ghulam Rasool's merit earns him many promotions that also allow his own relocations to cities such as Lahore, Amritsar, Simla, and Rawalpindi. Just before partition, the Indian Civil Service gives Ghulam Rasool the choice to remain in the service of India or to join the newly established Civil Service of Pakistan; he chooses the latter. The choice proves foolish as the flawed bureaucratic structures of Pakistan soon disenchant Ghulam Rasool, who dies in Lahore disillusioned and embittered.

At the end of the novel and the end of Ghulam Rasool's life, his wife tells him to "'[t]ry to cheer yourself up by thinking of the good times you and your family had together. Remember Rawalpindi, Amritsar, and Simla when the British were there'" (Ashraf 336). Her advice is meant to distract Ghulam Rasool from focusing on "the rot which had set in [in Pakistan] and which he was sure would eventually consume the iron frame which the British had taken such pains to build for over a century" (Ashraf 312). "Rot" invokes a metaphor of deterioration, a process that suggests some level of neglect in the new nation of Pakistan. At the same time, this metaphor also seems to establish the Raj as the high water mark of subcontinental achievement. Taken together, these two passages appear to be saying that the passing of the "good times" of the British colonial period should be lamented, not celebrated. Yet, while the metaphor's double-sidedness identifies some positive elements in the colonial experience, it also leaves a space for Pakistani agency. That is, if rot occurs because of neglect or a failure of meticulousness, then there does or did exist the possibility that effort could have been made to prevent the nation from rotting. To recognize the potential to avoid rot, even if retrospectively, does not necessarily make Pakistan's failure inevitable; that is, the rot metaphor avoids any determinism of the sort that has Pakistan failing even before it begins.[32] The metaphor's recognition of potential unrealized refocuses Ghulam Rasool's nostalgia from resting simply upon the bygone days of the Raj to being concerned with what could have been, a possibility only able to be articulated after seeing what Pakistan becomes. This type of nostalgia fits Jennifer Wenzel's definition of "anti-imperialist nostalgia," which "holds in mind hope for changes that have yet to be realized." As Wenzel further describes it, anti-imperialist nostalgia "acknowledges the past's version of the future, while recognizing the distance and the difference between that vision and realities of the present" (7).[33] Anti-imperialist nostalgia, then, links past, present, and future differently than do more conventional deployments of nostalgia: "Unlike other kinds of nostalgia, anti-imperialist nostalgia is a desire not for a past moment in and of itself but rather for the past's promise of an alternative present, the past's future" (Wenzel 17). To desire the "past's future" in the present means that one's perspective on the present is somehow at a tangent to any mainstream view that accepts the present as is. Ghulam Rasool's inconsolability at the novel's end puts him at this tangential relationship to his fellow Pakistanis who, in the face of corruption, rationalize, "'We are all brothers. Why should we try to create problems for one another'" by following rules or recognizing governmental authority (Ashraf 300). The alternative present, the "past's future" for which Ghulam Rasool seems to hanker, would recognize governmental authority if, the novel suggests, it were anchored in an ideology worthy of loyalty and capable of rewarding merit.

Ghulam Rasool's desire for an alternative Pakistani present derives not from any direct political participation on his part. In fact, the novel as a whole is remarkable for the absence of Congress/League talk. What political talk there is appears peripheral. At the time of Ghulam Nabi and Noorani's marriage in 1885, for example, the British arrest another Indian in the Indian Posts and Telegraphs

Department for preventing the delivery of the mail. In his confession, the perpetrator states that he took "only the dak [mail] of the military officers," for it facilitates British rule over India. His intention was "to kill those who bore ill will against us Indians" (Ashraf 16). This episode prompts the narrator to reveal that "[i]n his heart Ghulam Nabi was quite concerned about the creation of the Indian National Congress and was sure that the British had an ace up their sleeve as they were its creators" (Ashraf 17). Ghulam Nabi's concern isn't that the British are out to hoodwink the Indians; rather, he worries over the possibility that the Congress will disrupt British rule. In a similar vein, politics come up again in passing during a conversation Ghulam Rasool has with his father-in-law, Haji Jaffar, in 1940:

> [Haji Jaffar] mentioned the turmoil that was seeping into India due to the rising wave of nationalism. The haji felt sure that at some point in time the British would have to leave India which would be governed by its own people. He could not say whether that would be good for the Indians and whether the peace that existed now, so essential for trade and prosperity, would continue.
>
> (Ashraf 155)

For his part, "Ghulam Rasool abstained from being drawn into a political discussion..." (Ashraf 155). Ghulam Rasool demonstrates less reticence over nationalist politics than his father did decades before only because he refuses to engage. But, both men avoid public political stances, giving the impression of political quietism or, worse, toadyism.

Yet, the narrative's selective use of irony when characterizing Ghulam Rasool's first-hand interactions with the agents of Empire begins to outline what he is nostalgic about and, thus, to differentiate his views from Raj nostalgia. Ghulam Rasool first interacts with the British when he applies for admission to a government school in Delhi. Azmatullah, a local Indian barrister, gives the boy lessons on how to behave during the admissions interview. Prefacing his advice with the statement that "'[t]he English are a very finicky people,'" Azmatullah goes on to observe, "'We Indians tend to be fidgety, shaking our legs, picking our noses, or handling our private parts before others. Avoid these mannerisms like the plague because the English detest them'" (Ashraf 62). Just as Azmatullah begins with a gross generalization about British people, his characterization of Indians is similarly stereotypical, a point highlighted by the fact that nowhere in the novel is there an Indian described as engaging in any of these behaviors. The balance of Azmatullah's advice solidifies the stereotypes on both sides, which doesn't stop Ghulam Rasool from following the older man's directions (Ashraf 64). Success is Ghulam Rasool's, whose interview prompts "Professor Pringle, an avowed racist who washed his hands with soap every time he shook hands with a local, [to feel] that as long as Indians like Ghulam Rasool were around, the British would have no problems ruling over them" (Ashraf 65). Far from condoning Professor Pringle's view, the interview scene as a whole subtly mocks it by demonstrating how the professor fails to discern Ghulam Rasool's performance as a stereotypically acceptable babu-in-the-making.

Indeed, although Ghulam Rasool succeeds in school and his career to the point that Indians and British alike heap praise upon him, which suggests that Professor Pringle's view holds water, Ghulam Rasool refuses sycophancy. By 1924, Ghulam Rasool ascends to the Postmaster's position in Rawalpindi, and his residence sits across the road from the British Officers Club. Every afternoon, he goes to the club to play tennis and, one day, finds himself playing doubles with three British Officers. One, a Colonel Sanderson, asks him to join the trio: "'Hello Blackie! ...How about being my partner in a game against these two young majors?'" (Ashraf 177). The narrator reveals that "Ghulam Rasool had not liked the way he had been addressed, [but] he held back his reaction, proceeding to take out all his aggressiveness on the court..." (Ashraf 177). Their victory over the two majors insures that Colonel Sanderson seeks Ghulam Rasool out again for other matches and continues calling him "Blackie." Ghulam Rasool, who, the narrator confides, "started considering the appellation as a big joke," corrected the Colonel the one or two times the latter does refer to him properly by saying, "'Sir, call me by my nickname, "Blackie",' which left everybody doubling up in laughter and sent the message across to the colonel" (Ashraf 177). Ghulam Rasool's humor hinges upon his presumption of intimacy between himself and his "superior," the Colonel, for only friends, equals, go by nicknames. In other words, Ghulam Rasool refuses the condescension and racism, the inequality, that the racial slur entails. His wit and his tennis skills even the power imbalance, at least temporarily, thereby gesturing toward a more equitable system.

To be sure, the novel frames Ghulam Rasool's entire rise in the Indian Posts and Telegraphs Department as evidence of the possibility of such an equitable system. Ghulam Rasool assumes the Postmaster's position in Rawalpindi from an Englishman, Mr James Jones, and, thus, becomes the first Indian to hold the post. For his part, Mr James Jones cannot fathom the move:

> Postmaster Jones could not understand the department's logic in replacing him, a thoroughbred Englishman, but then he was convinced from his experience of a quarter of a century in the postal department that most things were increasingly turning from illogical to stupid with the indigenization of the department.
>
> (Ashraf 175)

Jones's view smacks of racism and leaves no room for the possibility that the likes of Ghulam Rasool may have earned his promotion or that the capabilities of employees like Ghulam Rasool prove the justice of the indigenization of the postal service, as well as the entire Indian Civil Service. Jones's insistence on his own "thoroughbred" pedigree demonstrates the absurdity of his stance rather than that of the British colonial government, which is finally acknowledging Indians' rights to self-determination. Immediately after Jones conveys his views, the narrator discloses that "well-informed sources within the postal circles who knew the [Jones] family" suspect that "he was not as pukka an Englishman as he claimed to be" (Ashraf 175). The rumored "impurity" of Jones's heritage highlights his own hypocrisy and, implicitly, the ridiculousness of a system invested in appearing "pukka" or socially acceptable because racially superior. Against this sham of a worldview, Ghulam Rasool's promotion and competence stand as a measure of earned worth and recognition, achievements in a meritocratic order.

The subtle reference to the circulation of gossip about Jones's mixed heritage points to one of the functions the postal service performed in British India. According to Christopher Bayly, the postal service was one of several pre-existing bureaucratic structures the British East India Company and, later, the Raj appropriated from Mughal India ("Knowing," 5–20). In addition to transporting and delivering the mail, the postal service also engaged in surveillance, collected information, and facilitated the transmission and circulation of these materials; in effect, the postal service was also an intelligence gathering institution (Bayly, "Knowing" 21).[34] As such, the postal service was "more than [a] useful adjunct to power and legitimacy," argues Bayly, it was "integral to them" ("Knowing" 5). The Raj's ability to systematize the existing postal networks and the information they gathered, often through the workings of "native informants" or Indian civil servants, facilitated the centralization of power (Bayly, "Knowing" 5). Further, the British accomplished this centralization of power by controlling what could be known and said. As Bayly contends, the British exerted "direct control of information agencies" through "strident rhetoric of imperial loyalty and racial superiority to control the boundaries of political language and information" ("Knowing," 30). Under British control, the postal system did more than connect the vast subcontinent; it also exerted a centripetal pull across the distances of this geographical mass, thereby establishing, for better or worse, a common touchstone.

The Postmaster gestures toward these extra-fictional functions of the postal service in British India. Spying within the ranks is frequent, for example. Indeed, the British authorities only come to know of the Indian who steals the mail of British military officers via their spy networks within the postal service, of which Ghulam Nabi is a part (Ashraf 11). Similarly, on the occasion of one of Ghulam Rasool's many promotions, his British superior in the postal service advises him to "'[r]emember that the post and telegraphs is a vital organ of British India and requires its staff to be constantly on the alert. The best way of doing so is to keep your eyes and ears open and your mouth shut'" (Ashraf 118). These examples demonstrate the thorough infiltration of a surveillance mindset within the novel's fictional Posts and Telegraphs Department. However, Ghulam Rasool's attitude toward his work is not a wholesale or uncritical reflection of the overarching British colonial ideology Bayly outlines. Ghulam Rasool's deportment on the tennis court at the Officer's Club in Rawalpindi highlights his resistance to the racialized hierarchy Bayly discusses. The novel's ironic treatment of other instances of claims of British superiority, such as the college admissions interview, also evidence the narrative's broader refusal of race hierarchies.

Ghulam Rasool does, nonetheless, hold to the idea of loyalty. After he makes his decision to join the Civil Service of Pakistan, for instance, he "visited the branch post offices to bid goodbye to those who worked there" (Ashraf 289). Ghulam Rasool's leave-taking involves the dispensation of advice; he tells the postal staff "to be as loyal to the new countries as they had been to the British sarkar" (Ashraf 289). The balance of his advice suggests that Ghulam Rasool is not advocating blind faith either to the British or to the new governments of India and Pakistan. He expresses to the staff his appreciation for the "cooperation that they had provided him and asked them to forgive him for whatever he may have said or done in the line of duty that may have caused offence" (Ashraf 289–90). The model of interaction Ghulam Rasool advocates here values teamwork and consideration; he even humbles himself before his "inferiors" by asking their forgiveness. This passage gives shape to the type of loyalty Ghulam Rasool endorses: one premised upon dutiful fellowship and reliability. Arguably, this understanding of loyalty represents the center that holds for Ghulam Rasool. And, in this way, the centralization that the postal service accomplishes works as a metaphor for social and even political interactions geared toward an idea of greater collective good.

The Pakistan into which Ghulam Rasool moves does not uphold or even strive for this grand idea of collective good. Early in his residence in the new nation, Ghulam Rasool encounters corruption. Because of his high placement in the Civil Service of Pakistan, for instance, Ghulam Rasool takes on responsibility for the allotment of some evacuee properties in Lahore (Ashraf 293). Believing he had received "honest answers" from a refugee from India, Ghulam Rasool allots the man "a bungalow near the university grounds" (Ashraf 293). Happening upon the house by chance, Ghulam Rasool stops to greet the refugee, who has rifled through the previous owner's possessions choosing for himself and his wife the finest clothes, jewelry, and housewares (Ashraf 294). Ghulam Rasool understands then that this refugee was "an uneducated and corrupt individual devoid of sensitivity who felt no qualms about grabbing and using the wealth of others as his own" (Ashraf 295). The episode leaves Ghulam Rasool "wondering how people like the [refugee] and his progeny would build and run the new state of Pakistan" (Ashraf 296). Greed appears, in Ghulam Rasool's view, to be the primary even the sole modus vivendi in this new nation. He worries, for instance, about finding suitable marriages for his daughters as "he had not bargained for a society where money would be the most important criteria for gauging the worth of a person" (Ashraf 316). Similarly, a colleague approaches Ghulam Rasool with an opportunity to make money on the side:

> "Sir, Pakistan was not made for angels but for human beings with all their failings. It was made for the deprived Muslims of the subcontinent, to improve their lot. The poorer you are the richer you want to be in the quickest possible time, and the sale of car permits is one such way to make money."
>
> (Ashraf 306)

The colleague's distortion of the idea of Pakistan rewrites the past in order to suit the present and, in so doing, legitimizes bureaucratic corruption as an appropriately nationalistic get-rich-quick scheme.

If at one point Ghulam Rasool thought the creation of Pakistan was meant "to provide equitable treatment for all who chose to live in it" (Ashraf 297), he comes to question, "What had the world come to after partition?" (Ashraf 317). The equality Ghulam Rasool thought would accompany the creation of Pakistan aligns with his definition of loyalty, which, arguably, secured his commitment to the British via his work at the Posts and Telegraphs Department. His disgust over the venality of life in post-partition Pakistan marks the distance between what Ghulam Rasool held as an ideal and the reality's present. This distance deepens his nostalgia at the novel's close. The trenchancy of his wife's advice to remember the "good times" and his own "rot" metaphor clearly develop from an ideal not realized, as Wenzel's notion of anti-imperial nostalgia would have it. Further, Ghulam Rasool's own refusal to accept the racialized hierarchies of British colonial rule, while still valuing how that rule centered a place as disparate as India by giving people something to believe in, shows that he is not merely nostalgic for a reductive notion of some time gone by. The past Ghulam Rasool would return to is an ideological disposition—an idea more than a place or a time—that casts Pakistan's future as full of the potential for its citizens to live equitably.

2   1971

Much of the English-language literary output—and some of the Urdu-language output, as well—on the 1971 war between West and East Pakistan (and, by December of that year, India, too) contributes to the mythologizing of muhajir identity.[1] In these fictions, the representation of muhajir identity functions less as an unassailable claim to belonging and more as a means of critique. That is, if, historically-speaking, muhajirs sacrificed the "most" for the new nation of Pakistan, their disappointment at what (West) Pakistan had become in its first twenty-four years of existence served as a trenchant criticism of the failure of the nation of Pakistan to embody the best features and ideals of the idea of Pakistan. The three titles I discuss in this section—Durdana Soomro and Ghazala Hameed's 2006 novel *Bengal Raag*, Shahbano Bilgrami's 2007 novel *Without Dreams*, and Moni Mohsin's 2006 novel *The End of Innocence*—depart from this trend and, instead, use the figure of the child to cast a range of affective attachments to the nation that hinge upon the degree to which the primary characters are vulnerable to the coercive powers of the state, made manifest here in the violent conflict between the two wings of Pakistan. Whereas those fictions concerned with the mythos of the muhajir acknowledge the failure of the nation, these three fictions examine how belonging is the prerogative of the privileged. Indeed, when considered collectively, these three novels go from uncritically celebrating this privilege of belonging to portraying those who can belong as weighed down by guilt as they grapple into adulthood with the suffering of others required to secure their own positions. Notably, the suffering the non-privileged characters experience ties again and again to the conflict between West and East Pakistan.

The prominence of child characters and narrators in Soomro and Hameed's, Bilgrami's, and Mohsin's novels establishes a link between the present discussion and the one involving Bapsi Sidhwa's *Cracking India* in the previous chapter. Sidhwa's text deployed metafictional awareness, I argued, to reposition Lenny's precociousness and her representation of her own memories. Rather than reading Lenny's youthful behavior or her memories as "genuine" portraits of her experience, the metafictional awareness invites a consideration of the deliberateness of these representations; that is, Lenny presents her memories via recognizable conventions so that readers accept them as memory while they also see what makes such memories narratable in the first place. Less a matter of unreliability, Lenny's metafictional tendencies consciously bracket her first-hand "experience" of the 1947 partition to encourage a broader recognition of the conventions used to tell stories of that historical moment. Two of the three novels I discuss in this chapter use memories of childhood, too, but without the metafictional bent. Instead, memory works in *Without Dreams* and *The End of Innocence* to illustrate the abiding guilt the privileged characters, who are both children and adults in their respective fictions, bear long after the traumas of their childhoods. In both instances, these traumas connect to the 1971 conflict, directly in the case of Bilgrami's novel, as one of the characters is Bengali, and indirectly in Mohsin's, which instead explores the implications of euphemistically framing the conflict as a "domestic disturbance." *Bengal Raag* functions as the counter example, as this novel figures the preservation of privilege, i.e. the ability to claim belonging to West Pakistan, as an indisputable "good." *Bengal Raag* frames these preservation efforts with an idea of childhood as apolitical and naïve. Bilgrami's and Mohsin's novels also take on this idea of childhood, but, through their use of memory, both debunk it. Nonetheless, as I explore at several points throughout the chapter, the prominence of the child in all three novels exemplifies how representations of this life stage often reflect adult desire rather than a universal truth about human development.

The events immediately preceding and precipitating the 1971 war fleetingly recuperated the possibility of democracy in Pakistan and, with it, the potential to inspire affective attachments to a national identity crafted from a transparently run state. After twelve years under two successive military regimes, Pakistan held its first "real" democratic elections in 1970. Yahya's dismantling of the One Unit plan created for the first time in Pakistani history the conditions for a one-person, one-vote election. The One Unit plan, hatched in 1956, "consolidat[ed] West Pakistan into a One Unit province [creating] parity with East Pakistan in the National Assembly [that] could thus be understood as an attempt to safeguard the centre from a populist Bengali challenge" (Talbot, *Pakistan* 126). By doing away with this manufactured parity, Yahya opened the door for the Bengalis to have a larger presence in national politics, and that's precisely what happened. The Awami League, the most prominent political party in Bengal, secured 167 out of 169 East Pakistan seats in the National Assembly, positioning Sheikh Mujib ur-Rahman, the party's leader, as Pakistan's next Prime Minister (Beachler 472). Yet, Yahya refused to convene the National Assembly at the start of 1971, thereby circumventing the rightful appointment of Mujib as Prime Minister. ZA Bhutto worked in concert with Yahya to obstruct the installation of the democratically elected National Assembly, in which Bhutto's Pakistan People's Party won eighty-one of the one hundred and thirty-eight West Pakistan seats (Talbot, *Pakistan* 200). Democracy thus made no return to Pakistan in 1971. By March, with East Pakistan experiencing political upheaval thanks to the parallel government the Awami League established there, relations between the two wings of Pakistan deteriorated to the point of violence. On 25 March 1971, the Pakistan Army conducted Operation Searchlight, inaugurating the armed conflict that would end only after India joined the fray in December of that year. Before 1971 closed, Bangladesh emerged from the violence.

If the scuttled elections of 1970 address "why" the 1971 war happened, several developments speak to "what" happened in the war's aftermath. ZA Bhutto became Prime Minister, unseating Yahya in December 1971, a move that bolstered Bhutto's popularity. Bhutto's success, at least initially, created for many a positive sense of belonging to the nation and a greater confidence in the state.[2] Further, Bhutto negotiated with Indira Gandhi to secure the release of the 90,000 Pakistani POWs held in India for two years after the war. While the circumstances of the POWs incarceration was a cause of national embarrassment—i.e. because of Pakistan's surrender to the Indians in December 1971—their return to Pakistan brought some qualified closure to the war. These developments inform the lived experience of the war's aftermath, suggesting that some Pakistanis were able to form or maintain a strong bond with the nation. At the same time, however, many aspects of the conflict remained (and remain) unresolved. "Stranded Pakistanis," the citizens of the united nation who were unable to evacuate Bengal and return to the west, exist in a national limbo as they are barred from repatriation in what is now Pakistan.[3] Moreover, nowhere within official Pakistani discourse has there been a proper reckoning or remembering of the events of that year. One of the government's most significant documents on the conflict, *The Report of the Hamoodur Rehman Commission*, which was compiled by a panel of three judges at ZA Bhutto's behest, was classified from its completion in 1972 until 2000, when portions of the *Report* and its *Supplement*, written upon the POWs' release in 1974, were leaked by an Indian news magazine.[4] The *Report*'s classification left a narrative vacuum, which implicitly facilitated a national amnesia on the subject. Combined, the "Stranded Pakistanis" and the classification of the *Report* create gaps between experiences of this historical event and national discourses about it.

Bengal Raag leaps over these gaps. Durdana Soomro and Ghazala Hameed's co-written 2006 novel is a veiled autobiographical fiction about twin sisters who, because of their father's job in the Civil Service of Pakistan, live and travel throughout what was once East Pakistan. More suited for an adolescent audience given the tone and appearance of the story (there are several drawings included in the text), *Bengal Raag* chronicles the adventures of Diya and Gaity from the time they are about seven years old and living in various locations such as Dacca and Chittagong until they become young women resident in Lahore. The twins' childhood and adolescence unfold from the late 1950s to 1971, so their lives are glancingly touched by larger historical events, including Ayub's military coup in 1958, the 1965 war with India, and the separation of East Pakistan six years later. Because the narrative point of view concentrates on the children's perspective with only an occasional nod to their adult understanding, the novel presents these larger historical events without any insight into their significance beyond self-centered references to the twins. The use of the child, or children, in this case, thus limits perspective without irony or metafictional effect, as in Sidhwa's *Cracking India*, for instance. As a result, the twins' concern for themselves and their report of their parents' concern for the family inadvertently highlight how privilege, which is here the authority of a West Pakistani identity, works to insure the family's "safety." Even more—and equally as inadvertently, one imagines— this "safety" relies upon an unabashed prejudice against Bengalis. Thus, the novel reads as a testament to West Pakistani superiority, figured in the "happiness" of the twins' family, which allows for the putatively ingenuous pathos the story expresses for the severing of the nation.

By the time of the civil war, the girls' family has relocated to Lahore, which, for their father, a Punjabi, is a sort of homecoming. But, the family lives in East Pakistan during the years that saw the rise of Bengali nationalism. Unlike many of the novels dealing with the 1947 partition that I've already discussed, these political events occur at a remove from the family's daily lives. The twins encounter Bengali nationalism, for instance, via their participation on the school debate team. The issue of the English language's position as a language of instruction is a perennial favorite for the team. Although the narrative voice establishes that Diya and Gaity are on the same debate team, it does not reveal which side of the English language issue they argue. Instead, readers learn that "English won the day but only just. Bengali was more than just a language to the Bengalis…" (Soomro and Hameed 91). At this juncture, the narrative also reveals the tensions between the East and West Pakistanis, noting that Bengalis possess a "resentment of the Urdu-speaking minority, who exploited their resources and bagged the best jobs" (Soomro and Hameed 91). Each language, then, bears an ideological charge; however, the narrative voice creates a distance between these tensions and the twins' positions in East Pakistan. In addition to presenting their side of the language debate ambiguously, the narrative also appears to place the family in an uncommitted ideological position. The twins' father is, for example, a West Pakistani, and, yet, according to his wife, he is "'more Bengali than the Bengalis themselves. You are always standing up for them…'" (Soomro and Hameed 99). For her part, the twins' mother, who was raised in Calcutta, is eager to purchase a plot of land in East Pakistan as a safeguard for when her husband retires: "It was Mother who fretted about what would happen when [Father] retired. She couldn't visualize herself moving into some small rented accommo- dation with her children and being thrown at the mercy of greedy landlords" (Soomro and Hameed 47). The mother succeeds in finding a plot, having a house built, and even renting the place while the family still enjoys living in government housing in East Pakistan. And, though the family does eventually lose claim to the house once they are back in West Pakistan and the 1971 war begins, the narrative presents the house's loss as more of an inconvenience rather than as part of the turmoil brought about by the nation's schism. All three of these examples make it difficult to pin down precisely how the twins' family relates to the broader political events of the 1950s and 1960s. The obscurity of their ideological position seems all the more remarkable given the father's position as a West Pakistani in the Civil Service of Pakistan who is stationed primarily in the east.

As the novel moves toward the events of 1971, its ideological investments become a bit easier to discern. The twins' maternal uncle manages to migrate from the east back to Lahore (and eventually Karachi), and the narrative voice, favoring the twins' perspective, reveals that "[e]ight months ago [in 1970] he had been the jolly uncle that they had all known and loved. But now he was an old man" (Soomro and Hameed 138). With their uncle's altered state and newspaper accounts providing testimony of the violent disintegration of the country, the family members who reside in Lahore greet the visit of the twins' eldest sister, Aynee, with some trepidation. While the family was still living in East Pakistan, Aynee married a Bengali and settled there. Later, when violence erupts, she and her two sons come to the West, but not permanently. Her visit's transient nature is due, the novel suggests, to the gap between the family's and Aynee's political views:

> Since Aynee's coming the situation at meal times was always a little tense. All of a sudden she had become the odd one out. No one agreed with what she said about Mujib's being a good-hearted man or about the Pakistan Army having been overly brutal. Instead Murtaza Uncle and the rest stuck to their point of view that now the Bengalis should not be given positions of power any more.
>
> (Soomro and Hameed 139)

Several aspects of this passage underscore that the narrative voice favors the twins' childlike perspective. First, it characterizes Aynee as the "odd one out," a marginal position that, in the twins' view, contrasts sharply to the central one they felt she had always enjoyed as the family's eldest child. Further, this passage groups "Murtaza Uncle and the rest" together without making clear that the twins also link their views with their uncle. The suggestion here is that the twins may still be perceived by their family as too young to have sound political convictions. Indeed, the novel only allows the twins to process the war in terms of their personal familial ties. In one scene, for example, Aynee's son, Zakir, asks Diya if he can sleep in her bed with her. As they drift off to sleep, the little boy warns his aunt that, were she to come visit him in East Pakistan, she had better not speak Urdu, for "'[o]therwise they will think you are a Bihari and shoot you'" (Soomro and Hameed 142). The boy doesn't specify to whom his "they" refers, and the narrative voice doesn't give any indication that Diya herself understands the likely reference to be the Mukti Bahini. Instead, the narrative voice discloses Diya's frame of mind as being emotionally "drained," for it seems "strange to her that a part of her family should have been so thoroughly assimilated into a different race" (Soomro and Hameed 142). The twins remain outside the political fray as the violence between West and East Pakistan escalates, yet their sympathies clearly veer toward West Pakistan's stance, a point made especially clear as Diya views her own nephews as racial Others.

In highlighting the twins' emotional rather than political involvement in the events of 1971, the novel reinforces a certain notion of childhood or a child's perspective. Although the twins age more than a decade over the course of the narrative and are, thus, at their oldest in 1971, their viewpoint remains immature in the sense that it does not encompass broader contexts. This depiction of childhood, then, reinforces a common construction of that life stage, one that emphasizes innocence and a lack of (adult) complexity. Jacqueline Rose's work on the "impossibility of children's fiction" examines this conventional ascription of innocence to childhood and locates innocence "not as a property of childhood but as a portion of adult desire" (xii). This "adult desire" is, for Rose, an "invest-ment" in childhood meant to "fix" or stabilize the concept of "child" (3–4). In effect, the impulse to fix the idea of childhood, Rose argues, develops from an interest in containing or stifling "something which cannot be spoken" (3–4). Thus, the issue with a child's perspective as a literary device is not whether children have any awareness of political events and their significance, for such a concern overlooks the role literary representations play in encouraging or limiting interpretation. The issue (or one of them) then becomes a concern over how the use of a child's perspective in a literary representation of an historical event, such as the 1971 war, presents the event's meaning. Further, according to Rose, the deployment of "myths of primordial innocence" frequently serve conservative politics or ideological stances (xii), which suggests the location of Soomro and Hameed's narrative. In *Bengal Raag*, the twins' perspective endows the 1971 war with emotional consequences that prioritize the "safety" of the west, as well as a deep-seated belief in differences anchored in racial essentialism.

There are traces of this racism throughout the novel. They emerge in the family's domestic dealings. When the man who eventually becomes Aynee's husband first approaches her parents, for instance, they are "rather taken aback." Fully aware that this young man intends to ask for Aynee's hand, her parents make "frantic efforts...to locate suitable Punjabi boys. All Mother's West Pakistani acquaintances, even the ones she wasn't terribly fond of, were contacted" (Soomro and Hameed 42). The twins' parents' desperation signals their bias, further underscored as the narrative voice indicates that the only West Pakistani boys who could be found "at such short notice...were all either too short, too dark or had some other unbearable impediment" (Soomro and Hameed 42). Without irony, the narrative voice concedes that Masud, the Bengali suitor, "was also short and dark" (Soomro and Hameed 42). Upon this foundation, Diya builds her conclusion that her nephews, the offspring of this marriage, are her racialized Other. In a similar vein, the twins' mother arranges for her eldest son's work transfer from Chittagong back to Dacca on the fear that he's made a love connection with a Bengali woman. The merest hint of this possibility brings home for the mother "the urgency of leaving East Pakistan" (Soomro and Hameed 96–7). The novel's presentation of the mother's preoccupation with "suitable" marriage partners for her children substantiates a racism otherwise undetectable in the twins' parents' other views, such as the father's "Bengali-ness" and the mother's interest in building their retirement home in the east. By embedding this racism in the intimacy of familial relations, the novel establishes a cordon around the family, one characterized by a notion of racial purity. And, given the twins' acceptance of their parents' views, evidenced by the narrative voice's lack of irony and Diya's view of her nephews, the family's prevailing investment in racial purity coincides with the narrative's construction of child-hood as innocent and uncomplicated. The connection of racial purity with the innocence of childhood removes politics from this racism, just as politics are at a remove from the novel's depiction of childhood.

The inviolability of the innocence characterizing this depiction of childhood manifests itself throughout the novel as an interest in "safety." The novel remarks upon the twins' safety at several different temporal and geographical junctures. In a chapter titled "Earliest Memories," the narrative voice locates the family during their first posting in Dacca, circa 1956 or 1957, when the twins are only four years old (Soomro and Hameed 5). The general temporal marker matters to how the narrator sets the scene: "In those days it was so safe that even though the girls were only four…, they would freely wander over to the neighbor's house to play" (Soomro and Hameed 5). The nostalgic tone of this reminiscence hints at a regret for how dramatically or drastically circumstances change; the implica-tion is, of course, that other days followed during which the girls were not safe to walk to their neighbor's. Insofar as nostalgia has a conservative bent, the manner in which the narrator frames this early chapter casts this time and place as idyllic. The narrator presents the family's move to Chittagong that follows in quick succession to the posting in Dacca in a similar fashion: "When the girls were not studying, they would be roaming over the adjoining hills. Nobody bothered them and they never got lost. It was really amazing how absolutely safe it was" (Soomro and Hameed 11). These memories' idyllic presentation may well draw additional affective force from the family's socioeconomic circumstances. The Chittagong house, for instance, sits on Commissioner's Hill, so named because the "British had built their residences and offices on these hills" (Soomro and Hameed 9–10). The twins' class position as daughters of the district commis-sioner does as much to insure their "safety" as does the relative calm of the historical moments during which they are resident in East Pakistan. As that calm disperses, the twins' "safety" remains of tantamount importance, as in the scene when their mother insists that their older brothers protect them from the "'Begali-speaking boys" and their "'*goondas*'" who are protesting Dacca University's presentation of an English-language play. One of their brothers turns proactive and dissuades the Bengali-speaking boys from protesting at all by promising them that "the next annual play would be in Bengali" (Soomro and Hameed 89). This scene emphasizes the family's privilege and its protection through staging the tensions around the production of an English-language play, a sign of the family's educated and, thus, elevated class status.[5] The novel's insistence on the "safety" of the twins' identities as children, then, furnishes a cover both for racial bias and class dominance.

The multiple purposes to which "safety" is put via the privileging of the twins' childlike perspectives ultimately shades how the narrative deals with the nation of Pakistan. During a "tour" of West Pakistan upon which the family embarks before taking up permanent residence there, for instance, they travel from Rawalpindi to Islamabad, a move apparently prompted by the fact that the national capital had recently moved there from Karachi and one that locates the narrative historically at the latter half of the 1960s (Soomro and Hameed 109). According to the novel, "Islamabad was chosen because of its perceived safety, being surrounded by hills, which also lent it a picturesque beauty" (Soomro and Hameed 109). Here, safety corresponds to protection, and the capital's move is thus strategic.[6] In the context of the novel, the motivation for the move, which makes Islamabad a metonym for the entire nation, takes on an added resonance. That is, if the twins' "safety" signifies class privilege and racial biases, then the nation's "safety" similarly involves such class and "race" considerations, considerations born out historically given the prevalent prejudices against Bengalis and West Pakistan's internal colonization of the East.[7] And, yet, given the novel's association of "safety" with childhood, the nation's "safety," as the novel represents it, may also take on the trappings of innocence and purity. If so, then *Bengal Raag* provides a narrative that endorses an unproblematized picture of the nation of Pakistan, which, given the historical context of 1971, supports when it's not exonerating West Pakistan's role in these events.

Shahbano Bilgrami's 2007 novel, *Without Dreams*, features a non-linear narrative that explores the memories of two key characters, Abdul and Haroon, who, in the novel's primary temporal plane, 1983, are both adolescent boys, age seventeen and thirteen, respectively. The prominence of these two adolescent characters introduces two contrasting ways to view how Pakistan's history from 1971 to 1983 shapes the lives of characters inhabiting markedly different class and ethnic positions: Abdul is a servant in Haroon's family home. Rather than present childhood as innocent and simple, as *Bengal Raag* does, *Without Dreams* desentimentalizes both boys' youths through their mutual concern for Haroon's mother, Tahira, who suffers abuse at the hands of Haroon's father, Javaid. Not only do Tahira's beatings disrupt whatever domestic idyll might exist in the family's upper class home, they also help Abdul conjure memories of his own once-forgotten past in East Pakistan and Haroon understand the way power works. That is, insofar as these beatings affect both boys' development, they do so as history lessons in addition to more intimate emotional ones. *Without Dreams*, thus, obliquely offers a critique of Pakistan as nation pursued through the intertwined concepts of sacrifice and passivity. Abdul's biography serves as the novel's example of sacrifice, and, at once, comments upon the history of subcontinental nationalisms while it also illustrates how the dynamics leading up to the events of 1971 are too often construed as a necessary propitiation for the rarefied existence of the West Pakistani elite. Haroon's understanding of his mother's abuse revolves around the concept of passivity, which, like Abdul's sacrificial role, also connects to subcontinental nationalisms. Yet, rather than prize passivity as effective and moral non-violent resistance, Haroon comes to view those who espouse passivity as complicit with existing power structures. Through both boys and their attendant concepts, then, Bilgrami's novel upturns the expected narrative of Tahira's victimhood into an unacknowledgeable history lesson that frames the nation of Pakistan that emerged after 1971 as unmistakably culpable for its abuse of East Pakistan.

The novel's most recent temporal plane unfolds in 2002 when Haroon travels from London back to Pakistan to set his family's long-vacant house in order. His return prompts his own recollections about the year he left Pakistan, 1983, which is also the year of his father's death. While, ostensibly, the novel is about uncovering the circumstances of Javaid's death, it really revolves around the relationships between the wealthy and their servants. The police conveniently accuse and convict Abdul for Javaid's death in order to protect Haroon and his family's highly esteemed social position. Approximately ten years before Javaid's death, Tahira finds Abdul begging while the family is visiting the seaside in what is presumably Karachi. Initially, Tahira treats Abdul, who, at the time, is only seven or eight years old, as a sort of adopted son, including him in the lessons she gives Haroon. As Tahira becomes increasingly aware of Abdul's not so filial affection for her, she discontinues her attentions and, instead, casts him in the role of houseboy. Despite her qualified rejection of him, Abdul remains loyal to Tahira, which necessarily means that he harbors a resentment toward Javaid because of his abusive treatment of her. Haroon shares this resentment, and he is the one who eventually acts upon it, pushing over a bookcase that crushes his father to death. Aside from the frame narrative that features an adult Haroon returning to Pakistan in 2002, most of the novel's events take place during the 1970s and early 1980s when both boys are children.

The novel's figuration of Haroon and Abdul as children throughout the plot's most significant events refuses both a sentimentalist and a developmentalist approach to the representation of a child's perspective. Unlike *Bengal Raag*, which uses the twins' childhood as a veneer to prevent the serious examination of West Pakistani "safety" brought about through privilege, *Without Dreams* casts childhood as an ambivalent and threatening period during which the two child characters harbor an awareness of their own lack of safety or innocence. The adult Haroon, for instance, vehemently rejects a romantic view of his own past: "Childhood. As if it was worth celebrating in poetry and books!" (Bilgrami 18). The narrative voice is even less sentimental as it describes how Abdul and the other beggar children live "frantically racing after cars, taxis, trucks, jeeps and motorcycles as if they were chasing their own lost childhoods" (Bilgrami 44). According to the narrator, these children had lost something, "a quality that couldn't be put into words without sounding trite or sanctimonious" (Bilgrami 44). The combination of "trite" and "sanctimonious" in this sentence indicates how quickly any attempt to frame childhood can turn into prescriptive moralization or an ascription of virtue to a period in life purportedly outside of social codes and influences. In light of these views, Jacqueline Rose argues that adult desire shapes representations of childhood, "fix[ing] the child and then hold[ing] it in place" so as to cover over what "cannot be spoken" (3–4). *Without Dreams* uncovers that desire through its depictions of Haroon's and Abdul's childhoods and, I contend, attempts to speak about West Pakistani complicity conducted through the twinned concepts of sacrifice and passivity. The boys' maturation, then, does not lead to a fuller sense of completeness or other telos, a point made evident, in part, through the novel's non-linearity.

Thus, *Without Dreams*, insofar as it manifests elements characteristic of novels of development, challenges the conventions Feroza Jussawalla associates with what she calls the "postcolonial *Bildungsroman*." According to Jussawalla, the postcolonial appropriation of this European genre allows authors "to define the birth of their new nations and to define their experiences in relation to colonialism..." (29–30). Postcolonial writers spin the traditional developmentalist ethos of the genre, in Jussawalla's schema, to promote anti-colonial critique. However, Jussawalla's correlation of maturation with coming into nationhood naturalizes both processes, suggesting an unproblematic inevitability that follows a single track.[8] Such mono-track thinking functions normatively, in that it enforces a fixed notion of adulthood, as well as one of nationhood. *Without Dreams'* multiple temporal levels, its desentimentalized depiction of childhood, and its thematic concerns of inequality and injustice played out via sacrifice and passivity reshape Jussawalla's paradigm. Tobias Boes's characterization of novels of development, following Mikhail Bakhtin, more aptly suits the dynamics of Bilgrami's text. Boes argues that this genre "situates its protagonist on the threshold between different historical eras" (236), and, depending on how one views the narrative unfolding of history, such a placement need not signify "progress." Jussawalla's interest in the anti-colonial novel of development can then be understood as only one instantiation of the postcolonial *Bildungsroman*, and a novel such as *Without Dreams* as another, in that it presents an aspect of the postcolonial condition beyond the historical moment of anti-colonialism. The threshold through which both Haroon and Abdul pass is 1971, that rupture between East and West Pakistan. The post-1971 era in which they dwell throughout most of the novel leaves Abdul unrepresent-able, as I discuss below, and Haroon markedly uncomfortable in what Pakistan has become. Thus, if, according to Franco Moretti, one of the functions of the novel of development is to induct the protagonist into the "'comfort of civilization,'" then *Without Dreams* once again challenges this convention by challenging the means through which such comfort is derived (116).

Tahira's marginalization of Abdul instantiates a larger pattern in his life: namely, a profound provisionality that leaves Abdul feeling both without family and without history, all in service to others' belonging. Indeed, he fixates on Haroon's nursery, especially the artifacts it houses, such as an old photo of Tahira holding an infant Haroon, as a physical manifestation of what it must mean to have a history, a sense of belonging, and, ultimately, a legitimate identity. Early in the novel, Abdul doesn't understand his fascination with the photo; all he knows is that "[i]t reminded him of something in his past, something he couldn't quite place yet" (Bilgrami 15). Much later, after Abdul more fully recollects his own history in East Pakistan, which involves the rape and murder of his mother at the hands of West Pakistani soldiers, Abdul wants to insure that the photo remains on the nursery shelf so that "Haroon's childhood was preserved" (236). Abdul's conceptualization of the photo as an integral part of what stabilizes Haroon's identity points to the apparent necessity of specific evidence to prove one matters, even while it demonstrates how Abdul serves as a sacrifice for this stabilization.

This photo testifies to Tahira and Haroon's connection, and its "rightful" position on the nursery shelf in the family's upper class home further suggests that only the privileged possess such proof, especially in a textualized or representative form. Furthermore, Abdul's focus on the legitimacy this domestic scene lends helps account for the novel's close depiction of specific locations, such as Saathpari (the family home), the market at Saddar, and the street corner where Abdul once made his living as a beggar. At the same time, the novel refuses to name in what city the plot unfolds or from what village Abdul hails. In lieu of place names, the novel offers scenic clues, such as Saathpari's relative proximity to the sea, suggesting that the main setting is Karachi, or the intense greenness and topographical flatness that suffuse Abdul's dreams of his very early childhood, which point to his East Pakistani origins. The contrast in the novel's treatment of place—focused on specific locations and abstruse about larger geographical ones—foregrounds an important theme: the submersion of a critical perspective on nationalist histories in service to the unjust entitlements of the privileged.

The connected concepts of sacrifice and passivity are central to the novel's development of how privilege functions. One extended episode detailing Javaid's abuse of Tahira provides both a thematic and structural touchstone for the novel's presentation of these two concepts. This beating, itself unremarkable, occurs the night before a large dinner party that Javaid has coerced Tahira into hosting. What distinguishes this beating from all the others is that Abdul intervenes. While he and Haroon have often witnessed Javaid's drunken rages, on this particular night, Abdul "emerged from behind the armchair," the vantage point from which he witnesses the beating Javaid administers, and "leapt between Sahib and Begum Sahib," providing Tahira the chance to move toward the door as Javaid passes out due to his intoxication (Bilgrami 87). As the narrative perspective shifts between Javaid, Tahira, Haroon, and Abdul, the perspectival voice repeatedly emphasizes that Abdul's actions mark each character's perception, howsoever hazy due to alcohol or memory, of the event. Haroon, for instance, not realizing at the time that Abdul is also watching his parents fight, remembers seeing only a "figure disappea[r] in a flash of yellow" as Abdul prevents Javaid's further assault and then hastily exits (Bilgrami 81). For his part, Javaid only "vaguely recollected that something strange had happened the night before" (Bilgrami 82). Abdul himself remains baffled at his own actions, as the narrator reveals that he "hadn't planned" to make his presence known at all (Bilgrami 86). And, finally, Tahira "couldn't believe what had just happened," largely because, after considering Abdul's possible motives for intervening, can only conclude that "he had *saved* her" (Bilgrami 88; emphasis in original). By presenting each character's recollection of the event, the novel highlights how multi-perspectival and limited any single understanding is. At the same time, however, as the episode reverberates, especially for Abdul and Haroon, such an insight gets quickly overshadowed as the episode provides a glimpse into how power shapes narratives.

Abdul's act of "heroism" ironizes the sacrificial role he otherwise plays throughout the novel. Tahira resists acknowledging that he "*saved* her" arguably because his low social status would seem to preclude his having any power over her. Indeed, as the narrative voice maintains its focus on Tahira's reflections on the event, it reveals that Tahira "lacked the necessary imagination" to see Abdul as anything other than the servant who brings her warm milk every night (Bilgrami 90). Tahira's failure of imagination points to the absence of available narratives that would allow a fuller representation of Abdul's identity, an absence that not only speaks to his marginalization as a servant but also to his negligible historicity. That is, time and again, the narrative voice underscores how Abdul feels that he has no significant or verifiable past:

> One of the few things that Abdul could count as being a part of his per-sonal history was a seemingly inexplicable attraction to the colour green, as if somewhere, in a past life, he was connected to the earth. Other than this, and fragments of memory and dream, he had little, by the time he was seventeen, to call his own. He sometimes felt that he had been denied something.
>
> (Bilgrami 63)

This passage makes an oblique reference to the greenness that predominates in Abdul's dreams and that eventually helps Abdul discover his East Pakistani connections and the reader his place in Pakistani history. And his involvement in this specific instance of Javaid's abuse of Tahira facilitates Abdul's discovery.

The link between Tahira's beating and Abdul's past could seem to unite them as fellow victims; however, insofar as Tahira's vulnerability triggers Abdul's memory and his eventual reclamation of his East Pakistani roots, the link serves rather to highlight Abdul's outsider status, which allows others to sacrifice him for their own benefit. The night after the beating, which is also the night of the dinner party, Tahira collapses before her guests due to the injuries she incurred at her husband's hands. For Abdul, "something in the way Begum Sahib suddenly fell to the ground…made him confront what that structure in the sea of green [about which he perpetually dreams] contained. There was an entire history there, if only he know how to reclaim it" (Bilgrami 122). Tahira's vulnerability to violence prompts Abdul to connect her victimhood to his dreams and memories, allowing him to eventually recall his own mother's vulnerability. As Abdul understands the dreams he has of greenness are actually set in East Pakistan and, thus, involve his own mother's suffering (Bilgrami 191–7), he also realizes he gains a history: "Slowly he was beginning to realize what it all meant, the woman's relationship to him…It wasn't easy, this business of having a past, a history rooted in a far-off place…" (Bilgrami 215). Abdul's identity, born of his recovered past, becomes burdensome precisely because it marks him as an Other in West Pakistan, quite apart from his status as a servant. When the police trump up charges against Abdul for Javaid's death, for instance, the public readily condemns him, for, in their (West) Pakistani eyes, "his ethnicity branded him violent, sulky, temperamental" (Bilgrami 234). Abdul comes to understand the inescapability of an historically-constructed identity inscribed on his body as he regards how his "dark skin," "[l]ike his newfound identity,…hung heavily on his soul" (Bilgrami 235). Beyond the fact that Tahira does not intervene on Abdul's behalf when it becomes clear that the police intend to frame him for Javaid's death, an act for which an adolescent Haroon is responsible, Abdul's inability to realize fully a relationship with his own mother that resembles even remotely the one Haroon has with Tahira blocks him out of any privileged belonging, which throughout the novel is tied to familial and class status. Even as his memories come back to him, Abdul understands that he has "no proof of an older past" beyond his skin color (Bilgrami 187). Without a textualized or material archive on par with Haroon's nursery, Abdul can never enjoy the security of belonging that Haroon does, despite his family's dysfunction. Indeed, at the novel's very end, an adult Haroon comes upon another photograph depicting a day at the beach he and his family, along with Abdul, enjoyed in 1983. Haroon contemplates the photo, realizing it is "the closest, perhaps, [Haroon] has ever gotten to an image of Abdul, and even then he is beyond the frame, outside the lens, voiceless, imageless and unrecordable" (Bilgrami 244). Much as Tahira recognizes that she cannot imagine Abdul beyond his two dimensional role as servant, Haroon understands that he cannot "see" Abdul, for his East Pakistani identity places him beyond representational frames.

Abdul's unrepresentability illustrates his sacrificial role. The more Haroon considers the photo that doesn't frame Abdul, the more he doubts Abdul's entire existence. Haroon estimates that he would find "[n]othing about [Abdul], for example, as a person. Nothing about his history, or where he came from" (Bilgrami 244). Abdul's invisibility ironically results from his history and where he came from, two immutabilities that allow others to sacrifice him for their own preservation. During the seaside picnic depicted in the photo Haroon contemplates, for instance, Javaid physically attacks Abdul for burning the food. Another servant, the driver, witnesses the attack but fails to protect Abdul. As the narrative voice briefly shifts into the driver's view, readers learn that he "acknowledged guiltily to himself that he had almost—yes, he would've, if he weren't a driver in the employ of this important man—he had almost jumped in to stop him, but at the last moment…had fallen back…a passive victim" (Bilgrami 183). The driver's acknowledgement damns him, as his passivity connects directly to his position of dependence on Javaid. The driver needs his job and, thus, decides not to act; he's fully aware of the need for intervention, of the operant power dynamics, yet decides not to act. In this way, Abdul's beating protects the driver's livelihood, for the driver's reliance on Javaid influences the former to the extent that he will allow injustice. And the driver knows this. The police officer investigating Javaid's death shares this awareness but with far fewer pangs of conscience. The novel metaphorizes the officer's desk chair to conjure the privilege this public servant secures as he deliberately falsifies his report on Javaid's death. This chair "support[s] the curved musculature of his thighs, raise[s] his back, somehow plant[s] his feet more firmly onto the cheap blue carpet beneath him" (Bilgrami 227). These benefits motivate the officer to "do anything to protect" his chair (Bilgrami 227). As a representative of the police, this officer obviously stands in for the sanctioned violence that the state wields over its populace. And, given the novel's oblique historical references to the 1971 war, during which the state of Pakistan deployed its soldiers against its own citizens, the parallel suggests the perpetuation of power achieved through overt force as much as through the "passive" kind the driver represents. In order to insure the successful perpetuation of this type of power, Abdul must be sacrificed. Securely seated, the police officer understands that his chair consolidates his own belonging to (West) Pakistan, as it "somehow plant[s] his feet more firmly" on the ground.

Abdul's sacrifice comes about through several types of (in)action, all in service to the preservation and perpetuation of a grander power that rules by intimidation, insecurity, and force. Haroon inadvertently gains this precise understanding of how power operates through school, one of the essential plot elements of novels of development, according to Gregory Castle (674). Haroon receives this lesson by questioning the received interpretation of Pakistani history as portrayed by his textbook. Significantly, this questioning punctuates the scenes in which Javaid beats Tahira and the dinner party that follows the next night. Such a structuring of these scenes expands the beating's meaning beyond the "domestic" and, instead, presents it as a tableau of nationalist power at work. The day after the dinner party, while at school, "Haroon sat slumped over his textbook, underlining glorious moments in his nation's history with a stiff wooden ruler" (Bilgrami 92). The use of "slumped" to describe Haroon's posture immediately gives the lie to the gloriousness of the nation's history as the text-book presents it. This history is "so replete with shining examples of heroic leadership and principles followed through wisely" that it makes Haroon's eyes "hurt." Associatively, his mind goes to his memories of the dinner party the night before (Bilgrami 93). At first glance, the association between the textbook history and the dinner party highlights the irony of the former made manifest in Javaid's decidedly unheroic actions. To read this initial reference to Haroon's history lessons in this way, however, too neatly posits Tahira in the victim's role, a position Haroon denies her. His denial is born not of insensitivity but of his intolerance of passivity, especially passivity passed off as virtue. Haroon comes to view his mother's passivity—which she herself refers to as her "dirty habit" (Bilgrami 88)—as indefensible complicity. Once Haroon makes that link between passivity and complicity, his insights forward a critique of post-1971 Pakistan and of nationalist mythologies that prize the virtuousness of non-violent resistance.

The tie to 1971 occurs in another punctuating scene set in Haroon's school. Entirely strung out from anxiety over his mother's beating and the resultant lack of sleep, Haroon experiences a paralyzing test anxiety that prevents him from even beginning his history exam.[9] As he consults with his teacher after the other students have submitted their exams, Haroon sees

> [t]he nearly unmarked blackboard loom[ing] in front of him with just one
> date casually scribbled on the side, near the small collection of broken bits of

chalk: 1971. Probably a leftover date from the senior history lesson that usually preceded theirs every Thursday.

(Bilgrami 107)

Much like the above quoted passage wherein Haroon slumps over his history textbook as he reads its heroic tales, this excerpt's significance hinges upon the juxtaposition of images. While the date, 1971, is "casually scribbled," the chalkboard looms in front of Haroon. From Haroon's perspective, the board's marking appears large, imposing, even intimidating. But, from some other perspective— perhaps that of the history teacher who wrote the date on the board—the date and the event it metonymically represents merits only casual notation. Indeed, that the date appears "near the small collection of broken bits of chalk" and is likely a "leftover" suggests that what it signifies to the teacher—who, incidentally, views history textbooks with some awe since they are "government-issued textbooks!" (107)—need not draw that much attention or consideration. The date's position on the blackboard parallels Abdul's at Saathpari: marginal, hardly worthy of notice. Yet, for Haroon, preoccupied by his family problems to the point that he cannot put pen to paper, this date hangs over him. This scene constitutes Haroon's interaction with his history teacher and loosely introduces the association Haroon makes between his mother's beating and 1971.

In order to solidify the connection between Haroon's home situation and the nation's history, the narrative perspective, favoring Haroon's interior, concentrates on how power functions. The boy's fear that his teacher will tell his parents about his poor test performance motivates Haroon to visit the school's library, where he borrows a history book with the intention of making amends with his history teacher. Haroon cannot get beyond the library book's first paragraph, which ends with "'The historical forces that have led to the creation of this great country...'" (Bilgrami 111). The ellipsis here signals Haroon's paralysis. The narrative visually illustrates how Haroon tries again:

And again:
"The historical forces that have led to the creation of this great..."
[...]
"The historical forces that have led..."
[...]
"The historical forces...."

(Bilgrami 111)

Caught in this cognitive stutter, Haroon finally breaks free "as it suddenly struck him": "'History is shaped by *force*'" (Bilgrami 112). Haroon's recognition of force's role in the shaping of the narratives he has already sarcastically labeled "heroic" make him skeptical, even cynical, about the other lessons he learns at school. The same history teacher mandates, for instance, that his students must attend a performance of Rabindranath Tagore's *Sacrifice*, for this play, according to the teacher, is about pacifism or "'*non-aggression.*'"[10] And, as the teacher explains, "'This isn't the last time the word crops up in the history of our region. In fact, when our nation was...'" (Bilgrami 129). This time, the ellipsis indicates Haroon's dismissal of the lesson, for he has already concluded that, since "great movements were shaped by forces or, more particularly, *by force*," "[n]othing could be achieved through inaction" (Bilgrami 123). Haroon's studential obstinacy at once calls into question the nationalist mythos that praises non-cooperation as appropriate anti-colonial resistance and the nationalist dismissal of the events of 1971. Both, in Haroon's view, are cover stories since only action—namely, forceful action—accomplishes ends. In the logic Haroon deploys, then, present circumstances derive from past actions and their perpetuation, which leaves nearly everyone accountable for what the present circumstances are.

To be more precise, Haroon equates non-aggression not necessarily with an absence of agency but with a *willful* choice not to act, for any action could achieve some outcome. Thus, not to meet force with force, act with act, is to allow the present to continue. In this sense, the intertextual references to Tagore's *Sacrifice* are doubly ironic. First, in the play itself, though the king puts an end to the sacrifice of animals (and at the risk of his own assassination), he nonetheless retains his life and his throne at the play's end. The power structure obtains. Second, the play's title resonates with Abdul's role throughout the novel, and his identity as an East Pakistani orphan gives the lie to the virtuousness of Pakistan's purported nationalist history of non-aggression. Even more, the play, insofar as it's a part of Haroon's history lesson, also relates back to his father's abuse of his mother. And, as I've suggested at several points above, Haroon's rejection of non-aggression as a credible nationalist narrative coincides with his refusal to grant his mother a pass given her victim's status. As Haroon's awareness of his parents' abusive relationship grows, he becomes increasingly incredulous of his mother's acceptance of this violence. As Tahira recovers after one beating, Haroon thinks, "He loved her, and yet at that moment all he could feel for her was contempt. Was she really that weak? Did people actually allow these things to happen to them? Passively?" (Bilgrami 97). Haroon's doubts here, coupled with Tahira's own admission that her acceptance of her husband's behavior was her "dirty habit" (Bilgrami 88), complete the direct ascription of victim's status to Tahira, at least at a metaphorical level. Instead, both Haroon and Tahira sense her participation in her own abuse. Indeed, in the scene when Haroon brings the bookcase down on Javaid, Haroon can openly admit to himself that he suspects just that: "He pushes [Tahira] roughly away, at once angered and amazed at the astounding passivity that makes her complicit with her husband's violence. He wants nothing to do with her" (Bilgrami 241). Tahira's refusal to deal openly with her husband's abuse parallels the driver's willful failure to come to Abdul's aid when Javaid is beating him. The driver does not intercede because his material well-being depends upon his submission to Javaid's authority, and the parallel here suggests the same may be true of Tahira, at least metaphorically. Moreover, Tahira cannot fulfill a sacrificial function as does Abdul because power works for her benefit, as is made blaringly evident when the police officer deliberately protects her and Haroon by framing Abdul for Javaid's murder. As the mistress of Saathpari, Tahira, like the house itself, "represent[s] old money, established roots, character" (Bilgrami 35), that is, a legitimate belonging. Tahira must remain that idealized mother holding the baby boy captured and frozen in the photograph gathering dust in Haroon's nursery, for this photo and what it represents prove that they belong.

As Moni Mohsin's 2006 novel *The End of Innocence* calls upon idea, nation, and state, it bears resonances with several other novels already discussed. The novel's focus on how the state—here the military and the police, as well as the powerful, land-owning Azeem family—structures everyday life links this fiction to Singh's *Train to Pakistan* and Ashraf's *The Postmaster*. And, as with Bilgrami's *Without Dreams*, Mohsin's novel examines what price belonging to the Pakistan that remains after 1971 exacts. Mohsin's novel announces its conceptualization of childhood through its title. Two child characters, Laila and Rani, experience the end of their innocence during the novel's primary temporal plane, 1971. The timing and location—several villages in rural Punjab—of their experiences coincide to conjure a specific regionally-inflected view of the Pakistani nation that pushes any nostalgia over the idea of Pakistan, as well as any assertions of bureaucratic or state-like power, to the margins. Belonging to the nation hinges upon capitulation to values and concerns that prioritize a gendered hierarchy ordered according to purity and honor rather than to a democratic vision, zamindari dominance, or even a recognition of military authority. In short, a particular definition of nation subordinates both the idea and the state (or state-like actors) of Pakistan.

Although the novel opens and closes on New Year's Eve, 2001, the bulk of the plot unfolds between October and December of 1971 through an omniscient third person narrative voice. In this two month span, fifteen year old Rani, who is the granddaughter of Sardar Begum's longest-employed servant, sees her first movie, a tragic Punjabi folk story about lovers denied, and, shortly thereafter, meets a young man with whom she indulges her own romantic tendencies only to find herself pregnant and terrified. Rani's attempts to solve her problem—by first seeking help from the local nuns and then prevailing, she thinks, upon her paramour to marry her—are in vain. Eventually her grandmother, Kaneez, and, circuitously, her stepfather, Mashooq, find out, and Rani is disavowed by the former and beaten to death by the latter.[11] Rani's grandmother's and stepfather's reactions manifest what the novel presents as the dominant regional ethos, one valuing honor, a word rife with gendered connotations. Kaneez and Sardar Begum, for example, insist that Mashooq be released from police custody even though he confesses to beating Rani to death, for to prosecute him would alert everyone to Rani's "sin." Tariq Azeem, Sardar Begum's son and Laila's father, capitulates to his mother's order despite his own commitment to law-and-order justice and, thus, facilitates Mashooq's release by using his considerable influence as the most powerful landowner in the district. To view this novel as a child's narrative of development is to acknowledge a significant revision of the conventions associated with that genre. If, traditionally, narratives of development, according to Gregory Castle, "duplicat[e] in literary form a cohesive set of cultural codes whose primary function is to govern social integration in such a way that young men and women *fit into society*" (22), then *The End of Innocence*, as a postcolonial iteration of the genre, reveals at what cost this integration takes place, not just for the protagonist but also for the so-called community the protagonist is called to join. In this sense, Mohsin's novel refines further critical redefinitions of the postcolonial narrative of development, for, rather than "emphasiz[ing] the pernicious effects of the dissociation between the protagonist and the society to which he belongs," as Jose Vazquez has it, Mohsin's novel uncovers the pernicious effects of belonging at all.

The novel links Rani's increasingly desperate situation with the violence and coming war with India in East Pakistan, suggesting that her stifled development parallels or reflects that of the nation itself. This structural linkage functions chronotopically, allowing the novel to represent the events of the fall of 1971 through the specifics of a precise regional location. Mikhail Bakhtin defines chronotope as *"time-space"*: "Everything—from an abstract idea to a piece of rock on the bank of a stream—bears the stamp of time, is saturated with time, and assumes its form and meaning in time" (42). This emphasis on historicity requires a consideration of context, and Bakhtin elaborates on what context means by spatializing it as well: "time…is localized in concrete space, imprinted on it… [T]here are no events, plots, or temporal motifs that are not related in an essential way to the particular place of their occurrence, that could occur anywhere or nowhere…" (42). With respect to the history upon which Mohsin's novel draws, the dissolution of Pakistan can only be understood as its dynamics manifest themselves in the characters' attitudes toward them, for example, and, as I discuss, these attitudes themselves develop from specific locations, social and geographical. Bakhtin formulates his idea of the chronotope to address how novels of emergence, his phrase for the *Bildungsroman*, represent the protagonist's own development; the protagonist "emerges *along with the world* and he reflects the historical emergence of the world itself" (Bakhtin 23). The context or history in which the protagonist develops is not static or fixed, according to this view, but is as subject to change as the protagonist herself. Any appearance of fixity or intractability, then, represents an exertion of power or a more complete saturation of place by a given historical narrative. That Rani first realizes her dissatisfaction with her life's prospects after seeing a romantic movie illustrates this point. She's careful to point out to Laila that the film, *Heer Ranjha*, is in Punjabi, not Urdu or English (Mohsin 10). This distinction matters because it locates the film in a specific location and culture. Even more, Laila's ayah identifies the story as a Punjabi folktale (Mohsin 19). Bakhtin points out that folktales "intensify the native soil" as they "interpre[t] and saturat[e] space with time, and dra[w] it into history" (52). Thus, the inclusion of this filmic adaptation of a Punjabi folktale introduces into the novel the power of narrative to spatialize history and, as a result, to legitimate specific claims of belonging. Ironically, despite the folktale's "native" origin, the pull of its narrative on Rani brings her into violent conflict with other "native" narratives that disallow the romantic transgressions the film idealizes.

With their chronotopic functions in mind, the links between the narrative of Rani's development and the violent conflict embroiling Pakistan and, eventually, India in 1971, articulate how history and identity take on meaning according to location specific narratives. Rani is buried on 3 December 1971, the day hostilities between India and Pakistan officially break out (Mohsin 335). A trench servants dig to bury an Indian light bomb reminds Laila of Rani's grave (Mohsin 344). These structural linkages between Rani's developmental narrative and the 1971 war hinge on the theme of domestic violence, literal in Rani's case, metaphorical in the nation's. During her first assignation with her boyfriend, for example, the young man brags that his brother is killing Hindus and "'smashing those scrawny Bengalis' faces for trying to break away from us'" (Mohsin 40). Since any mention of political turmoil falls outside the romantic script Rani desires, she's left wondering "[h]ow...the conversation [had] come to scrawny Bengalis?" (Mohsin 41). In the moment, this reference to the situation in East Pakistan comes off as just an opportunity for the young man to perform his own masculinity, a performance partially lost on Rani. But, the image of the (West) Pakistanis "smashing" the faces of their compatriots foreshadows the injuries Rani sustains, including a "'smashed nose,'" broken jaw, and "'considerable damage to her skull'" (Mohsin 290), at Mashooq's hands. The connection between the violence embroiling the two halves of Pakistan and the punishment meted out to "bad" girls such as Rani gets strengthened and naturalized by the Army representative, Colonel Butt, the CO at the nearby district cantonment. He dismisses Tariq's question about the "'atrocious things going on in East Pakistan'" by saying, "'Civil war is not a polite, sanitary affair. It's like war within a household. Between a husband and wife, if you will'" (Mohsin 105). By casting the relationship between West and East Pakistan as governed by heterosexual norms in which, for instance, a man is responsible for preserving the family's "honor," this metaphor effeminizes the East Pakistanis and casts them as deserving of the treatment they receive at the hands of the West Pakistanis and, indeed, as responsible for their "sins" as Rani is. This mindset blunts what other affective or intellectual responses the characters may have to Rani's death or the hostilities between East and West Pakistan (leaving off the coming war with India) in that it reinscribes and, thus, prescribes the view necessary to be included in the larger collective.[12]

National belonging emerges in *The End of Innocence* as the preservation of and submission to a place-specific idea of honor. What it means to be Pakistani, then, takes shape at the localized sight of Sardar Begum's haveli in Kalanpur, whose ethos dominates even Tariq's estate and factory in the adjoining village of Sabzbagh. Sardar Begum voices the predominant view, which relies on a rigid hierarchy:

"When people forget their place, they step out of the bounds decided by Allah. That's when the devil begins his work. Now, what are the Bengalis doing but forgetting their place? Allah has decreed a place for everyone—one for me, one for the sweeper, and one for the Bengali. As long as we remember it and honour it, all will be well."

(Mohsin 180)

Posited as intractable and absolute, the structure Sardar Begum values requires strict adherence, either through coercion enforced by social pressures or by violence, as her reference to the Bengalis makes clear. Sardar Begum's insistence at the novel's close that Mashooq be released after he confessed to killing Rani maintains this structure. She tells Tariq, "'It is not for you to give justice. That is for Him. And this is not about *your* conscience, either. It is about *their* honour, *their* loss'" (Mohsin 331; emphasis in original). Sardar Begum contrasts Tariq's desire for law-and-order justice, which shapes his conscience, to Rani's mother's and grandmother's honour and loss, with the latter prevailing. To quell Tariq's resistance to her command, Sardar Begum explains, "'Rani committed a sin. She paid for it with her life. She had stained her family's honour. Mashooq, rightly or wrongly, removed the stain'" (Mohsin 331). Sardar Begum's equivocal stance on Mashooq categorizes his act as beside the point given that Rani's actions "stained her family's honour." The removal of this stain is of greater concern than the technical illegality of Mashooq's actions, the illegality that Sardar Begum reduces to Tariq's "conscience." What's at stake in the preservation/restoration of Rani's family's honour is the reification of the hierarchy upon which Sardar Begum's worldview depends. Rani's "sin" evidences her transgression of her decreed place as a "good" girl who should only have sex with her husband in a marriage based on obligation and respect.[13]

The necessity of stain removal in service of the preservation of honor finds its echo in how the characters react to Pakistan's surrender to India. At stake here, just as with Sardar Begum's hierarchy, is the preservation/restoration of a rigid order that adjudicates who belongs and where. When Tariq's driver, Barkat, learns of the surrender and, thus, of his son's fate as a POW, he tells Tariq, "'I dreaded receiving that telegram telling me that my boy had died fighting. That was my worst fear. I never for a moment thought he would lay down his arms meekly like a girl. Death, I think, would have been preferable to this disgrace… How will I ever live down this shame, this stain on our honour?'" (Mohsin 343). If Sardar Begum's dictate, premised on the essential need to remove Rani's stain, demands submission and silence, so then, the novel suggests, will what remains of Pakistan; to claim belonging at the local and at the national level, that is, will be to acquiesce to an enforced amnesia.[14] The prevalence of the mindset that justifies West Pakistani dominance through the metaphor of domestic violence finds its logical extension here in the notion of stained honor, and, significantly, Barkat emasculates his son. This notion manifests itself in both the national and private arenas, amplifying the interpellative function of a mutually enforced governing narrative.

Mohsin's novel dramatizes the interpellative process by showing how this narrative subordinates other forms of power, both liberal and conservative, as well as other sites of affective attachment. In other words, the pull of national belonging, howsoever locally defined, trumps emotive attachments to the idea of Pakistan and the bare power wielded by bureaucratic functionaries and other structural powers such as landowners. Sardar Begum's ability to corral Tariq represents one example of how state-like power falls in line behind this specific vision of national belonging. Throughout the bulk of the novel, Tariq represents the benevolent zamindar whose liberal politics and practices grant Sabzbagh, his village, "a prosperous, well-fed look" (Mohsin 13). Tariq starts a cooperative on his land in order to provide the village women a skill set that will enable them to earn money, and he underwrites Rani's education at Kalanpur's school for girls. The Army's powerhold on the country disgusts him, as well (Mohsin 287). Despite these progressive views, Tariq nonetheless values and revels in his unassailable role as village patron: "All this prosperity, this progress, it was his doing. And the villagers', of course" (Mohsin 156). What he has accomplished in Sabzbagh far outstrips any contribution he could have made in the Civil Service, for "those labyrinthine bureaucracies...have made not a jot of difference to anyone" (Mohsin 156). All of Tariq's efforts at creating this prosperity enhance his already elevated position as the only son of a landowning family that has lived in this area of rural Punjab for eleven generations (Mohsin 209). Tariq possesses influence enough to have given the police inspector his job (Mohsin 316), and, thus, the inspector defers to Tariq's authority when it comes to extracting Mashooq's confession (Mohsin 317–28). All of these examples illustrate Tariq's power and the ideological convictions that drive its deployment. And, yet, when Sardar Begum orders him to use this influence to effect the ends she seeks, he yields. Indeed, she cements her coercion of him by asking, "'And have you thought how you will appear to the world, Tariq Azeem, publicly fighting for the rights of a girl who has brought shame and dishonor on her people?'" (Mohsin 331). Sardar Begum's trump card blatantly disregards rights discourse, thereby undercutting state-related edicts, even as she appropriates Tariq's zamindari powers to bolster the hierarchy she wants maintained. Tariq possesses complete awareness of his mother's actions and thinks to himself, "Now he knew he was about to taste humiliation" (Mohsin 333). He swallows this humiliation because "he belonged here. This was his home, his place" (Mohsin 156).

The military is the other site of bare state power brought to heel by Sardar Begum's dictates and, ultimately, by this specific understanding of national belonging. Throughout the novel, the Army as a site of power stands in contrast to the zamindari power Tariq possesses. Colonel Butt, the CO at the district cantonment, holds a "general antipathy...for people with privileged back-grounds," and, in his new environs, this means Tariq. Equally as suspicious of politicians as Tariq is, Colonel Butt tells him that "'[t]he true guardian of this country is the military'" (Mohsin 209). This statement is only the first that hits the mark, endowing the Colonel's views with qualified legitimacy. He continues, for instance, by mentioning that "'some people'" regard the zamindari system as "'feudal'" and that he understands why Tariq didn't stay abroad or in Lahore, for in Sabzbagh, Tariq "'gets to run the show. If I were in your place, I, too, would want to come back to this house, this status, this certainty'" (Mohsin 208). By setting Tariq and Colonel Butt as opposites, the novel highlights their structurally similar positions. Both hold power because of a rigid hierarchical system, and both, it can be argued, benefit economically at others' expense.[15] At the level of plot, both have a hand in solving Rani's disappearance and murder as it's the Army that finds her body in a canal and, given the obviousness of her injuries, conducts a post mortem. The Colonel makes a point of telling Tariq that the Army has treated Rani's body "with respect," to which Tariq responds with the requisite gratitude and then adds,

> "But crimes of passion like this one are common here. Have been for centuries. I don't know as yet who killed her and why, but I am ready to bet that she was a victim of her own naivety. Some ruthless, ignorant bastard took advantage of her innocence and killed her."
>
> (Mohsin 292)

The Colonel mocks Tariq's response as a declaration of privilege: "'That's convenient! Blame the girl for her own death. "What did she die of?" "Oh, she died of innocence!" It certainly let you off the hook, Tariq Sahib, for bringing her murderer to justice'" (Mohsin 292). This scene takes place before Tariq questions Mashooq, who is brought to the police station only for public drunkenness. Thus, Tariq hasn't yet elicited Mashooq's confession. Nonetheless, his speculations over Rani's demise align with his mother's way of thinking in that they refer to the idea of honor as motivation for crimes, an idea that does implicate the victim in her own death. The Colonel voices the progressive view, here, anticipating the very outrage Tariq later vents when his mother tells him to secure Mashooq's release. Once again, the novel posits a parallel between these two figures and the state structures and powers they represent and highlights how both end up toeing the line Sardar Begum spools out. She tells Tariq simply to lie to the Colonel about his progress in finding Rani's murderer (Mohsin 332). Tariq does so, and the lack of follow-up suggests that the Colonel accepts Tariq's word.

The affective resonance of the idea of Pakistan similarly falls to the wayside, representing how this locally-articulated definition of national belonging marginalizes yet another alternative. All but tangential to Rani's story, Laila's "normal" life takes place largely in Lahore, where she attends a convent school and lives with her Nani or maternal grandmother.[16] Nani is fully cosmopolitan, having been the successful wife of a Pakistani diplomat. The narrator, privileging Laila's views of her grandmothers, describes Nani as "a lot more fun" in comparison to Sardar Begum. Indeed, "[w]hereas Sardar Begum was always reminding [Laila and her sister] to think of the hereafter…and urging decorum…, Yasmeen [Nani] encouraged them to be adventurous" (Mohsin 246). The novel distinguishes Yasmeen from Sardar Begum primarily along the lines of "modern" views, especially with respect to gender, education, and personal independence. While Sardar Begum's politics emerge through her conservative and, at times, prejudiced attitudes, Yasmeen's are explicit: she defined her duty as an ambassador's wife in terms of the efforts they had made for the "country they had fought so hard to liberate" (Mohsin 51). Similarly, Yasmeen reminds her daughter and son-in-law of her abilities to withstand the dangers of wartime Lahore by invoking her memories of the 1947 partition:

> "[I]t was a dangerous time...But also a very exciting time. We were getting freedom. And our own country, Pakistan. We'd fought for it for so long. We'd marched on the streets and protested and gone on strike against the British. And Mr Jinnah, so ill, so emaciated and yet so resolute. He was up against a whole stableful of wily Congress wallahs, aided and abetted by that ghastly Mountbatten. But, in the end, he trumped them all."
>
> (Mohsin 251)

In this passage, the novel's sole reference to the politics leading up to the 1947 partition, Yasmeen reinforces Muslim nationalist mythologies by casting Jinnah as a champion facing seemingly insurmountable odds. As a statement of an affective ideal, much hinges upon Yasmeen's "our own country": to whom does the "our" refer? Yasmeen continues, lamenting, "'We had such high hopes of this nation...I never imagined it would unravel so fast'" (Mohsin 252). To Tariq's speculation that, perhaps, Pakistanis never were a nation, Yasmeen offers the idea of Pakistan as a homeland for India's Muslims, irrespective of the language differences and geographical distances that may, in 1971, appear to be the causes of conflict. This scene concludes with Yasmeen "whisper[ing] in a husky voice," "'We weren't meant to split, to shatter. I was there when this country was made. I remember'" (Mohsin 252). Yasmeen's emotional reaction to the current political events illustrates her affective investment in the idea of Pakistan, itself made manifest in her references to Jinnah and the orthodoxies of Muslim nationalism. Yet, there is no place for Yasmeen and the affective investment she makes in Sabzbagh's and Kalanpur's dominant ethos. Indeed, despite Fareeda and Tariq's insistence that she join them in the countryside to escape the threat of war-related violence in Lahore, Yasmeen opts to stay. The narrative leaves Yasmeen behind after this scene, suggesting that her attachments, her claims to belonging, are out of place in the main storyline, just as she is out of place in rural Punjab.[17]

In effect, Laila's positive associations surrounding Yasmeen represent another way Mohsin's novel employs the figure of the child. The extension of this argument, then, also places Laila outside the affective bonds Sardar Begum reinforces. The novel locates Laila's position outside these affective bonds as independent of but amplified by Rani's tragedy. The chapter that follows the one in which Rani first meets with her young man begins with Tariq and his wife Fareeda "listening to the BBC's World Service. Again" (Mohsin 47). Laila attempts to get her parents' attention only to have them "brus[h] aside her queries with false smiles and a swift change of subject" (Mohsin 47). Just as the image of "smashing" faces foreshadows Rani's fate, Tariq and Fareeda's efforts to dismiss and shield Laila establish the pattern that perpetually situates Laila disadvantageously to the reality of the moment. The use of "false" to modify "smiles" suggests Laila's growing awareness of her parents' efforts to do just that. Indeed, the end of Laila's innocence involves her discovery of adult perfidy and how it contributes to her unknowingly providing Mashooq with the motive he needs to proclaim his own belonging through killing Rani. The novel centralizes Laila by deferring the explicit revelation of Rani's pregnancy until Mashooq kidnaps and murders her. By doling out only hints, the novel foregrounds Laila's childlike understanding even as it provides a space for Laila to voice her suspicions over how Rani and the adults rebuff and redirect her questions. Laila's interest in directness and honesty foil the novel's outcome, calling into question the price of belonging and, through the narrative frame set in 2001 and delivered via Laila's first person narration, leaving her marginalized and inaccessible even to her own family. Thus, while it is Rani who undertakes the passage from childhood to adulthood through her sexualization, it is Laila's continuing status as a child that provides the critical vantage point from which to view what belonging to the nation involves. The narrative of Laila's development involves, then, her reckoning with truths in ways that others will not or cannot validate.

Part 2

Islamic Nation? Islamic State?

3   Islam before Pakistan

The desire for a homeland for India's Muslims formed the basis of the idea of Pakistan. The "two-nation theory" justified the All-India Muslim League's call for special consideration that, at first, did not also entail a demand for a separate country.[1] This theory, formulated by Muhammad Ali Jinnah in 1937 (Jaffrelot, *Nationalism* 12), held that the differences between Muslims and Hindus were stark enough to warrant the creation of separate states; as Christophe Jaffrelot observes, the two-nation theory gave the League and, eventually, Pakistan a *"nationalist* ideology…which has been formulated *against* India, the 'other nation'" (*Nationalism* 7–8).[2] A "Muslim" identity, thus, occupied a central place in the articulation of the idea of Pakistan, which isn't to say that the idea was intrinsically an Islamic vision. As all students of Pakistani history know, "fraught" best describes the relationship between Islam and the state throughout Pakistan's history. Indeed, according Ayesha Jalal, Pakistan has been on a "desperate quest for an officially sanctioned Islamic identity" ("Conjuring" 74). Nine years after Pakistan's creation, for instance, the constitution declared the nation an Islamic Republic. And, yet, the project of defining "Islam" in this context has vexed the country since.[3] After partition, Ali Usman Qasmi explains, the question "was not about the admissibility of the role of Islam in Pakistan but the *kind* of Islam to be established and the extent of its influence in the working of the state" (1200; emphasis in original). Qasmi's stress on the word "kind" calls forth a long-standing debate over Islam in South Asia, both in terms of what has become the ideological foundation of Pakistan and that which dis/ allows the belonging of Muslims in other South Asian nations. One of the recurring themes in this debate involves the syncretistic or composite nature of Islam in South Asia.

Much like Masroor's *Shadows of Time*, all five of the novels in Tariq Ali's Islam Quintet—*Shadows of the Pomegranate Tree* (1992), *The Book of Saladin* (1998), *The Stone Woman* (2000), *A Sultan in Palermo* (2005), and *Night of the Golden Butterfly* (2010)—feature syncretistic cultures in action, as well as violent efforts to purify such cultures. The first four novels foreground syncretism by highlighting the interrelations between Muslims and Christians, between Muslims and Jews, and even within Islam as it is practiced in different locations throughout the Islamic world. Further, each of these four novels fictionalizes moments of major historical transition affecting Moorish Spain in the early sixteenth century (*Shadows*), Arab Muslims in what is now called the Middle East at the end of the twelfth century (*Saladin*), Ottoman Turkey at the close of the nineteenth century (*Stone*), and Arab Muslims in present day Sicily in the middle of the twelfth century (*Sultan*). Only the last novel, *Night of the Golden Butterfly* (2010), deals with Pakistan, and, notably, this novel's treatment of syncretism has little to do with Islam itself. Indeed, *Butterfly* departs significantly from the four novels that precede it, as its setting mostly at the end of the first decade of the twenty-first century prevents it from being historical fiction and its plot doesn't fictionalize a momentous historical transition in the Islamic world. *Butterfly* does, nonetheless, share with the first four novels a concern with the merging of cultures and ideas. That is, the "politics of difference and identity" that characterizes syncretism, according to Peter van der Veer, binds all Ali's novels (van der Veer 196). In this section, I take Reed Way Dasenbrock's suggestion that Ali's Islam Quintet tells a "'whole story'" in order to argue that the first four novels' explicit treatment of the theological, cultural, and social pluralities operating around and within Islamic civilizations at the times Ali fictionalizes establishes a critical perspective that, when brought to bear on *Butterfly*'s more muted interest in Islam, calls into question the very possibility of articulating a claim to belonging to the Pakistani nation. Unexpectedly, then, Ali's novelistic series, focused through four volumes on the most triumphant and most tragic moments in Islamic history, largely bypasses the promise of the Idea of Pakistan and contends instead with the nation's failures to bind the people collectively. Although Ali's Quintet does not treat the idea of Pakistan or the era of South Asian decolonization, it shares with *Shadows of Time* more than just a thematization of syncretism. Similar to Maheen's ultimate disillusionment with Pakistan over that nation's inability to foster creative expression, the five volumes discussed here focus on cultural production. More specifically, Ali's Quintet cumulatively examines how representation and interpretation work and, ultimately, identifies the significance of self-generated representations and interpretations.

Ali's five volumes all evidence a self-consciousness over representation and then use this self-consciousness to examine the politics of syncretistic cultures. That is, the metafictional draws attention to the role power plays in structuring (inter-)cultural interactions and the narratives that define such interactions. The first four novels concentrate on representations of the violent responses to pluralism and/or the merging of cultures at specific historical moments: the Inquisition drives the Moors out of Spain at the beginning of the sixteenth century (*Shadows*); Saladin retakes Jerusalem from the Crusaders at the close of the twelfth century (*Saladin*); the Ottoman Empire crumbles at the end of the nineteenth century (*Stone*); and the Christians drive the Muslims out of Sicily and mainland Italy in the middle of the twelfth century (*Sultan*). Critics argue that the absence of a neat historical linearity across the first four volumes initiates the series' broader metafictional concerns. Ahmed Gamal, for instance, sees the achronological order of the novels as enacting a movement/countermovement dynamic, which allows readers to see both the decline and ascent of various Islamic cultures and, thus, sketches an historiographic alternative to the notion of forward progress ("Rewriting" 9–10). Similarly, Dasenbrock contends that the historical jumps between the first four novels allow readers to look "backwards and forwards at the same time" (26), a double vision that can shift contemporary perspectives on Islam's sociopolitical position in the present. Klaus Stierstorfer's labeling of the four novels as "antifundamentalist utopias" hints at the critical work the metafictional elements undertake (153). My own analyses add to this conversation by contending that *Butterfly* develops the metafictional in its treatment of Pakistan to point toward—but, markedly, not to represent fully—who and what historical narratives leave out.

Understanding what is at stake in the arguments over the definition of "Islam" in a Pakistani national context allows for a fuller appreciation of the Islam Quintet's critique of Pakistan's failure to cement an inclusive national belonging around "Islam" as a lived culture. To attempt to define "Islam" in a Pakistani national context is, in part, to identify Pakistani singularity. As Adeel Khan observes, nation-states need to "define their individuality" (*Politics* 68), a nationalist impulse inherited, according to Syed Akbar Hyder, from colonial historiography (24).[4] For Pakistan, the articulation of national uniqueness necessarily involves a repudiation of syncretism understood as the merging of Islamic and un-Islamic practices and beliefs. Yet, the notion of a subcontinental "composite culture," a narrative favored, according to Javed Alam, by both liberal and Marxist histories, obstructs claims to uniqueness. Beyond the purported overlap of folkways shared by pre-partition subcontinentals from an array of religious identifications, in the post-partition era, this effort to individuate Pakistan proved/ proves daunting. The obstacle emerges because, as A. Khan continues, "the demand for Pakistan was a secular nationalist demand of a section of Muslims who felt threatened, not religiously but economically, by the Hindu majority... But there is no denying that the rhetoric and slogans for the demand were couched in religious symbolism" (*Politics* 69). So what of the millions of Muslims who remained Indians? The division of the 'umma, or community of believers, complicated any ready and inextricable linkage between Islam and Pakistaniness. Very simply, an acceptance of the composite argument threatened Pakistan's distinctiveness in that it elided the differences that would distinguish Pakistan from its neighbors, especially India.

At the same time, the deployment of "religious symbolism" to attain geographical nationhood created, in A. Khan's terms, an "ideological quagmire" domestically involving precisely what role "Islam" plays and what the term means (*Politics* 70). Barbara Metcalfe contends, for example, "official Pakistani ideology was founded on [the] binary" between what the state viewed as "Islam" and its native variants, wherein the former was dominant (xxii). This binary implies that, whatever constitutes the "native," it is by the logic of the binary opposition not "Islam." The result of the homogenizing impulse behind official Pakistani ideology, A. Khan argues, includes the state's denial of the "diversity and difference" abounding in the "composite [nature] of various regional and ethnic cultures, which cannot be defined as Islamic or un-Islamic" (*Politics* 70–1).

The suppression of internal diversity and external ties to other cultures in the subcontinent creates, in Magnus Marsden's view, "a lingering tendency for Pakistan specialists to depict 'Pakistani Islam' as unique and distinct," a point that would suggest that the framers of Pakistani nationalism through the decades have indeed succeeded in individuating the nation (982). S. Sayyid and ID Tyrer make a similar point, pointing out that Pakistan's apparent singularity achieved through the denial of syncretism frames the nation as a "pre-determined entity almost independent of broader social and political transformations" (66–7). Or, to adapt Hyder's terms, Pakistan appears "frozen" both inside (domestically) and out (subcontinentally) (25). The maintenance of this putative stasis requires the exertion of power. In Pakistan's history, these efforts to fix the meaning of "Islam" constitutionally and culturally have consistently veered toward the homogenizing, hierarchizing, and orthodox, shunting public discourse into prescribed, state-legitimated formats. The plurality of cultural practices involving Islam throughout Pakistan have not and do not necessarily conform to these centralized prescriptions, resulting in a fragmented rather than solidified collective Islamic identity.

Returning to Metcalfe's point regarding the deployment of a binary between Islamic and native cultural elements in "official Pakistani ideology" also helps shift this discussion to an evaluation of the broader theoretical implications, especially in terms of historical agency, of the debate over syncretism in Pakistan. This debate is by no means news, for, as Metcalf points out, it reached its apogee in the 1980s (xxii), but its dynamics resonate throughout every decade of Pakistan's history and in the nation's cultural productions, as well.[5] Veena Das's assessment of the debate points out that syncretism's proponents and detractors both figure top-down "Islam," or what Das refers to as "normative" Islam, as "a single pattern of perfection which seems to be in the nature of an unchanging essence" (294). Metcalf's own evaluation of the debate mirrors Das's charge of essentialism, with the former going even further in her determination that the debate relies upon a "two-sided homogeneity" as it casts both normative and syncretistic practices as wholes unto themselves (xxii). The upshot to these essentializing dynamics highlights an irony: both normative and syncretistic arguments about Islam's status in the subcontinent and in Pakistan fall prey to what, in another context, Mahmood Mamdani calls "Culture Talk." "Culture Talk" reads politics ahistorically, as an outcropping of a culture's very essence (Mamdani 17). Moreover, "Culture Talk" strips people of their historical agency. Mahmood argues that, in an Islamic context, "Culture Talk focuses on Islam and Muslims who presumably made culture only at the beginning of creation, as some extraordinary, prophetic act" (18).[6] From that moment in time forward, Mahmood contends, this viewpoint would have Muslims simply conforming to that frozen culture rather than actively making and living their culture through history (18). If, as Das and Metcalf argue, both sides of the syncretism debate essentialize and homogenize, then only the actors proclaiming and recording the official definition of "Islam" in Pakistan via historically-significant documents and laws act with any purpose. This connection between agency, "Islam," and official discourse illustrates van der Veer's point that "the notion of power is crucial to understanding" syncretism (185).

So far, I've tried to highlight what is at stake in discussions about Islam and syncretism specifically in Pakistan and South Asia, as well as to identify the broader theoretical issues, including essentialism and agency, operating in these discussions. My analyses of Ali's Quintet comment directly on how the debate of syncretism in Pakistan forecloses upon an inclusive collective Pakistani identity informed by Islam. The use of metafictional elements in Ali's fictional series targets the historiographic exclusions that result from the partisan delegation of historical agency. At the same time, the serial nature of Ali's project continuously draws attention to what remains under- or unrepresented. Other critics, including Gamal, Dasenbrock, and Stierstorfer, argue that the destructive and constructive dynamics of Ali's series serve as correctives to hegemonic Western-oriented histories that overwrite the vibrancy and importance of Islamic cultures; I contend that the destructive and constructive dynamics in the series as a whole culminate by pointing out what the novels themselves leave out. That is, the novels focused on past historical eras do indeed function as counternarratives while they also build up to *Butterfly*'s critique of contemporary Pakistan's narrative exclusions.

The highly anticipated unveiling of a triptych in *Night of the Golden Butterfly*'s last chapter serves as a culmination of the entire series' concerns over representation, interpretation, and exclusion. In many ways, the first four volumes contribute to this anticipation, since the triptych's subject depicts the events covered in the earlier novels. As such, the artwork metafictionally urges a doubling back, so to speak, to reconsider how the stories about al-Andalus (*Shadows*), al-Kuds (*Saladin*), Turkey (*Stone*), and Siqilliya (*Sultan*) contextualize *Butterfly*'s story of contemporary Pakistan, and vice versa. The entire conceit of Ali's final installment in his Quintet makes the necessity of this doubling back clear. The plot revolves around Plato—friend, old mentor, dissident artist—commissioning his friend Dara to write "a novel based on his life" (*Butterfly* 3). Dara agrees and informs Plato that, to complete the project, "the period would have to be invoked, the social milieu excavated, and navel-gazing resisted" (*Butterfly* 5). In response, Plato argues that "a setback...could be transformed into a victory through a work of art" (*Butterfly* 5) or, in other words, that art can encourage a re-evaluation of the circumstances out of which it emerges and in which it is received. To prove his point, "[Plato] was working on a triptych that would be a call to arms...A work that would set Fatherland [Pakistan] on fire" (*Butterfly* 5). Plato dies soon after he finishes the triptych, and the work's unveiling to an audience of his friends occupies center stage in the novel's final chapter. As "creator" of Plato's fictionalized life, Dara holds a privileged position as key interpreter of his old friend's work, and, indeed, Dara is the one who reads the first panel as satire, the second as idol worship, and the last as Plato's autobiography in images. Thus, the very premise of *Butterfly*'s plot announces the narrative's self-consciousness: namely, meaning can only come from a consideration of context even while this meaning may change what the context itself signifies. Further, the possibility of ongoing meaning construction that emerges from this exchange between context and interpretation creates a dynamism that refuses the homogenizing tendencies characteristic of both sides of the syncretism debate. This dynamism better accommodates a sense of lived culture.

Images focused on both the destructive and constructive power of representations recur throughout the five volumes.[7] *Night of the Golden Butterfly* draws attention to the destructive and constructive power of representations. This novel ends, as I mention, with the posthumous unveiling of a triptych created by Plato, a character who, as a young man, serves as mentor to the narrator, Dara, and who, later in life, becomes an important if critically undervalued painter. The paintings' subject matter, as well as how the novel presents this subject matter to the reader, enacts a culmination of the previous four novels' overlapping preoccupations with representation, destruction, and construction. The novel builds anticipation for the paintings' revelation by having other characters, namely Zaynab, Plato's patron, describe the first panel to Dara long before the entire project's completion. Zaynab repeats to Dara Plato's own words: "'Look at this one. My last work. This huge cat is me and I'm watching Fatherland. Look, here are Fatherland's four cancers: America, the military, mullahs and corruption. For the cat there's just a single one, but the cat will die first. Fatherland is on intensive chemotherapy'" (*Butterfly* 165). Highly self-referential, Plato's painting or, rather, its indirect description, emphasizes the possibility of art's opposition to politics and ideology. Clearly, Plato's satire metaphorizes the forces destroying post-9/11 Pakistan as cancers, a figuration that crystallizes this representation's attempt to critique how power operates presently in the "Fatherland." Significantly, these forces are both external and internal to Pakistan, illustrating the government's failures to negotiate multiple interests within its borders and beyond them. The first panel of the triptych, thus thematizes destruction, even while its existence marks an investment in art's constructive potential.

The Quintet's other volumes extend *Butterfly*'s concern with destruction. In the prologue to *Shadows of the Pomegranate Tree*, set in 1492, the Crusaders confiscate and burn nearly all the volumes comprising the learning and culture of Moorish Spain. Not entirely ignorant to these volumes' value, "scholars in the service of the Church had convinced Cisneros [Queen Isabella's confessor] to exempt three hundred manuscripts from his edict" (*Shadows* 2). More furtive efforts also helped preserve additional books. The third person narrator describes how some Christian soldiers "understood the enormity of the crime they were helping to perpetrate," and, so, these men "would deliberately discard a few manuscripts in front of the tightly sealed doors" of Gharnata's/Granada's Muslim inhabitants (*Shadows* 3). The Believers then hid these treasures. The scene of the conflagration measures the devastation visited upon the Muslim community, as the "sky itself seemed to have become a flaming abyss…It was as if the stars were raining down their sorrow" (*Shadows* 4). Casting the stars as sorrowful, this scene's indulgence in a pathetic fallacy effectively conjures the Moors' apocalypse, visited upon them by the Church of Rome. Very explicitly, the burning of centuries of Muslim learning amounts to the destruction of their culture on the

Iberian peninsula. The prologue closes with the narrator revealing that Cisneros, "more than anyone else," "understands the power of ideas" (5), underscoring the necessity of the eradication of Moorish culture if Christian Spain is to prevail.

And, indeed, throughout the balance of *Shadows* and the other two volumes set subsequent to the fifteenth century, the bonfire of the books in 1492 represents the erasure of Moorish culture. The Baron, a German character in *The Stone Woman*, hypothesizes that the Catholic Church feared the power of Islamic ideas to such an extent that, rather than "be overwhelmed by argument" and the intellectual superiority of Islamic thinkers, the Church framed its interactions with the Moors as a "Holy War," which, of course, successfully removed the Muslims from Spain (127–8). Additionally, in *Butterfly*, as the characters discuss "the fate of Islam in the West," one remarks, "'[T]hey [Westerners] wanted us to swallow our history, our culture, our language, our entire past, and all that is not so easily digestible" (173). As *Shadows* represents the bonfire scene, however, it is not entirely destructive. At the same time, the scholars' pleas to preserve three hundred volumes and the soldiers' efforts to secret away even more acknowledges, howsoever surreptitiously, the value of the interactions and blendings that result in syncretistic cultures, a point voiced by *Stone*'s Baron: "'[N]ew ideas develop best when they are in struggle against orthodoxy. The synthesis is usually original and exciting'" (128). Ali's Quintet returns again and again to the positive potential of synthesis, the cultural and intellectual growth that can occur amidst plurality. And, significantly, just as often, Ali's novels stress that such plurality exists within Islamic cultures, a point I develop below, as well as between Islamic cultures and those of the Christians and the Jews.

Destruction within Islam also serves as a major theme throughout the novels. In the first panel of *Butterfly*'s triptych, for instance, Plato's visual depiction of Pakistan's toxic complicity in its own self-destruction through its ill-considered foreign and domestic policies tops off the recurring theme of self-destruction that runs throughout the preceding four novels. The metafictional treatment of the self-destruction theme in *Butterfly* recontextualizes its appearance throughout the Quintet. In addition to self-destruction's plot-level significance, this metafictional dimension problematizes the representation of a single or monolithic "Islam" in these historical moments. Each of these earlier novels highlights the tensions within their specific Islamic cultures alongside the conflicts between the Muslims and the Christians/Western world. This attention to the internal dysfunctions of Ali's fictionalized Islamic cultures supplements the representation of intercultural pluralities, which throughout the series leads to violence, with insights into the issues of intracultural pluralities. In *Shadows*, a character known as al-Zindiq, or the Skeptic, articulates most fully and frequently how the Moors in Spain contributed to their own downfall. Al-Zindiq argues, "'[W]e underestimated our own capacity for self-destruction...[T]he self-styled defenders of the faith quarreled amongst themselves, killed each other, and proved incapable of uniting against the Christians'" (*Shadows* 34–5). Unity amongst Muslims, al-Zindiq posits, would have protected the Moors from the Christians' incursions.

And, yet, as al-Zindiq expounds at later points in the novel, the unity he envisions thrives on sharp intellectual debate rather than staid, oppressive homogeneity. Al-Zindiq repeatedly challenges the charges of heresy attached to the great thinkers from al-Andalus's past, claiming that the perpetuation of these charges occurs only because "'the ignorant spread ignorance'" (*Shadows* 83). Pointedly, in al-Zindiq's estimation, this ignorance springs from adherence to religious orthodoxy, which, when dictated by those in power, mutates Islam's tenets to serve political ends. Further, the prevalence of such ignorance stands in stark contrast to the intellectual liveliness of Islam's past, which, as al-Zindiq points out, had allowed Muslims to lead "'the rest of the world in the realms of science and architecture, medicine and music, literature and astronomy'" (*Shadows* 127–8). The first meeting of Salah al-Din and Ibn Yakub, the sultan's Jewish scribe, in *The Book of Saladin*, echoes al-Zindiq's views. Ibn Yakub, acting as first person narrator, describes his inaugural visit to the sultan's palace in Cairo; as he peruses the library, he comes across Abul Hassan al-Bakri's *Sirat al-Bakri*, a biography of the Prophet "denounced" as blasphemy in the city's main mosque. Salah al-Din catches Ibn Yakub reading the "offending book" and comments, "'To dream and to know is better than to pray and be ignorant'" (*Saladin* 11). Markedly, the narrative puts these words in Salah al-Din's mouth, the sultan who re-takes Jerusalem or al-Kuds from the Crusaders. Doing so preempts a charge of heresy and, instead, separates belief that coexists with intellectual inquiry, on the one side, from the unquestioning performance of prayer meant to signify "true" belief, on the other. Idrisi, the character favored by the narrative perspective in *A Sultan in Palermo*, ponders a similar theory as he casts the history of Islamic cultures as a contest between urban- and desert-dwelling Muslims. The former were responsible for Islam's great cultural and scientific accomplishments, while the latter were "puritans [who] burnt books of learning, outlawed philosophical discourse, punished scholars and poets, thus beginning the process that would allow the enemy to enter through the pores of our weaknesses and destroy everything" (*Sultan* 70). The quelling of this intellectual vibrancy resulted, in al-Zindiq's view, in the Muslims' inability to "'find the road to stability and a government based on reason'" (*Shadows* 127–8). Collectively, these characters' perspectives rest on the contention that what made Islamic cultures great in the past was precisely their tolerance of questioning and inquiry, that is, of plurality. These cultures spell their own demise when they begin to stifle the uniqueness and ingenuity that results from the merging of a variety of perspectives.

These arguments in favor of heterogeneity within Islamic cultures introduce the Quintet's interest in the constructive power of representations. *Butterfly*'s build up to the unveiling of what turns out to be Plato's triptych also stresses the constructive power the painting possesses. Returning to the scene I referred to above, Zaynab, having relayed Plato's own description of the painting, can subsequently only remark to Dara, "'It's a horrific painting…He wants you to write about it'" (*Butterfly* 165). Zaynab's insistence that Dara write about Plato's last work adds to the meta elements of the painting's initial presentation in the text, which emphasized Plato's intentionality. Alongside the artist's self-insertion in the painting, the viewer's interpretation—that is, Dara's interpretation—will construct meaning. Ironically, however, long before Dara actually views the painting, which he thinks has remained unfinished due to Plato's death, he bestows upon the work a title, mindful of Zaynab's parameters that it be "'[s]omething simple and nonprovocative, like Unfinished...'"; Dara's suggested title is "'Artistic Structures of Political Meaning in an Unknown Country. Unfinished, 2009'" (*Butterfly* 171). While Zaynab's interest in avoiding provocation signals her own incomprehension of the oppositional role that art can play in society, she nonetheless approves of Dara's proposed title. For Zaynab, "Unknown" serves as an as apt modifier since the country to which it refers—i.e. Pakistan—is "'unknown to its rulers'" (*Butterfly* 172), a group who, nonetheless, possess the lion's share of historical agency. The "actual" painting, revealed as the first panel of Plato's triptych in *Butterfly*'s concluding chapter, maintains the depiction of the four cancers but, as Dara narrates, "much changed since the early drafts" (265). The biggest change, as Dara notes, is Plato's addition of "the wall of humanity with which the painter had encircled the canvas" (267). In depicting the masses, people who are, in Dara's words, "not unlike the ten [laborers] who had carried the painting into this hall" (267), Plato's addition amplifies the "unknown," that is, the distance between the rulers and the ruled.[8]

Beyond plot level, the language of the painting's title transposes Plato's critical intentions onto the main narrative itself. "Unfinished" suitably describes the Quintet as a whole, as it accounts for the volumes' traversal over vast swathes of history and geography. That is, the necessity of (re-)telling the story abides, even as cultures rise and decline. Such a reading of Dara's suggested title dovetails with both Stierstorfer's and Dasenbrock's points regarding how the novels imagine history otherwise, how they entertain the seemingly counterfactual, in their attempts, first, to challenge dominant Western/colonial histories of these periods and, second, to think through the "what if" scenarios that may have allowed these Islamic cultures to attain internal harmony as well (Stierstorfer 157; Dasenbrock 28). Moreover, connecting "unfinished" to Zaynab's appreciation of "unknown" develops the insight a bit more by bringing the contemporary Pakistani context into focus. For Pakistan to be "unknown to its rulers," for instance, suggests that the elite political class fails to recognize the day-to-day realities of the Pakistani people. Plato's work of art, presented as it is in a fictional text, implies that artistic representations can construct a Pakistan known to its people *through the act of interpretation*. In other words, Zaynab's directive by proxy that Dara write about Plato's "horrific painting" foregrounds the significance of analyzing representations, in addition to or even above heeding the artist's intention. Further, Dara's use of "unfinished" in the title indicates the irresolution of the interpretive act. Such open-endedness eludes the foreclosure of meaning orthodoxy desires, enabling the flexibility or plurality common to syncretistic environments and traditions.

The possibility that representation, especially in narrative form, can foster inclusivity through making an idea, a belief, a question known or knowable to viewers/readers threads through Ali's Quintet. And, this possibility works in concert with the destructive elements the volumes also share, collectively creating a sense of historical agency through acts of interpretation and the conviction that the "unfinished" holds promise even in the face of historical moments pockmarked by violence and attempts to eradicate a variety of cultures and lifeways. While, as other critics argue, the first four volumes' use of metafictional elements makes clear the Quintet's counterfactual impulses aimed at (re-)telling the histories of encounters between Christendom and Islam, it also encourages an examination of what stories or ideas get left out of the internal narratives of Islamic cultures. That is, just as with the preceding discussion of the theme of self-destruction within Islamic cultures, this theme of construction involves an internalized turn, focusing on two additional types of stories whose inclusion in the broader narratives of these historical moments would provide a fuller (but not exhaustive) view. The first type of story emerges from the "heretical" philosophers and intellectuals in Islamic cultures; the Quintet presents these figures' contributions as marginalized by dominant orthodoxies. The second type of story amounts to more of a gesture that continually points toward what viewpoints still need to be told, thereby manifesting the "unfinished" quality of the entire Quintet's critical examination of syncretistic cultures and identities.

The second panel of Plato's triptych takes these "heretical" philosophers and actors as its subject, demonstrating, once again, how *Butterfly*'s conclusion, the quintet's closing frame, urges a re-evaluation of how the entire series provides commentary on contemporary Pakistan. The inclusion in the paintings of the "heretics" who appear throughout the Quintet—Ataturk, al-Ma'ari, Ibn Hazm, Ibn Sina, Ibn Rushd, and even the real Idrisi—initially prompts Dara to title the panel, "The Good Muslim" (*Butterfly* 271), a clear endorsement of the entire series' investment in the value of challenging orthodoxy. But, upon the discovery of a James Joyce allusion, the viewers collectively decide to name the panel, "'The Obscure Soul of the World'" (*Butterfly* 272). The title itself comes directly from *Ulysses*; the passage, to which Plato directs the painting's viewers by including the page number, names Ibn Rushd and Ibn Maymud (whom Ali also fictionalizes in *Saladin*) as "'dark men in mien and movement, flashing in their mocking mirrors the obscure soul of the world, a darkness shining in brightness which brightness could not comprehend'" (*Butterfly* 271–2). The "mocking mirrors" of this intertextual reference to Joyce enhances the metafictional impulse behind the act of interpretation taking place in the scene. The mirror image draws attention to how these "heretics" refract orthodox "realities" in their own work, creating a paradoxical "shining" darkness. By labeling, via Joyce, these intellectuals' contributions "darkness," Dara's interpretation of Plato's painting connects back to both the "unknown" and the "unfinished" from the triptych's first panel: genuine intellectual inquiry has no prescribed or definitive conclusions. Further, in reflecting on the aptness of the Joyce allusion, Dara concludes that Plato was "[t]hinking of the tortured history of his country, his continent, and his religion" (*Butterfly* 272), suggesting that critiques and satires, such as those launched by Plato's art, Joyce's writing, and, implicitly, by the book Dara will write about Plato's life, as well as the book Ali has written, are similarly "bright" darknesses.

The inclusion of the "heretics" in the second panel of Plato's triptych encourages a careful tracing of their appearances throughout the previous four volumes of Ali's Quintet. The first volume, for instance, presents a sympathetic portrait of Islam's "heretical" thinkers, including Abu'l Ala al-Ma'ari (*Shadows* 28) and Ibn Rushd, known to the Christian world as Averroës (*Shadows* 83). In the face of the heresy charges against these thinkers, al-Zindiq repeatedly defends the value of their contributions. When Zuhayr, the young scion of the al-Hudayl family in *Shadows*, proclaims that "'our religious scholars'" deem al-Ma'ari "'an infidel'" (*Shadows* 28), for instance, al-Zindiq replies, "'I have learnt more from one of his poems than from all the books of religion. And I mean *all* the books'" (*Shadows* 29). Similarly, in *The Book of Saladin*, Halima, Salah al-Din's favorite wife and Ali's complete fiction, invokes both al-Ma'ari and Ibn Rushd, saying of the former that he "'never allowed any authority to set limits to the kingdom of reason'" and that the latter was "'also inclined to doubt'" (*Saladin* 125). Both thinkers, in Halima's estimation, challenged faith-based tradition and its "'code of conduct, by which we must all live'" (*Saladin* 125). Al-Zindiq's privileging of poetry over religious books, which pointedly includes the Koran, along with Halima's appreciation for how al-Ma'ari and Ibn Rushd call into question the orthodox strictures on everyday living, emphasize the role of interpretation, especially as it encourages critical reflection on received traditions.

In *A Sultan in Palermo*, the narrative point of view, which favors Ali's fictionalized Idrisi, begins the whole novel quite self-consciously: "The first sentence is crucial" (3). This line serves to induct the reader into both textual and ideological considerations. As the novel's opening, the sentence fails to orient the reader adequately, for it provides no characters' names or setting's details. By the close of the novel's first paragraph, while Idrisi's name remains unknown, the narrator does reveal that "he," Idrisi, "envied [the ancients] the choices [of beginnings] their world had made possible, their ability to search for knowledge wherever it might be found" (*Sultan* 3). Idrisi's envy situates textual beginnings ideologically, indicating that Idrisi writes under epistemological constraints. Within pages the details of this ideological context become clearer, as Idrisi wonders explicitly "why [he] should start [his book] *In the name of Allah, the Beneficent*...just like every other scholar in his world. Why?" (*Sultan* 10). The use of the pronoun "his" before "world" indicates Idrisi's awareness that other "worlds" or realities exist outside orthodoxy's parameters. Idrisi resolves his intellectual crisis by opening his own personal edition of his book with this sentence: "*The earth is round like a sphere, and the waters adhere to it and are maintained on it through natural equilibrium which suffers no variation*' (*Sultan* 17; emphasis in original). At the opening of all the other volumes, Idrisi decides, "he would praise Allah, the Prophet, the Sultan and anyone else who had to be flattered" (*Sultan* 17). Idrisi's use of the word "flattered" underscores the banal conventionality of dedicating knowledge to the powerful, be they divine or mundane. Enthralled to neither divine nor mundane power, Idrisi views such conventional openings as ego stroking, a perspective intentionally at a remove from what is socially, politically, and religiously acceptable.

Ali's fictionalization of Kemal Ataturk in *The Stone Woman* works to much the same effect; that is, the novel presents Ataturk as an iconoclast. In what amounts to a cameo appearance, the unnamed Ataturk, made identifiable by references to his connections to Salonika (*Stone* 193), distinguishes himself as a promising young officer who, like the narrator's brother and husband, is a member of the Committee for Union and Progress (the Young Turks). This young officer invites Nilofer, the first person narrator, to be a part of the Committee's secret proceedings, a gesture neither her husband nor brother think to make, with the rationale that "'like-minded women'" aid the cause (*Stone* 180). In the course of the Committee's proceedings, other progressive ideas come to light, such as the Latinisation of the Turkish script, abolition of the clergy's power, mandatory education for all children, and the removal of the veil (*Stone* 192). Strikingly, Ataturk's appearance in the second panel of Plato's triptych differs from the mode in which Plato paints the other historical figures, who Plato represents "almost in Socialist Realist style" (*Butterfly* 269). Dara points out that Plato painted Ataturk in a surrealist style, though the figure is recognizable enough due to "[t]he famous hat, the cryptic smile, the cigarette, the tilted face" (*Butterfly* 269). Plato dresses his Ataturk "in tights and his legs were posed in a fantastic pirouette. Rudolf Nureyev or a whirling dervish? The choice was ours" (*Butterfly* 269). Dara's interpretive ambivalence or leeway over Plato's painterly decision to represent Ataturk surrealistically breaks the neat alignment of the painting's and the earlier novels' portrayals of the other heretical thinkers and actors. In other words, Dara's unresolved views on the painting's representation of Ataturk explicitly heightens the open-endedness of the interpretive act even more than does the questioning and doubt the other heretical figures metonymically embody. This open-endedness may have something to do with the historical proximity of *The Stone Woman*'s plot to the present day; unlike Ali's other historical fictions whose events are centuries in the past, the disintegration of the Ottoman Empire and Ataturk's creation of a "new" Turkey itself remain an "unfinished" project, much like Pakistan.

The appearance of these heretical figures in Plato's triptych amplifies the metafictional thrust of Ali's Quintet, as the recurring references to their unorthodox contributions to their respective Islamic cultures emphasize the series' investment in the constructive impulses born of pluralism. Alongside these "heretics," Ali's Quintet also repeatedly gestures toward the stories that remain untold. No end limit exists in syncretic processes; as a process, syncretism can't be swamped. These five novels illustrate the endless potential of syncretism through their historical span and their gesturing toward the untold stories. In *Shadows*, very little survives of the Banu Hadyl after Ali's fictionalized Cortes butchers the family, burns their house, and razes the entire village. Hind, the family's second daughter, lives on only because, upon her marriage, she relocates to the Maghreb with her husband. Zuhayr, her brother, also lives, but only because he is not at home when Cortes arrives; the narrative hints that Zuhayr's death is imminent, however. At the novel's end, Zuhayr sends al-Zindiq's papers, his life's work, to Hind, asking her to "[*l*]*ook after them well*" (*Shadows* 239; emphasis in original). Al-Zindiq's philosophy becomes a narrative yet to be told, aligning his own "heretical" views with those of the intellectuals he championed throughout the novel.[9]

Additional gestures toward untold stories in Ali's other novels draw attention to the power dynamics operating through the act of narrative assertion. I have noted how other critics read Ali's Quintet as oppositional in the sense that the series counternarrates these already well-known historical moments. Yet, mounting this opposition by no means guarantees full inclusivity. Clearly, Ali's novels value the challenges posed by heretical thinkers and, thus, attempt to incorporate them, even if obliquely, into the histories the novels re-imagine. At the same time, however, these novels replicate the silencing they're correcting, sometimes by making their exclusions explicit and sometimes by speaking for the groups they silence. In the paratextual "explanatory note" Ali includes in *The Book of Saladin*, for example, he clearly states that Ibn Yakub, the Jewish scribe who Salah al-Din enlists to chronicle his life, is Ali's fictional creation (xiv). Thus, when Ibn Yakub mentions that his wife "wanted [him] to return home to resume [his] work on the history of our people. That, for her, was far more important than becoming a court scribe" (*Saladin* 43), the metafictional impulse draws attention to how the writing of Salah al-Din's story supersedes the writing of Jewish history. The narrative itself makes its exclusions explicit.

The Stone Woman presents a more oblique example of narrative assertion resulting in narrative exclusion. While this novel features a first person narrator in Nilofer, its conceit—a geological feature, the Stone Woman, serves as a confessional for all the characters—allows for other characters to tell their own stories, too. This confessional premise allows the novel to include the voices of characters long since gone and to dole out information that is otherwise outside of Nilofer's knowledge. And, yet, even this type of structural and narratorial inclusion has its limits. In what initially comes off as a digression, Nilofer recounts what transpires when her family sits for a formal portrait. One of the photographs of Nilofer's father, Iskander Pasha, ends up "travel[ing] the world and appear[ing] in most of the books on early photography" (*Stone* 96), a fact that prompts Nilofer to go off on a tangent about the photographer, Giulio Bragadini. His photo of Iskander Pasha finally brought the Bragadini name the fame "denied by the old Sultans" for generations (*Stone* 96–7). Nilofer cuts herself off, though, stating, "The fantasies of the Bragadinis have no real place in this story…The past is difficult enough" (*Stone* 97). This assessment of the past's difficulty operates on both personal and broader historical levels, as, over the course of the novel, Nilofer learns that the Pasha isn't her biological father and that the Young Turks plan to create the new nation of Turkey out of the ruins of the Ottoman Empire.

And, yet, Nilofer's direct denial of the Bragadinis' relevance to the story, especially the "public" one involving Turkey's emergence as that modern thing called a "nation" from that old-fashioned thing called an "empire", runs counter to Nilofer's otherwise expansive vision of her country's future. After meeting the unnamed Ataturk, for instance, Nilofer engages her husband, a member of the Committee for Union and Progress, in a conversation about "purity" in post-Ottoman Turkey. Claiming that some members of the Committee "'want native plants only to be nourished'" in the new nation, Nilofer objects, "'In our cities and villages different communities have lived side by side for many centuries. Turks, Armenians, Greeks, Kurds, Jews and heaven knows how many smaller groups'" (*Stone* 193). In Nilofer's objection is the recognition that to become Turkish is to exclude, whereas being Ottoman means living amidst syncretism. Although the Bragadinis are Italians who have lived in Istanbul for centuries (*Stone* 94), Nilofer's dismissal of their relevance to the story of how the Ottoman Empire ends and Turkey begins renders her complicit in this dark foreshadowing of the violence yet to occur between the new Turks and their minority populations. The untold story of these minorities in *The Stone Woman* does play out indirectly through the murder of Nilofer's Greek husband, an event that happens off-stage, so to speak, and, thus, at a remove from the Committee's proceedings at Nilofer's family's home outside of Istanbul.

Similarly, this theme of the untold story appears in the first panel of Plato's triptych as the "wall of humanity" (*Butterfly* 267). Again, Plato added this image to the painting, in which "[t]he people on the edge were part-hedge, part-fence," as a boundary around the four cancers (*Butterfly* 267). Dara's immediate response to this wall image is to liken the "walled" figures to the laborers working at Zaynab's Sindhi estate. Significantly, Dara's description does not individuate any of these laborers. Instead, Dara describes their work: as he and his friends await the unveiling of Plato's painting, they are "interrupted by the slow march into the space of a team of ten brawny peasants" who are carrying the massive triptych (*Butterfly* 264). Once these workers set the painting down, Dara continues, "[m]ore retainers rushed in to help uncover it" (*Butterfly* 264). The presence and physicality of these workers contrasts starkly to that of the assembled audience, all of whom enjoy wealth, privilege, education, etc. In a sense, this scene enacts the very distance Zaynab hits upon with her gloss of the word "unknown" in the painting's title. Dara's likening of the figures in the "wall of humanity" to these "peasants" and "retainers," who might as well be beasts of burden and serfs, suggests that the painted figures also lack any humanizing (self-)representations. In his role as chief interpreter and narrator, Dara nonetheless offers his reading of the wall's meaning, deciding that, by presenting the masses as a wall, "Plato is stressing [the] collective strength" that prevents them from being "simply victims" (*Butterfly* 267–8). Dara's interpretation endows these figures with a purity that, he seems to suggest, can only belong to the poor. In a blurring of the artist and the interpreter, Plato/Dara speak for this walled humanity: "There is no blood on our consciences" (*Butterfly* 268). Dara hopes that the walled image manifests Plato's "last utopian shout": a revolution from below that would allow the masses to reclaim Pakistan so that it would become the "future" muhajirs and other Muslims thought it would be in 1947 (*Butterfly* 268). In effect, the entire unveiling scene, which starts with the laborers bringing the triptych into the room, subtly points toward the untold story of the laborers, the peasants, the retainers, all those who Plato/Dara romanticize in the "wall of humanity." Indeed, Dara's reading of the painting metafictionally signals the disjuncture between the story he narrates and the painting he interprets. Not a fault of Ali's narrative, Plato's and Dara's reductive representations of the Pakistani masses furnishes the entire Quintet with yet more narrative arcs to trace, other stories to include in a syncretic process that produces an inclusive Pakistani identity. The triptych's identification of the masses' untold stories also suggests/advocates a radical turn away from seeing only the elite as historical actors and toward recognizing the agency deployed in everyday living.

4   Zia's Islamization

Zia ul-Haq's Islamization of Pakistani political and public discourses from 1977–1988 fixed a spotlight on the place of Islam in Pakistan's national self-conception. From "encouraging" workplaces to accommodate daily prayers to institutionalizing zakat in the banking industry and promulgating the Hudood Ordinances, which spelled out very specific guidelines for testimony and punishment in criminal cases, Zia's Islamization program sought to alter religious practice from private piety to public injunction. While Zia himself often proclaimed his intention to bring Pakistan "closer to the precepts of Islam" (Kennedy 307), his regime's concerted right turn marks, in the opinion of many scholars, a significant departure from the idea of Pakistan. Iftikhar Malik, for instance, argues that Pakistan "was achieved by worldly and reformist elites largely banking on a Muslim identity yet disclaiming any ideas of a theocracy" ("State" 676). Jinnah and the Muslim League, Malik claims, viewed "*Islam* and *Muslim* [as] two distinct constructs" and, accordingly, used the latter, which they viewed as a "more general ethno-cultural identity," as the basis of a "non-theological Islam embedded in syncretic traditions" to construct their version of Pakistani nationalism ("State" 682–3).[1] From an historical long view, then, Zia's Islamization of Pakistan contributes, in Malik's estimation, to Pakistan's being misunderstood, externally and internally ("State" 676). Zia's positions as Chief of Army Staff at the time of his overthrow of ZA Bhutto's democratically elected government (1977) and later as Chief Martial Law Administrator and eventually as President only compound his religious hard sell in the sense that the alterations he made to the legal system, the Constitution, and other institutions exercising state control drove a wedge between the people and "Pakistan."[2] Zia's regime also dictated the terms of a normative Pakistani identity by imposing an idea of a proper Islamic order and, by extension, a "good" Muslim through alterations to the state's functions. To dissent from or critique these terms automatically places people outside of the established norms, precluding their claims to belonging.

Islamization in Pakistan under Zia emblematizes a refusal of syncretism in concrete form. My analyses in the previous chapter of Tariq Ali's Islam Quintet used the theoretical stakes of an argument in favor of syncretism to assert that self-consciousness over interpretation and representation running through Ali's novels continuously point toward the stories that remain untold, the voices unheard, when homogeneity overpowers plurality. As Ali's novels repeatedly advocated for the necessity of "heretical" views in any formulation of an inclusive Islamic order, I claimed that *Butterfly* ultimately illustrates the absence of an affectively relevant definition of the Pakistani nation as Plato's triptych can only represent the people as "masses" and "faces in a wall." The four novels I discuss in this section—Uzma Aslam Khan's *The Geometry of God* (2009), Ali Sethi's *The Wish Maker* (2009), Mohammed Hanif's *A Case of Exploding Mangoes* (2008), and Kamila Shamsie's *Broken Verses* (2005)—similarly champion the idea of dissent in an effort to create a space not only to critique Zia's Islamization program and its aftermath but also to re-assemble an affectively compelling sense of belonging to the nation. For these narratives, the state-sponsored incursions into everyday living alienate characters from collective cohesions, played out again and again as domestic and interpersonal dramas. This alienation also signals a wider detachment from social networks that connect characters productively to community and nation. In addition to unfolding in part or in whole during Zia's tenure, all four novels also share two interrelated elements: conspiracy thinking along with homosocial dynamics and homosexual identities.

The coincidence of these elements shapes plot and characterization while also inviting a queer postcolonial critical disposition. Hanif's *A Case of Exploding Mangoes*, for instance, satirizes the authority of Zia's political order by putting into play several conspiracy theories that attempt to account for the aircraft explosion that killed Zia in 1988. The satire develops out of the gallery of rogues intent on bringing down Zia that the narrative assembles, and it gains its anti-authoritarian edge from the narrator's homosexual relationship with his fellow Air Force cadet. Their redirected sexual desires upset the prescribed hypermasculinity the novel associates with the reigning regime and its religious predilections. The playfulness of Hanif's text torques the irresolution of the real life conspiracies surrounding the still unknown causes of Zia's death and, thus, suggests the possible ridiculousness not only of conspiracy thinking but also of the extant social order. The other three novels also launch critiques of Zia's Pakistan while attempting to imagine routes out of conspiratorial thinking as well. Shamsie's *Broken Verses* explicitly employs what Eve Kosofsky Sedgwick calls "paranoid reading," a characteristically queer hermeneutic, to forward the plot, while extra-narratorially encouraging an acknowledgment of this methodology's limits. The identification of these limits matters, for the novel also attempts to locate some form of agency that will allow the characters to re-assemble a narrative of belonging. Sethi's *The Wish Maker* shares this tendency toward re-assembly as its narrator crosses the threshold of heteronormativity to demonstrate the sterility of what Lee Edelman calls "reproductive futurism" (3). *The Wish Maker*, thus, establishes a connection between the postcolonial politics of Zia's regime and gender dynamics that reinforce the putative legitimacy of the broader socio-political order. Whereas Sethi's novel makes this connection via the homosexuality of its narrator, UA Khan's *The Geometry of God* situates its characters in a series of erotic triangles that emphasize, as Sedgwick has argued, how homosocial bonds between men bolster existing power regimes through asymmetric gender relations. However, Khan's novel does not just replicate this familiar homosocial convention; rather, the narrative allows two female characters to provide their perspectives on these triangles, thus highlighting not only an awareness of the power asymmetries but also gesturing toward an alternative, more balanced order. As all four of these novels expand the possibility of affective attachment to the nation by challenging in queer terms the dominant definition of "good Muslim," they also extend the critique of Muslim nationalism launched by Shah Nawaz's *The Heart Divided*, which similarly seeks to expand the definition of "good Muslim" from a feminist perspective.[3]

As I note above, Zia's Islamization of Pakistan's legal and public discourses represents a departure from the idea of Pakistan. Indeed, Malik even uses the word "syncretic" to modify Jinnah's attitude toward Pakistan's Islamic cultural inheritance. I use the word "cultural" deliberately, for, again, as Malik reminds us, the League conceptualized "Muslim" as a cultural identity as much as a religious one. Pakistan as a homeland for India's Muslims is not necessarily coterminous with Pakistan as an Islamic nation. Indeed, given the diversity of the territory that eventually comprised the nation of Pakistan, Lawrence Ziring argues that Pakistan, post-Zia, would be better served to operate as an Islamic Republic rather than an Islamic State ("Dilemmas" 799). According to Ziring, as a republic, Pakistan could adopt an "amorphous secularism that offers the best possibility for the achievement of 'balance' between the diversity of Muslims, between Muslims and non-Muslims, between fundamentalists and nonfundamentalists, between nationalities and ethnic groups, and tribal orders and provincial interests" ("Dilemmas" 799).[4] Ziring's preference for an Islamic Republic signals a gesture toward state structures and a conceptualization of the nation that are more inclusive for being more tolerant of Pakistani plurality. The inverse, as Nikki Keddie and her co-authors explain, is a "government-sponsored Islam [which] is bound to be a more centralizing, neo-traditional kind of Islam where everybody should believe the same thing and follow the same laws" (40). All four of the novels I analyze in this section identify the wedge Zia's Islamization drives between state operations and a cohesive national affect.

Zia announced his vision of the nation from the moment of the 1977 coup. William Richter reports that, immediately after overthrowing ZA Bhutto, Zia "left no doubt of the Islamic thrust of his administration" (548). While, by 1977, Pakistanis were no strangers to military rule having already seen Ayub and Yahya at the helm just before the nation's first democratic elections in 1970, Zia's rule inaugurated a new political disposition. As Hasan-Askari Rizvi points out, Zia's regime marked the first military dictatorship in "Pakistan's history [wherein] the ruling generals…openly declared that they were conservative in their orientations and…forged political ties with several groups of the Right," including most notably the Jamaat-i-Islami ("Paradox" 542).[5] By 1979, Zia promulgated the infamous Hudood Ordinances, legal codes that dictated very specific requirements for admissible testimony and severe punishments for crimes of theft, rape, adultery, and fornication.[6] The remarkable gender imbalances associated with the evidentiary requirements of the Hudood Ordinances—that four adult males must

witness penetration for a charge of rape to stand, for instance (Weiss 15)[7]—
contribute to their notoriety, prompting Malik to comment that "Zia's Islamization
policies took away the few constitutional and civil rights that women had
gained in the near past" ("State" 678–9). Historically, then, Islamization under
Zia signals a distinct and deliberate shift, promoted at the very highest levels, in
the definition of the Pakistani nation accomplished through alterations in state
functions.

Not surprisingly, Islamization has had serious concrete effects on both
civil society and the possibility of democracy in Pakistan (quite aside from Zia's
disinclination to call for genuine elections).[8] In terms of public discourse,
Zia's regime selectively censored free expression and curtailed public demonstra-
tions. Stephen Cohen and Marvin Weinbaum, writing in 1982, observe that
"coordination of opposition activities and plans for wide civil unrest were
stymied. Press censorship denied the regime's critics the desired mass audience"
(138). At the same time, Cohen and Weinbaum also make plain that "many
professional groups remained free to publicly criticize the regime, and the newspapers sometimes subtly conveyed anti-government information" (138). The
hierarchical structure of Martial Law endowed Zia with the power to manage
access to and the content of public discourse. Such a vice-like grip on public
discourse allowed Zia to position himself, in the words of Hasan-Askari Rizvi,
as "God-ordained...a ruler in an Islamic State [who] is performing his duties
in accordance with the Quran and Sunnah" ("Paradox" 538). With God on his
side, Zia could then "poin[t] out that those who opposed or demonstrated against
his government could be accused of waging war against an Islamic government
and therefore indulging in anti-Islamic activities" (Sayeed 220). In such a bifur-
cated discourse that collapses the state's political functions and religious identities, dissenters are automatically outside the national *and* religious folds, even if
they could find a location from which to speak in such a heavily regulated public
arena. According to Rizvi, ironically enough, opponents to Zia's Islamization
sought not to decouple Islam fully from political discourse but to promote a
"participatory and an egalitarian Islamic system" that contrasts the "punitive and
regulative aspects" of the system Zia implemented (546).[9] Zia's stifling of civic
discourse in the public sphere precludes the kind of participation these opponents
favor, leaving little doubt as to how well democracy fared during his tenure.

In fact, Islamization under Zia had little truck with democratic principles
or structures. Zia's alterations to the 1973 Constitution lead Cohen and Weinbaum
to the conclusion that the government did not "vie[w] representative institutions
as fully compatible with the concept of a just and stable Islamic order" (141).
Malik makes the same point, claiming that Zia viewed "the representative system
as 'un-Islamic'" ("State" 1081), while also observing that the general's stronghold meant less governmental accountability and a stubborn refusal to decentral-
ize ("State" 1080). Couple the centripetal force of Zia's power with his outlawing
of political parties in the elections he did finally hold in 1985, and the result, as
Rizvi points out, was the enhancement of the "political relevance of parochial
identities and particularistic orientations. Appeals [during this election] based on

language, ethnicity, and religious-sectarian differences were quite common" ("Civilianization" 1070). The fragmentation of the electorate ironizes Zia's centralizing efforts under the heading of "Islam," to be sure, but, at the same time, it also exacerbates the possibility of a shared national identity under any banner.[10] Such fractionalization further stokes the economic, ethnic, linguistic, and religious enmities that have plagued Pakistan since its inception. The political and public climate endemic to Zia's eleven years of power, thus, effectively marginalized the potential for tolerance and inclusive plurality by, on the one hand, threatening opponents with the charge of being "un-Islamic" and, on the other, by (unintentionally?) encouraging the perpetuation and prioritization of regional and even sectarian identities over a cohesive national one. In other words, this sort of environment fueled fear and distrust, as any foray into political or civic discourse could run afoul of the stark boundaries Zia's regime drew around a "Pakistani" identity.

In a sense, then, Zia's Islamizing agenda penned a definition of "Pakistaniness." This idea of a deliberately narrated national identity situates Zia's Pakistan within a larger discursive context wherein alternative narratives, such as those offered by literature, can supplement, critique, or challenge the one Zia imposed. From this perspective, Ziring's conclusion that Zia may "have misread the Pakistani story" ("Dilemmas" 799) serves as an invitation to position other readings of Pakistan's story alongside this dominant one. The novels I discuss in this section demonstrate that some of these readings take the shape of conspiracy theories. As Aasmani, the narrator of Shamsie's *Broken Verses*, observes, "The art of storytelling, so ingrained in this nation, had turned— in all the years of misrule and oppression—into the art of spinning conspiracy theories, each one more elaborate than the one before" (*Broken Verses* 37). The pressures of yet another stint of military rule morph what Shamsie's narrator deems a national impulse toward storytelling into a conspiratorial compulsion, a claim that certainly influences the reception of the story Aasmani herself tells and, in turn, colors all attempts to narrate the nation. In a broad analysis of the effects of military rule on the potential for democracy in Pakistan, Marvin Weinbaum identifies a tendency toward a politics of suspicion and a penchant for conspiratorial thinking throughout the nation's history. One reason for this abiding tendency, Weinbaum argues, is that the trappings of democracy were slow in coming to Pakistan. The government didn't promulgate a constitution until 1956, by which time its citizens had already witnessed the assassination of Prime Minister Liaquat Ali Khan.[11] This rocky start prompts Weinbaum to declare, "The democratic myths that so often sustain a system were thus only weakly instilled…" (642). Weinbaum's use of the word "myths" highlights the role of story or narrative in grounding a sense of belonging to the nation. Any reading of the story of Pakistan, then, needs to account for democracy's tenuous position. Indeed, so shaky are the democratic grounds in Pakistan, Weinbaum contends, that "despite [its] revival…from time to time, it [is] predictably held in suspicion" (642). Such an interpretive disposition leads Weinbaum to read the resistance specifically to Zia's regime as "above all an absence of trust in authority" rather than an instance of democracy in action (643). Still with reference to Zia's Pakistan, Weinbaum further argues that this distrust of authority views all governmental actions, including the "implementation of Islamic policies, its reports of economic progress, the country's military posture, the legal protections of minorities and women, and so on," as "public fictions" (647). The flimsiness of these fictions promotes in Pakistanis a "paranoid syndrome," according to Weinbaum, that "conspicuously employs conspiracy theories to explain political outcomes" and ultimately ends up fueling widespread political apathy that is "corrosive to civic culture" (648–9).[12] When conspiracies are rife, alienation from the state occurs.

From a literary perspective, however, conspiratorial thinking can promote other dynamics, as well. The four novels upon which I focus in this section all indulge in conspiracy thinking, effectively embedding conspiracy's narrative form within their own. Recognizing the embedded nature of these conspiracy theories matters, because the literary deployment of these theories heightens their tendency to "oscillat[e] between the figural and the literal," to borrow Clare Birchall's words (41). That is, if, as Birchall contends, conspiracy theories are a "knowledge-producing discourse" (34), then their incorporation into literary narratives that explicitly name these plot elements as conspiracy theories draws attention to how the characters interpret and make meaning. Moreover, conspiracy theories interpret to explain phenomena, irrespective of the availability of information or the theorist's partiality.[13] The reader, thus, engages with a primer on interpretation and can gauge the viability of the character's or narrator's explanatory attempts while also reflecting on her/his own interpretive processes. This doubled act of interpretation informs the formal features of conspiracy theories, as well as the cultural work they do when embedded in a larger narrative structure like the four novels of concern here.

Like all narratives, conspiracy theories have conventions. A readily identifiable convention: the conspirators often figure as omniscient and certainly secretive. Also: no bit of evidence or occurrence is random; as Birchall puts it, "contingency is dismissed in favour of conspiracy" (46). The theorist's position is a third convention. He or she is frequently marginal and eccentric, though, at the same time, heroic.[14] David Coady identifies the conspiracy theorist as occupying "an important specialized social role," as this person/character "investigate[s] officialdom" ("Conspiracy" 133). Coady's interest in weaving the conspiracy theorist into a larger social fabric suggests that the theorist's appearance of eccentricity or marginality is an effect, an effort by the "powers that be" to discredit him/her, which takes place in a broader context or field of signification. At the same time, the theorist's heroic marginalization oversimplifies his identity, just as the conspirators' purported omniscience oversimplifies (through amplification) their identities. With respect to both the conspirators and the theorists, then, conspiracy theories as narratives endow these figures with a high degree of agency, a tendency that also emerges in the cultural work conspiracy theories do, as I discuss below. An irresolute conclusion is another convention. Birchall refers to this irresolution as a "non-depletable opening" in the place where other narratives claiming explanatory power seek closure (48). Conspiracy theories' refusal of closure matters, because it leaves the narrative's futurity ambiguous, uncertain. While Peter Knight sees this type of uncertainty, especially as it surrounds "causality, agency, responsibility, and identity," as working against conspiracy theories' abilities to make meaning effectively (4), this "non-depletable opening" can also be read more optimistically as an invitation to an ongoing and public effort to construct shared meaning.[15]

This invitation, along with these other conventions, speaks to the contributions conspiracy theories make in the literary narratives I discuss in this chapter. Brian L. Keeley argues that conspiracy theories offer an "ordered universe," meaning that, through the bestowal of full agency on conspirators and theorists alike, conspiracy theories promote a worldview in which "events are *capable of being controlled*" (123; emphasis in the original). And, since these theories relate all "loose ends" to the plot at hand, their proffered worldview is also highly unified (Keeley 119). And yet, when conspiracy theories function as plot elements in other narratives, when readers see theorists interpreting these "loose ends," the theories also "highlight the excess produced by any reading that claims full knowledge or attempts closure" (Birchall 53). This emphasis on excess represents the doubling of interpretation I mention above. For Gary Walton, this doubling enacts the "defamiliarization of information structures" (par. 2), a point Birchall echoes by recognizing how conspiracy theories are "both familiar and unfamiliar[; they] retur[n] to us as simultaneously ours and not ours" (29). To acknowledge how this doubling of interpretation works, then, is also to see how the literary deployment of conspiracy theories reconfigures agency and belonging. Whereas, on their own, conspiracy theories indulge in fantasies of full agency and full disempowerment, literarily embedded theories illustrate for the novel's reader their processual nature. As a process, conspiracy theories "put on display a possibility of reading, or rather, a perceived 'impurity' of reading," according to Birchall (55). The difference between a "pure" and an "impure" reading is perspective and power, both of which show how conspiracy theories are, in Michael Baumann's words, a measure of the "quality of collective knowledge acquisition" (151). That is, conspiracy theories as an example of reading practices prompt an evaluation of the grounds upon which knowledge claims are made. While for some critics, such evaluative impulses are precisely what make conspiracy theories anathema to political efficacy, as they are deployed in these four novels, such theories invite collective identification and solidarity.[16] Though the theorists themselves may obsess over the nefarious forces at work within the plot, the theories' inclusion within the larger novels emphasizes participation in the meaning making process, in the construction of the nation's story, wrested free of the precepts of the state.

Not to be paranoid, but the appearance of conspiracy theories and explicit homosocial and homosexual identifications in these four novels is no coincidence. In addition to the specific ways I'll be borrowing aspects gleaned from queer theory, including the erotic triangle and alternative futurities, for my analyses of each novel, bringing key insights from this critical field to bear on these

novels' engagement with Zia's Islamization agenda adds important considerations to my ongoing discussions of belonging or constructing an alternative
affective attachment to a national collective through acts of interpretation. With
respect to how these novels' queer elements contribute to efforts to belong,
I consider the queer/postcolonial interface or what Murat Aydemir calls the
"sex/culture divide."[17] Three of the four novels I discuss in this section feature
homosexual acts and/or characters: *A Case of Exploding Mangoes*, *Broken
Verses*, and *The Wish Maker*. None of the characters who identify as homosexual
or who engage in homosexual activity do so openly; that is, none of them are
completely "out." Their semi-closetedness literally and figuratively marginalizes
these characters, especially since all three of these novels foreground heterosexual desire or couplings. At the same time, the qualified revelations of each
character's sexuality, which occur privately either just between the narrator and
the reader or between one character and another, possess significant explanatory
power. That is, the disclosure of sexuality answers questions, connects dots,
solves mysteries—in short, plays into the conventional expectations of the
embedded conspiracy theories—and, as a result, distinctly individuates the queer
character and endows greater significance to his/her relationships with the
other (straight) characters.

This explicit individuation or deepening of character calls to mind—without
exactly replicating—what queer and postcolonial theorists alike have identified
as a problematic irony in formulations of the queer subject. One ironic aspect
of this formulation is the process of individuation itself. Aydemir argues
that "individuation hinges on sexuality,...the enunciation and exercise of
desire," as these two actions contribute to a sense of self-determination (14).
At the same time, the process of individuation detaches, so to speak, the subject
from "his or her cultural environment" (Aydemir 14–15). Now constituted as
a self-determining individual freed from "family, religion, community, and tradition," the individuated subject who has embraced his or her sexuality resembles
the "paradigmatic" Western subject (Aydemir 14–15). And, as Andrea Smith
points out, "The Western subject is universal [in his/her individuality], while the
racialized subject is particular" (42). Indeed, for Aydemir, the racialized subject's
particularity, his/her non-universality as a self-determining individual, allows
for the relegation of the racialized subject into the anonymity of the "masses,"
for the "liberal sex/culture split distributes sexual and cultural forms of life
in discrete, mutually exclusive universes" (Aydemir 16). The racialized subject
has no individuated "personhood," as his/her cultural identity serves as the most
salient aspect of identity. The "queer" achievement of Western universality
through individuation comprises another ironic aspect of this formulation,
because a basic tenet of queer methodologies is, in Anthony Slagle's words,
to "rais[e] fundamental challenges about the essential nature of identities"
(130–1).[18] In other words, queer theories should trouble the purported acontextu-
ality of the Western subject not benefit from its hegemony as queer goes global.

The presence of queer characters and elements in this section's novels highlights this ironic tension between the essentialized universality of the subject and

the need to contextualize identities in cultural and historical specificities in an effort to challenge Zia's Islamization. Insofar as Zia's "Islam" defines what it means to be a Muslim *and* a Pakistani, this conflated identity strives to be universally applicable across the nation's territory. In that regard, "Pakistani" as an identity becomes individuated, just as queer identities do when they detach from culture and tradition by asserting their sexuality. Mindful of Aydemir's sex/culture divide, the queer characters in the novels at hand do not come out fully nor do they renounce their cultural attachments; these characters are both/ and. Therefore, their marginal positions vis-à-vis the novels' dominant heteronormative orders represent both the characters' "real" sexual[t]y and the diversity otherwise quashed by Islamization's homogenizing powers. The literal and figurative significance of the characters' queer identities mirrors how the literary embeddedness of conspiracy theories in these same novels highlights acts of interpretation, as I point out above. Further, these queer identities specify those interpretive acts by grounding them in the historical circumstances of Zia's Pakistan and its legacies, showing how their reading of the story of the nation refuses to accept (only) Zia's definition of a proper Pakistani.

My assertion that all four of the novels I analyze in this section attempt to establish viable affective attachments to a collective identity outside of the precepts of Zia's Islamized state derives from how the novels' queer elements shift the conspiracy theories' interpretive concerns. Conspiracy theories are acts of interpretation, as I discussed above. Conspiracy theorists project a skeptical ethos, a paranoia even, that, as I note, trumpets a lack of evidence as proof of their theories' accuracy. In other words, conspiracy theories rely on the hidden and the deliberately, diabolically obscured. This critical impulse toward exposing the concealed aligns almost precisely with critiques of queer theory's dominant interpretive methodology, one characterized by "symptomatic" reading.[19] Eve Kosofsky Sedgwick was one of the first queer theorists to call attention to the rote and static tendencies behind what she calls "paranoid reading," a concept she bases on Paul Ricoeur's "hermeneutic of suspicion" ("Paranoid" 4). Rita Felski characterizes such interpretive dispositions as possessing an "uncompromising wariness and hypervigilance," as well as a "disdai[n for] the obvious" (28–9). Re-evaluations of a "hermeneutic of suspicion" explicitly wonder about what can be gained when one concentrates on the obvious or engages in what Heather Love calls "shallow reading" (383). "Surface" readings may, indeed, be fitting, for "paranoid reading" has its limits. Sedgwick locates the appropriateness of "paranoid reading" in contexts wherein "violence would be deprecated and hence hidden in the first place" (16). However, Sedgwick notes that "social formations" exist in which "visibility itself constitutes much of the violence" ("Paranoid" 17). The workings of power in these types of social formations do not seek the cover of night, so to speak.

In the glaring light of day, then, the aim of critical practices should be, in Sedgwick's estimation, to encourage the realization "that the future may be different from the present," as well as "that the past, in turn, could have happened differently from the way it actually did" ("Paranoid" 22).[20] The adoption of an interpretive process that bears a future-orientation and an acceptance of the past without heavy handed prescriptions shifts the critical focus of conspiracy theories as acts of reading. According to Sedgwick and many others, we must rethink interpretive practices so that our acts of reading are reparative, a type of "queer reading that can attune [critical practice] exquisitely to a heartbeat of contingency" rather than the sense of inevitability so "closely tied" to "paranoid reading" ("Paranoid" 23). Felski argues in much the same vein, encouraging acts of reading that "look carefully at rather than through appearances, [that] respect rather than reject what is in plain view" (31). Both Sedgwick's and Felski's contributions encourage perceptive interpretations keyed to identifying and analyzing the literary features and devices—or what Felski calls "aesthetic attachments" (32)—to which readers respond. This queer reading strategy can thus alter the interpretive thrust of conspiracy theories. Embedded as they are within the larger narratives of these four novels, the conspiracy theories with which I'm concerned do deal with exposure at the level of plot, but, as plots within plots, they also signal an aesthetic appeal. This interest in the theories' aesthetic appeal specifies the doubled act of interpretation I discuss above. More precisely, the point then becomes to speculate over why conspiracy theories invite aesthetic attachment and how these attachments may encourage collective identifications that do not neatly accord with officially sanctioned ones.

Kamila Shamsie's *Broken Verses*, set in 2002, revolves around a hoax meant, in part, to convince Aasmaani Inqalab, the novel's first person narrator, to believe that her mother's lover, referred to simply as the Poet, is still alive. Aasmaani is susceptible to conspiratorial thinking given what remain for her unanswered questions about her mother's "disappearance" two years after the Poet's alleged death. The hoax is plausible because the Poet, composer of incendiary verse, purportedly dies under mysterious circumstances, likely at the hands of Zia's henchmen. Samina, Aasmaani's mother, also engages in anti-Zia activism, but her chosen outlet is straightforward political protest against the Hudood Ordinances. No one other than Aasmaani subscribes to the theory she begins to spin based on clues she receives through Shehnaz Saeed, a famous actress and old friend of her mother's. By novel's end, Aasmaani uncovers the hoax, perpetrated by Shehnaz's son Ed, who, for the briefest of moments, is also Aasmaani's lover. With all mysteries solved and loose ends tied, the novel enacts a bait and switch: the conclusion's too neat resolution suggests that Aasmaani's search for meaning, rather than any definitive statement on the Poet's or Samina's fate, constitutes the narrative's central problematic. Aasmaani becomes the paradigmatic "paranoid reader," to alter slightly Sedgwick's phrase, in her desperate attempts to verify that the Poet and her mother are still alive. Yet, Aasmaani's interpretive frameworks, structured according to naturalized heteronormative gender scripts, return her again and again to the same hopeless conclusion: Samina chose the Poet over Aasmaani. This prescribed interpretive process pushes Aasmaani to become politically apathetic and, thus, accepting of the fragmentation of any collective sense of resistance against oppression— under Zia or Musharraf—or of national belonging. In this way, the novel locates the limits of "paranoid reading." At the same time, however, *Broken Verses* reclaims some measure of agency by challenging through the introduction of a queer character the very gender precepts that structure Aasmaani's reading practices. More precisely, Aasmaani's "paranoid reading" doesn't equip her with the analytical skills to detect Shehnaz's homosexuality, so Shehnaz's qualified coming out catalyzes a paradigm shift that encourages a re-reading of Samina's story and, ultimately, a reconceptualization of what belonging to the nation might mean.

Even before Aasmaani receives the coded messages in which Ed ventriloquizes the Poet, she exhibits a wariness toward other characters' tendencies to associate her with her mother or her mother's politics. In the novel's early pages, Aasmaani interviews for a job, any job, at a television station. When some employees note Aasmaani's resemblance to her mother, she thinks to herself, "What was amazing was the way women in Pakistan took one look at me and assumed they were entitled to instant familiarity…" (*Brroken Verses* 10). Further, Aasmaani arrives at the studio without "'a CV or references'" (*Broken Verses* 9) yet refuses the CEO's offer of hosting a political talk show, a job he thinks would suit Aasmaani even if she has only "'a fraction of [her] mother's fire'" (*Broken Verses* 10). The CEO "looked offended" by Aasmaani's rebuff but ends up offering her a job writing trivia questions for a quiz show anyway (*Broken Verses* 10). As far as first impressions go, Aasmaani comes off as defensive and suspicious of others' motives; in short, she's a prime candidate for "paranoid reading." For Sedgwick, "paranoid reading" seeks to expose the hidden, as I point out above. This objective positions the paranoid reader as skeptical, if not cynical, and, in a sense, as a know-it-all who, as Sedgwick sees it, harbors an "anxious paranoid determination that no horror, however apparently unthinkable, shall ever come to the reader as *new*…" ("Paranoid" 22; emphasis in original). Often a step ahead, frequently keener, the paranoid reader employs a logic based on causality and inevitability ("Paranoid" 23). Such tendencies foster interpretations of the present and future that look much like the past. Despite her occasional yearnings to view her present circumstances otherwise (*Broken Verses* 39), Aasmaani's sense of how history affects her life testifies to her paranoid tendencies; as she criticizes Ed's apparent obliviousness, for example, she marvels that "someone who'd grown up in Pakistan could [behave] as though history hadn't been breathing down our necks all our lives" (*Broken Verses* 46). Aasmaani's own childhood, punctuated as it was by her mother's and the Poet's anti-government activities and their consequences, instantiates the incursion of history into everyday life. The lines between political participation and personal identities blur for Aasmaani, creating a pattern that ties Aasmaani to Pakistan. Aasmaani allows this pattern to structure her life, predisposing her to "paranoid reading."

But, because *Broken Verses* embeds a conspiracy within its larger narrative, Aasmaani's predilection toward "paranoid reading" emerges as a meta-interpretation even as it also bears, at the level of plot, some legitimacy. Her reading of Pakistan's political climate in the novel's past and present hits the mark, for example. Aasmaani's memories of the years under Zia's rule are "all about fear" (*Broken Verses* 91). Aasmaani recalls how the passage of the Hudood Ordinances prompts the Poet to wonder, "'How can words be used for such indignity?'" while causing her paternal grandfather to weep "himself to death" over such "laws being passed in the name of Islam" (*Broken Verses* 91). Aasmaani endures the Poet's repeated incarcerations and exiles, not to mention witnessing her mother's beatings at the hands of security forces quelling protests against Zia's regimes. The Poet's alleged death in 1986 at the hands of the government culminates these years of turmoil (*Broken Verses* 95–6). Pointedly, the novel links Zia's military dictatorship with Musharraf's, going so far as to suggest that the latter regime may be even more dangerous. Aasmaani wraps the Zia regime in nostalgia, despite the fear-filled years, simply because the "battle-lines were so clearly drawn then with the military and the religious groups firmly allied, neatly bundling together all that the progressive democratic forces fought against" (*Broken Verses* 73). Fast forward to Musharraf's coup, and politics are all in "disarray," from Aasmaani's perspective, because "the religious right [is] talking democracy better than anyone else" (*Broken Verses* 73). With Musharraf unwilling to cede any meaningful control over the legislative process, however, Aasmaani concludes that Pakistan, circa 2002, bears only a "democratic façade" (*Broken Verses* 73). The government remains a force to be feared.

Rather than spur Aasmaani on to greater political participation, though, her reading of Musharraf's disingenuous democratic rumblings amplifies her alienation both from Pakistan and from her own past. Her conspiracy-mindedness bears a cynical cast. Musharraf's regime proves that democracy has still not taken root in the nation, prompting Aasmaani to judge the Poet's and her mother's efforts under Zia's regime as "farcical" (*Broken Verses* 73). The joke, then, isn't so much the government, which, after all, has the power to kill, as it is the idea of resisting oppression or participating in the democratic process. Indeed, Aasmaani takes this conclusion as her great revelation, which she experiences when Zia's plane explodes:

> When the news reached me of his death, that was the moment I saw all my mother's stories of contentment and repose as nothing more than fairy stories…That was the moment I broke. All those years she had fought against Zia's government—she and the Poet—with rallies and speeches and poems… It had got him tortured and killed; it had got her—well, there were no words for that, either…All those noble means of resisting came to nothing. But then someone—no one even knew who—put a bomb in a plane, and the General exploded, and already, within hours of his death, they were saying, there really might be elections now, real elections…Because someone put a bomb on a plane…That is how you resist tyranny. By becoming it, by becoming it absolutely.
>
> (*Broken Verses* 139)

Zia's assassination proves to Aasmaani how successfully his regime imposed a system, a prescribed manner of conducting affairs, premised upon tyrannical violence, both discursive and material. This system only recognizes fear, threats, and destruction, rendering any act of non-violent resistance or counternarrative meaningless. In such a system, Samina's life "as an activist," according to Aasmaani, "was a lesson in futility" (*Broken Verses* 287).

Ironically, Aasmaani's cynicism locks her into an interpretive tyranny that similarly curtails recognition of anything outside its parameters. Her attempts to understand Samina's fate repeatedly fall back on a knowable category: the good mother. Unable to accept Samina's suicide two years after the Poet's death, Aasmaani clings to the lack of evidence—no body—to maintain the hope that one day Samina will return. And yet, to Aasmaani's mind, Samina's extended absence—even if it holds the possibility of her return—proves hurtful, for it confirms Samina's preference for the Poet over Aasmaani. Aasmaani remembers her mother saying, "'I would not allow them [the dominant social order] to tell me there was a choice to be made between motherhood and standing up for justice,'" even while Aasmaani admits to failing to ask in response, "'But what about the choice to be made between motherhood and romantic love?'" (*Broken Verses* 90). For Aasmaani, Samina "left. She chose to go" (*Broken Verses* 128). Plagued for years, Aasmaani rehearses the same old recriminations: "Even if you wanted to come back, that does nothing to change the fact that you left to begin with. It's not natural. Mothers aren't supposed to choose anyone else over their children. You unnatural woman" (*Broken Verses* 254). While in some respects, Aasmaani's mother issues can be read as the "work/life balance" chestnut, her sense that Samina's multiple roles are irreconcilable also plays out the tyrannical logic of Zia's system in terms of identity politics: Samina can only be *this* and not *that*. Aasmaani clings to an interpretive framework that only allows her to find meaning in either/or postulations. This framework's inflexibility, its desire for clear lines, functions tyrannically, just as Zia's system did. The visibility of Zia's tyranny illustrates Sedgwick's point about the limits of "paranoid reading": the violence is apparent; it needs no exposing.

Aasmaani's incorporation of this tyranny into her own "paranoid reading" practices further illustrates these limits. The novel ends well in the sense that it doesn't strand Aasmaani at this interpretive impasse. Although she's crushed by Ed's deceit, Aasmaani begins to re-interpret her mother, as well as the possibility of belonging to the nation in a meaningful sense. Shehnaz's coming out to Aasmaani occasions these changes in interpretation. Given her predisposition to essentializing motherhood, Aasmaani accepts without question the gossip that, years ago, Shehnaz abandoned her wildly successful acting career "to devote time to 'preparing for and raising'" children (*Broken Verses* 6). Apparently, "paranoid reading" only applies in certain contexts. In other words, this story appeals, because its logic works for Aasmaani: a mom wants to mother more than do anything else. As a category, "mother" holds tremendous, implacable explanatory power. Late in the novel, however, Shehnaz sets Aasmaani straight: "'I don't know how that story got started. I never publicly gave any reason. Well, I suppose that is how the story got started"" (*Broken Verses* 299). Aasmaani's uncritical acceptance of so blatantly inaccurate a story stands in stark contrast to the interpretive cynicism she exhibits toward nearly all other "public" stories she hears.

Relatedly, Shehnaz's disclosure of her sexuality catches Aasmaani unawares. When Shehnaz reveals her marital arrangements—her second husband needed her to act as a beard (*Broken Verses* 294)—Aasmaani sidles up to the obvious though impolite conclusion: "'But…But you're Shehnaz Saeed. You could have found plenty of men who would have given you financial stability and also…'" Shehnaz finishes the sentence: "'Sex?'" (*Broken Verses* 294). Aasmaani's heteronormative reflex marks the extent to which her interpretive framework relies upon rigid gender and sex categories. Shehnaz's embodiment of "mother" and "wife" disrupt Aasmaani's previously unchallenged notions. This shift also uses gender to address other types of identity formation. Shehnaz's explanation for how she overcame the shame she felt about her sexuality makes the scope of this shift clear. Samina's the one who helped Shehnaz accept herself:

> "I've never liked mangoes[, Samina said]. People say it means I'm not a true Pakistani, but I've never liked mangoes. Nothing to be done about it, and frankly I don't see why I should bother to try. The way I see it I'm just expanding people's notions of what it means to be Pakistani."
>
> (*Broken Verses* 296–7)

Samina's distaste for mangoes metaphorizes a challenge to essentialist categories. Markedly, Samina analogizes her own unconventional Pakistaniness with Shehnaz's homosexuality, making explicit how the latter offers a new way to define the former. Or, to reverse that formulation, Samina's mango analogy highlights the neat, rigid alignment of a sanctioned Pakistaniness and heteronormativity. Linking homosexuality and Pakistaniness forces a realignment of both identities, bridging Aydemir's "sex/culture" divide and opening new identity formulations. As Shehnaz comes out to Aasmaani, she points the younger woman in the direction of new ways to claim belonging within the family and within the nation.

Although somewhat pat, the novel's conclusion emphasizes how this possibility for newness has taken root in Aasmaani's interpretive framework. For years Aasmaani clung to the conviction that her mother's and the Poet's efforts to resist tyranny amounted to nothing. Tyranny only recognizes other forms of tyranny. After this hoax, however, Aasmaani proclaims, "That's what they did, Omi [the Poet] and Mama: they gave meaning to the world when it seemed senseless" (*Broken Verses* 335). Aasmaani knows she's "just creating another story for myself," but this version inspires her to re-enter the "world," which she does by "volunteer[ing her] services as a researcher for a documentary about the women's movement in Pakistan, to be broadcast in time for the twentieth anniversary of the Hudood Ordinances" (*Broken Verses* 335). The porousness between the nation's history and her personal one no longer oppresses Aasmaani's life; no longer a "paranoid reader," Aasmaani breaks the power of the pattern she has used to understand her life. Now Aasmaani sees that connection as a way to articulate a common identity in spite of Zia's legacy.

Mohammed Hanif's *A Case of Exploding Mangoes* satirizes an event in Pakistani history that may well be the source of more conspiratorial speculation than any other: Zia ul-Haq's death in an airplane crash in the summer of 1988. Pak One, Zia's plane, exploded shortly after take-off on 17 August, killing the President, many of his top generals, and Arnold Raphel, the US Ambassador. Through a surfeit of conspiracy theories, the satire illustrates the distance between the state and the characters' abilities to establish meaningful, collective identities. More specifically, the novel entertains several possible conspiracies and other explanations for the crash, whose cause remains unsolved extra-fictionally. These possibilities vary in plausibility, but the novel's point is not to advocate or prove one over the others or even to insist on any of the theories' viability. Rather, the sheer number of possible explanations, which constitute a range of interpretations of Zia's Pakistan, invite a consideration of how and why any of the theories appeal. At the same time, the satire queers the logic of power. That is, the conspiracy that involves Ali Shigri, a cadet at the Pakistani Air Force Academy who serves as a first person narrator in roughly half of the novel's chapters, complicates the satisfaction associated with finding out "what really happened," redirecting the novel's satirical focus to the possibility of other narrative structures that may provide a sense of satisfaction or satiation. Ali's homosexual relationship with Obaid, another cadet, introduces this possible alternative.

The novel entertains a wide array of conspiracies launched from seemingly every quarter. Zia's number two, General Akhtar, heads the Inter-Services Intelligence agency until Zia's suspicions get the better of him and Akhtar is replaced by General Beg. Both Akhtar and Beg, working independently, hatch plots to assassinate Zia. Akhtar covers his bases: he uses Ali Shigri as a pawn while he also formulates a contingency plan—filtering poison gas into the air ducts of Pak One—to accomplish his goals. As with any good conspiracy, however, Akhtar isn't working alone. His underling, Major Kiyani, helps with the details. But, the real mover behind Akhtar's plan is the US, or so it seems. In a scene that highlights the contingencies of interpretation, Akhtar believes the CIA has given him the green light to eliminate Zia. The narrator establishes the setting—a party at the US embassy in Islamabad—as a self-aware simulacra:

> The party moved down to the den, a large basement hall with leather sofas, a forty-four-inch television screen, and a bar; a blatant exercise in suburban nostalgia. Arnold [the Ambassador] had arranged for some of his American staff to see the recording of the Redskins versus Tampa Bay Buccaneers in the previous week's NFL playoff.
>
> (234)

The "den's" furnishings reek of middle class America, which the narrator knowingly diagnoses as "suburban nostalgia." Akhtar, identified in this scene as the "veteran spymaster," does not process the flimsy artifice of the den and, instead, assesses the location, with all its activity, as "the perfect backdrop for sounding out Coogan," the CIA station chief in Pakistan (235). Akhtar's interpretation of the setting is clearly incomplete, as the pre-recorded game makes clear: "The Saudi ambassador sat on a divan with a wad of fifty-dollar bills in front of him, taking bets on the game. Somebody had forgotten to explain to him that the game was eight days old and that the Redskins had trampled the Buccaneers" (235). Just as the Americans willingly swindle the Saudi ambassador by making bets with him, Akhtar will surely be had by Coogan. Akhtar's attempts to engage Coogan in a conversation about how to deal with Zia meet with limited success, but Akhtar surmises that "in the subtle art of spycraft, this noncommitment was also a kind of commitment" (236). These glimpses into Akhtar's interpretive process, which show how he derives great significance from comments and gestures that could hold any number of meanings, signal how desperate Akhtar is to achieve his goals. Fed up with being Zia's number two—the relationship between the two men is likened to "two dogs stranded on a glacier, each sizing up the other, trying to decide if he should wait for his comrade to die before eating him or…make a meal out of him immediately" (196)—Akhtar, an embodiment of the worst excesses of the state as the head of the ISI, nonetheless feels alienated from power. The novel cleverly captures the perverseness of this disjuncture between being so powerful and yet feeling alienated by having Akhtar defile the very idea of Pakistan: he installs a camera in the portrait of Jinnah that hangs in Army House so as to spy on Zia (170). His conspiratorial efforts, seek to reconcile his realities with his ambitions. Thus, when Coogan, seemingly wrapped up in the Redskins-Buccaneers contest, declares, "'Go get him,'" while "winking at the general," Akhtar concludes that he has just received the CIA's directive to assassinate Zia (237). Given the not so clever ruse the assembled Americans are playing on the Saudi ambassador, Coogan's enthusiastic outburst could well be an attempt to pull Akhtar into that joke, but those subtleties are lost on the Pakistani spymaster.

Other assassination plots similarly derive from a sense of alienation from the state, but their motivations seek not to (re-)consolidate power, as do Akhtar's, but to right the injustices perpetuated by Zia's regime. Not surprisingly, characters who represent the oppressed and underserved spearhead these interconnected plans. While incarcerated in the basement of the Lahore Fort, Ali "meets" the Secretary-General of the All Pakistan Sweepers Union, who is imprisoned as a result of a set-up, or so he says. This man targets Zia because the latter's "'coup d'état was a historic setback for the workers' struggle against the nationalist bourgeoisie'" (146). The story the Secretary-General tells Ali involves the government's infiltration of the Union, all in an attempt to weaken the Union's political base. The regime's attempt to co-opt National Cleanliness Week pushes the Secretary-General over the edge, however, as the government wanted the Week's slogan to be "Cleanliness is half the faith" (147). This slogan offends the sweepers, because, according to the Secretary-General, they "'are either Hindus or Christians'" (147). "Rubbish" and "purity" function as the lynchpins of this particular conspiracy. In a material sense, the Sweepers Union literally facilitates everyone's daily lives, a point the Secretary-General makes: "'We called a strike...And in three days the rubbish piles were mountain-high and all the gutters were clogged and your civilian bourgeois brothers had to carry their own rubbish to the dumps'" (147). The sweepers are human infrastructure, the very basis of how the state operates. Yet, the government takes them for granted. At the same time, the religious identities of the Union members also signal their metaphorically "impure" status under a regime bent on conflating a national identity with a religious one. Doubly excluded, the Secretary-General seeks to disrupt the ruling regime in an attempt to gain acknowledgment.

The plot the Secretary-General launches while incarcerated at the Lahore Fort draws in a third inmate, blind Zainab, a rape victim who has been sentenced to death for adultery under the Hudood Ordinances. Zainab's conviction proves to be a source of much vexation for Zia. The *New York Times* assails him (150–2), as do stray activists who manage to infiltrate Zia's "widows and orphans" photo-op events (135). Bringing to mind the extra-fictional case of Safia Bibi, a thirteen-year-old blind girl convicted of adultery after having been raped, the narrative takes aim at the inhumanity of Zia's purported piety.[21] From the fictional Zia's perspective, the public and international outcry over blind Zainab's conviction represents a "legal dilemma," not a moral or ethical one (152). Seeking clarity, Zia phones a "ninety-year-old Qadi, his man in Mecca, who had retired as a judge of the Saudi Sharia court thirty years ago and since then had never missed a prayer in Khana Kaaba. The man practically lived in the House of God" (153). Zia's reverence for the aged Qadi suggests the former's understanding of the law, any law, as acontextual, a poorly thought-out universality that shows the costs of Islamization's homogenization. At the same time, the Qadi's literal and metaphorical distance from Pakistan and from day-to-day living points toward the irrelevance of his perspective to the particularities of Zainab's or anyone's case. Zia presents the Qadi with the vaguest of descriptions of the Zainab case; the Qadi, after much ridiculousness, concludes,

> "If she [the alleged victim] is married, her husband will have to establish in the court that she is of good character and then we'll need four male Muslims of sound character who have witnessed the crime...And if the woman is not married, she'll have to prove that she was a virgin before this horrible crime was committed."
>
> (154–5)

While Zia "felt much better" after this conversation, his wife, who agrees to help her husband deal with the resulting public relations mess, nonetheless sees right through the farce that is this legal reasoning: "'But how is the woman [Zainab] supposed to prove that she is a virgin if a bunch of men banged her for three days and three nights?'" (155). The narrative's inclusion of this exchange between Zia and the Qadi illustrates how, in a heteronormative patriarchal order, men "seek mastery and domination over each other through a woman [in order to] cement the larger social bonds" (Kramer 120).[22] Much like the sweepers, blind Zainab, who represents disenfranchised women (rather than the begums, like Zia's wife), experiences an unjust alienation due to the state's mandates. Her role in the Secretary-General's conspiracy, thus, also serves to right the state's wrong.

Zainab helps the Secretary-General by passing a letter penned by him to Ali (239).[23] Because the contents of the letter remain unknown, the narrator invites the reader to play conspiracy theorist by planting clues as to its contents. When Ali is first imprisoned in the cell next to the Secretary-General, the latter tells the cadet that, prior to leading the All Pakistan Sweepers Union, he was a simple mango farmer who unionized his fellow farmers (158). This detail matters for it connects to yet another conspiracy about Zia's death: a grenade secreted within a case of mangoes on board Pak One. Indeed, Zia is quite excited about hosting a mango party on the plane, sharing his "'gift from All Pakistan Mango Farmers' Cooperative'" (286), which just happens to be the collective formed by the Secretary-General. The suggestion is that Ali passed along the letter Zainab places in his possession. The narrative's positioning of the reader as a conspiracy theorist through the instrumentalization of these three characters— the Secretary-General, who represents the laborers and the minorities; Zainab, who stands in for oppressed women; and Ali, the novel's affective center—in this particular conspiracy invites sympathy, especially as the presentation of this particular plot contrasts so significantly to the absurdity of the one Akhtar hatches. While the case of mangoes may not have included a grenade, that the narrative leaves the possibility open provides some satisfaction, as both the Secretary-General's and Zainab's causes seem just. Their causes' appeal, thus, encourages a collective bonding outside the state's dictates and in spite of its power.

Zainab's involvement in the Secretary-General's plot and her triangulated relationship to power between men shows how this conspiracy plot, like Akhtar's, proceeds either along prescribed gender lines or in contravention of them. That is, the operating logics remain familiar in both instances: patriarchal and heteronormative. Indeed, these two terms structure the dominant order. For instance, Zia reveals his awareness of the necessity of establishing himself as top dog. A brief flashback to the first meeting Zia calls of his top generals after they overthrow ZA Bhutto's government illustrates the deliberateness of his efforts to secure his power. Zia "knew that he couldn't take [the generals'] loyalty for granted. He would have to kill the cat at the very beginning" (37). "Killing the cat," as the narrative goes on to divulge, is a highly gendered metaphor for establishing masculine dominance in a heteronormative context. Folding a flash-back into a flashback, the narrative returns to Zia's wedding night, when General Zia was still just a captain, and a virgin. His uncle advises him to "'[k]ill the cat on the first day,'" but, naïve, Zia "found no cat to kill that night" (37). Instead, Zia experiences a "fumbling failure" in his matrimonial bed, as his new bride "turned her back to him and went to sleep" (37). In Zia's view, his inability to consummate the marriage on his wedding night "had resulted in a marriage in which his authority was never fully established" (37). Zia calls that object lesson

to mind "[t]wenty-seven years later [on] the morning after his midnight coup...
He intended to kill the cat, bury it, and hoist his flag over its grave" (37). Zia's
transposition of the cat killing metaphor from his wedding night to the first meeting he presided over as Chief Martial Law Administrator establishes a direct
connection between his failure to cement his masculine dominance in his
marriage and his desire to avoid making the same mistake as a military dictator.
The logic this transposition imposes on political matters is clearly heteronormative and patriarchal: equality between genders or even the possibility of a woman
exerting her authority over a man is unacceptable; masculinity in this formulation
is intolerant, competitive and ruthless, even when presented as Muslim piety; and
beta males are submissive and effeminate.

The narrative defamiliarizes these logics by positioning Ali as another in a
long line of conspirators. In this role, Ali defamiliarizes the future, a process
made possible through his homosexual relationship with fellow cadet Obaid, or
Baby O. In other words, Ali's role as queer conspirator alters the significance
of the end goal, which is to assassinate Zia, by leaving unspecified what this
goal would mean. Whereas Zia's death would mean a consolidation of power for
Akhtar or the triumph of the dispossessed for the Secretary-General and Zainab,
its import for Ali remains amorphous, and this indeterminacy holds within it the
possibility for an entirely different futurity.

Ali's motivation to assassinate the dictator derives from his father's alleged
suicide. Colonel Shigri, who was integral to Pakistan's handling of CIA resources
during the Soviet-Afghan war, purportedly hanged himself from a ceiling fan,
though Ali wonders:

> Ceiling fan.
> Bedsheet.
> His eyes popping out of their sockets.
> The colonel weighed a bloody ton. Where were the laws of physics?
>
> (47)

Ali doubts the "official" story of his father's suicide, but Major Kiyani, an ISI
agent who arrives on the scene of the "suicide," coerces Ali's signature on a
"statement that said as the only male member of the family, [he] didn't want an
autopsy, [he] didn't suspect foul play, and [he] had found no suicide note" (73).
Given Ali's role as first person narrator, the narrative skews to his perspective.
This bias notwithstanding, Ali does uncover information that complicates his
image of Colonel Shigri as a betrayed national hero. For instance, when Major
Kiyani transports Ali to the Lahore Fort to interrogate him about Obaid's disappearance with a fighter jet, one of the Major's underlings informs Ali that his
father "'built this place. On two weeks' notice'" (125). The interrogator clarifies
that he means the torture chambers—"'all this stuff underground'"—not the
actual Mughal fort (125). As his father's complicity sinks in, Ali can barely ask,
"'Did he order this [torture] as well? Did he use to...' I wave my hand towards
the barber's chair and the chains hanging from the ceiling" (125). The torturer

views such work as merely "'doing his duty'" (125), confirming for Ali what he can't actually articulate.

Ali receives further confirmation of his father's "duty" from the Secretary-General before the latter knows that Ali is the Colonel's son:

> "They sent in their best man to interrogate me. Zia's right-hand man. Colonel Shigri. On the very first day, he had electrical wires put on my privates, but after he couldn't break me, he became a friend. He moved me into a cell with a window. A very fine man. He must be a general by now."
>
> (160)

Ali receives this information with a "shudder of loathing" but maintains his incredulity over the possibility that his father committed suicide (160–1). What redeems the Colonel in Ali's eyes is the former's repugnance for becoming a "pimp" for the US and Pakistani governments (89, 263, 264). In retaliation and with the help of a young Ali, Colonel Shigri burns twenty-five million American dollars, which he was supposed to funnel into the pockets of the ruling elite (265). The narrative's gradual revelation of Colonel Shigri's complicity in and resistance to Zia's regime complicates any easy condemnation of the government, on the one hand, or any ready heroicization of the Colonel, on the other. These muddy waters compromise the righteousness of Ali's vengeance: he deplores Zia for the latter's corruption and perfidy, and yet Ali learns that his father bore these traits, as well. Thus, at the level of plot, this knowledge sullies Ali's motivations on both personal and political/ideological levels.

The problems with his motives notwithstanding, Ali's goal as a conspirator is the same as the novel's other plotters: to kill Zia. However, the insertion of homosexual desire into Ali's scheme confuses the end game. The novel's homoerotic elements suggest an alternative future not invested in "killing the cat." Allusions to the homoerotic attraction between the two cadets pepper the novel. As narrator, Ali repeatedly draws attention to Baby O's heart-printed silk underwear (23, 54). Their physical proximity elicits arousal: when Obaid "put[s] his hands on [Ali's] shoulders," for instance, Ali "stiffened," a coy double entendre that just as likely signifies arousal as good posture. And, as if penning a sonnet to one's beloved, Ali makes frequent reference to the sweetness of Obaid's breath (141, 142, 180). More overt encounters amplify the sexual tension. They hold hands while walking to Ali's family home (258). During their jungle-survival training, Ali carries Obaid "out of combat," and, while being ferried away on Ali's back, Obaid "dug his heels into [Ali's] thighs...[Ali] flung him down on the ground when [Obaid] nibbled his earlobe." The flirtation culminates with Obaid jokingly replying to Ali's dictate that the "'first rule of survival is that you shall not screw your saviour'" with, "'Not even when it feels so good?'" (261). Ali's frequent references to the sexual connection between him and Obaid contrasts the otherwise heavily heteronormative ethos of the military as it's presented in the novel, signaling the military as one target of the narrative's satire.

At the same time, however, the cadets' relationship also introduces—though doesn't completely play out—an alternative structuring logic. In the most overt encounter between Ali and Obaid, Ali indicates his uncertainty over what the experience means. Their physical interaction starts as a fight over Ali's unwillingness to allow Obaid to help with his conspiracy to kill Zia. Ali communicates his refusal with a "limp-wristed mime," a gesture that "killed" Obaid (182). Obaid strikes Ali in response, and, as the two tussle, Obaid "plant[s] both his knees around [Ali's] hips, [and then] start[s] to pull [Ali's] vest out of [his] trousers" (182). Ali's arousal intensifies, but, uncomfortable with Obaid's being able to see his reactions, Ali closes his eyes (182). By shutting his eyes, Ali refuses to see, which, in the context of the novel's interest in conspiracy theories, amounts to a repudiation of both the conspirator's and the conspiracy theorist's vigilance, as both roles require a heightened, a paranoid, attentiveness. Significantly, however, Ali does not refuse to participate in the sexual encounter. The only reticence Ali confesses involves kissing: "I was scared of the lips that were gently brushing their way towards my chest. I was scared of being kissed" (182). As the encounter intensifies, Ali does eventually open his eyes, for he reports seeing Obaid with "[h]is eyes shut and [with] a gentle smile [that] was spreading around his lips" (183). Following on his own resolution not to see, Ali's fear over being kissed, over the heightened intimacy that act signifies, coupled with his observation of Obaid's pleasure and satisfaction, suggests both an uncertainty over— what would it mean to kiss Obaid?—and a recognition of an alternative connection between men. The homosexual encounter between Ali and Obaid introduces a new, unconventional logic that governs relations between men, one not premised on the intolerance, competitiveness, and ruthlessness that characterizes Zia's heteronormative and patriarchal order. This scene represents the apogee of Ali and Obaid's homosexual desire, and, with Obaid's death in the very crash that kills Zia, the novel does not develop the implications of the alternative logic the cadets' desire introduces into the narrative. This lack of development does not, however, diminish the potential futures toward which this new logic points. Indeed, this lack of development may well indicate the absence of suitable forms of representation.

Unlike *Broken Verses* and *A Case of Exploding Mangoes*, Ali Sethi's *The Wish Maker* does not directly involve its characters in conspiracy plots. Instead, by anecdotally retelling Pakistani history from partition to post-9/11, the novel builds an environment conducive to a culture of conspiracy and suspicion. Further, the historical span that the novel traverses draws attention to how narratives use and connect origins and futures. The anecdotes that piece together a sense of the nation's history and that illustrate each character's chosen way to narrate her belonging to the nation all derive from the experiences of the members of a single family, one dominated by female characters: Daadi, the grandmother and matriarch; her two daughters, Suri and Hukmi; Zakia, her daughter-in-law; and Samar Api, her niece. The narrative mediates the transmission of these characters' experiences through its first person narrator, Zaki, who is Zakia's son. At times, a third person narrative voice takes over, making it seem as though

Zaki's control doesn't extend over the entire story. But, subtle markers within the text signal Zaki's presiding direction, even as they establish his distance or detachment from the stories he relays.[24] Zaki's centralized if sometimes obscured narratorial perspective matters, because it sparks questions about narrative structure. The novel ends and begins in the narrative present, some point in post-9/11 Pakistan, with Zaki returning to Lahore from university in the States for Samar Api's wedding. Every chapter in between, however, dispenses with linear or even reverse chronology in favor of a jumpy temporality that allows for the revelation of significant moments in each of the main characters' lives. Notably, these moments align with periods of political turmoil in Pakistani history, including the 1947 partition, Ayub's regime, Zia's regime, and several points in Benazir Bhutto's tumultuous rises and falls. And, equally as important, the female characters are at odds in their political dispositions, making it appear as though they represent opposing worldviews. However, Zaki's role as narrator also allows him to reveal in his own terms his homosexuality. This aspect of his character, combined with his role as controlling yet, at times, detached narrator, suggests that the correlation of the personal and the historical is an effort to illustrate the mutual co-reliance of these spheres rather than champion one political perspective over another. In other words, the co-reliance illustrates that even the differing political convictions his family hold depend upon the same structures; that is, these convictions employ similar origins and forecast similar futures.

The novel's opening image establishes Zaki's narratorial perspective. The introduction is a single sentence chronicling Zaki's literal return to Lahore, and its dominant image encapsulates the airplane's descent:

> The clouds approached from below and went upward and onward until they had left behind the view; it was of turf, gray turning to green and brown, a mosaic that now grew zones and roads and began to show the specks, expanding into vehicles, that were moving and heading in the pale morning light to destinations of their own.
>
> (3)

Zaki's perspective of the clouds *below* inverts any accustomed, grounded point of view. Immediately, then, this sentence creates a sense of Zaki's unique narrative angle, one without ground. In other words, Zaki's initial up-in-the-air vantage point distances itself from the taken for granted grounds of most other perspectives. The plane's descent metaphorizes Zaki's gradual submersion into the grounded perspectives shared by the individuals driving the vehicles on the plotted "zones and roads," that is, across the state-planned and regulated spaces. This opening image situates Zaki's viewpoint and his narrative voice as different from the norm or expected.

Significantly, the return affords Zaki this view, a point that emphasizes the importance of his (qualified) diasporic identity. Zaki's immersion into American college life facilitates his coming out, at least in that location. By the fall of his first term, he's involved with politically active organizations on campus, including a magazine called "*Peace and Justice*" (416). Zaki participates in protests, too, developing "new kinships" (416). These burgeoning connections prompt Zaki to go to the "Nineties Dance, to the South Asian Dance, to the Islamic Society Banquet, and [he] went to the Queer Dance, and stood beneath the colors of the rainbow, which were [his]" (416). University life cements new solidarities for Zaki between groups that speak to the various facets of his identity: he's involved with the South Asian group, the Islamic Society, and the Queer organization. In effect, Zaki's experiences at college in the States provide him the opportunity to begin to bridge what Aydemir calls the "sex/culture" divide. That is, Zaki fosters all the aspects of his identity—the cultural, religious, political, and sexual—without having to choose one over any other.

The explicitness of the image of Zaki standing under the rainbow flag contrasts the previously closeted way he, acting as narrator, represents his sexuality at other moments in the novel. A pre-adolescent Zaki experiences his first homosexual encounter with a neighbor boy, who shares with Zaki a "discovery": his erection (161). In a game of "I'll show you mine" that goes too far, Zaki also experiences shame over his interests, as the neighbor tells him that he's "dirty and wanted to do dirty things" (161). Years later, Zaki has another encounter with a school friend, Karim, and, instead of shame, senses that he's "arriv[ed] satisfactorily at what [he] already [knew]" (318). Nonetheless, this young Zaki doesn't tell his mother or Samar Api, his closest confidant, about his sexual orientation. And, his decision not to disclose this aspect of his identity to anyone but the reader before he leaves for the States stands in contrast to the public drama starring Samar Api, whose raging heterosexuality courts scandal. Given that Zaki returns for her marriage, however, Samar Api finds redemption in the form of a marriage proposal. While there's no indication that, in the novel's present, Zaki comes out to his family, his very visible embrasure of his homosexuality at college—his bridging of the "sex/culture divide"—inflects his narrative perspective. Zaki's queerness extends beyond his sexuality to how he represents the stories he conveys about his family.

In the majority of these stories, Zaki plays only a bit part, as the female characters occupy center stage. However, in a moment that appears late in the novel but, chronologically, occurs just before his return to Pakistan, Zaki locates his viewpoint at an angle from those shared by his relatives. In this way, his diasporic location also functions metaphorically, allowing him to distance himself from his family's various origin stories. For example, Zaki subscribes to *Women's Journal*, the political magazine his mother edits. Upon reading her editorial about recent government activity, Zaki sends his mother an email:

> Read "Supremacy of Parliament" (*WJ*, 20–27 Sept.) and disagreed completely. How can you ask the same people—the very same people— to come back and run the show? Can you give me a better example of compromise?
>
> (416)

Zakia's replies, "[W]e have to work with what we have. But I am glad you disagree. It would be boring if you didn't!" (416). Although Zakia reads Zaki's objections as a mere difference of opinion, his dispute can also be read as a challenge to the very structures of the system, a point made more manifest by Zakia's insistence that one has to work with what one has. In effect, Zaki wants to work with something different, and it's this interest in finding alternatives outside the existing system that queers politics by setting his perspective apart from his mother's, which, structurally, mirrors even the most conservative political views of other family members, as I illustrate below. Further, this queer perspective also informs Zaki's presentation of the rest of the story.

This presentation relies upon the connection between Pakistani politics, personal experience, and forecasting the future early on. As I note above, the novel opens with Zaki's first trip home to Lahore since he started university in the United States. His time away defamiliarizes the daily routines of his family's home, so he spends much of the first chapter observing everyone's activities. Zaki notes that the family's old servant Naseem watches television as she begins her morning chores. What follows is a long paragraph whose structure calls to mind the endless stream of shows Naseem reviews as she switches channels. An emergency news bulletin interrupts the regularly scheduled program to announce a failed assassination attempt against Musharraf (11). Conspiracies swirl immediately: "There was talk of the establishment, talk of America and its allies, its interests and its changing relations with the Pakistani military. There was talk of 9/11 and the Jews. And there was talk of Islam, a religion of peace that was being misunderstood" (11). The channel review continues, covering programs dealing with aspects of Islam, including whether "nail varnish [was] haram or halal," until the channel surfing pauses on a women's call-in show. "A housewife from Rawalpindi" doesn't know what to do: her daughter watched one of her husband's pornographic movies (11). Unconcerned with the fact that her husband has these movies, since he is "unstoppable," the mother wonders whether there is any way "to undo those things and take them back out of the child's mind" (11). The women on the show, some of whom "held degrees in subjects such as child psychology," counsel the mother against worry, for children, curious, always break out of the "sheltered environments" their parents create. Every generation of parents builds these environments, and every generation of children moves beyond them; "'It is always going and going in circles,'" says the show's host (11–12). The specifics from the call-in show conclude the paragraph, which begins with "politicians cut[ting] ribbons and mak[ing] speeches," switches abruptly to violence, and moves through the many facets of Islam to land, finally and mundanely, at this mother's struggle to understand her daughter's burgeoning sexuality, made manifest via exposure to heterosexual pornography. This progression establishes associative links between the content on these channels. The power that sustains politicians and makes them vulnerable to violence connects, in Pakistan, to specific interpretations and contextualizations of Islam. The gendered order that shrugs its shoulders at a man's "unstoppable" interest in pornography fits into this power structure, as does the mother's worry over how her daughter's sexuality takes shape. In addition, given that this channel review ends with the host emphasizing generational transmission, the paragraph's progression also forecasts the future: here's what the nation is, here's where it comes from, and here's what it will be.

This progression, as it associates politics, violence, Islam, gender, and sex, while also forecasting the future in terms of the past, specifies Lee Edelman's concept of "reproductive futurism." This concept relies upon a rigid logic that imposes an "ideological limit on political discourse as such, preserving in the process the absolute privilege of heteronormativity..." (*No Future* 2). For Edelman, the figure of the "Child," by which he means the "perpetual horizon of every acknowledged politics" (*No Future* 3), represents this ideological limit. The "Child" functions as an "emblem of futurity's unquestioned value" but, as "Child," defines this futurity in terms of heterosexual reproduction (*No Future* 4). The ideological limit imposed in the name of the "Child" recognizes only those discourses articulated in its terms, no matter if those discourses bear apparently oppositional labels, such as "conservative" or "liberal." Edelman illustrates this point through his rhetorical question: "How could one take the *other* 'side,' when taking any side at all necessarily constrains one to take the side *of*, by virtue of taking a side *within*, a political order that returns to the Child as the image of the future it intends?" (*No Future* 3). Memorably, Edelman refers to "reproductive futurism" as a "Ponzi scheme" (*No Future* 4), emphasizing how the status quo benefits from its own discursive self-replication. And this status quo extends beyond sexual relations, as the progression established by Naseem's channel surfing illustrates. A political order—even a contested one—that operates according to staid gender roles buys into this Ponzi scheme even if no actual children are involved. As a vision of the future, "reproductive futurism" is also highly narrative. As Andrea Smith argues, "[N]ormative futurity depends upon an 'origin story'" (47). Depending on the specific present, any given "origin story" can be, for instance, a pre-lapsarian paradise or a retroactive extension of the present into the past (Smith 46, 47). The forecasted future lines up accordingly as the chance at redemption or as the unbroken continuation of a glorious tradition.

The correlations between the historical and the personal that emerge as Zaki tells the stories of his female relatives illustrate how their seemingly opposed political convictions, which define their familial positions and identities to a large degree, foster "reproductive futurism." These characters' perpetuation of the logic of "reproductive futurism" operates at several levels, from the interpersonal to the overtly political. Zakia and Daadi's personal relationship exemplifies one narrative aspect of "reproductive futurism": the origin story. These two characters couldn't be farther apart in disposition. The distance between them is clear immediately after Zakia moves into Daadi's home after marrying Sami, Daadi's son. Because Sami is in the Air Force, Zakia, soon pregnant, is often alone with her mother-in-law. Uninterested in the heavy foods Daadi has sent to her room, Zakia refuses them, inadvertently offending Daadi (120). Small problems such as these accumulate until Zakia realizes she must fare for herself, which she does by getting a job as a journalist (121). Sami's death in an airplane crash while Zakia is still pregnant with Zaki only raises the stakes between the two women. Zaki reports that his grandmother "taught [him] to recognize his father in the pictures on her mantelpiece" (31). Daadi uses these photographs as evidence for the idea of Sami she imparts to Zaki, prompting him to observe a contrast: "My father was a dashing young man in Daadi's room. But in my mother's room he was someone else, a scattered man who lived in many things" (32). When Zaki receives a detail about Sami from his mother, he tells his grandmother, who says, "'I don't know about that'" (33). Zakia responds nearly in kind when Zaki tells her details imparted by Daadi: "'It's wishful thinking'" (33). To reconcile the difference, Zakia tells Zaki that Daadi has to hold on to her version of Sami "'[b]ecause she's his mother. She's had to keep him alive. People need things to believe in'" (33). Zakia's explanation points to the function of origins in narratives. In order to continue living after Sami's death, Daadi needs to posit a certain idea of who her son was, according to Zakia's explanation. What Zakia doesn't admit, however, is that her version of Sami works in the same way. Both characters construct a Sami story that helps them live beyond his death and acquaint Zaki with his father; the details make the difference, but their structural function as origin in their respective narratives is the same.

Suri and Hukmi, Zaki's paternal aunts, illustrate another aspect of "reproductive futurism": its predictability. Their uncanny interchangeability satirizes the highly conventionalized scripts of heteronormativity. Zaki's description of his aunts' upper middle class comforts, for instance, barely differentiates between the two. Enjoying financial security, thanks to their husbands, Suri and Hukmi

> had restyled their homes: the driveways of both houses sloped gently outward past steel gates, and the names of the owners were nailed to the outside walls. Inside too there had been changes: the upstairs bathrooms were fitted with Jacuzzis and modern showers; there was wallpaper on the walls; there were split-level air conditioners with remote controls in the living-dining areas and also in the bedrooms; and there was wall-to-wall carpeting downstairs, for which the removal of shoes was required.
>
> (15)

Oh, and they're neighbors with adjoining—not just adjacent—lots. The humor here is subtle: one wonders if the same wallpaper adorns the walls in both houses, as the sentence's grammatical structure suggests. Both sisters have two children—a boy and a girl, same birth order—cousins who are, of course, inseparable. Suri and Hukmi finish each other's sentences (17), and they wear the same outfits (184). Beyond gently mocking the predictable signifiers of bourgeois life, Zaki's description of his aunts' lives and homes presents this domestic ideal as scripted to the point of indistinctness.

That Zakia doesn't live such a life, that she works outside the home—first as a journalist and, in the novel's present, as the editor of *Women's Journal*, a political magazine—makes it seem as though she represents an alternative to the futurity that Suri and Hukmi perpetuate. However, the correlations between history and personal experience foreground the structural similarities of the characters' perspectives, illustrating how "reproductive futurism" extends into spheres seemingly unrelated to the "Child." The relationship between Zakia and Daadi also illustrates this point even though they seem a study in contrasts. Compounding their other differences, the two characters have starkly contrasting political convictions. When Benazir Bhutto gets elected in 1988, Zakia "said it was historic" (62). Daadi has none of it, proclaiming instead that Benazir's triumph over Zia's legacy "was just another story, a story that had been made up to fool people like Naseem and to make people like [Zakia] feel good about themselves" (62). Daadi doesn't stop there, continuing on to lambast ZA Bhutto, as well, claiming that "he had done some terrible things to his opponents in his time, things only caesars and pharaohs had done to their enemies to set examples" (62). Where Zakia sees the return to democracy via the Bhuttos' Pakistan People's Party, Daadi sees the continuation of a corrupt lineage not at all unlike a power drunk monarchy. With such vehement views, neither woman can brook the charges of corruption that dog their favored politicians and instead argue that conspiracies are at work. During Benazir's second stint as Prime Minister, for example, Zakia struggles, both personally and professionally, with the corruption charges levied against the ruling government:

> "We know there is corruption[," Zakia says. "T]here has always been corruption. But why do we look now? Why are we looking *only* at this government? Why don't we look at the corruption of those who rule with guns, and have ruled with guns for so many years and are even now waiting in the wings?"
>
> (263)

In response to Zaki's question about who has the guns, Zakia replies, "'The establishment,'" which prompts Daadi to interject, "'It is a word...A long, empty word'" (263). Evidence mounts against Benazir's administration, seriously undermining Zakia's conviction that the Prime Minister is the target of conspiracies and forcing Zakia to acknowledge that, if the *Women's Journal* continues to support Benazir, it is "'tantamount to quietism'" (264).

While Zakia's reluctant admission of Benazir's fallibility seems to prove Daadi right, at the same time, the older woman similarly finds herself conflicted due to her political loyalties. A stalwart supporter of Nawaz Sharif, Daadi refuses to accept Zakia's estimation that Benazir's successor seeks only to consolidate his own power. The novel alludes briefly to Sharif's effort to pass the Fifteenth Amendment in 1998 after the international community levied sanctions against Pakistan for the nation's nuclear tests (330–1). When Zakia condemns Sharif's intentions, telling Daadi that the older woman's "'savings and [her] spending, all of it has been for this,'" meaning Sharif's self-interest, Daadi dismisses the evaluation: "'It is all exaggerated,'" she says (331). As Zakia has done in the face of anti-Benazir criticism, Daadi now similarly ascribes anti-Sharif views to conspiratorial thinking. And, again like Zakia, Daadi eventually comes to acknowledge the dire political situation as the two watch footage of Musharraf's 1999 coup. Both characters say, one after the other, "'Martial law'" (333). Although these two characters have markedly different political loyalties, their positions within the structures of political discourse mirror one another. If both characters' life narratives after Sami's death require the positing of a specified image of him as their origin stories, then, similarly, these narratives take shape from the scripts made available through the dominant political discourse. Thus, again, despite apparent differences in detail, the two characters inhabit similar structural positions within an order arranged around the inviolability of the "Child."

The correlation of historical moments and personal experiences does more than illustrate the characters' structural similarities. These correlations also suggest how a broader atmosphere of suspicion comes about. To capture the genesis of this atmosphere, the novel, through Zaki, posits two versions of Pakistan's origin story through both Daadi and Zakia. These origin stories matter, because they locate the narrative basis for the future Zaki implicitly critiques. Prompted by photographs, a flashback accounts for Daadi's youth in Lahore. The violence of partition ruptures her neighborhood. As late as 1946, "[t]he word 'Pakistan' had been on people's tongues, a word they used mostly in slogans, and their lives in Lahore were unaffected by it" (347). But, by 1947, "The Hindu family next door, the Parsi gentleman who lived in the secretive double-story house and ran the laundry on Mall Road, and Amrita's family, a Sikh family— all of them had locked their houses and gone away" (347). Daadi's memories of Lahore, which straddle the creation of Pakistan as a territorialized nation, indicate, first, that the idea of Pakistan hadn't infiltrated "their lives" in any meaningful way, suggesting that, as a "slogan," "Pakistan" had little affective resonance for Daadi. Second, these memories reveal how much the creation of Pakistan cost, at least in Daadi's estimation: nationhood comes at the expense of the neighborhood's plurality. Even as rumors begin to circulate about the rise of communal violence during partition, Daadi's father councils, "'Don't be so narrow-minded'" (350), a clear expression of his faith, transmitted to his daughter, in the bonds of social trust and community. However, when the violence becomes palpable, when their non-Muslim neighbors sneak away in the night, narrowly avoiding murderous mobs comprised of their Muslim neighbors, "Daadi's father didn't tell her to broaden her mind" (352). Through personal memories, the narrative thus establishes the trauma of partition as both the origin of Pakistan and of Daadi's tendency toward suspicion of all things political. Not only does the idea of Pakistan hold no sway over Daadi, but the founding of the nation itself initiates for her an apprehensive disposition that later manifests as a willingness to indulge in conspiracy thinking. More broadly, Pakistan's founding, rather than instilling trust in the government and in fellow Pakistanis, inaugurates an atmosphere of political suspicion that, in relation to the articulation of a collective identity, functions exclusively. This formulation of what the transition from idea to nation brings about suggests that partition imposed the discursive constraints of "reproductive futurism" on definitions of Pakistaniness.

The second origin story, though different in the details, works in much the same way. Conveyed through a flashback, Zakia's biography establishes her muhajir identity. Her parents migrate to Pakistan after the death of Zakia's paternal grandfather (77). Upon their arrival in Karachi, Zakia's parents "had to sleep in camps that were set up in public places, camps that lacked water in the dry season and were flooded in the rainy season. When people protested they were beaten with batons and tear-gassed" (78). And, although Zakia's parents eventually prospered in Karachi, they continued to feel "belittled and ridiculous." Further, no amount of material success could eclipse, in her father's mind, the home he'd left in India: it was the "best house in the best lane of a mohalla" (77). Nostalgia figures here as a powerful pull, especially in light of the state-enforced obstacles muhajirs faced. As the child of muhajirs, Zakia experiences some cognitive dissonance; she can only compare her parents' stories, which weren't her own experiences, to how her textbook presents Pakistani nationhood:

> At school [Zakia] learned every day about the country they called their own, the country with the sea and the desert and with the mountains in the north…, the country that contained so many languages and ways of dressing in clothes, where Sindhis wore ajraks and the Baloch wore turbans, where Pathans herded mountain goats and wore hats that looked like pies placed on their heads, and where Punjabis, most memorably, carried pots on their hips and moved swayingly through mustard fields. [Zakia] was sure this country existed.
>
> (76–7)

The textbook's idealized image of Pakistani plurality seems as remote to this young Zakia as the idea of Pakistan, used as a slogan, seemed to the young Daadi. Both characters feel at a remove from these visions of collective belonging purportedly materialized through the functions of the state. Despite her certainty that this Pakistan exists, for instance, Zakia "just didn't see herself in it" (77). And, just as the trauma of partition embeds a tendency toward suspicion in Daadi, Zakia's inheritance of her parent's muhajir displacement likewise encourages her own suspicious bent. The second origin story filtered through Zakia's experiences takes on both the centrality of muhajir mythology in definitions of Pakistaniness and any celebratory framings of that identity in terms of diversity. The two visions of the future depend upon the acceptance of muhajirs into the plurality that existed (and continues to exist) in the territory that became Pakistan. Thus, these visions, as well as the framing of partition as the achievement of freedom for those already living in the territory, facilitate Pakistan's unique version of "reproductive futurism." And, this "future" fuels distrust in politicians and conspiracy thinking among ordinary people. Zaki's "queer" narration highlights this atmosphere of suspicion, how it delimits structures, and, in the process, signals the possibility of a different future.

Uzma Aslam Khan's *Geometry of God* touches upon many of the points, including a focus on acts of reading and an illustration of the narrative function of origin stories, I've already discussed in my analyses of Hanif's, Shamsie's, and Ali's novels. Similarly, then, this novel explores the distance between state-sponsored ideologies and characters' efforts to articulate a meaningful sense of collective belonging. In addition, UA Khan's novel brings together conspiracies and male homosocial/homosexual bonds to demystify their overlapping relation to power. *Geometry of God* employs congruent erotic triangles to represent how females mediate male relationships, be they hostile or affectionate, and, in doing so, become objects of exchange. Yet, because the plot contains a very real and lethal conspiracy that involves one of these triangles, the novel also showcases an inversion of such relationships, wherein female characters rescale the triangle's asymmetry. This inversion allows the female characters to scuttle the allocation of power, suggesting the possibility of piecing together a less restrictive narrative of the "real" Pakistan.

As the novel opens, Zia's regime holds power, and the narrative presents his Islamization program through the Jamaat-e-Pediash or Party of Creation (24), whose members fill the ranks of the Academy of Moral Policy (49). Noman, one of the novel's three first person narrators, becomes involved with these organizations when his father, a firm supporter of Zia's regime, enlists his son as his personal secretary. Little vexes the Academy more, at least initially, than Zahoor, a paleontologist fixated on the marine life that once inhabited the ocean whose now empty basin comprises the mountains and valleys outside of Islamabad. The Party of Creation opposes Zahoor's emphatic insistence on evolution as the explanation for humans' existence. To these proponents of Zia's "Islam," the double meaning of "*fuzool*," the Urdu word for both "nonsense" and "fossil," says it all. For the likes of Zahoor and his colleagues, however, fossils are the only kinds of "writing" that represent "reality" (3, 5). Indeed, for Zahoor, the fossil record he and his team uncover in Islamabad's environs constitutes the "real" Pakistan: "'Pray five times a day and be a *real* Pakistani! [Zahoor exclaims.] Speak Urdu and be a *real* Pakistani, or English and half as Pakistani! Well, here's my answer. Study whales and be Pakistani!'" (6). Immediately, then, the struggle over origins becomes apparent. The contest pits Islamization as the sole discourse capable of defining Pakistan versus the "rational" approach represented by a scientific inquiry focused on the specificities of the place itself: top-down or ground up. These conflicting dynamics mirror the tensions between "pure" Islam and syncretism. Much as Noman's father recruits his son, Zahoor drafts his granddaughter, Amal, another of the novel's first person narrators, into his scientific quest. At the novel's start, Amal is only eight, but neither her age nor her gender prevent her from accompanying Zahoor on a dig, during which she discovers a fossil of an 'S' shaped ear bone of a prehistoric land-roving whale. Amal's discovery provides Zahoor with just the proof he needs to continue developing his theory about the ocean's existence, while it also inspires Amal to pursue paleontology herself. Several factors derail Amal's ambitions, however, including Zahoor's penchant for controversy, Amal's gender, and her little sister, Mehwish, the last of the novel's narrators, who loses her eyesight when she's only a baby. Amal becomes her sister's eyes, but this domestication obstructs the full development of her intellectual curiosity. Despite these obstacles, Amal maintains a close relationship with both her sister and her grandfather.

These struggles over origins and the ways they are cross-hatched with the characters' personal relationships give shape both to the novel's major conspiracy and its erotic triangles. Unlike any of the other novels I've discussed, *Geometry of God* gives credence to an actual conspiracy. Noman, in an effort to please his father, exaggerates Zahoor's influence, thus setting in motion a series of events that snowballs into lethal violence. Tensions first flare when, coincidentally, Zahoor is giving a lecture at the same hotel where the Academy of Moral Policy is holding a meeting. Dispatched as a spy to the lecture, Noman witnesses nothing much; that is, Zahoor's lecture draws a small—though largely disinterested— crowd (89), who awaken only when Zahoor turns his fossil talk into a political diatribe. Arguing that intellectual curiosity, a gift, motivates him to search endlessly, Zahoor claims, "'This gift is a great threat to some, inside and outside our country'" (92). Such an inclination to search rather than to settle on or merely accept answers threatens power, because, as Zahoor continues, it can't be controlled (92). Zia's Islamization, however, is trying to do just that, and, as a result, according to Zahoor, "'We are suffocating between brass and beard, tank and creed!'" (93). Those audience members who do protest take issue with how Zahoor's mixed science and politics (94), missing the point that knowledge claims of any type relate to power and, thus, to politics. Despite Zahoor's tears, the lecture is unremarkable, and, yet, under pressure, Noman embellishes the audience's reaction for the Academy. In his capacity as first person narrator, Noman reveals his motives and reservations:

> If Zahoor wants a public, Aba wants an enemy…I'll help both by exaggerating Zahoor's influence.
> But if I exaggerate Zahoor's influence, what will these men do to him?
> (97)

Noman signals from the start that he's aware of how his participation in what one member of the Academy calls the "'Islamization of Thought'" has material consequences (81). With this understanding, Noman can identify himself as a "Zia baby," that is, "a child who blows with a small wind and bats for both sides" (98). Noman's self-labeling accurately diagnoses his lack of ideological conviction while also critiquing the "Islam" of Zia regime's as crass opportunism. At the same time, this awareness of the very real consequences of his participation does not, however, prevent Noman from anonymously issuing Zahoor two warnings—veiled threats, really.[25] Amal later shares an excerpt from one warning letter: "*Dear Sir, Godlessness is a cancer whose favorite organ is the pen…*" (143). These warnings work as intended, at least on all the characters who care for Zahoor if not on him directly; that is, the warnings successfully and legitimately provoke conspiratorial thinking amongst Zahoor's family and friends.

By having "rational" scientists engage in conspiratorial thinking, UA Khan's novel calls into question the irrationality, the just plain loopiness, often associated with conspiracy theorists. This inversion of the conspiracy theorist stereotype highlights how the Academy, as an offshoot of Zia's regime, lacks, in David Coady's words, the "epistemic authority" required to legitimate belief in their pronouncements ("Irrational" 199). While the Academy and the government may lack this type of authority, they do still retain the brute power to exact consequences for Zahoor's dissent: with Noman's knowledge, the Academy manufactures blasphemy charges against Zahoor, who is in and out of prison for years until a judge finally acquits him. Physically depleted and aged by the experience, Zahoor now relents to his friends' demands that he hire guards. After one of his guards is murdered, Zahoor goes into hiding, which, of course, means that he's no longer pursuing his paleontological quest. Unsatisfied, those who conspire against him plot an assassination attempt at Amal's wedding, and, though Zahoor survives, his companion Junayd dies, and both Mehwish and Noman are injured. Through the use of violence, precipitated by Noman's ambivalent participation in the Academy's Islamizing project, what the novel frames as the repressive forces prevail.

And, yet, the triangulated relationships that link the characters complicate the entire concept of repression in the novel. As Sedgwick contends in her seminal argument on erotic triangles, such formations schematize the distribution of power, which, with respect to gender, is always asymmetrical ("Between" 598). Working from Sedgwick's contribution, Beth Kramer asserts that conventionally triangulated relationships illustrate how men "seek mastery and domination over each other through a woman," thereby "cement[ing] the larger social bonds" (120). Women's positions within these relations, Kramer continues, "is always demeaning" as they are figured "objectively and symbolically as contested property" (123). Early on, the novel establishes two significant triangles that operate in these ways: the first is between Zahoor, his companion Junayd, and Amal; and the second involves Zahoor, Noman, and Amal/Mehwish, as the two sisters manifest different aspects of the same function. In the Zahoor-Junayd-Amal triangle, Amal serves as the witness of the two male characters' homosexual attachment. One of the novel's first scenes has an eight-year-old Amal mediating between her grandfather and his friend, as the latter two argue over the possibility of knowing God. Amal notices a lull in the conversation and describes what she sees: "When I look up again, I notice Nana [Zahoor] and Junayd are not talking any more but staring at each other, and their eyes smile" (8). Offering no additional commentary, Amal's participation in the scene as observer validates, in a sense, the connection between the two friends simply by witnessing it. She continues, signaling to the reader the erotic dimension of the interaction: "Then Nana tears himself away to refill Junayd's glass" (8). Her position vis-à-vis her grandfather and Junayd abides, for years later, she silently communicates their intimacy to Noman when he asks after Junayd. This scene takes place after Zahoor is acquitted; his time in prison ruins his health, and Junayd cares for him, which is what Amal and Noman view:

Zahoor's coughing violently, Junayd beside him. He covers Zahoor's knees with a blanket. Brings cough syrup. Wipes Zahoor's forehead with a hanky drawn from his shirt pocket.

…

"He never married—Junayd?" [Noman asks Amal.]
…. Amal looks at me and we both fall silent.

(319)[26]

As the keeper of the couple's secret for all these years, Amal's participation in the triangle is passive—observe and remain silent—even while it gives form to the attachment. To be clear: no textual evidence exists that Amal objects to her grandfather's relationship with Junayd. Rather, the point is, her triangulation of their dyad reinforces the bond.

This bond between Zahoor and Junayd encompasses not only their personal relationship but also their broader social and political positions as legitimate knowledge producers. And, although targeted by the Academy for Moral Policy, Zahoor's and Junayd's roles as knowledge producers make them powerful. Once again, Amal's triangulated relation to both male characters sustains their power. An early scene situates this triangle within the context of knowledge production. Amal, just a girl, accompanies Zahoor, Junayd, and several others on a dig outside of Islamabad, and she finds a fossil of the ear bone of a prehistoric, land-based whale. Zahoor tells her that the fossil is, "'possibly, proof of the evolution of whales. What we were looking for and would not have found, if not for you'" (31). Amal, thus, plays a key role, howsoever inadvertently, in the construction of the origin story in which Zahoor invests. Further, in assisting in her grand-father's scientific endeavors, Amal also provides him and Junayd more fodder for their playful, ongoing debates on whether science or art best cultivates knowledge of the world (9). As he and his fellow scientists build upon Amal's fossil, Zahoor incorporates Amal into this narrative. Years later, at the very lecture Noman later uses to condemn Zahoor in his father's eyes, Zahoor tells the audience that his granddaughter "'was only eight years old when she found this,' he picks up a bone, 'a copy of the diamond key'" (92). When the narrative returns to Amal's perspective, she relays, "So this is how it is. Nana praises me to everyone. I'm the girl who found the fossil skull of the oldest whale" (101). In recognizing her own oxymoronic futile indispensability, Amal also recognizes a bitter irony:

The girl who slipped the diamond key into his hands has become the girl that's talked about. She's the anecdote. She spices his speeches to give them a human touch. *Sweet.* She's the audience. Not the player. She's *she.*

(101; emphasis in original)

The sentence structures in this passage illustrate Amal's slippage between being an active subject to being a passive object. Moreover, Amal's assessment of her shifting roles in the production of knowledge fulfills a prediction she makes, as narrator, about her eight-year-old self: "The men [Nana's colleagues] compliment me on being a clever eight-year-old and talk to me as if I'm eighteen, which is more seriously than anyone will talk to me when I *am* eighteen" (11). As an eighteen-year-old young woman, Amal occupies a subservient position because of the presumed correspondence of her gender and heterosexuality, both of which preclude her further participation in knowledge production even as they bolster the male characters' participation in that very process.

This presumed correspondence of Amal's gender and sexuality prefigures her own and her sister's roles in a congruent triangulated relationship, this time involving Noman. From the moment Noman spies on Zahoor's lecture, the younger man harbors a genuine—as opposed to strategic—desire to know the scientist. The triangle that connects him to Zahoor also initially includes just Amal, but as Mehwish approaches sexual maturity, she shares the third angle with her sister. Homosocial rather than homosexual, Noman's desire to know Zahoor develops out of his "Zia babyhood" or his ambivalence over helping his father and the Academy of Moral Policy. In retrospectively contemplating his own potential for perfidy, Noman remembers "feeling a sudden, surprising urge to know [Zahoor]...The adoring grandfather of a curly-haired girl and her blind sister. The one who didn't flinch when others threw insults and chairs at him. Who didn't say what they wanted to hear. My opposite" (100). The fact rather than, necessarily, the content of Zahoor's convictions appeal to Noman. And, pointedly, that draw encompasses Amal and Mehwish. If Zahoor is Noman's opposite, then the relationship Noman wants with the sisters has to be different from the one Zahoor has with them: rather than paternal, sexual and more. Noman narrates his own self-examination of the family's gravitational pull: "The first time I saw them [at the lecture], it was Zahoor and the older girl that intrigued me" (131). Indeed, Noman often describes Amal in sexually charged terms, noting her "voluptuousness" (94) and her "full mouth half-bored, half-amused" (66). Later, when Noman transfers his desire to Mehwish, he tempers the overtly sexual impulses of his desire but not its drive to possess: Mehwish's "face is delicate. Her skin, thin, translucent. It's a beauty I don't want to consume, like strawberries. It's a beauty I want to receive, like light" (251). Mehwish's draw is strong enough that Noman worries whether "Zahoor is right to pull her away from me" (252). Indeed, Amal speculates that Zahoor's initial interest in Noman derives from the older man's awareness of the younger's sexual attraction to his granddaughters (257). Very explicitly, then, Mehwish becomes a conduit of exchange between the two male characters, while she also operates as a proxy for Noman's interest in Zahoor. Amal reports, for instance, Mehwish's jealousy over the "growing attachment" between Zahoor and Noman (192). As Mehwish becomes Noman's romantic fixation, Amal serves as his not-quite sexually neutral intermediary with Zahoor. "Not quite," because Amal clearly remains a strawberry: Noman still admires "the fullness of her hips" and notes how her sweater "hid[es] her breasts" (304). The older man sends Amal to Noman's, olive branch extended, to relay his willingness to forgive Noman's hand in the manufactured blasphemy charges (302).[27] Thus, Amal, too, functions as a means of exchange. Both sisters thus strengthen the links between Noman and Zahoor and, as a result, reinforce their power, howsoever oppositional the two male characters' positions seem.

Geometry of God closes with a final triangle that functions in a markedly different way than the conventional ones geared toward reinforcing masculine bonds and the dominant social order. This triangle inverts the dynamics of the others in the novel even though it involves Amal and two of her male colleagues. Despite her long history of being the "anecdote" her grandfather tells as part of his origin story, Amal does manage to earn a university degree and get a job in a paleontology lab. Her new credentials notwithstanding, Amal still cannot do field work because of her gender. Further, her male colleagues even use her gender to obstruct Amal's lab work; as Amal narrates, "Behind them all, I become *she*" (273). The power dynamics operating in the Zahoor-Junayd-Amal triangle operate between Fawad-Ibrar-Amal, as well. And, since Fawad and Ibrar are "members of the…student offshoots of the Party of Creation" (271), their relation to Amal also includes the more material power dynamics that characterize the Noman-Zahoor-Amal/Mehwish triangle, too.

Amal refuses, however, to allow the replication of these forces, the continuation of her repression. She recognizes that the order Fawad and Ibrar represent assigns gender to realm in the following way: "To woman: microcosm. To man: macrocosm" (288). But, Amal also understands that the new narrative to which she wants to contribute "is higher than our petty prejudices, [so] why [would she] let herself get tangled up in microscopic meannesses?" (288). Amal's refusal of the petty signals her efforts to find an alternative structure into which she will fit her work and its meaning. In action, these efforts amount to a refusal to be provoked:

> In the lab one day, Ibrar hovers around me while I remove the latest set of rocks brought back from a dig. I lean across the table. He peers down my neck. Then he pushes a slab off the table. Fawad laughs…I pick it up…The rest, I start to clean. A rib? A manatee's? An oddly calming chemical begins to course through me.
>
> (312–13)

Ibrar and Fawad mix their ideological intolerance for science with a sexual intimidation in order to fix Amal at her angle. She carries on, ignoring them: "So what if their theology is as mixed up as this backbone? As the spine takes shapes [sic], Fawad recedes. Eventually, all of him vanishes to the place that he had, till now, succeeded in putting *her*. I don't become she" (313). Less a renunciation of her gender or even her sexuality, for that matter—in fact, this passage is intercut with Amal's narration of her sexual encounters with Omar, the man she ends up marrying (312, 317)—Amal's emphatic "*her*," her refusal to "become she" amounts to a positive, active construction of a different story. Her subsequent participation in a dig, achieved through significant argument and negotiation, further develops this story. Amal and her team find another important fossil of a previously unknown prehistoric whale species. The existence of this new creature poses more questions than it answers, and it also fulfills Amal's desire: "I have only ever wanted to be a humble voice in a mighty chorus. I have only ever wanted to be a small flame in a greater fire. Tonight, I am" (364). Where the stories Zahoor and Noman's father wrote bore origins, suggesting a singularity befitting their large personalities, Amal's narrative comes to voice through a chorus, a plural endeavor. *Geometry of God* thus approaches a redefinition of a "good Muslim" or a "real" Pakistani by challenging Amal's relegation to object status. As she becomes subject, Amal reshapes identity narratives, opting for collaboration and tolerance.

Part 3

Multicultural nation, privileged state

5 Karachi

In the context of Pakistani history, Karachi occupies a unique position. The country's capital upon independence in 1947, Karachi was also the target destination for Indian Muslim migrants, called muhajirs, who crossed the newly established border from India to Pakistan to re-establish their lives in the newly anointed homeland for Indian's Muslims.[1] Oskar Verkaaik characterizes the Karachi of 1947 as belonging to a "period [of] mythological time because the memory of it is deeply structured by stories that describe a conveniently arranged city that, as in a myth of origin, emerged out of the very beginnings of the Pakistani nation" (68). Framed as a site suitably and even ideally situated to represent the newness of Pakistan, Karachi, as Verkaaik further contends, emerges in this historical moment as the "exemplary Muhajir city" and the "South Asian city par excellence," where migrants would find a "safe haven and, importantly, would make a new start and finally live up to [the city's] full potential" (69). The Karachi of 1947 serves as a metonym for the optimism of the nascent Pakistan. And, yet, these mythological origins prove ironic, as the Karachi of subsequent decades mounts challenge after challenge to Pakistani national cohesion. The muhajirs of 1947 were only the first major migrant influx Karachi sustained. While the muhajirs' numbers swelled the city's population to over one million in 1951 from only a half million in 1947 (Hasan 174), subsequent immigrants busted the city's seams, as the population more than tripled in the next two decades (Hasan 182). By the 1960s, the majority of immigrants were coming from other parts of Pakistan, adding languages and cultural traditions to the already tense Sindhi-Urdu mix (Hasan 182). By all accounts, the city and the nation were unprepared to handle Karachi's unfathomable growth, a failure of infrastructural anticipation that surely complicates any single explanation for the violence that began to erupt in the mid-1960s (Ahmar 1032).[2] S. Akbar Zaidi, for one, reads the violence that has characterized life in Karachi for the last four decades or more—violence that is frequently read in class and/or ethnic terms—as a struggle "against the State itself" (387). Similarly, Moonis Ahmar observes that Karachi and other urban areas of Sindh were once "vehement supporter[s] of a centralized political structure" until a "radical shift in attitudes and perceptions" made these areas "the most serious threat to Pakistan's political order since the loss of East Pakistan in December 1971" (1035–6). With this turnabout in mind, the history of Karachi as an actual Pakistani city and as a signifier traces the changing resonances of my three key terms: idea, nation, and state.

As I suggest above, any explanation for Karachi's transmutation from model capital to frighteningly violent city that relies on a single factor—be it class, ethnicity, or politics—proves inadequate. In Iftikhar Malik's view, analyses of Karachi require the consideration of "interlinked themes including demography, pluralism, ethnicity, class, religion, state structure and the role of various personalities and parties" ("What" 2219).[3] Given these multifarious concerns, claims of belonging to Karachi are similarly complicated, especially when assessing the extent to which those claims do or do not also entail a broader claim to "Pakistaniness." In keeping with this site specificity, I characterize all four novels I explore in this section—Kamila Shamsie's *Kartography* (2004), Bina Shah's *The 786 Cybercafe* (2004), Adam Zameenzad's *The 13th House* (1989), and Maniza Naqvi's *A Matter of Detail* (2008)—as Karachi novels, meaning that each of these novels foregrounds what it means to live in *this* city. Thus, my primary focus will be on setting as a literary device or, in other words, how these fictions represent the city.[4] Although these novels are all relatively recent, they do cover the full span of Karachi's existence as a Pakistani city, allowing for an assessment of how contemporary literary narratives about this location stand in relation to dominant historical and anthropological accounts. It's against these accounts that I project my literary analyses, which, as a group, cast Karachi in perpetual motion or, in Edward Soja's terms, as a "megacity": an "increasingly discontinuous, fragmented, polycentric, and almost kaleidoscopic socio-spatial structure" (235).[5] Soja's string of adjectives captures the complexity of claims of belonging to Karachi. The city's dynamic identity stands in some tension with boundary-laden discourses that demarcate identity in ethnic or class terms, for instance.

In this section, I argue that these Karachi novels manifest a preoccupation with the city's history in their formulations of affectively appealing identities or claims to belonging to the localized site of the city and to the broader location of the nation. The concept of mobility figures in my analysis of how each novel views history and, accordingly, how all four novels engage with Pakistan as idea, nation, and state. Many of these fictions include the mythological Karachi of which Verkaaik speaks. The recurrence of this nostalgia for the Karachi of 1947 presents an idealized Karachiite identity deeply invested in the idea of Pakistan and that idea's promise of a unified national identity as "Pakistanis." Further, this nostalgia connects the novels discussed here with Ashraf's *The Postmaster*, which features Ghulam Rasool's "anti-imperialist nostalgia," an affective yearning for the promise of Pakistan yet unrealized. In contrast, the nostalgia present in these fictions about Karachi represents an historical stuckness that attempts to limit or contain transgressive mobility. In other words, this nostalgia has none of the critical impulses that Ghulam Rasool's does. The critique emerges, however, because none of these novels allows this nostalgia to prevail; so a Karachiite and Pakistani identity shaped exclusively by the idea of Pakistan or by the nation's early years doesn't stand. The various characters' disillusionment with the state introduces a wedge between the idea of Pakistan and the definition of national unity that follows from that idea. Much as the nostalgia operates, the representations of the state's presence in these fictions rely upon another kind of stuckness, one that contains the city through leveraging politicized identities. Mobility can function in tension with nostalgia and representations of the state to outline alternative Karachiite identities characterized by movement within the city. These alternatives cast a skeptical look at the weight of historically dominant identity categories, while also separating themselves from the inherited notion of a unified Pakistani identity.

The historical context in which I want to situate my literary analyses involves the nearly unfathomable changes Karachi has undergone since the creation of Pakistan. In Steve Inskeep's view, contemporary Karachi is an "instant city": "a metropolis that has grown so rapidly that a returning visitor would scarcely recognize it" (2). Under British rule, Karachi was certainly an important if modest port city. Convinced of its unique character, Karachiites successfully lobbied in 1936 for a separation of Karachi from the Bombay Presidency, the organizational unit of which the city was a part under the Raj (A. Khan 218). This pre-partition Karachi was a diverse place in a different sense than its contemporary incarnation; Hamida Khuhro and Anwer Mooraj note that the "Bohras, Khojas, Memons, and Hindus lived cheek by jowl" in this still-colonial version of the city (x). Come 1947, Adeel Khan points out that Karachiites were "initially sympathetic" to the muhajirs' plight, a compassion likely made possible due to the fact that Sindh saw considerably less violence that did Punjab ("Sindhi" 218). Characterized in these ways, the Karachi of 1947 and before becomes the stuff of nostalgia, as post-partition brought about many alterations. A. Khan speculates, for instance, that the radical changes that took place once the muhajirs settled permanently in Karachi motivated a perspectival adjustment among those already living there. One major change had to do with language, as Urdu replaced Sindhi, an unprecedented linguistic shift, given that Sindhi had always been the lingua franca even during the colonial period (A. Khan 218). From a "native"—i.e. pre-1947—Karachiite perspective, then, the city would seem unrecognizable almost immediately in the early years of Pakistani nationhood.

Despite the changes that their arrival inaugurates, muhajirs indulge in their own nostalgia that similarly fixes Karachi, or so the dominant narratives go. Over and over again, one reads that, for migrants, the allure of the idea of Pakistan resided in its promise of a homeland for India's Muslims, as well as the related promise of a shared identity as "Pakistanis." Through a favored narrative that often emphasizes sacrifice, these migrants traveled across the newly created borders to embark on a new national experiment and to embrace a new national—and unified—identity. The Karachi many muhajirs found was, in some sense, a vacated city, an urban space waiting to be re-inhabited. Pre-1947 demographics show that Muslims were in the minority, comprising only 3.5 percent of the population compared to the 42 percent share held by Hindus; percentages shifted radically after 1947, as the city witnessed the departure of most of its Hindu community, which also comprised an important faction of the city's economic base (Hasan 171). The incoming muhajirs swung these percentages so that, by 1951, 96 percent of the population was Muslim and less than two percent were Hindu (Hasan 174). With their higher literacy rates and more developed vocational skills, the muhajirs quickly filled the socio-economic and cultural gaps left by the populations that departed for India and embraced life as the new Pakistanis living in the new nation's capital city. Karachi's early years as a Pakistani city were, thus, the golden age for the newly arrived muhajirs.

But, the demographic changes occurring in 1947 were just the start, and, so, the muhajir golden age wanes as did pre-partition Karachi. As Khuhro and Mooraj state, Karachi "helter skeltered in a demographic onslaught only a few cities in the world have matched" (viii). Khuhro and Mooraj's choice of terms— "helter skeltered" and "onslaught"—calls to mind a confusion born of violence, and violence brought about through a variety of factors emphatically punctuates Karachi's permutations in the decades following partition. Internal migration within Pakistan brought still more groups into the midst of old-time Karachiites. According to Arif Hasan, in the 1960s, the most significant number of migrants to Karachi came from the North West Frontier Province, and their movement south "was supported by the political patronage that was offered to them by the military rulers [i.e. under Ayub's regime], whose leaders also belonged to the NWFP" (182). The arrival in Karachi of Pakhtoons and Hazarawals from the NWFP (Hasan 182), thus, introduces not only additional ethnic and economic considerations, but it also signals the political dynamics that contribute to the more complex—when compared to the nostalgic renderings of pre-partition Karachi—diversity that contributes to the city's overall sense of perpetual movement or even, when taking the increasing outbreaks of violence into consideration, instability. Ahmar identifies 1964–5 as the first time when "ethnic" clashes between the muhajirs and the newly arrived Pathans occur in Karachi, for instance. Given the political context in which the Pathans migrate to Karachi, however, to label their tensions with the muhajirs "ethnic" provides only a partial account. Indeed, the political stakes at work in Karachi through the subsequent decades help illustrate the inadequacy of only an "ethnic" diagnosis for the city's troubles. Muhajirs also clashed with the Pakistan People's Party, whose stronghold is Sindh, in the 1970s (Ahmar 1032–3). This tension serves as just one example of political rather than strictly "ethnic" conflict, for as Adeel Khan chronicles, Sindhis were more likely to back the PPP's agenda than a Sindhi nationalist one from the 1970s–1990s (226). Further, A. Khan argues that Zia backed the Muhajir Quami Movement (MQM) in the 1980s and the ISI had a stake in leveraging unrest in Karachi and the rest of Sindh through the 1990s (225–6, 227–8).[6] Military actions throughout the region in the 1970s and 1980s also resulted in the influx of yet more migrants with still other languages and cultural traditions, and constitute additional examples of the extra-ethnic pressures on Karachi (Hasan 188). Of these actions, the US's covert war in Afghanistan contributes to some of the most dangerous developments in Karachi.

As the entry point for the arms the US, with the help of Zia's government and the ISI, was funneling to the mujahideen in Afghanistan, Karachiites old and new witnessed the kalashnikovization of their city's culture.[7] This development prompted perhaps the only clear line of demarcation in Karachi's identity: that between the rich and the poor. Possessed with the ability to up sticks and leave, the rich cleared out of the old city and, instead, established their own enclaves in Clifton and Defense; or, as Hasan puts it, the increase in violence lead to the "ghettoization of the rich" (188). Given that, for the elite, as Malik has it, "ethnicity is merely a misnomer," their own movement within Karachi exemplifies how economic concerns also shape the city's identities ("What" 2220).

The cultural, social, economic, and political forces factoring in these radical shifts in Karachi's demographics amplify the failures of the Pakistani state, first, to anticipate migrants' choice of Karachi as a destination in 1947 and, later, to manage in any meaningful way the effects on the city's growth brought about by the country's historical circumstances. While observing that the city's growth illustrates how "many Karachis [...] exist simultaneously," Sayantan Dasgupta also points out that large portions of the city have developed and continue to develop in unplanned ways (306). The later migrants—that is, those who don't identify as muhajirs—came with lower literacy rates and less vocational training, thus putting a strain on Karachi's economy. Compounding this strain, as Ahmar argues, these population increases also contributed to a "growing demand for housing, public services, [and] education that [Karachi's] deteriorating infrastructure could not provide" (1040). Unsupported, many of these later migrant groups get caught up in exploitative systems that hold out the promise of providing the services that the state has failed to furnish. Dasgupta notes, for instance, that "entrepreneurs" took advantage of the housing shortage by carrying out housing deals for illegal, semi-permanent settlements called katchi abadis, veritable shantytowns that mushroomed throughout the city (306). From the 1960s onward, municipal plan after municipal plan got shelved or simply failed (Hasan 182), creating a power vacuum in the city. Predictably, Karachi's kalashnikovization only exacerbated the city's problems by rendering the state subservient to the arms and drug trades (Hasan 188). The breakdown of a reliable state- or municipal-supported infrastructure in Karachi arguably affects the terms with which Karachiites claim belonging to their city and their nation. Hardly remaining the "model South Asian city" it was touted to be in 1947, Karachi's identities, instead, permutate diachronically and synchronously.

Throughout the decades of its existence as a Pakistani city, decades defined by alterations in size, national standing, and character, Karachi remains the economic leader of the country.[8] And, while economic prosperity has not proved to be a panacea for the city, this fact, along with the demographic changes—and the social, economic, and political dynamics that accompany them—provide the historical context for my analyses of these four Karachi novels. I conduct these analyses through three key terms: nostalgia, mobility, and corruption. In acknowledging the deteriorating infrastructural conditions, the frightening violence, and the class inequities, these fictions break with nostalgic renderings of the city. That is, they not only put a distance between their claims of belonging to the city and whatever promise the idea of Pakistan may have held, but they also signal the inability of the state to bind the city's inhabitants via a collective identity. Yet, despite incorporating the material realities of the actual urban space in their fictionalized representations, these novels, together, hold out an optimism for continuing change or mobility, linked to Karachi's economic reality, and hint at the possibility of achieving a "better" life, which, although commonly defined in material terms, also signifies greater inclusivity. Thus, change, Karachi's defining feature, also serves as the affective tie that binds the novels' characters to place, i.e. to city and to nation. And, again together, these novels also suggest that only a corruption of the idea of this identity formulated through change hampers the characters' abilities to realize and strengthen the ties that would link all city dwellers as Karachiites.

Nostalgic renderings of Karachi bestow a sense of belonging on the characters who indulge such affective attachments, but, at the same time, these renderings also fasten their identities to historically predominant scripts. In her discussion of the distinctiveness of "urban nostalgia," Tamar Katz points out that "a study of the city and its representations must by definition be a study of the rhetoric of loss" (811). While it may seem obvious, nostalgia is an affective response to changed circumstances, a way of re-anchoring oneself in a moment (and the places tied to that moment) when one thinks, in the present, one felt more secure or more able to make sense of one's environment. Nostalgia attaches meaning to the past, endows the ability to make sense, to know the past with some confidence, and helps secure the affective attachment that centers the subject claiming to know. But what Karachi has been lost? Katz's observation that "[m]odern life has been theorized as a constant encounter with change; in this view, cities are exemplary modern social spaces because of the speed with which they are transformed" seems to capture post-partition Karachi perfectly (811). Conventional definitions of nostalgia would then diagnose the loss mourned as a simpler, more static time, likely experienced in a rural setting. And, yet, the "urban nostalgia" Karachi inspires in these fictions focuses more on the era of transformation from colonial port to capital city or, more abstractly, on the achievement of modernity that accompanied the achievement of nationhood.[9] In this sense, the nostalgia for Karachi these novels manifest possesses a kind of irony that Andreas Huyssen, writing of the contemporary fascination with ruins, sees as a "nostalgia for modernity that dare not speak its name" (7). Huyssen's point resonates with my analysis of nostalgia in these Karachi novels in that it indicates the draw of Karachi as the model city, the new capital of the finally-achieved homeland for India's Muslims. The affective attachment nostalgia facilitates for these characters allows them to fantasize about themselves as thoroughly modern. And, insofar as "urban nostalgia" entertains the possibility of an authentic identity born of a secure belonging—that ability to make sense of the city that I mention above— Karachi nostalgia implies that to be an authentic (and new) Pakistani is to be modern. The deflation of the nostalgic framings of Karachi, then, signals not an l4

affective departure from allure of a modern identity, at least for some characters, but, rather, the narratives' alternative framings of the terms by which the characters belong to the city and claim to be modern.

Maniza Naqvi's *A Matter of Detail* features "urban nostalgia" for Karachi, an affective yearning for the wholeness and belonging that an "authentic" identity promises. The narrative in its entirety does not allow this nostalgic indulgence to go unproblematized, however, suggesting that the much-desired authenticity follows from dominant identity markers that do not align well with what the novel sets as actual lived experience as a Karachiite. Set in 2004 and punctuated with flashbacks to earlier historical moments, especially the partition era, *A Matter of Detail* centers around one family made up of Razzak, his two co-wives, Hajra (Bari-ma) and Zareena (Choti-ma), and their five daughters, Sara, Kulsum, Amina, Resham, and Shireen. The settings prove just as significant as these central characters. The daughters were raised at a dwelling referred to by its address, 43-G, and Razzak and his two wives, now elderly, still live there. Hajra also owns a flat on Lawrence Road, which was her family's home for generations, in one of Karachi's oldest neighborhoods near the Saddar, an important early site of commerce. The novel's opening quickly establishes that, two months prior, Hajra departs 43-G to re-settle in her girlhood home on Lawrence Road. These two locations anchor Hajra's urban nostalgias between which she is stuck, as her idealized visions can't accommodate all the aspects of her identity.

Residence at the Lawrence Road flat allows Hajra to dwell in a remembered Karachi of idealized diversity. In large measure, the Karachi Hajra associates with Lawrence Road is located in the late 1940s and early 1950s, the city's national golden age. Hajra recalls her years at university before she marries Razzak in 1953 as cosmopolitan, even though she doesn't leave Karachi. At that time, the "Saddar was alive with sounds," as "[s]hopkeepers and vendors shouted out the latest items for purchase to passersby" (11). These goods hail from the world over: China, America, Japan, India. Further, the culture was permissive and the Saddar crowded enough that Hajra and Razzak, yet unmarried, could visit coffee houses, cafes, and bookstores without censure (11). Hajra's nostalgia is rooted in something deeper than the delights of this cosmopolitan consumerism, however. What makes this era a golden age for her is how, as she tells her daughter Sara, for "'us old Karachiites, there was a strong sense of community and caring'" (29). This sense of community among long-time Karachiites matters to Hajra in the novel's present, because she has decided to resuscitate her traditional religious practices as a member of Karachi's nearly extinct B'nai Israel community. According to Hajra's vision of Karachi's past, the city in 1953

> was a place where people went to jamaat khanas, and temples, and churches, and synagogues and imam bargahs…This was all part of the way of this city…No one thought anything of it. We were all equally strange, equally queer…All of us were the same because of our differences. But really, we were just shades apart. Just shades apart…And this was alright. This was

the way it should have remained. And no one from the outside looking at
all this could tell one from the other.

(30)

With its emphasis on the plethora of religious identities to be found in Karachi at
this time, Hajra's framing of the city hits upon Karachi's more explicitly diverse
past, as historical demographics show, and holds that this demographic diversity
equaled a more tolerant society. Importantly, Hajra also distinguishes between
"insiders" and "outsiders," a distinction that coincides with her self-identification
as an "old Karachiite." But, Hajra's inclusive/exclusive dynamic works more
to prop up early-1950s Karachi as a national beacon rather than to rip it out of a
national context entirely. For, as Hajra explains, these "old Karachiites" "'held
together as best we could when the world around us started to fall apart at the
seams and change so rapidly. The whole world had gone crazy, the country was
slowly going crazy'" (29). Hajra's use of the adverb "slowly" suggests a gradual
departure from the sanity of the thoroughly modern Karachi, the new nation's
capital. To endanger this modernity with the violence of the times is to descend
into madness. An authentic Karachiite identity and, by extension, an authentic
Pakistani identity, then, derives from staying true to this model of diversity,
demographically evident and, clearly, affectively desired.

If the Lawrence Road flat represents for Hajra the tolerant diversity of
Karachi's early years as Pakistan's national capital, the house at 43-G brings
up a more forced urban nostalgia for her. Hajra's idealization of this location, one
shared with her husband, co-wife, and daughters, counters the highly valued
cosmopolitanism Hajra associates with the Lawrence Road flat by illustrating
how Hajra's "difference," her Jewishness, needed and still needs to be hidden
over the course of decades. This need to hide and even erase for a time Hajra's
identity offers a commentary on Karachi's increasing religious homogenization
but also shows a crack in Hajra's equation of diversity and tolerance in Pakistan's
first capital city. In other words, the erasure of Hajra's Jewishness casts doubt
on Hajra's own mythological origins: that cosmopolitan vision of Karachi as
the nation's first capital. On the surface, 43-G seems idyllic. It's Hajra's marital
residence, and it is spacious enough that Hajra and Zareena frequently entertain
the possibility of all five of their daughters taking up residence in their own wings
of the house once again. Thus, 43-G signifies domestic plenty and contentment.
And the family's affective attachments to the place reflect this domestic bliss.
Late in the novel, for instance, Amina, a December Pakistani in from New York,
wants nothing more than to remain at 43-G where she's convinced she's "relevant." One of the most emphatic shows of the house's affective resonance
involves Hajra's preservation/restoration efforts. While in residence at Lawrence
Road, Hajra learns that Sara and Zareena had the dining room floor at 43-G pulled
up in the rumor-fueled hope that they would find gold, left by departing Hindus
in 1947, buried beneath the original mosaic tiles (55–6). With this glimpse of the
house's past, that is, that it belonged to Hindus who left in 1947, the narrative
establishes 43-G as a site of change, even if the house's inhabitants refuse to

incorporate this fact into their sense of belonging to the house. Hajra is, for example, apoplectic over the floor, wailing, "'My beautiful floor, my house!'" exclaiming her primacy in the house as first wife (56). Hajra eventually enlists Rehana, a young woman from a modest background who has an academic interest in Karachi's architectural past, to reconstruct the floor as best she can. Following Hajra's command that "'we will put back the floor exactly as it was'" (62), Rehana, the professional restorationist, succeeds to such an extent that Hajra's other New York-returned daughters—Kulsum, Resham, and Shireen visit Karachi, too—remark "in unison, 'This looks great! I really don't see a change!'" (427). Hajra's insistence on restoring the floor rather than replacing it with wood or marble, as Zareena and Sara advocate, illustrates how the floor signifies the family's identity; Hajra views the marble and wood options as "'upstartish ideas,'" suggesting that the old mosaic floor testifies to the family's rootedness in place (63). But, such a claim of long-standing permanence obscures the house's provenance, hiding a history that does not square with Hajra's vision of her belonging to the house and to the city.

Yet, Hajra's claim to 43-G is more complicated than her possessive pronouns indicate. She marries Razzak without her family's knowledge or permission, and her father disowns her (28). Up until the novel's present in 2004, Hajra, Razzak, and Zareena perpetrate an elaborate ruse, keeping from their daughters the fact that Hajra is a Jew and not a Parsi who converted to Islam upon her marriage to Razzak (29). As with 43-G's past, Hajra's Jewishness gets erased. The fact of this ruse, despite Hajra's insistence that, in 1953, "'[e]veryone then knew my background. If they didn't say anything, it was out of respect for me and my family and respect for [Razzak]'" (29), challenges Hajra's attempt to fix an idealized Karachi through her nostalgic renderings of both Lawrence Road and 43-G. Further, it hints at a tension between Hajra's preferred narrative of the past and the reality of the life she has lived since marrying Razzak.

This tension is made manifest by the event that precipitates Hajra's departure for Lawrence Road two months prior to the novel's opening. Intent on re-embracing her Jewishness over fifty years after her marriage required her to put it aside, Hajra couples the revelation of her heritage to Sara with the announcement that "'now that [Sara does] know, we will start celebrating Yom Kippur, Roshashana, Purim, and Passover'" (32). Sara, upset over the initial revelation, and Zareena, who is consoling her, "both looked at Hajrabai, their identical eyes widened," and, in an "aloof tone," Zareenabai asks, "'What do you mean we will start celebrating? Who will start celebrating, where?'" (32). Hajra's response that she expects to celebrate her own traditions at 43-G, her long-time home, elicits from Zareena an unexpected exclusion: "'[W]e are Shia and these are not our traditions'" (32). The narrator explains that Hajra left for Lawrence Road the next day (32). Hajra's exile from what had become her family domicile is, as the narrator states, a matter of "harming herself to save herself" (32). What selves are at stake for Hajra? The self she thinks she's saving is one that accords with the vision of Karachi made manifest by the Lawrence Road flat, a self frozen in an era when Karachi represented the promise of a new Pakistan. The self she harms is one defined by Hajra's most immediate and domestic relationships as co-wife and mother: Hajra "missed her position [at 43-G] acknowledged every day by an army of people who referred to her as Bari-ma. She was Bari-ma to the entire household and to everyone who visited there" (33). At the same time, Zareena's objection to Hajra's interest in celebrating Jewish traditions takes on added resonance given the former's muhajir identity (277). The apparent irreconcilability of these two selves, underscored as it is by Zareena's insistence that they are Shia, problematizes the authenticity which Hajra's idealization of both sites seeks. Hajra's actual existence as a Jewish woman, co-wife, and mother cannot be lived in either location, for the actuality of life at Lawrence Road tells a different story than the one Hajra memorializes, and the prevalence of Zareena's perspective points to the power of the muhajir mythology to overwrite other identity scripts at 43-G. In other words, *A Matter of Detail* presents Hajra's yearnings to reclaim her "authentic" identity as a Jewish woman, manifested by the Lawrence Road flat and predicated on her account of Karachi's cosmopolitan past. And, yet, Hajra's life at 43-G, especially her efforts to fix that structure in its own idealized past, points toward the inability of either location to secure her identity.

The loss upon which Hajra's Lawrence Road nostalgia in particular focuses corresponds to the conceptual rudderlessness left in the wake of the loss of the idea of Pakistan. In effect, the achievement of a homeland for India's Muslims signaled, to borrow Thomas Blom Hansen's characterization of the end of apartheid in South Africa, "the disappearance of the blockage…that prevented true self-realization and thus could explain a range of problems and shortcomings in everyday life" (298). No longer the largest minority in a united India, the new Pakistanis achieved the power of self-determination when they achieved nationhood, or so the idea of Pakistan seemed to promise. Yet, the achievement of nationhood proved to be "a moment of uncertainty, compounded by changing relations among local, regional, and global forces," a series of changes that left "everybody in the country…to rethink themselves" beyond the alluring terms of that initiating idea (Hansen 298). Although the India-as-arch-nemesis narrative continues to predominate in both real and imagined terms in contemporary Pakistan, the uncertainty and the necessity—or opportunity—to "rethink themselves" informs the nostalgias seen in *A Matter of Detail*. Hajra, in the face of changes, returns to a vision of the past, which is also an absence or loss. But, as I've shown, Hajra's nostalgias don't stand unchallenged in Naqvi's novel, and in the context of all of these Karachi novels, the turn is toward a future orientation that locates belonging in change, movement, potential. That is, these Karachi novels identify new terms with which to articulate belonging both to the city and the nation, and these terms rely heavily on the concept of mobility.

Mobility does stand in contrast to fixity, to be sure, but, for my purposes, mobility also invites a re-purposing of familiar ideas, especially the idea of being modern that is so central to Hajra's nostalgic and idealized view of Karachi. The underlying impulse to anchor place and identity through nostalgia, evident in Hajra's efforts and desires, posits a view of place, in Peter Adey's words, "as a container—both fixed and discrete" (78). But, as Adey argues, place possesses an "inherent relativity, the inherent relatedness of things through which places actually *take* place" (78; emphasis in original). Adey's contention draws attention to how the structural elements of place, which seem permanent and largely immovable, come into meaning through processes similar to those that endow subjective identities with meaning. For Adey and for others engaged in the field of mobility studies, the putatively "solid" structures of place take on and grant meaning based on human interactions with place. In Nick Scott's view,

> [M]obilities...textur[e] the built environment in particular ways. In other words, city space, be it a building, billboard, or superhighway, gains meaning and agency through the way it variously affords and stymies the movement of bodies and other objects.
>
> (151)[10]

Thus, there's another way to look at Hajra's apparent tendency toward stasis. The security of a "modern" Karachi identity that Hajra attempts to gain by residing at Lawrence Road, for instance, attempts to stymie movement or the articulation of other claims to belonging to Karachi, be they more progressive or regressive than the one to which she is attached. Hajra is stuck between two nostalgias, neither of which will allow her to claim all the aspects of her identity.

Adam Zameenzad's 1988 novel *The 13th House* also illustrates how characters get stuck in dominant identities that, while used to explain Karachi's troubled past, do not, according to these fictions, account fully for what it means to belong to the city and to the nation. Using an unnamed first person narrator who often claims omniscience, Zameenzad's novel is set in Zia's Pakistan and also uses a house to emblematize the characters' stuckness. In this case, Zahid, a muhajir approaching middle age, rents a house for his family that represents to him an arrival of sorts, as the house's spaciousness—a sitting room plus two bedrooms—would allow him, his wife, and their two children to live like gentlefolk (6). To Zahid, in short, the house was "the fulfillment of a dream" (4). But, through his darkly comic lens, the narrator, who's known Zahid since the latter took care of him as a child, links Zahid (or, more precisely, his persistent confusion), the house, and the failures of the government, presenting the house as a symbol for how the state falsifies the very terms it uses to define citizens' belonging. The house, thus, symbolizes Zahid's misplaced affective attachment to an idea of the "nation" that best serves the state's interest. Insofar as mobility is, according to Tim Creswell, "related to power and does involve motion" (60), Zahid's confusion stands in for his limited mobility or his submission to being defined via dominant scripts. Mobility also operates out on the streets themselves, however, pointing to the reclamation of an agency the narrator deems democratic and, therefore, at odds with the power the state attempts to enforce.

Zameenzad's novel qualifies as a dark comedy for its presentation of the implausible. The novel's implausibility derives from the narrative voice itself. While an embodied character through much of the story, the narrator reveals himself at the end to be a ghost stuck at Zahid's house forever. Throughout most of the novel, this ghost narrator voices his skepticism over the mystical dynamics of the house that pull Zahid into a world populated by what the narrator subtly—and not so subtly—presents as charlatans. This disjuncture—a ghost casting suspicion on the existence of the supernatural—illustrates how, as Gillian Pye argues, "black" humor "uses implausibility as a form of 'comic insulation' against anxiety" (67). By creating a distance between the plausible and the implausible, dark humor such as the type Zameenzad's narrator deploys encourages an indirect examination of the "sites of social anxiety" (Pye 66). The use of a ghost narrator provides leeway, as can been seen by the frequency with which the narrator indulges in diatribes all of a kind with the following:

> As well as open abuse of the people by the government, open abuse of the government by the people was reaching new heights—at least in so far as it was safe to do so under the so called Defence [sic] of Pakistan Rules. These made a mockery of civil rights, but still the strikes gained momentum and demonstrations and mass rallies got larger, uglier and more frequent. Students, as usual, joined the happy throng and educational institutions (pardon the misnomer) were once again brewing trouble. Religious fanatics looted wine shops and emptied out the bottles, often orally, in order that the weaker ones might be protected from the evils of intoxication. The beards of mullahs trembled with righteous rage at obscenity and immorality, which they saw in anything that had an opening, or by any stretch of the imagination could be construed as vaguely perpendicular, round, oval, pendulous or receding. The strain on their genitalia was unbearable, and they lashed out screaming obscenities at anything 'obscene', which was practically everything. You could feel their sphincters tightening in orgiastic fury as under the tattered garb of chastity angry erections kept popping up, aching symbols of a sexually deprived society.
>
> (46)[11]

As this invective gains momentum, the narrator's critique grows more scathing and his humor more gauche. The narrator descries stifled democratic practice, an appropriate point of protest, with the mild humor of his parenthetical insertion "(pardon the misnomer)." Moving to the topic of hypocrisy, he becomes downright ribald, hedging the possibility that the response to his comments will either be outrage or knowing laughter. When ultimately placed into the context of a narrative told by a ghost, tirades such as this one beg the question of which is more absurd: Pakistan's current political conditions or a story told by a ghost? The novel's use of dark humor suggests that both register rather high on a scale of the implausible. At the same time, the humor allows for the direct acknowledgment of "sites of social anxiety."

These diatribes pepper the bulk of the narrative, which centers on Zahid's relationship with his house. Zahid's residence in the house serves not only as the novel's primary setting but also as its primary plot-driver as it is what motivates Zahid's search for help from a guru. Beyond representing to Zahid the achievement of a certain standard of living, the house also holds narrative significance because of its reputation for being haunted. Zahid knows about this reputation from the start, but he conceals this information from Jamila, his wife, nonetheless (Zameenzad 4–5, 9). Zahid is strangely unaffected by the house's "'stories'" and instead feels confusion over the happiness it brings him, for he always interprets happiness as "a harbinger of bad news." He reasons, though, that his happiness is just as likely as anyone else's, only then to become "somewhat confused as he wasn't too sure about anybody else either" (Zameenzad 4). Politics, religion, and commuting to work all join happiness as phenomena that confuse Zahid, creating an overall sense of his inability to act with purpose (Zameenzad 10, 13, 23). Inevitably, Jamila learns about the house's reputation, and her fear of the house increases after their son, who has developmental issues, has two "fits" that Jamila attributes to the house's evil. Equally as spooked by the fits, Zahid seeks out the help of a guru he meets purportedly by chance when seeking medicine for his daughter, Azra. This guru, the Shah Baba, captivates Zahid from the first. Yet, the narrator's representation of their initial meeting casts suspicion on the Shah Baba's authenticity. The guru says to Zahid, "'Children are God's greatest blessing, next only to parents. Yet both can cause great pain'" (Zameenzad 29). Preoccupied with his daughter's illness and recently conflicted over not having to care for his now deceased parents, Zahid, hearing the Shah Baba's pronouncement, feels a "current of high-voltage electricity cut through the centre of [his] being. The generality of the statement made it all the more meaningful to him'" (Zameenzad 29). Zahid's reading of the specific in the general in this instance matches his behavioral tendencies, as evidenced by his penchant for horoscopes, whose "vagueness only strengthen[ed] his faith in some mysterious way" (Zameenzad 5). The narrator connects Zahid's belief in horoscopes to his belief in the Shah Baba, a link that renders the latter suspect. This link also calls into question the Shah Baba's motives behind and abilities to bless the house, not that Zahid acknowledges this doubt. Indeed, the Shah Baba is perhaps the only force that quells Zahid's persistent sense of confusion. After his first meeting with the Shah Baba, for instance, Zahid finds himself transformed into a "strangely confident man, confident in the knowledge that all would be well…" (Zameenzad 32). And, later, the narrator reveals that, "[i]n search of security [Zahid] had to create a despot, and who more worthy than the Shah Baba?" (88). Zahid refuses to doubt the Shah Baba at his own peril; he is later arrested and incarcerated for the murder of the narrator, an act probably committed by the Shah Baba's lackies. Further, by analogizing the Shah Baba with a despot, the narrator creates a link between the guru's manipulative power—based on religious gullibility—and Zia's authority, allegorizing Zahid's relationship to the Shah Baba as a way to understand the affective pull of Zia's Pakistan.

In order to belong to his own house (and, allegorically, the nation), Zahid submits to constraints on his own figurative mobility; that is, he allows the place to define him. As the narrative progresses, the house takes on agency, holding Zahid "in the palm of its hand," for instance (Zameenzad 9). Or, later, the house takes residence in him, a dynamic the narrator describes through likening Zahid's relationship with the house to an unnatural pregnancy: "So would the house never be born but live within him and yet without him and do whatever it liked whenever it liked" (155). This metaphor endows the house itself with control over Zahid, linking his life indissolubly with the house's will. Immediately after offering this metaphor, the narrator poses a question that takes up its own paragraph: "Was it 1982, or 1971, or 1965, or 1947; or all the years in between; or could it be all the years to come?" (155). Character's link to setting also becomes the link to historical context. By first listing dates and then wondering which year it actually is, this question suggests that there's no differentiating between specific historical moments in Pakistan. Rather, the implication is that all moments bear the same dynamics, the same identities, over and over again. The associative chain created via the connections between Zahid, the house, and Pakistan's undifferentiated history foregrounds the idea of stuckness in this novel.

As I've noted, the drama played out between the house, Zahid, and the Shah Baba functions as an allegory for the political maneuverings of the state under Zia's rule, which themselves create a specific notion of the nation. And this allegory highlights how Zahid's affective attachment to the house amounts to an acceptance of the rigid identity scripts the state enforces through its politicization of Islam, as evidenced in the narrator's invective, and its corruption of the political process. At the level of plot, Zahid fixates on the idea that the Shah Baba can exorcise the house of whatever evil that is causing his son's fits. When the Shah Baba does come to the house, Zahid feels "as honored as if God in person had knocked" (156). Zahid's religious reverence for the Shah Baba coupled with his likening of the guru to a despot makes of the Shah Baba a symbol for the power resulting from state-sponsored ideas of the nation, especially during the Zia era when that dictator mutated Islam to meet political ends. The narrator makes the connection between Zahid, the house, and the nation very explicitly: "Zahid's own life was to follow the pattern of the nation in a strangely hypnotized way as if under the spell of the country's political tick-tocking. Whether the house was a silent spectator or an active instigator of events is not for me to say" (Zameenzad 48). "Hypnotized" aligns with the reverence with which Zahid approaches the Shah Baba, while also indicating the absence of Zahid's agency: he can only act at the Shah Baba's or the government's behest. "Pattern" speaks to the repetition or recurrence of the identity scripts that constrain Zahid's mobility, tying him to the house, which, despite the narrator's disingenuous demurral, operates in Zahid's mind as an agent.

What emerges is an image of Zahid enthralled by powers he cannot resist. Thus, Zahid fails to see the signs of the Shah Baba's artifice, such as the latter's inexplicable fluency in English, spoken completely without accent (123), and his impossible claims of old age, given his "strong, muscular thigh covered with a thick matting of curling hair beneath which the skin shone smooth and pearl-white" (30). So, when one of the guru's minions tells Zahid that the Shah Baba "'never touches money, literally,'" but only accepts donations for the mosque he wants built on the site of the dera in Karachi once he departs (Zameenzad 90), Zahid believes this claim to be true. Zahid's credulity is also responsible for the narrator's murder. Buffeted by his own misfortunes, the narrator decides his recovery, facilitated by the millions of rupees his mother has saved for him, depends on his departure from Pakistan. He withdraws all his money and comes to spend his last nights in the country at Zahid's house and, while there, offers Zahid and Jamila a significant sum of money to pay for their son's long-term treatment. While reticent to accept the entire sum the narrator offers—Zahid says that the narrator's generosity has "'left me too confused'" (Zameenzad 193), a sure sign he'll turn toward the security the Shah Baba represents—Zahid predictably takes five hundred rupees to donate to the Shah Baba's mosque fund. When Zahid presents the money to the Shah Baba, he "could feel a change in the air" at the dera. "There was a long, stunned silence" (Zameenzad 195). Having extracted all the requisite details about the narrator's fortune, the Shah Baba's coterie arranges for Zahid to be held up at the dera and for the narrator to be present at Zahid's house (Zameenzad 197, 199). Although the narrator's murder isn't recounted, the set up and the subsequent disappearance of the Shah Baba, his retinue, and his dera points to their involvement (Zameenzad 200). Incarcerated and tortured, Zahid spends the rest of his life "lying in the foetal position in a corner of the bleak cell like a bloodied question mark [and] looked more ridiculous by the day," if one had the sense of humor, the narrator contends, to appreciate his posture (Zameenzad 202). This final image of Zahid makes for an uncomfortable joke, one that's clearly not funny, but it nonetheless highlights the absurdity of the entire story, one told by a ghost.

Zahid's incarceration for a crime he does not commit signifies his constrained mobility, his stuckness in an identity sealed by his affective attachment to the house. As a foil, the novel offers a more expansive mobility that imagines moving through the city rather than grounding one's identity in a house. Through move-ment in the streets, the novel establishes an alternative conceptualization of belonging to the city and to the nation. The starkest example of this type of mobil-ity occurs when Zahid, his family, and the narrator are returning to the house after a day at Clifton Beach. The narrator has borrowed a friend's car, and, while being driven in a private automobile provides no end of thrill for the family, it also creates a sense of isolation as they find themselves cut off from the route back to Zahid's house. A protest obstructs their passage. With the ability "neither [to] backtrack nor [to] move forward" (75), the car's occupants watch the police "shooting real bullets this time" and engaging in "hand-to-hand combat" with the demonstrators (76). With the demonstration eventually broken, "the wounded and the dead were so speedily removed in police vans that were it not for the broken windows, looted shops and a raging fire you wouldn't have thought that the peace had been disturbed in any way at all" (Zameenzad 77). Despite his veiled sarcasm, the narrator sees these street-based activities as "a hopeful sign" (Zameenzad 76). Hope resides in an interpretation of the demonstration as "a democratic process of sorts" that serves as "proof that the government had failed" (Zameenzad 76). This interpretation emphasizes how "the people were succeed-ing. They did protest. Disastrously. But they did…Clamouring, demanding their rights, aware that they *had* rights" (Zameenzad 76). The masses' turn to the streets constitutes real democratic participation, in the narrator's view, even if the government meets this participation with state-sponsored violence. Indeed, the state's response highlights the distance between its view of proper citizenship and the people's efforts to define it in their own terms. For the narrator, these efforts prove that a "nation that had become conscious of such fundamentals [as rights] could, even if the government did nothing, achieve great things for itself" (Zameenzad 76). Significantly, the narrator distinguishes between the "nation," which he aligns with the demonstrators, and the "government," which violently suppresses the "nation." This specific idea of the nation is the most explicit example in the novel of affectively appealing identities that refuse the dominant categories the state would impose. As such, Zahid's position as unwilling spectator effectively trapped in a car only underscores the extent to which he embodies a stuck and submissive identity.

Moreover, the narrator's own observations of the lives of the less privileged also prompt his revision of what "nation" signifies. In the course of his own plotline, the narrator falls out with his wealthy father and takes up residence at a shabby hotel, a world far removed from the rarefied atmosphere of the elite. Seated at a table in the hotel's café, whose walls "were decorated with mirrors of different shapes" (Zameenzad 107), the narrator notices the many differences amongst the clientele: "[d]ifferent faces, different moulds of faces, different colours of skin, different languages, different dress, different cultures, different attitudes, different values" (Zameenzad 108). Paradoxically, "[o]ne mirror reflected all" of this variety (Zameenzad 108). The mirror metaphorizes a vision of the nation, as the narrator's subsequent reflections indicate: "If it was one nation, the whole of pre-partition India was one nation. If that was two nations, it was many. If these were one because of Islam, what about Bangla Desh, Afghanistan, Iran, Turkey; Muslim countries all over the world? What of the Muslims in India now?" (Zameenzad 108). The narrator calls into question the very foundations of the Pakistan movement by expanding the concept of "nation" to envelop diversity rather than merely accept the dominant definition of nation as homogenized group. His questions also challenge post-partition Pakistan's insistence on the unifying power of Islam, a favorite emphasis especially under Zia's rule. Much like the vision of democracy the mass demonstration conjures, the customers at the café represent to the narrator a "nation" defined by the seemingly unbounded multiplicity of Karachi itself.

Kamila Shamsie's 2002 novel, *Kartography*, also adopts a focus on the streets as a way of representing Karachi's multiple and multiplying identities. This diversity lies at the base of the novel's preoccupation with dominant historical narratives or patterns. Shamsie's novel exhibits a tension between what I've been calling stuckness in historically dominant identities, on the one hand, and efforts to represent in alternative ways the changing demographics and belongings characteristic of Karachi, on the other. As I note above in my discussion of the explanations for Karachi's turbulence, a focus on any single vector is partial.[12] Moving beyond an argument for the novel's class or ethnic concerns, I focus on how the novel attempts inclusivity, a broader understanding of claiming Karachi and the nation, through an interrogation of the putative determination of the present by the past.[13] Mobility figures into this analysis through the transgression of boundaries, literal and figurative, that throws into bold relief the pressures and the privileges of a circumscribed identity.

Kartography opens in 1986 and focuses on the friendship between Raheen and Karim, upper class thirteen year olds whose parents are also longtime friends. The chapters that follow a straight linear chronology record the intimacy of this friendship and the stresses it comes under as Karim's parents, Ali and Maheen, decide to migrate to London, partially due to the increasing violence of 1980s Karachi and, one surmises, partially in an effort to save their failing marriage. Their parents' respective marriages puzzle Raheen and Karim, because these partnerships result from a fiancé swap that occurred in 1971. Where once Zafar, a muhajir, was engaged to Maheen, a Bengali, he's now married to Yasmin, who was formerly Ali's fiancée; these overlapping love stories unfold in flashback chapters set in 1970 and 1971. The reason behind the swap—an unforgiveable outburst of anti-Bengali abuse by Zafar, Raheen's father—prompts an estrangement between Raheen and her father in the novel's advanced present, set in 1994. Through interchapters set in 1970 and 1971, the novel reveals that Zafar's real fault was his desire to live as though outside of history, as if his youth and privilege insulated him from the inequities and prejudices of the era. The breaking of his engagement with Maheen thus comes off as Zafar's efforts to protect himself from the social disadvantages of being linked to a Bengali. Karim fears that Raheen is genetically predisposed to act only in her own privileged self-interest, just as he thinks her father did.

As this brief summary suggests, the novel examines ethnic and class boundaries. Raheen, in her role as first person narrator, accurately comments that "class bound everyone together" on their side of Clifton Bridge, which is the "right" side, "in an enveloping, suffocating embrace, with ethnicity only a secondary or even a tertiary concern" (*Kartography* 160). Her choice of "enveloping" and "suffocating" to modify "embrace" and, thus, characterize her own and Karim's privilege, sets the parameters of how their mobility in Karachi defines their identity. Ironically, given the characters' privilege, a theme of constraint runs throughout Raheen's description of her life in Karachi. In the novel's early pages, for instance, thirteen year old Raheen and Karim are packed off to a farm in rural Sindh by their panicked parents who fear Karachi's escalating violence. The children's initial explorations of the countryside force Raheen to realize "how strange it was that we never walked in Karachi, not from Karim's house to mine, not from Sind Club to the Gymkhana, not from anywhere to anywhere…" (*Kartography* 17). As she grows accustomed to the rural expanse, she thinks to herself, "In Karachi we never had this freedom, this space to wander in. Too dangerous to walk around…" (*Kartography* 27). A function of her privilege, these limits on Raheen's mobility define her elevated class position. Even the opportunity to transgress these boundaries only happens because her parents have similarly wealthy friends—"decadent feudals" (*Kartography* 12)—who own a farm in Sindh.

The explicit incursion of outright "ethnic" concerns into the characters' lives introduces additional ways of understanding mobility, including in terms of the transgression of boundaries. As young adults, Raheen, Karim, and their friend Zia find themselves literally out of place when Zia's car breaks down in Mehmoodabad, the wrong side of Clifton Bridge. Much like the irony of the constraints accompanying their privilege, here the friends' literal means of mobility—Zia's car—forces them to contend with other ways of understanding how Karachi's political and material landscape shapes identities. The car troubles precipitate an encounter with a man who announces himself as a car thief and a muhajir, and who Raheen as narrator refers to as "fake-Nike man" (*Kartography* 159). The man puts both Zia and Raheen on edge, rendering her attempt to establish common ground with the man disingenuous: "'We're Karachiwallahs, too,'" she tells him, self-consciously choosing not to use "Karachiite," which would mark her as anglicized (*Kartography* 160). To Raheen's dismay, Karim is the one who connects with the man:

> "You're Muhajir," I heard Karim say to the man. For God's sake, what was he trying to do!
> "Yes, hero. What are you?"
> "Bengali."
> Zia and I both looked at him in surprise. I'd never once heard Karim identify himself that way.
>
> (*Kartography* 161)

Karim's self-identification as Bengali situates the car thief's muhajir identification as an ethnic categorization rather than an identity born out of the specifics of Pakistani history. The boundary between cultural and historical identities blurs but leaves intact the force of these markers. At the same time, Zia and Raheen's surprise at Karim's declaration of Bengaliness crosses their familiar class lines of identification, made all the more explicit by the understanding that seems to pass between Karim and the car thief, as the latter replies to Karim's revelation, "'We didn't learn anything, did we? From '71'" (*Kartography* 161). In the face of this proffered solidarity, Zia and Raheen trot out their own ethnic affiliations— hers muhajir, his Sindhi and Punjabi—as "almost a set routine—which deflected the differences in our backgrounds" (*Kartography* 162). They, too, attempt to re-establish cohesion based on their shared class position and despite Raheen's muhajir identity that logically links her to the car thief more readily than any of the other identity factors at play. Beyond once again underscoring how their limited mobility in Karachi defines the friends' privileged identities, this scene in Mehmoodabad emphasizes the movement across boundaries that complicates any single explanation for Karachi's troubles or definitions of "Karachiwallah" or "Karachiite." In other words, the rising and falling saliency of the ethnic and class identifications in this scene unstick the dominant identity categories that would otherwise disallow Karim from relating to the car thief or align the man with Raheen because of their shared muhajir identities.

These shifting identities become legible in part because of how mobile these four characters are or are not.

This scene, which brings up how structural inequities bear on mobility and enforce prescribed identities, also foils the novel's stake in promoting a different mobility through maps. "Fake-Nike man" shares his biography, telling the three friends that he "'wanted to join the civil service. I'm an educated, literate person, you know'" (*Kartography* 160). Karim quickly surmises that Sindh's quota system, which historically worked to "balance" the representation of ethnic groups in government jobs, blocks the car thief's employment opportunities. Neither Zia nor Raheen buy the man's tale, but Karim, deeply affected, comments to his friends as they leave Mehmoodabad that he "'shouldn't have come back'" to Karachi at all (*Kartography* 163). The Mehmoodabad episode brings to a head Karim's long-standing anxieties about the privileged ways he and his friends belong to Karachi. Maps become the outlet and symbol of Karim's anxieties. But, rather than fixing the city textually, Karim's many maps, some of which Raheen incorporates directly into the narrative, revise the city's topography always with an eye toward a self-aware perspective. In this way, the maps match the image of the spinning globe with which Raheen opens the novel, while emphasizing mobility and change (*Kartography* 1). Indeed, Karim's idea of a web-based inter-active map illustrates how the inhabitation of place informs a variety of identities and, as Caroline Herbert argues, how "Pakistan's identities, and Karachi itself, [are] in constant motion…" (171). In Karim's description, the interactive map is inclusive:

> "You start with a basic street map, OK, but everywhere there are links. Click here, you get sound files of Karachiites telling stories of what it's like to live in different parts of town. Click there, you get a visual of a particular street…Choice of languages in which you can read the thing. Sounds files in all kinds of dialects. Strong on graphics for people who are illiterate."
>
> (*Kartography* 300)

Envisioning the map's perpetual construction as a "'lifelong project,'" Karim also envisions cross-class access, predicting that in "'a few years…an amazing number of people will have access to [a computer] even if they don't own it themselves'" (*Kartography* 300). The open-endedness of Karim's web-based map defies the constraints and closures of the dominant identity categories imposed by the state through programs like the quota system. Further, Karim's interactive map invites participation by Karachiites on their own terms, in their own dialects and languages, creating a heterogeneous community through the map rather than a homogenous one enforced via reductive labels. Knowing and belonging to Karachi, enabled by the map's dynamism and articulation of mobile identities, thus results from telling one's own location-specific story.

The kind of belonging Karim's interactive map enables bears the potential to defy stereotypes and other types of constraining identity constructs. In facilitating the telling of individual, site-specific stories, the map could show the disjuncture

between the assumptions that lie behind an identity category and the lived experience of the person claiming that identity. In other words, the map's facilitation
of mobility, understood figuratively here, animates the everyday transgression of
categories. So, even while the novel sometimes frames mobility ironically, it also
presents mobility as a challenge to determinism. Again, the Mehmoodabad
episode illustrates this point. Skeptical of the car thief's story, Zia concludes,
"'He's probably with the MQM and you just don't want to get involved with
someone who has anything to do with these political groups'" (*Kartography*
162). Although similarly skeptical of the car thief's trustworthiness, Raheen
nonetheless takes issue with Zia's hasty conclusion, which he attempts to reinforce by claiming, "'It's the Muhajir Qaumi [sic] Movement, isn't it? And he's a
Muhajir with grievances. Two plus two equals four'" (*Kartography* 162). Raheen
challenges this math by stating, simply, that she, too, is muhajir (*Kartography*
162). Just as these cross-hatched identifications problematize any single explanation for Karachi's troubles, they also invalidate the easy correlation of identity
category and political outlook, a correlation, the novel suggests, that would serve
the government's interests. Later, amidst escalating violence, for example,
Raheen as narrator indulges a digression: "And there was a split in the MQM—
the work of the intelligence agencies, so the rumour went, who saw (or thought
they did) the efficiency of getting a group to break in two, each side turning
bloodily on the other" (*Kartography* 283). Stories told from the ground up, as
they would be in Karim's map, would similarly challenge the determinism to
which her friend Zia subscribes.

This challenging of determinism expands beyond the too easy paralleling of
identities and politics to address historical determinism as well. The car thief's
allusion to 1971, for example, signals one of the many instances in which the
novel draws on that particular era in Pakistani history in an effort to situate 1980s
and 1990s Karachi in a longer historical trajectory. When "fake-Nike man" tells
Karim that Pakistanis have learned nothing from their own past, he implies that
the discrimination he experiences as a muhajir in 1994 Karachi connects to
the discrimination against Bengalis that fueled the schism between the two wings
of Pakistan. The novel doesn't allow such an alignment, which would render
Pakistani history "stuck," to stand unchallenged, however. Rather than wholly
endorse such parallels, the novel, through Raheen's perspective, also offers many
examples that call into question this type of historical determinism. Raheen's
and Karim's parents' fiancé swap prompts the novel's treatment of 1971. Herbert
argues that this domestication of national history amounts to a movement
"towards the excessive narrativization of the *personal* in the absence of an official, *public* engagement with the losses [caused by the war] in the context of
censorship and martial law" (163; emphasis in the original). Pakistan's national
amnesia regarding 1971 can't be gainsaid, to be sure. But, the domestication
of that period by the fiancé swap storyline also invites an analysis of how power-
fully "privatized" discourses affect identity formation. In other words, the
novel plays out the extent to which Raheen's and Karim's parents' actions and
views inform their children's outlooks. Although highly individuated, this

context does allow for an examination of the validity of identifying historical parallels.

And, the novel encourages such an examination. At several points after learning of her father's anti-Bengali outburst, Raheen wonders "[w]hat...something that happened nearly a quarter of a century ago [had] to do with our lives?" (*Kartography* 211).[14] Rather than an attempt to ahistoricize her own identity, Raheen's question instead promotes a recognition of the contingencies that do shape but don't determine identities. Such a recognition counters Karim's line of thought; he accuses Raheen of being her father's daughter:

> "[Zafar] thought he could pretend the war and everything going on had nothing to do with him, or with [Maheen]; he pretended and pretended that the outlines in which they lived didn't matter, until one day it was at his door and things inside him that he never acknowledged, never tried to deal with, came out.
> ...
> "And you're the same. You're the same, Raheen."
>
> (*Kartography* 219)

Karim's generational conflation mirrors the car thief's ethno-historical one. Both examples confuse how the past relates to the present, however. That is, Karim and the car thief read determinism and inevitability in the relationship, illustrating one of the ways the present makes use of the past or how history gets stuck. For her part, Raheen appears to accept her mother's logic. Without justifying Zafar's words or actions, Yasmin holds that the entire incident forced Zafar "'to look [at] the country straight in the eye'" (*Kartography* 251), by which she means that "'he didn't pretend like [the incident] hadn't happened'" (*Kartography* 252). Rather than determinism, Yasmin's point speaks to historical mindfulness. Such an attentiveness gives due consideration to the past without rendering previous eras as equivalent or even analogous to the present. A mindful attitude's approach to the past's relation to the present aligns with the ground-up dynamic Karim hopes to incorporate into his interactive map. Belonging can then come about through the unique or idiosyncratic terms that characterize the habitation in or mobility around geographical place and identity narratives.

In Bina Shah's 2004 novel *The 786 Cybercafé*, two places—Karachi itself and the titular café—highlight mobility or the ways that movement within and between places endows identities with meaning. Jamal, the novel's central protagonist, is a twenty-something "entrepreneur" striving for success amidst the forces of overpopulation and underemployment in early twenty-first century Karachi. With drive but no resources or technological know-how, Jamal must rely on his friend Yasir, who has money thanks to his father's success, and his own younger brother Abdul, who has studied computers and technology at university, in order to realize his dream of opening a cybercafé on Tariq Road, a busy commercial center in Karachi. The three young men succeed in their venture, but not without difficulty. The virtual openness and freedom of the internet attract trouble both from those who would exploit these attributes and those who would censor them completely. As a result, the café becomes a target for arson, which puts an end to the three young men's collaboration. Jamal, however, remains undaunted and, with sheer entrepreneurial grit, re-opens another cybercafé with his own resources. This brief plot summary identifies some rather conventionalized markers of a suitably "modern" identity, at least from a twenty-first century standpoint: access to the internet and the technological education necessary to run a business that grants such access, not to mention the socio-economic benefits of entrepreneurship. Yet, these markers remain at the surface of a more deeply humanistic definition of belonging to Karachi. While problematic in its theoretical foundations, the humanism the novel promotes is unlike the allure of the idea of Pakistan and the promise of self-determination that the new nation held out for India's Muslims. Instead, this novel creates an affectively compelling sense of belonging out of a full awareness of Karachi's constraints and limitations. Further, via Jamal's ambition and resiliency, and even Yasir's rebellion against his father, the novel's figuration of belonging stands in opposition to the bureaucratization of identity that the state enacts, a dynamic brought to the fore by a blackmail scheme targeted at the café.

Karachi serves as more than a backdrop in Shah's novel. The city's fungal growth and attendant if paradoxical economic vibrancy initially provide the primary set of obstacles to the type of life for which Jamal and Yasir strive, thus helping to illustrate how movements, constrained or enabled, contribute to the construction of the identities of places and individuals alike. From the novel's opening paragraphs, Karachi takes shape as a grueling city "punish[ed]" by a scorching heat "with depressing regularity." The city's weather dictates how its inhabitants live:

> Most of the people of Karachi (the eighty seven percent who could not afford air conditioning) greedily sucked cold drinks through cheap plastic straws, touched their faces to slabs of ice from the local ice-seller, stole a few hours' rest in the cool of an air-conditioned mall or cinema hall. But the relief was always temporary; the heat made it impossible to think, or plan for action.
>
> (11)

The temporariness of the reprieve most Karachiites enjoy and, importantly, the impotence caused by the unrelenting discomfort metaphorizes the constraints under which these Karachiites live: the city's most basic conditions weaken the majority of Karachiites, making the expenditure of any effort bootless. The third person omniscient narrator details just how hopeless the situation is by locating "Jamal and his friends" among the "thousands of young men just like them [who] roamed the streets of Karachi, knocking on the same doors for the same few hundred jobs" (12). Starkly different from the Karachi Hajra idealizes and inhabits in Naqvi's *A Matter of Detail*, the reality of these limited opportunities squares with what Jamal has always known about Karachi, having grown up there, the narrator tells us, in the 1990s. During this time and through to the novel's present, Karachi is a "wasteland of failed opportunities," except for where that other thirteen percent who are unaffected by the city's heat are concerned (30). Naturalized through the weather metaphor, the obstacles, phrased as class restrictions, which Karachi puts in front of the likes of Jamal produce lethargy rather than agency.

Yet, by also involving Yasir, Jamal's privileged friend, in the café, the novel introduces another sort of mobility not bound by the same environmental constraints. By showing the differences between how Jamal and Yasir experience Karachi, the novel begins its project of developing an affectively appealing identity not easily categorized by staid identity markers, such as class or even ethnicity. Jamal's friend since school days, Yasir deliberately defines his identity in a much different way than his friend; whereas, early in the novel, Jamal has "sharp ways," a "need to cut others short, [and] the desire to do it quickly and sneakily" (34), Yasir wants to develop the café with "truth, decency, and honor," characteristics that align with Islam and that are not, in Yasir's estimation, "incompatible with life even in a big city as fast-paced and cutthroat as Karachi" (36). Both young men understand how Karachi operates. But, while Jamal initially sees the necessity of working the system, Yasir appears to hold a much more optimistic view of Karachi, perhaps one informed by the ease with which he moves around the city as the son of a wealthy businessman. As evidenced by the names he gives his sons—Saddam and Osama—Yasir's religiosity seems to verge on the extreme, but his motives for embracing Islam so explicitly point to another story. Deemed by the narrator to be more of a "Muslim hippie than a Muslim fundamentalist," Yasir uses religion as the "Eastern equivalent of tattoos, weird hairstyles, and punk clothes that tormented Western teenagers' parents" (40). As this analogous list of attributes hints, Yasir's religiosity constitutes his rebellion against his father, an acting out motivated by his father's "cold-hearted materialis[m]," for, despite the fact that his father "paid taxes and zakaat," the older man refused to lend money without interest (40). Yasir's turn away from the privilege his father's success affords him coincides with his turn toward a life he deems more fulfilling because less materialistic, a turn toward developing the cybercafé with Jamal. Thus, Yasir's association with the venture shifts what the entire project is about: not wholly class-related, the café also promises defining and achieving success via an alternative route not entranced by pure profit.

Moreover, the café allows for the articulation of identity not bound to ethnicity markers either. The novel presents Yasir's father's success as a feature of his muhajir identity, rooting this community's prosperity initially in "the firmament of the fledgling nation" and then attributing the achievements of the subsequent generation to which Yasir's father belongs to the "values and attitude of survival" these first Pakistanis passed on to their children (39). Yasir's rebellion against his father stands in for a refusal to embrace this ethnic identity and its reigning mythology. Indeed, on a surface level, Yasir's defining identity category is Islamic, but, more notably, it also signifies the diminished allure of the idea of Pakistan and how the muhajir community in Karachi adapted this idea into the foundation of their definition of belonging to Pakistan. Yasir's long friendship with Jamal further illustrates how their shared stakes in the café gesture toward an alternative identity with strong affective appeal. Yasir's father, the narrator reveals, has never been able to figure out why the two boys are friends, for, to him, Jamal is a "rascal, a good-for-nothing punk" (42). Read historically, the father's antipathy may well stem from Jamal's Sindhi identity. And the reverse applies as well. Just as Yasir inherits (and later rejects) his father's muhajir myths, Jamal receives his own father's view that "the Sindhi man in Karachi had been born at a permanent disadvantage" (23), unlike the "Punjabis and Mohajirs [who] were at the very top of the order, having taken over and manipulated all the systems in order to serve their own interests…" (24). Jamal, like Yasir but to a lesser degree, also rejects his father's ethnic-based views, as evidenced by his personal and business relationship with Yasir and even his own decision not to accept the status quo as handed down by his father. Both young men, thus, reject the existing identity discourses that would prescribe their opportunities—for good and bad—and deny the very possibility of their friendship.

The Karachi into which both Jamal and Yasir are born—that is, the experience of place predicated upon their familial ties, which are themselves created by history—delineates the horizon of each character's movement, thereby shaping their identities in ways both characters find unfulfilling. The cybercafé functions as an alternative place that, although nestled within the larger metropolis, counters Karachi's constraints. For both Jamal and Yasir, the café signifies the possibility of change. Although Yasir asks for his father's help in securing the retail space for the café, the younger man's participation in the venture allows him to test his conviction that one can conduct business in Karachi with "truth, decency, and honor" (36). The café's very name, The 786 Cybercafe, which is "the numerical code for 'Bismallah', In the Name of God" (33), impresses Yasir. And, later, he finds his own misgivings about the service the café provides uninformed: "Yasir's fears about the 786 Cybercafé centered on the fact that all sorts of vulgar things existed on the internet. But he'd had no idea that people were using the net to put out the word of God" (175). In terms of mobility, Yasir's ability to see the internet as an instrument through which he can further develop his piety illustrates how his interaction with this place enables an identity he has chosen over one he received through the circumstances of his birth, which endow him with familiar identity markers including class and ethnicity. The idea that the cybercafé as place facilitates a fuller sense of agency hints at the humanism that lies at the base of the novel's new definition of belonging to Karachi and to the nation. Tied to this power of choice is the possibility of change.

The cybercafé resonates in much the same way for Jamal. The prospect of proprietorship makes Jamal feel "as though he were evolving from a subhuman into a noble, mighty figure" (45). As Jamal starts to feel human, a sense he's experiencing for the "first time" in his life (45), he starts to alter his understanding of how he'll move through Karachi in the future. Out celebrating with Yasir and Abdul, for instance, Jamal sees "garish billboards that advertised Pepsi and mobile phones and huge, larger-than-life chocolate ice cream bars." This visual spectacle hypnotizes Jamal, "lull[ing] him into thoughts about the good life" (67). And these thoughts feed his pride, for, as the owner of the cybercafé, Jamal now knows "he wouldn't always be the passenger in a small car, dwarfed and over-taken by people whose cars were larger and faster..." (68). Unmistakably marked by a recognizable consumerism and rather cliché, Jamal desires to get out of the passenger's seat through his entrepreneurial efforts. As it does with Yasir, the cybercafé as place endows Jamal with a humanistic sense of agency notably lack-ing in his sense of his earlier status in Karachi. The narrator's use of an automo-bile metaphor to convey this agency also emphasizes the idea of mobility as identities changing because of how they travel amidst places. Further, the novel posits these identities through mobility as directly connected to Karachi and to Pakistan. By the novel's epilogue, set a full year after most of the plot's events, Jamal has achieved enough success to buy himself a Suzuki, a feat he accom-plishes by "presenting himself [to the car dealer] as an entrepreneur with a stead-ily growing business" (308). In terms of literal mobility, the novel establishes early on that Yasir has a car, while Jamal must rely on mass transit. Jamal's newly acquired Suzuki signals the degree to which he acts with agency and, thus, has secured his belonging in Karachi. In fact, Jamal drives his brother, Abdul, to the airport when the latter departs for Canada to continue his education. While admitting some envy, Jamal "had a feeling that he was tied to Pakistan. He couldn't leave, the way Abdul could" (311). In a concrete sense, the resurrec-tion of the café after the arson binds Jamal to Pakistan and to Karachi more specifically. But, by pointing out that "a new tenacity had been born in him" (312), the narrator also makes the point that Jamal prioritizes this strong sense of belonging even over the possibility of material gain. Further, Jamal's "tenacity" is a future-oriented conviction that his own aspirations will shape Karachi.

The novel cements Jamal's affective appeal by representing his encounter with corruption in masculine terms. The café as place is a "man-made domain" (296), a "dream come true for hundreds of boys" (121). The café's gendered space thus becomes the proving ground for competing masculinities: on the one side is Jamal, Yasir, and Abdul, with their aspirations and largely good inten-tions; on the other is Mushtaq, a city functionary, who is described repeatedly as a "small man" (182, 183). Mushtaq cases the café as if a rat, "scuttling around the alleys, casting his yellow eyes on the walls of the cybercafé" (181). Intent on extorting bribes from Jamal because of the café's illegal operation of VoIP technologies, Mushtaq manages to make the cybercafé feel "like being in Karachi Central Prison" (191), a location preeminently associated with the law-and-order functions of the state bureaucracy. The authorities prohibit the operation of such internet protocols, as the narrator explains, for they take business away from the state-run phone company. Demanding a cut of the profits, Mushtaq forces Jamal to continue operating the VoIP even after Yasir and Abdul have shamed Jamal for setting it up in the first place (194). Mushtaq clearly embodies the corrup-tion of the state structure. More damning, however, is how he leverages funda-mentalist suspicion over the open access of the internet by spreading rumors that the café is un-Islamic, because it doesn't censor websites (185) and then extorting even more money from Jamal for protection from "'religious mobs, over-inquisitive investigators, and...[his] superiors'" (194). Jamal sees the entire situation as "so predictable that it would have made him laugh, if it hadn't been happening to him" (193). This predictability makes a connection between the corrupt state structure and Karachi's social and cultural tensions. That is, the novel suggests that the state itself exploits and politicizes the explanatory power of ethnic, religious, and/or class conflict to cover its own self-serving interests. Further the Mushtaqs who operate in the structure view the world as "dog-eat-dog," meaning that they expect everyone else to fall into their pre-assigned spot in the structure.

Jamal's eventual triumph over Mushtaq, the café's unsolved arson notwith-standing, resolves these competing masculine identities in the former's favor, thus signaling the ascendancy of the affectively appealing identity Jamal repre-sents. Not aware of the amnesty announced by the PTCL (Pakistani Telecommunication Company Ltd.) that would overlook the "'unscrupulous activities [of those who] are taking valuable revenue away from the state body'" (281), Mushtaq comes to the café to collect his bribe. As he demands payment, the narrator describes how "[h]e drew himself up to his full height of five foot six and stretched his neck so that the Adam's apple bobbed up and down in his scrawny throat" (283). In contrast, the narrator immediately reminds the reader of "Jamal's good looks, his restless, wiry body" (284), highlighting the latter's greater appeal. Armed with the amnesty, Jamal can laugh at Mushtaq's threat to tell the police about the VoIP. Jamal's laughter infuriates Mushtaq, while it also renders him impotent: "The balance of power was shifting away from him, as if solid ground had turned to sand and was suddenly falling from under his feet" (285–6). In the face of Jamal's masculinity, his fortitude, and his good luck, the corrupt bureaucratic structure that Mushtaq represents and tries to impose on Jamal crumbles. And, given that Jamal re-opens the café a year after it burns to the ground, the identity Jamal embodies prevails into the future. Jamal's ability to change, enabled to a large extent by his interaction with place or, in short, his mobility, represents a new vision for belonging, far preferable to the inflexibility and rapaciousness of bureaucratic structures interested only in exploitation.

6   The Zamindari System

One way to understand the idea of Pakistan is as a coming to consciousness of a collective uniqueness that required political distinction. As much of the fiction dealing with the 1947 partition and the 1971 war indicates, this idea intertwined Muslim political self-determination with lofty ideals for the construction of a just and equitable society. As idea became nation and as the trauma of national disintegration provided another opportunity for collective reflection on the transition from idea to nation, the fictions I've already discussed present a spectrum of reactions to and critiques of the challenges of implementing the agenda of a political party as the basis of new nation. While Shah Nawaz's *The Heart Divided*, for example, concludes optimistically with both Zohra and Sughra hoping that the new nation of Pakistan can live up to their socialist and feminist ideals, Shahbano Bilgrami's *Without Dreams* outlines Pakistan's failure to achieve such lofty goals as evidenced by the break-up of the two wings of the nation. Moreover, some of the fictions dealing with the transition from idea to nation figure the nation's bureaucratic structures—its manifestation as a state— as the locus of affective attachment. In other words, if the affective resonance of the idea of Pakistan as represented in these fictions is one way of measuring the idea's trenchancy and success, then the transition's success also hinges in part on the ability of the state to posit and promote the new nation itself as the affective center that holds its citizens together. In Khushwant Singh's *Train to Pakistan* and Sorayya Khan's *Five Queen's Road*, the abstraction of the nation gets concretized through its bureaucratic structures, such as the civil service and the various property acts. These fictions suggest that such bureaucratic structures facilitate (or obstruct, as the case may be) the characters' senses of belonging to the nation through their abilities to include or exclude.

As the fictions I discuss in this section demonstrate, however, affective attachments to the nation as a broad collective identity do not always result from characters' reliance on state structures. This chapter extends the region-specific focus inaugurated by Singh's *Train to Pakistan* through its concentration on the connections between urban and rural locations in the Punjab. But, unlike Singh's novel, which posits the state as a force that enables the transition from colony to nation, thereby drawing affective attachments, the fictions discussed in this chapter locate the zamindari class as the affective center, signaling an end run around any state or national formation. That is, this section's focus on urban and rural locations in the Punjab reveals that belonging derives from regionally-based relationships, often calibrated by class, that can flagrantly contravene the dictates of the official state. Unlike how the state mediates national belonging in some of the fictions I've already discussed, in this section's fictions, the sense of belonging conferred by the state-like actors supersedes and, given its absence, appears to obviate the need for a broader national belonging. Further, given the long history behind regional hierarchies, these fictions suggest that the state-like actors' centrality in any given location hinders if not obstructs the nation's ability to attract and hold its citizens affectively. More precisely, Nadeem Aslam's *Season of the Rainbirds* (1994), selections from Daniyal Mueenuddin's *In Other Rooms, Other Wonders* (2009), and Mohsin Hamid's *Moth Smoke* (2000) all figure the power of the land-owning or zamindari class as dominating the structures that punctuate the characters' daily lives. In this way, the zamindars themselves function as state-like actors as they establish the norms governing these locations and adjudicate with what seems to be inviolate authority. The zamindar's dominance refracts even what appear to be the types of differences, especially between the rural and the urban, that would otherwise challenge the unity of collective identification. Yet, the unity of identification under the zamindar's authority isn't always a re-enforcement of a broader national identity. In the end, the zamindari system serves as the center that holds for the characters involved, even as that center alternately marginalizes and includes.

In a recent special issue of *Modern Asian Studies* entitled *From Subjects to Citizens: Society and the Everyday State in India and Pakistan, 1947–1970*, editors Taylor Sherman, William Gould, and Sarah Ansari identify the concept of the "everyday state" as a productive critical avenue into the "development of popular, public cultures" during this period in South Asia (2). Mindful of the "ambiguity and complexity of the boundaries between state and society," the issue's editors and contributors "explore the interplay between the rhetorical, ideological platforms set out in New Delhi and Karachi and the interpretations of these agendas in different localities" (2–3). In this section, I adopt this concern with the development of public cultures encapsulated in the phrase "everyday state," but rather than examine "official" state proclamations and actions, I analyze Hamid's, Aslam's, and Mueenuddin's works to see how they represent the state in their fictionalized settings. My analyses produce not a picture of the Pakistani state itself but rather one of a competing state-like actor: the zamindar. These fictions frame the traditional landowning class as the center that holds, both materially and affectively, thereby blurring the line between what could be recognized as a national "fellow feeling" and the state. The zamindar provides employment, food, counsel, even while he also manipulates his dependents and the state's authority itself, both explicitly and implicitly, so as to preserve his privilege and power. Despite the stark difference in setting—from posh Lahore to rural Punjab—these fictions, I contend, illustrate the ineffectiveness if not the irrelevance of the Pakistani state and, in its stead, posit the zamindari system as the state's more powerful shadow. My literary analyses focus on the workings of gossip in each text to illustrate how the zamindar substitutes for the state itself. Aslam's, Hamid's, and Mueenuddin's works all represent zamindari authority or, more properly, its maintenance through gossip and rumor, both in content and in form. I will develop in detail below how each of these fictions' structures manifest gossip's dynamics. More broadly, gossip as a type of discourse has a distinct and shifting relationship to power. While conventional views hold that gossip is frivolous and "idle," scholars in various fields, including anthropology and literary studies, contend that, in some instances, gossip can reinforce collective norms and, in others, can work to subvert them.

"Feudal" is the adjective that most frequently modifies the zamindari system in Pakistan. For precision's sake, I adopt Ayesha Siddiqi's definition of the word, which she says "denotes a set of economic and political relations and a pattern of social behaviours" (174). Add to Siddiqi's formulation of the zamindari system its other infrastructural functions, such as providing basic services and maintaining a version of law and order on a localized level, and the ways this system operates not only in a state-like fashion but also as a broader affective force become clear. That is, the role of the land-owning class expands any notion of the "everyday state" to include relations played out in arenas normally placed outside the purview of the official state. Indeed, Aslam's, Hamid's and Mueenuddin's fictions illustrate how the zamindar's authority exceeds that of the state's, subordinating bureaucratic, religious, and legalistic institutions even as it pervades the most intimate aspects of characters' lives. As the zamindar's authority serves to structure and delimit the characters' lives, it becomes the affective center that binds collective identity, oftentimes by demarcating through gossip who does and does not belong. Further, the zamindar's authority maintains its power through the social, political, and economic relations it structures and polices. Christophe Jaffrelot characterizes the zamindari system as "interdependent" in that laborers and others within the zamindar's sphere of influence put his interests above even those of their own kinship network (203). Talukder Maniruzzaman describes this interdependence less generously as a "beck and call" relationship wherein tenants do "the bidding of their landlords," especially in political contexts (85). Economic power coheres to political power, making the zamindar the foundation of his underlings' material survival. The zamindar's influence over and regulation of social relations follow from this consolidation of economic and political power.

The zamindari system's centrality, its (infra)structural and affective positioning, derives from a history that pre-dates Pakistan, both as idea and as nation. According to Siddiqi, social, economic, and political power began to consolidate around landownership because of British colonial practices, post-1857. The British bought "allegiance in exchange for land" (180), a transaction that was intrinsically feudal in that it "involved benefitting from the creation of local social classes that would guarantee the interests of the colonial masters" (Siddiqi 181). Although a practice meant to solidify and centralize British authority, this land-for-allegiance policy was also place-specific. The social class created by this practice—the zamindar class—was, thus, integrated at a local level even while it served as a conduit or intermediary for the colonial authority.[1] As David Gilmartin argues, "The British imperial state legitimized its authority...by acting as the central systemizer and protector of an indigenous structure of local, kin-based social organization" (*Empire* 37). At the localized site, the creation of the zamindari system "impacted on relations within society," Siddiqi contends, "since individuals, groups, tribes or clans required state patronage to enhance their power and financial worth" (181). From its colonial inception, the functions of the modern land-owning class have consistently blurred the lines between state and society, existing as a network of relations that has adhered for generations.

The Pakistani state reinforced these colonial land policies. Siddiqi argues that, in 1965, the Pakistani government "updated" the British Colonization of Land Act 1912, which itself was a reinscription of the Alienation of Land Act 1900 (180–1). This latter legislation insured a "stable agrarian society," in Gilmartin's view, over promoting "the free working of natural economic laws" (*Empire* 28). Part and parcel of this political stability was the British affirmation of the "significance of the tribal structure" (Gilmartin, *Empire* 28). More pointedly, Gilmartin frames the Alienation of Land Act 1900 as an instrument of the legitimation of zamindar authority, as the "[c]ontrol of land had increasingly come to dictate social and political status in the Punjab" (31). Further, through his reference to the comments made by a British official in the years immediately following the Act's passage, Gilmartin illustrates how the Alienation of Land Act 1900 made plain that the British "'identifie[d] political advantage with [the zamindar's] contentment and well-being, not with the contentment and well-being of the whole mass of its subjects'" (qtd. in Gilmartin, *Empire* 32). The historical construction of the zamindari system by both the British colonial system and the Pakistani state creates and reinforces a class of powerful people who, initially, acted as proxies for the state and have come eventually to function as a shadow of the state, a shift that surely complicates Pakistan's attempts at establishing a functional democracy.

Pakistan's long history of toothless land reforms illustrates how the contemporary zamindari system both obstructs genuine democratic practices and, often, circumvents the authority of the state itself. Talukher Maniruzzaman contends that, as early as the late 1940s and early 1950s, land reform legislation was ineffective (86–7). Ian Talbot observes that, although land reforms under Ayub were "hailed at the time as a major landmark which abolished feudalism," they were, in fact, "far from being radical" (165). Siddiqi joins Talbot in this assessment, and both scholars claim that ZA Bhutto's attempts at land reform were similarly lacking in substance (Talbot 231; Siddiqi 79). Indeed, Bhutto's reforms proved ironic, in Talbot's estimation, for, instead of reducing landlord power, they "encouraged Punjabi landlords to enter the PPP's ranks in order to safeguard their position" (231). In the decades following, Pakistan's return to military dictatorships saw not just the continued ineffectiveness of land reforms but also the streamlining of the zamindar's authority under Zia and how it directly benefitted the Army under Musharraf (Siddiqi 175, 185). The failure of the Pakistani government's land reform legislation appears inversely related to the increase in zamindari power, as the latter class officially infiltrates the nation's political strata, thereby complementing the "unofficial" powers they have traditionally wielded.

One of the most explicit ways to gauge the increase in zamindari authority from the colonial to the national setting is through its ability not only to circumvent but also to subordinate the state's authority. If, in an ideal democratic context, a state's purpose is to provide the (infra)structural support necessary to bring about social, economic, and political equality, then the zamindar's ascendency tarnishes that ideal insofar as land ownership on this scale represents, in Maniruzzaman's terms, "a cynical pursuit of sheer power" (87). Similarly, Siddiqi argues, in contrast to India's post-independence abolition of feudal landownership, "Pakistan's leadership [...] did not offer any substantive national goal" (75). Instead, scholars trace the rise of zamindar authority to the point that, in Maniruzzaman's estimation, "even the Deputy Commissioners and Superintendents of Police had to seek the patronage of feudal lords to remain at one station" (94). Moreover, Siddiqi argues that the rise of what she calls "military agriculturists" (183) transformed the Army from a powerful state institution into adherents of the "arcane feudal-colonial tradition" (181). As such, "the military became an instrument of feudalism and part of the feudal class" (Siddiqi 184). The key word here is "instrument." Siddiqi's argument shows a shift in the zamindari class's position from intermediary between state power and the masses to the base of power that now has its own intermediaries (i.e. the Army). Further, the Army's instrumentality, from a zamindari perspective, also demonstrates how the landowning class subordinates elements of the official state to its own state-like authority. The fictions I discuss in this section all figure the landowning class as a state-like authority. Even more, they represent the zamindar's influence as pervasive, subordinating, and, to some extent, even "moral." Gossip becomes the key literary device for the circulation and reinforcement of the zamindar's authority. But, as I discuss below, gossip, as it informs these fictions' structures, also identifies the weak spots in this authority.

If, as scholars contend, an interest in the "everyday state" is a way to analyze a collective's shared experience of the state's quotidian functions, then gossip presents itself as a reasonable site at which to examine the interface between state (or state-like) authority and social relations.[2] Gossip is, after all, the "very blood and tissue of [community]" (Gluckman 308). Further, given that my purpose is to illustrate how these fictions use gossip thematically and structurally to represent the zamindari system as the dominant state-like actor, Gabriela Hilti's observation of gossip's etymology proves suggestive. According to Hilti, gossip derives from "godparent, a figure who acts as a replacement or substitution for the biological parent" (41). In the Christian traditions that include the concept of a godparent, there is also the idea that this "substitute" parent is responsible for the godchild's moral upbringing. If we take "gossip" as a generalized concept rather than as an individual person, then gossip can represent a substitute system of norms.

Quite apart from its moral status, gossip can reinscribe or contest social norms.[3] According to Max Gluckman's seminal anthropological treatment of gossip, this form of communication provides social cohesion since it "maintains [a community's] values" (308). Patricia Meyer Spacks makes a similar point, arguing simply that gossip "expresses a worldview" (15). Hardly monologic, such a worldview takes shape through "extended interchange" (Spacks 19), a dynamic that leads Spacks to conclude that gossip's "[p]articipants assure one another of what they share" (22). The assurance comes about through gossip's maintenance of values, achieved via hierarchies and exclusions (Gluckman 309, 311). Gossip allows everyone to know their place. Importantly, gossip as "extended interchange" or, as Stacey Margolis puts it, a "network" (717) suggests its thorough permeation throughout all social levels. And, because it's a form of communication that relies on participation, gossip also grants its participants an active role in the interchange, thereby encouraging a sense of purposeful collaboration in a system that may not otherwise bestow much agency on individuals. The point here is that gossip's power, whether oppressive or subversive, is also diffuse, making the question of context integral to understanding what norms gossip reinscribes or contests (Gluckman 312).

At the same time, gossip as a literary device can also locate the vulnerabilities in the power structures associated with the zamindari system as these fictions represent it. To engage in gossip is to be in search of the latest news, the additional detail. While the individual who has the "juicy gossip" may have power, this power is transitory, for the very possibility of yet more breaking news means that power can shift between participants. This process of interchange, as Alla V. Tovares describes it, shows how gossip defers definitive closure:

> [G]ossip as a speech genre is a dialogue…where participants' rejoinders contribute to and co-construct the on-going conversation. [It is also] polyphonic in the sense that speakers weave a number of different, sometimes contradictory, voices into the tapestry of their conversation and by doing so create new meaning…
>
> (469)

The shared construction of meaning Tovares describes suggests the open-endedness of gossip: there's always more to the story. Gossip's irresolution has several more implications. According to Hilti, the impossible desire to know the story fully results in its being "told again and again in different versions…" (42), which, for Spacks, illustrates to a pronounced degree how "filtered" the story is (8–9). Structurally, this narratorial variety can take a patchwork shape, wherein the text (in)directly includes letters, overheard conversations, etc. (Vermeule 103). Such narratorial variety, moreover, insures that the story's "meaning can never be 'anchored'" (Johnson 52–3). Or, as Margolis contends, meaning is delayed or interrupted, two "technical difficulties of gossip" (714). Together, these insights into the functions of gossip illustrate how fictions that employ gossip structurally as well as thematically refuse the certainty of the very power or social forces that motivate the act of gossip in the first place.

Aslam's, Mueenuddin's, and Hamid's texts all further develop the interactions between gossip, the zamindari system, and the everyday state through their structures. In the abstract, "structure" is a key feature of all three of these terms. Gossip implies a pre-existing and hierarchized social structure, as I mention above, that supports the relations between individuals and makes gossip worth knowing and sharing. The above discussion of critical attitudes toward gossip also establishes that this form of discourse can work to reinforce or challenge this structure's dominant norms. The sociopolitical contexts in which I am situating my analyses of Aslam's, Mueenuddin's, and Hamid's fictions specifies this social order by identifying the zamindar as the authoritative and, at times, affective center of these norms. The zamindar's centrality leads directly to another structural consideration: that of the everyday state. Once again, a concern with the everyday state includes an examination of infrastructure, manifested as the institutions and authorities that inform custom and that shape individuals' experiences of collective belonging on a daily basis. Thus, my analyses of these fictions' narrative structures serve as both a logical and obvious way to explore how gossip involving the zamindar imagines the workings of the everyday state.

Nadeem Aslam's 1993 novel *Season of the Rainbirds* focuses roughly on a week in the life of an unexceptional rural Punjabi village during which a number of extraordinary events, including the murder of a judge, the delivery of mail presumed lost for nineteen years, and an assassination attempt on General Zia's life, take place. Alamgir Hashmi's observation that the novel conjures an atmosphere of ordinariness ("Survey" 224), coupled with Tariq Rahman's assessment that the novel features "the trivialities of existence [...] and the small but vital details which make up a world" ("Review" 219), immediately calls to mind the "everyday state." Set in 1982, the novel revolves around Maulana Hafeez; Azhar, the Deputy Commissioner; and Mujeeb Ali, the zamindar, and features a third person narrative voice, which frequently favors the perspectives of the maulana and the Deputy Commissioner. The relations between the three primary characters elaborate on the "state" aspects of that phrase, showing how the zamindar performs the functions of the state while also fulfilling additional social, political, and economic roles. The novel also includes five short italicized sections, narrated in the first person, whose connection to the main plotline remain irresolute. I use gossip as a focal point in my examination of both the main narrative and these italicized interruptions. With respect to the novel's primary narrative line, gossip circulates information often before official outlets do. Nonetheless, the gossip frequently extends the zamindar's authority, which is the only consequential site of power. Just as my above discussion of gossip contends, however, the novel's structure, its seemingly random juxtaposition of italicized first person segments amidst the main storyline, refuses the otherwise totalizing authority of the zamindar by presenting snippets of stories at some indeterminate remove from this authority.

Each of the primary characters embodies a different type of authority or influence over the rest of the novel's characters. Clearly, Maulana Hafeez represents a traditional religious perspective, though not one whose hold is absolute.

The village has a second mosque, led by Maulana Dawood, whose narrative presence is in name only. Azhar stands in for state authority, making his involvement with Elizabeth Massih, a Christian woman, all the more salacious and problematic for the villagers. As a member of the landowning class, Mujeeb Ali controls most of the village's and villagers' affairs through overt force, coercion, and straight up tradition. The extraordinary events of this single week in the village's life highlight the relational dynamics between these three characters, thereby making explicit the zamindar's ascendant position over both the state and religion. And, gossip is the means by which power circulates within these dynamics, thereby demonstrating the discourse's plot-level function in addition to its structural influence.

Mujeeb Ali serves as the locus of the village's power dynamics. The third person narrative voice of the novel's primary storyline specifically historicizes Mujeeb's lineage. The Ali family's fortune and power result from nineteenth century British largesse. Over the decades since, the family's "wealth has increased tenfold...mile upon mile of fishing rights, hundreds of acres of woodlands, hundreds of acres of farmland...The family owned twelve towns" (*Season* 67). Notably, this passage equates the Ali family's ownership of a dozen towns with its control over land and water rights, conflating the control of the socioeconomic life of manmade organizations with control over natural resources. The implication is that the Ali family similarly determines and polices the use of the inhabitants of these towns. Mujeeb Ali inherits and perpetuates this conflation. When an elderly illiterate laborer protests to Mujeeb Ali's overseer because the latter refuses to pay him his wage, for instance, Mujeeb does not intervene directly to insure the old man's welfare. When he does finally get paid, the old man "boldly" offers, "'I've worked on your lands since the days of your grandfather'" (*Season* 35–6). Despite the old man's assertiveness, he remains subservient to the generations-old tradition Mujeeb Ali represents.

Indeed, the novel deploys much symbolism to establish Mujeeb Ali's traditional centrality. As Azhar, the Deputy Commissioner, surveys Mujeeb's estate, the narrative voice relays how the family owns most of the "richest agricultural land in the country" (*Season* 37), positioning Mujeeb Ali, his forebears, and, presumably, his descendants as national providers. Water bounds these lands on three sides, a geographical reality that allows Mujeeb to remind "a gathering during the run-up to the last elections [that they were] surrounded by water and on the fourth side [by his] family's land; so if [they] won't support [the family, he] will drive [them] into the water" (*Season* 38). Mujeeb consolidates political power around himself through the exploitation of topographical coincidence, thereby suggesting the naturalness of his authority. Azhar's presence in this scene implicates him in Mujeeb's authority, as well. Azhar appears in the narrative only once prior to this interaction with Mujeeb, and that introductory scene unfolds at the house of the murdered Judge Anwar. The narrative offers no explanation for Azhar's visit to Mujeeb, but, during their meeting, the Deputy Commissioner informs the zamindar that he has "appointed himself the examining magistrate, which means that...he was responsible for collecting evidence and conducting investigations. In principle, he had to gather all the facts relating to the death, weigh them up with proper objectivity, and determine whether a case should proceed" (*Season* 36–7). Absent any legal or bureaucratic reason for Azhar's informing Mujeeb of his official responsibilities, the narrator's use of the phrase "in principle" casts a subtle suspicion over the Deputy Commissioner's ability to be properly objective. There is enough ambiguity in this passage— delivered as indirect discourse rather than actual dialogue—to suggest that Azhar may be inclined to shield Mujeeb's possible involvement in the judge's murder, a crime that remains unsolved. A final example: immediately after the narrative conveys the report of Mujeeb's fluvial threat it notes that "a portrait of the Founder of the state" hangs above a locked cupboard in Mujeeb's office (*Season* 38), the very site at which the old man stages his protest. The presence of Jinnah's portrait in Mujeeb's office invokes an affective attachment to the idea of Pakistan and, at the same, suggestively extends the portrait's affective resonance to encompass Mujeeb, as if the Quaid-i-Azam offers his benediction over Mujeeb's undertakings. These examples begin to sketch the many dimensions of the zamindar's centrality.

Gossip illustrates not only Mujeeb Ali's political and economic dominance but also the extent to which he influences social relations, thereby expanding his role as a state-like actor. The two primary topics of gossip in the novel revolve around the resurfacing of some mail bags that had been presumed lost in a train wreck nineteen years earlier and the scandal surrounding Azhar's intimate relationship with Elizabeth. The surprising reappearance of the long lost mail stirs up considerable anxiety in the village, especially for Mujeeb Ali. Yet, the root cause of Mujeeb's anxiety remains hidden as he manipulates gossip's workings to suit his own ends, whatever they may be. In an exchange with Maulana Hafeez, Mujeeb links the judge's murder with the reappearance of the letters; Mujeeb says, "'[Gul-kalam, the night watchman] was involved in Judge Anwar's murder. They paid him to guard the street for a few hours and also got the layout of the house from him'" (*Season* 68). Maulana Hafeez, standing in for the similarly uninformed reader, asks to whom Mujeeb's "they" refers. In response, Mujeeb avers: "'We're not sure yet...They're [the police] still working on him down at the barracks. Something to do with those letters, some mess from nineteen years ago'" (*Season* 68). Mujeeb's use of the first person plural pronoun "we" reinforces his position as the authority, even though, technically, the police are conducting the interrogation. Under the auspices of this authority, Mujeeb asserts a connection between the murder, Gul-kalam's guilt, and the mail. Yet, his "something" and "some mess" lack precision and, thus, for the reader if not for Maulana Hafeez, spark suspicion. What motivates Mujeeb's desire to connect a real crime to the mail's reappearance? Maulana Hafeez doesn't pose this question, and the novel leaves it unresolved, casting the workings of Mujeeb's power as ever more pervasive for being unaccountable.

Indeed, Mujeeb's power emerges as persuasive and manipulative as he pulls off a rhetorical sleight of hand in order to convince Maulana Hafeez to do his bidding. Starting just this rumor, Mujeeb warns the maulana that the murder and the letters will "'become so strongly linked in people's minds that in future the one is bound to lead to the other'" (*Season* 69). To avoid this outcome, Mujeeb asks Maulana Hafeez to talk to the postmaster about delaying the delivery of these "lost" letters until they've been examined, saying, while "feigning resignation," that he "'would talk to [the postmaster himself] but...'" (*Season* 68). The ellipsis here underscores Mujeeb's feigned resignation, signaling, once again, his manipulation of the maulana. The zamindar appeals to the cleric's moral stature in the community, too, claiming that the village has "'already had a *death* because of [the letters],'" even while the narrator characterizes Mujeeb as speaking to Maulana Hafeez "as though to a little boy" (*Season* 68). To the maulana's objection that to withhold the mail "'would amount to theft and betrayal'" (*Season* 68), Mujeeb replies:

> "Nothing will be suppressed, Maulana-ji. The majority of [the letters], perhaps all of them, will only be delayed. We'll examine each letter and withhold any that might result in the kind of crime that has already taken place."
>
> (*Season* 69)

Once again, Mujeeb displays the centrality of his authority through his use of the first person pronoun "we," and, once again, Maulana Hafeez asks to whom he refers. "'A group of people, responsible citizens, chosen by...chosen by yourself and Maulana Dawood,'" says Mujeeb (*Season* 69). Clearly a tactical appeal—again, the ellipsis signals a calculated move—to the Maulana's moral stature, Mujeeb's response also plays on the illusion of citizenship in a system that resembles more a monarchy than a democracy. The maulana acquiesces.

Despite his success convincing Maulana Hafeez to speak to the postmaster, however, Mujeeb Ali's efforts to suppress the mail also reveal the susceptibility of his power to gossip's critiquing function. When Maulana Hafeez approaches the postmaster with Mujeeb's request to withhold the "lost" mail, he parrots the zamindar's rumor linking the letters and the murder, and adds, "'It will benefit the whole town if those letters were examined before being sent out'" (*Season* 85). Unmoved, the postmaster responds, "'It's not the whole town, Maulana-ji. It's just the rich people that seem worried'" (*Season* 85). Maulana Hafeez stretches the zamindar's concerns so that they envelop the whole town, as if Mujeeb's agenda considers their collective well-being, but the postmaster will have none of it. When rumors and influence fail to achieve the suppression of the mail, Mujeeb resorts to outright physical threat in the form of a four-man patrol that manages to run the postmaster out of town, but not before the latter succeeds in delivering the mail (*Season* 89, 96). Both the postmaster's flight and Mujeeb's strong arm tactics become the subject of village gossip. The butcher and the barber, for instance, criticize both maulanas and Mujeeb for their hand in the postal scandal; the butcher says, "'Look what happened at the post office last night. But neither of these two [maulanas] will talk to Mujeeb about it'" (*Season* 99–100). Warming to his topic, the butcher continues in praise of the postmaster's courage:

> "Right under the noses of Mujeeb Ali's men who were patrolling the streets...I myself would have gone one step further. I would have written some letters myself, one to each person in town, listing the crimes the rich have committed against us since the beginning of time."
>
> (*Season* 100).

This conversation displays gossip's potential to undercut authority and, indeed, even to empower, if only through hyperbole, the disenfranchised. Nothing comes of the butcher's bravado, of course, as Mujeeb has already "'posted goondas outside the [post office] door,'" according to the barber's report (*Season* 100). Nonetheless, the butcher's commentary correctly diagnoses another pervasive and connected social ill: how religion, in the person of the two maulanas, bends to the zamindar's will.

The clear-sightedness of this example of gossip receives affirmation from Azhar, extending the sense of Mujeeb's vulnerability. The former questions Mujeeb over his installation of the four- man patrol, to which Mujeeb replies, "'two policemen [were] with them last night,'" emphasizing the extent of his control (*Season* 124). Azhar, nonetheless, asserts his own authority, "look[ing] Mujeeb Ali straight in the eye[:] 'And I would like your men out of the post office'" (*Season* 101). Mujeeb's "curt smile" given in response to this request for removal seems to signify Azhar's impotency. Yet, the Deputy Commissioner's reminder that Mujeeb is "'just a citizen'" and that he himself has "'divisional superiors to report back to'" appears to have the desired effect: Mujeeb assures Azhar that he'll "'have the post office keys sent to the barracks'" (*Season* 126). This confrontation between the landowner and the representative of the repressive state apparatus that is the police crystallizes the tension between these two powers as they seek to anchor the village's daily life or, in other words, to fulfill the role of the "everyday state."

The gossip surrounding Azhar and Elizabeth's relationship, however, works to re-center—violently—conservative social norms and, thus, also re-secure Mujeeb's centrality. The relationship is the subject of gossip throughout the novel, involving main characters, such as Maulana Hafeez and Mujeeb, and bit players, including unnamed police officers and local women, alike. While some of the gossipers relish the salaciousness of the situation, most voice objections on moral and communal grounds. Maulana Hafeez, who initially counsels discretion rather than gossip (*Season* 23), later publicly names and shames Azhar and Elizabeth by condemning their relationship in his Friday sermon (*Season* 165). Before that, however, the maulana asks Mujeeb to speak to Azhar, since the maulana is unable to work up the nerve. The maualana's request is for Mujeeb to convince Azhar to "'mend his ways,'" thereby indicating the reinstitution of a moral norm (*Season* 106). The maulana's appeal to the zamindar once again demonstrates religion's subservience to the landowning class. Further, in a reversal of Mujeeb's disingenuous appeal to Maulana Hafeez's moral stature, the latter's decision to seek Mujeeb's help on this matter of moral import suggests that Mujeeb is the one who anchors the village's moral code. Thus, efforts to maintain and reinforce that code contribute to Mujeeb's power, a point not lost on the maulana, as the narrative voice suggests: "Maulana Hafeez [...] watched [Mujeeb] until he disappeared into the great marble house that dominated one side of the street. Then, ordering his thoughts, he began walking slowly back towards the mosque" (*Season* 106). This topographical vision lays out the power structure with Mujeeb's "marble house" dominating the streetscape along which the cleric moves slowly.

The novel's culminating event is not the revelation of the judge's murderer but rather the public humiliation of Elizabeth Massih. While the narrative does not directly relay what happens to Elizabeth, gossip fills in part of the picture. Maulana Hafeez and his wife hear shouting as the attack begins (*Season* 180), and, the next day, he asks her, "'Hasn't there been any news of [Elizabeth]?'" (*Season* 191). Another husband and wife argue about the event when the wife, seeking the protection of the community, tacitly endorses Elizabeth's attack: "'If people can come out against a born-last-Friday Christian harlot then they will also come out to protect a respectable Muslim woman'" (*Season* 188–9). The husband condemns this logic for how it unthinkingly naturalizes the violent imposition of moral "norms" on an outsider, i.e. a Christian: "'No need to think about how or why it happened. Let's just talk about it as though it's the most natural thing in the world...That's the whole harami country's policy'" (*Season* 189). Beyond how the butcher and barber's exchange pinpoints the unjust exercise of power, the husband's condemnation identifies how complicity, figured here as talk or gossip, reifies violence. Though neither the wife nor the husband identifies the "they" who came out against Elizabeth—indeed, the novel also neglects to identify her assailants—Mujeeb's previous installation of his own night patrol provides a link between Elizabeth's attack and his power.

Moreover, the narrative suggests that Mujeeb has grown impatient with Azhar's insubordination. Not only does he offer a "curt smile" to Azhar before he agrees to the Deputy Commissioner's request for the keys to the post office (*Season* 125), suggesting he has taken offense, but when Azhar broaches the subject of Mujeeb's visit to Elizabeth in Azhar's absence, "[t]he dark skin under Mujeeb Ali's eyes had tightened" (*Season* 161). The tenseness of Mujeeb's face signals, once again, how close Azhar comes to overstepping the boundaries Mujeeb thinks should contain him. Indeed, Azhar may well have stepped across those boundaries when he closes the conversation in which Mujeeb tells him to end his affair with a simple, "'We'll see'" (*Season* 161). These examples of the changing dynamic between Azhar and Mujeeb, along with the presence of Mujeeb's private security force, collectively hint at the zamindar's role in Elizabeth's assault. Further, the village's acceptance of it, emblematized by the exchange between the husband and wife, and even the event's rapid eclipse by news of national crackdowns on perceived threats to Zia point to a return to homeostasis, a condition marked by the centrality of Mujeeb's authority.

Aslam's novel connects Mujeeb's seemingly all-encompassing authority to the extra-fictional context of Zia's regime, specifically a 1982 assassination attempt on the general's life, suggesting that the novel's historical referent may well exert a similarly stifling grasp on everyday life. The newspaper shared at the barber shop, for instance, includes a story about how "[t]he General had threatened the death penalty for any 'wayward' journalist who dared 'denigrate' his regime" (*Season* 58). Indeed, the one journalist who comes to the village to cover the story of the reappearance of the mail suddenly disappears or goes into hiding after the attempt on Zia's life. For their part, the villagers can't get a straight story about the assassination attempt. BBC World Service radio touches upon the story briefly, while Pakistani national radio offers nothing at all (*Season* 150–2). As the villagers put together what little they know about the attempt, contradictions emerge: "'The BBC said it was the hanged prime minister's son. But according to the All India Radio it was the guerrillas from Baluchistan,'" says Yusuf Rao, a local lawyer (*Season* 173). The fragmentary and unreliable nature of the information about the assassination attempt the villagers receive mirrors neatly how gossip itself operates in the novel. While the villagers can comment on the harshness of the regime's treatment of the "free" press and the shortcomings of the one officially sponsored by the nation, Zia's regime, nonetheless, remains capable of imposing its authority, violently if necessary.

The prevalence of gossip in these contexts prevents the totalization of this authority, however. As Brian Johnson points out, gossip's reliance on repetition means that "new contexts are introduced and content is altered[;] its meaning can never be 'anchored'" (52–3). Always open-ended, gossip depends, by definition, on excess, on what might next be known and what can't ever be known. While, at the level of plot, the gossip in Aslam's novel reinforces the existing hierarchical power structure, at the level of form, the novel presents its own excess: five brief italicized sections that bear no explicit relation to the main body of the narrative. Unlike the rest of the narrative, these sections feature a first person narrator—sometimes singular, sometimes plural. They also represent a greater awareness of how history is "present" in everyday life by relaying memories from 1947, 1971, and the turbulent 1980s. On the whole, then, these italicized sections display how these characters' lives do not fully conform to the dictates of power.

The first italicized section, for example, implicitly reclaims Islam from Zia's Islamization. Told in a first person plural voice that favors children's perspectives, this section distinguishes between men with black beards and men with white ones, pointing out that the latter "are kind and gentle" (*Season* 2). The narrators' Uncle Shujahat has a black beard, and, when he comes to visit, "[h]e takes our dolls and masks from us, breaks them in two, and then hands them back. He says images of God's creatures are not allowed in the house, not while he's visiting" (*Season* 2). His views clash with those of his sister, the narrators' mother, who challenges her brother: "'You're using religion as an exercise to withdraw from the world. [....] Father-ji was religious but he kept things in proportion. He even sent me, a girl, to Lahore to get a university degree. [...] And that was twenty years ago'" (*Season* 2). The mother's assessment of her brother's religious fervor strikes upon how this zealousness seeks to freeze the world rather than to deal with it, and this assessment could well be a comment on how power treats history: as static and fully evident rather than as fluid and contingent. In the context of Zia's Pakistan, the mother's recognition of the difference between her father's and her brother's religiosity—one in proportion and the other, presumably, out of bounds—extends as a broader critique not only of the narrowness of that regime's definition of "Islam" but also of its disregard for the nation's own recent social history, wherein the mother could be sent, without censure, to university.

The third italicized insertion, told from the first person singular point of view of a young girl, features Izmayal, a veteran of the 1971 war, who, according to the narrator, "exists outside the domain of mundane happenings" (*Season* 90). Izmayal's outsider status derives from his being a veteran, for, as the narrator relates, "We lost that war and when he came back everyone spat at him" (*Season* 90). In addition, Izmayal strikes the narrator as exceptional because "[w]hat is manifest to him is news to me" (*Season* 90). The suggestion here is that Izmayal's wartime experiences in what was East Pakistan so radically alter his views that his broader vision seems novel to the narrator and flat out offensive to the other Pakistanis. The narrator concedes that Izmayal is "alternately execrated and idolised" by her (90), indicating that he succeeds, in part, in encouraging her to consider his outsider's views. More specifically, during a conversation about shooting stars in which the narrator tells Izmayal that they are "arrows of fire hurled by Allah against the evil djinn," Izmayal laughs and replies, "'There's no Allah, girl'" (*Season* 91). This exchange features Izmayal's direct contradiction of the lesson the narrator learns from "the cleric's wife" (91). At the same time, Izmayal's laughing dismissal of the narrator's explanation challenges an entire Islamized—i.e. Zia-fied—worldview. Izmayal embodies an unassimilable aspect of the past that questions the inevitability of a unified nation and the infallibility of a centralized state.

Set off by appearance and, at best, tangential in relation to the main plotline, these italicized sections structurally represent the excessive nature of gossip, its endless irresolution. As these sections link history to everyday life through first person voices, they also pull away from the centripetal force of Mujeeb's and Zia's authority, which would institute norms and views aimed at upholding their power rather than recognizing the variety of meanings these characters attach to their everyday experiences. As these italicized sections interrupt the main storyline and situate the characters' everyday lives in large-scale historical events, they also exceed the boundaries of the local. When, for instance, the unnamed narrator reveals the abuse Izmayal suffered when he returned from Bangladesh, she widens the geographical scope of these interruptive narratives, suggesting that, in these broader contexts, Mujeeb Ali's locally-centralized powers no longer exert as strong a gravitational pull. Belonging may exist outside the zamindar's orbit, but these italicized sections resist positing an easy identification with Pakistan as either nation or state in the zamindar's absence.

Indeed, the disorientation these italicized sections create for the reader may mirror the disorientation of an unanchored belonging.

Like Aslam's *Season of the Rainbirds*, Mohsin Hamid's novel *Moth Smoke* undertakes a structural experiment. Unlike Aslam's novel, however, *Moth Smoke* represents zamindar power as expansive and extreme, while it also offers the most explicit challenge to this power through its narrative form. In keeping with the critical focal points of the rest of this section, my discussion of Hamid's novel also examines how gossip both reinforces and/or challenges the zamindar's ability to centralize the norms that comprise the "everyday state." In addition to how gossip works as part of the story's plot, I explore how the novel's very structure mimics gossip's elements. More specifically, Hamid's novel unfolds within a doubled frame that both invites an allegorical reading and resists such a reading's determinism. This narrative resistance manifests itself in journalistic exposés, suggesting that a voice railing against injustice and corruption can serve as an alternative affective center.

Moth Smoke's primary plot involves the deterioration of Darashikoh Shezad, aka Daru, a young man who squanders his promise and all available means in an attempt to keep up with the luxurious lifestyles of the actually rich and famous in 1998 Lahore. Ozi, Daru's best childhood friend, and his wife Mumtaz are the most immediate representatives of the privileged set, though the novel introduces other examples of this group, including members of the zamindar class. The disadvantaged exist, too: Murad Badshah and Daru's servant Manucci are the two most fully developed characters of this type. Daru's futile pursuit of privilege likely instigates his growing drug addiction and, ironically, leads to his unemployment and eventual involvement in drug selling and boutique robbing. Daru's desire to move up the social ladder, a feat he thinks should happen meritocratically, relates inversely to Mumtaz's drive to provide a public forum for the disenfranchised through her journalistic work. Their affair appears to spark the plot Ozi constructs to frame Daru for the hit and run death of a boy, a crime for which Ozi himself is responsible.

The novel's structure presents this story as part of Daru's trial for this crime, allowing Daru, Mumtaz, Ozi, and even Murad, Daru's partner in crime, to alternate as first person narrators or narrative focal points. These chapters appear within two sets of frames. The first frame, set in italics, tells the story of Shah Jahan and his warring sons, an episode out of subcontinental Mughal history that invites an allegorical reading of the constancy of destruction resulting from the desire for power. That Shah Jahan's sons serve as the namesakes for the main players in the plot proper suggests the determinism of this allegorical reading. The second frame, situated immediately within the italicized one, locates Daru— unnamed in both the opening and closing frames—in a prison cell during the trial that comprises the bulk of the main plot. This frame is, thus, the novel's most up-to-the-moment present. Speaking in the first person, Daru describes receiving an envelope upon which his name appears. By the point at which this frame closes, readers know that the envelope contains another of Mumtaz's exposés, this one laying out Daru's innocence. Although situated within the allegory of the italicized frame, this second frame story promises to exonerate and perhaps partially redeem Daru, a narrative intervention not possible or permissible in the determinism of the allegorical tale, which mainly tells the story of Aurangzeb's dominance.

Read through the metanarrative laid down by the italicized frame story, the alternating narrative perspectives reinforce a centralized authority. The italicized frame narrative locates power within the ruler and, hence, within the state. A dying Shah Jahan, fearing the division of his empire at the hands of his warring sons, "*commanded his workers to redouble their efforts*" to complete the Taj Mahal before his own death (Hamid, *Moth* 3; emphasis in original). This edifice, a monument both to Shah Jahan's wife and to the greatness of his rule, symbolizes the concentration of power in the figure of the emperor and suggests the hierarchized relation between him and these "*workers*." Aurangzeb's speedy defeat of his brothers and especially his deployment of the "*Holy Law*" to justify Darashikoh's execution also illustrates the centralization of power in the figure of the emperor and, even more, the subordination of religion to state authority (Hamid, *Moth* 4; emphasis in original).

The historical Aurangzeb's ruthless victory creates the readerly expectation that his namesake, Ozi, will exhibit the same characteristics and assert the same dominance. In addition to framing Daru for the hit-and-run of which he is guilty, Ozi uses his narrative contributions to rationalize his dominance. Describing Pakistan through a broad metaphor of theft, Ozi claims, "People are robbing the country blind, and if the choice is between being held up at gunpoint or holding the gun, only a madman would choose to hand over his wallet rather than fill it with someone else's cash" (*Moth* 184). Ozi offers this metaphor of violent self-interest as an elaboration of his money laundering activities—a charge to which he avers, "Well, it's true enough" (*Moth* 184)—as well as to counter the rumors he suspects swirl around Lahore: "And regardless of what you've heard, I'm not a bad guy" (*Moth* 184). This apparent forthrightness works in two ways: first, it presents his dominance as deserved and without apology; and, second, it establishes Ozi's awareness of his involvement in gossip about corruption. All aspects of this story testify to Ozi's success at maintaining his dominance. Toward the end of the novel, for example, in a chapter entitled "Judgment" and addressed via the second person to the reader, who stands in as the judge, the prosecuting attorney arguing Daru's guilt dismisses the possibility that Daru has been framed as a "fantasy," for there are no "interests powerful enough to corrupt the professionalism of the police, wealthy enough to bribe their legions of witnesses…" (*Moth* 235). Clearly, Ozi's influence also bends the legal profession—the state prosecutor, no less—to his will. In the novel's contemporary plot, the power Aurangzeb exercises in the allegorical frame emerges in Ozi's behavior, with the significant difference being that Ozi is not a head of state but rather a member of a highly privileged class. Authority, thus, remains centralized but it shifts locus so that the wealthiest function as state-like actors.

Ozi is a recent addition to this elite class, which, the novel suggests, is comfortably the province of the zamindars. Two quick examples illustrate this point.

Daru loses his job at an important bank because of his poor handling of a wealthy landowner. Lacking circumspection or suffused with the anger of the masses, Daru's treatment of the zamindar prompts the man to say, "'Young man, I don't like the way you're smiling'" (*Moth* 20). Daru's interior voice responds, "I'm not one of your serfs, you bastard" (*Moth* 20), even while it also concedes that Daru is "limited in [his] choice of responses to Mr. Jiwan's attempt to impose feudal hierarchy on [his] office" (*Moth* 21). Mr. Jiwan prevails: Daru is fired. Occurring early in the novel's plot, this episode demonstrates how the zamindari class wields power over the banking system, an institution that should only be subject to state regulation, while it also dictates Daru's everyday life. Daru falls victim to another demonstration of zamindari power when he sells drugs to an underage Shuja, yet another character who is a namesake from the drama unfolding in the italicized frame narrative. Shuja is the young scion of a "big feudal family" (*Moth* 181), and, when his father discovers that the boy bought drugs from Daru, the zamindar has Daru severely beaten (*Moth* 182–3). Daru goes to the hospital but lies about his injuries: "'Auto accident'" (*Moth* 183). The zamindar's justice prevails. Significantly, upon first meeting Shuja at a "kiddie party" (159) attended by others of Shuja's class, Daru thinks to himself, "It's a big lawn, and I stand in the middle, watching the house, wondering how many of these kids will grow up into Ozis. Quite a few, probably. Our poor country" (*Moth* 161). This linkage of Shuja with Ozi amounts to an expansion of the zamindari class to include the nouveau riche, like Ozi and his father, who make their money through corrupt business and civil service practices rather than through land ownership. Although Daru wonders if Shuja will grow up to be like Ozi, in effect, it's Ozi who has grown up to be like a zamindar. Thus, *Moth Smoke* shows the extension of the zamindar's power from the country to the city *and* the expansion of that class's authority to include other members of the elite.[4]

In addition to establishing Ozi's dominance, his narratorial contributions also acknowledge the gossip that swirls around him. Ozi's efforts to counter "what you've heard," rumors that include how his father is "frequently investigated but as yet unincarcerated" (*Moth* 11), prompt his own gossip-mongering about Daru: "let me tell you a thing or two about good old Daru" (*Moth* 185). Regardless of the details of Ozi's story about Daru, what matters is that Ozi possesses the power to make the story "true," as is evidenced by the very fact of the trial. That is, Ozi's false claim that Daru "killed the boy" (*Moth* 194) becomes the basis for the entire plot. So, despite the reader's access to the truth of the hit-and-run accident, courtesy of Daru's own first person narrative contribution, Ozi's take on the situation prevails to the extent that the entire criminal justice system buys into it. Ozi's gossip exemplifies how this discourse can reinforce the powerful and how the powerful subsume the state itself.

While the rumors Ozi's narration endorses end up dictating the function of the "everyday state" through their control of the criminal justice system, they also highlight how the novel's entire structure replicates gossip's discursive dynamics. In addition to Ozi's point of view, the novel also gives Murad Badshah, the proprietor of a rickshaw fleet and a drug dealer, an opportunity to contribute or testify. And, as Ozi does, Murad uses his narratorial opportunity to promulgate rumors. Murad concedes that he "encouraged rumors" about his lethalness (*Moth* 67), while he spins a yarn that frames him as a modern day Pakistani Robin Hood: "You see, it is my passionately held belief that the right to possess property is at best a contingent one" (*Moth* 64). Self-styled as a man of the masses, Murad none-theless reinforces Ozi's power when the former offers his own narrative as testimony against Daru, who, in Murad's view, "revealed his capacity for cold-blooded murder" (*Moth* 69) during one of their boutique heists. The structural inclusion of multiple testimonies, including Murad's, which is itself preoccupied with rumors and gossip, illustrates Blakey Vermeule's contention that the incorporation of such perspectives, as well as "frame narratives or letters," functions "preeminently [as] conversation overheard" (103). In this sense, the reader, who is at points referred to as "you" and implicated in Daru's judgment, serves as another node in the gossip network the entire volume constructs. The text's ability to implicate the reader in the plot's gossip through its structure tests the reader's partiality: the evidence presented should sway the reader's judgment, while the manner in which it is presented should alert the reader to the possibility of yet another version. This expectation of a deferral of the story's conclusion mimics gossip's dynamics, wherein the latest news or hottest rumor can shift the entire story's meaning.

Moth Smoke signals just this type of deferral through its second frame narrative. In the opening segment of this frame, Daru, speaking in the first person, receives from the prison guard an "envelope smooth and sharp against my fingers" (*Moth* 5). Adding to the envelope's description as "smooth" and "sharp," Daru next refers to it as "white" as he reads his "name in the handwriting of a woman [he] know[s] well" (*Moth* 6). At this early narrative juncture, Daru doesn't open the envelope or read its contents; he merely remarks upon the "damp imprints [his] fingers begin to leave in the paper" (*Moth* 6). Since this frame begins the novel's main plot, the reader knows nothing of Daru or the circumstances that land him in jail. Rather, the reader encounters an unknown letter, presented in terms, such as "white," that connote purity or even truth. Further, Daru's mention of what could be his tears dampening the envelope suggest the emotional turmoil of the wrongly accused.[5] The frame's closing returns to the same moment, wherein the "envelope glows" in Daru's hands. When Daru finally opens it, he finds a manuscript "Mumtaz has written, 'The Trial, by Zulfikar Manto,'" her pseudonym (*Moth* 245). Daru recognizes the exposé as "the story of my innocence. A half-story," that he continues reading "until [he] notice[s] the paper getting wet, the ink blurring into little flowers" (*Moth* 245). Mumtaz's article on Daru joins a litany of other explosive pieces she's written, including an article on prostitution (*Moth* 80) and another on how elites moved their money to offshore accounts before the government froze foreign currency accounts after the 1998 nuclear tests (*Moth* 165). Zulfikar Manto, Mumtaz's suggestive pseudonym, derives from the extra-fictional Manto's socially-charged literary output, while her need to take on a pseudonym acknowledges the degree to which she, as Ozi's wife, is implicated in the privilege she critiques in her exposés. Significantly, though Mumtaz contributes her "testimony" to the actual trial, the text of her exposés is never reproduced. Instead, Mumtaz reveals the reactions her work elicits; her prostitution article, for instance, received a "'big response,'" as her editor was "'swamped with calls'" that were "'mostly furious'" (*Moth* 80). Nonplussed by even a rock thrown through the newspaper's window, Mumtaz revels in the fact that "'people read it'" (*Moth* 80). These exposés disrupt complacency; they reveal the workings of power and inequity that shape the everyday lives of the elite and the non-elite alike. These articles' absence in a narrative replete with multiple perspectives and testimonies that both instantiate and mirror gossip suggests that they operate as a different type of discourse. Indeed, their ability to evoke highly emotional responses positions these exposés as an affective center that challenges the dominance that the elite—that expanded zamindari class—sees as its due. Such an alternative affective center also calls into question the determinism suggested by the broader narrative frame, which implies an historical determinacy set by Shah Jahan and his warring sons.

Daniyal Mueenuddin's 2009 short story sequence *In Other Rooms, Other Wonders* expands setting while remaining "in time," having characters move between rural and urban settings, in effect bridging the locations featured in Aslam's and Hamid's novels. In Mueenuddin's stories, however, the zamindar class remains centralized no matter the changes in setting. The stories' synchronic portrait of life in the city and in the country pushes the limit of the zamindar's power beyond village life in a rural locality and illustrates its reach into urban centers, locations usually assumed to have more "modern" forms of power. Further, the sequence provides little if any suggestion thematically or structurally of this translocal power's vulnerability, unlike *Seasons of the Rainbirds* or *Moth Smoke*, which do so structurally and thematically. As a result, *In Other Rooms, Other Wonders* presents the zamindar as the affective center that binds through inequality and prevails over any draw the nation, howsoever reimagined, might exert.

As with the other fictions discussed in this section, the zamindari class's power constitutes the everyday state. I focus on three stories in particular as they feature most prominently both the zamindar and his dependents: "Provide, Provide," "In Other Rooms, Other Wonders," and "Lily."[6] Thematically, in these stories, gossip reinforces conservative norms, just as it does in Aslam's and Hamid's novels. Structurally, each story's characters connect to the major zamindar figure—KK Harouni or Makhdoom Talwan—providing these individual stories and the entire cycle with a common touchstone throughout, a touchstone linked to the social, political, and economic role of the zamindari system more than to Harouni or Talwan as individuals.[7] The zamindars' structural pervasiveness, their very position as the center of the sequence, thus offers the counterexample to how Aslam's and Hamid's structures gesture toward power's vulnerability.

"Provide, Provide" features both major zamindars in order to situate its protagonist, Chaudrey Jaglani, within the hierarchy and affective order of this system. While, on the one hand, Jaglani, who is Harouni's estate manager, takes advantage of Harouni's financial misfortune (62), on the other, the rise of Jaglani's status to that of minor zamindar still leaves him under the patronage of Makhdoom Talwan, another major zamindar (79, 91). Jaglani views his opportunism as acceptable since, in his eyes, he maintains "his feudal allegiance to KK Harouni" (64). Further, as he accumulates more land and power, Jaglani "ruled his area in the old way" (80), thus maintaining the centrality of the zamindar's position to the point that "he felt he had risen so far, had become invulnerable to the judgments of those around him..." (74). On the rise, Jaglani considers himself to be above the gossip and the possibility of social censure that surrounds his affair with his housekeeper, Zainab, whom he eventually and, at first, secretly takes as his second wife. For the villagers, however, the affair and marriage are no secret, as Zainab is fully aware; she tells Jaglani, "'The villagers! They knew the first night. They leave me alone because they're afraid of you'" (70). Aside from illustrating Zainab's prescience (and Jaglani's lack thereof), this explicit acknowledgment of what the villagers already know characterizes how they are bound to Jaglani and, by extension, to any zamindar: through fear. The affective attachment, then, isn't positive. This point seems lost on the zamindar himself, the narrator suggests, as Harouni, for instance, "sentimentally thought that the people of Dunyapur [...] revered his family" (64). If the zamindar—be he Harouni or Jaglani—creates and maintains the structures of the everyday state as is evidenced by the careful accounting of who is dependent upon whom for their livelihoods (75, 76), these dependencies do not guarantee loyalty born of affection or gratitude but, rather, loyalty born of coercion that ends up replicating the inequitable power dynamics common to the relationship between the zamindar and the villagers.

Evidence of the perpetuation of this dynamic of inequity emerges from the gossip itself, showing its conservative tendencies. Jaglani's diagnosis of and rapid decline due to cancer provides an opportunity for Zainab to get her "just desserts," since she no longer has Jaglani's protection. Emotionally unconcerned, the nameless many who are subject to Jaglani's power "thought only of the changes to come, new men up, old men down, Jaglani's adherents thrown down" (92). Resigned, these people know that the system remains no matter who's on top, and that the fallen deserve no sympathy. For his part, Jaglani resents that "Zainab would go on, she had life in her, vitality, many years ahead. He didn't want her to live on after him" (92). Zainab may live on, but it's with an awareness of "the enormity of her loss, the failure of her preparations against abandonment" (83). Zainab falls prey to the social and economic censure of both Jaglani's family and the villagers, an ostracism made mundane in her final appearance in the story: having been summarily ejected from Jaglani's family home, she weeps and keeps "saying to herself, 'And they didn't even offer me a cup of tea'" (93). The social order, constructed on the zamindar system, refuses Zainab even the most rote and customary acts of hospitality, marking how far outside its norms she has been thrust.

Zainab's ejection from Jaglani's house illustrates the geographic expansion of the zamindar's influence, as this house is Jaglani's "city house" rather than the one in Dunyapur, the rural location that has served as the exclusive setting for his relationship with Zainab (85). The narrator reveals that the inhabitants of this "city house" view Zainab as a "vulgar Punjabi," for she harangues Jaglani's sons and servants "like women screaming over the common wall of their village huts" (92). While Zainab is clearly out of place in the city—and made more so by her expulsion from Jaglani's house—Jaglani's authority *isn't* out of place. That is, the zamindar's power travels beyond the confines of the rural locations that provide his material land base. This expansion of zamindari authority occurs throughout Mueenuddin's stories. Jaglani himself defers to Harouni's power when he visits the more powerful landlord in Lahore; the narrator refers to Harouni as Jaglani's "master," and Jaglani "keep[s] himself rigid" during their interactions (62). Jaglani's submissiveness before Harouni at the latter's house in Lahore shows the extent to which the zamindar's power infiltrates even the more elite echelons of one of Pakistan's largest cities. It is to this house in Lahore that Husna ventures in the titular story looking for Harouni's protection. Much like Jaglani does with Zainab, Harouni initiates an intimate relationship with Husna, extending his beneficence across class lines. And, much like Zainab, Husna suffers at the hands of gossipers after Harouni dies. At Harouni's "*jenaza*" (139), for instance, "[t]wo society women sat uncomfortably on the floor next to Husna, whispering, gossiping, and she heard one say to the other in English, 'Oh, isn't that *delicious*'" in reference to Husna's being in attendance (140; emphasis in original). Whether alive or dead, Harouni as zamindar would be immune from gossip's sting, but Husna, whose very presence may well be what makes these "society women" uncomfortable, remains vulnerable to gossip's conservative tendencies. Like Zainab, Husna, who, importantly, has always been a city dweller, is ejected from Harouni's house. The image of the "society women" savoring Husna's misfortune in "In Other Rooms, Other Wonders" fore-shadows the likely future of Lily in the story by the same name. "Lily" extends the expansion of the zamindar's authority from rural to urban settings by demon-strating how that authority exerts a gravitational pull on even the city dwelling, continent hopping, English- speaking elite. At the end of this story, knowing that her husband "Murad would be rich and powerful" as he inherits his uncle Makhdoom's mantle, Lily resigns herself to "becoming one of those thin sharp women from the cities who can hold their liquor but are dessicated by it" (220), women much like the ones who ostracize Husna in "In Other Rooms, Other Wonders."

These stories from Mueenuddin's sequence develop my focus on gossip, the zamindar, and the "everday state" to encompass not only rural settings but urban ones, too. The pervasiveness of the zamindar's authority that these texts suggest matters, because it begins to break down the perceived barrier between reigning social powers and location. That is, these stories position the urban elite as being held under the sway of the landowner just as the destitute peasantry is. The result is an image of power emanating from a rural base. Of course, any literary exam-ination of representations of the country and the city brings to mind Raymond Williams's work on the topic. While often faulted for failing to analyze properly how imperialism shapes/shaped rural and urban life in Britain and its colonies,

Williams's insights into the dynamics between country and city are nonetheless germane to the Pakistani context for they refuse the binary that would entirely separate the lifeways of the two types of locations.[8] Instead, Williams argues, "[A]s we gain perspective, from the long history of the literature of the country and city, we see how much, at different times and in different places, it is a connecting process, in what has to be seen ultimately as a common history" (288). Williams's use of the words "connecting" and "common" prove both vexatious and relevant in the present context given its concerns with how literary representations of rural and urban life portray affective attachments to collective identities. Surely the zamindari system connects disenfranchised peasant to English-speaking party girl in Mueenuddin's stories. The "common"-ness of their history, if read as "ordinary," may have more to do with the zamindar's centrality as the "everyday state" than with any other viable or acknowledge-able sense of shared concerns, however.

In Other Rooms, Other Wonders certainly illustrates how gossip centers the zamindar's authority and how that authority functions as the "everyday state." Unlike *Season of the Rainbirds* and *Moth Smoke*, however, Mueenuddin's text casts the zamindar's centrality as more saturating, an effect created not only by how the stories connect country and city but also how they link together as a short story sequence. I affix the word "sequence" deliberately to Mueenuddin's volume, for, as Robert M. Luscher argues, stories in sequences are not "completely closed formal experiences[s]" (148). This openness aligns one of the short story sequence's generic characteristics with gossip's: both refuse closure or both rely on the supplement. Another shared characteristic is both forms' reference to orality. Short story sequences derive their narrative structure from oral cultures, according to Paul March-Russell, and, thus, encompass that tradition's "mutability of storytelling and social structure" (107).[9] Similarly, gossip bears the potential to challenge and/or reinforce social structures through the critique or imposition of norms.

The paralleling of Zainab's, Husna's, and even Lily's experiences as objects of gossip illustrates the structural dynamism of the short story sequence. These three characters occupy much different social and geographical locations: Zainab is a poor rural woman; Husna is a lower middle class city dweller; and Lily is a globe-trotting cosmopolite. Yet, despite these differences, each character finds herself caught up seemingly by choice in intimate relationships with the zamindar figure. The structural similarities of each female character's entanglement highlight an unexpected commonality. Relatedly, each of the zamindar figures— Jaglani, Harouni, and Murad—appears different: Jaglani actively makes himself into a powerful landowner; Harouni benefits from family lineage; and Murad, though also related to a zamindar family, represents progressiveness given his agricultural entrepreneurship. The volume's sequential nature deploys these differences to conjure the variety of ways that the zamindar's power structures everyday life, creating a sense of scope that spans rural and urban locations, as well as class hierarchies and ideological divides.

Part 4
Failed state, nation in crisis

7 9/11

Despite the horrific material destruction wrought by the hijackings that occurred on September 11, 2001, "9/11" signifies both a peculiar absence and an ineluctable abstraction. The iconicity of the World Trade Center towers in New York City's skyline creates, post-9/11, a disorienting absence, and, while (plans for) memorials exist at the Pentagon and in Shanksville, Pennsylvania, these two sites infrequently appear in broader conversations and debates about the status of "9/11" in the American cultural imaginary. At the same time, as many have commented over the years, the US-led "war on terror" radically shifts conventional notions of international conflict as the "enemy" is an abstract noun, an affective response, rather than a nation. And yet, ironically, the two geographical locations at which the US focused its "war on terror" call to mind the very material concerns of history's unfinished business: that is, the Taliban's ascendancy in Afghanistan connects to the US-backed covert war against the Soviets in the 1980s; and Saddam Hussein's deposition in Iraq completes a project begun in the first Gulf War, which is to say nothing about his rise to power. The recollection of these historical circumstances suggest that the abstraction clinging to the "war on terror" itself works to absent considerations of other perspectives or alternative courses of action.

The novels I discuss in this chapter—Nadeem Aslam's *The Wasted Vigil* (2008), Mohsin Hamid's *The Reluctant Fundamentalist* (2007), Kamila Shamsie's *Burnt Shadows* (2009), and HM Naqvi's *Home Boy* (2009)—counter this dominant tendency to absent and abstract through historicizing impulses made manifest through a revision of postcolonial migrancy.[1] Each novel engages with the events of September 11 or its aftermath through death or violence, but these narratives also feature absences that pre-date the events of that day. These pre-existing absences, I contend, change the emphasis US-centered representations—literary, media, political—place on 9/11 by challenging their decontextualization of "terror." The trope of migrancy as it operates in a variety of ways in these fictions asserts historical specificity in the face of this decontextualization. Migrancy as a concept, thus, takes on a different inflection from its more conventionalized usage over the past twenty years in postcolonial discourse. These novels' deployment of migrancy has none of the free-floating or archimedian privileges associated with cosmopolitanism or certain versions of transnationalism. This migrancy isn't about hybridity or translation, either. Instead, these fictions figure and, in some cases, ironize migrancy as a brutal encounter that is, because of its emphasis on a longer historical perspective, neither a pre-determined, inevitable clash nor a necessarily optimistic exchange. Each migrant example, thus, specifies and concretizes cross-cultural and international relations, pinning down the abstractions incumbent to the "war on terror."

By incorporating absences that chronologically pre-date the losses of 9/11 and grounding them through migrancy, these four novels amplify and complicate their characters' relation to collective national attachments and to the workings of the state. Amplification emerges from the variety of nations that serve as settings within these stories. The characters' movement between locations suggests, at times, an effort to transcend the pull of a shared national affect and, at other moments, the strong draw such attachments have in contexts overdetermined by conflict. Much of this overdetermination derives from the characters' understandings of the coercive power of the state, usually figured as violence or its threat. Coercion colors the characters' willingness or ability to claim belonging to a nation, as the narratives demonstrate how such claims require a compromise of the characters' own ideals or those long perpetuated as part of a nation's own mythologies.

Any effort to interpret how these fictions speak to attachments to Pakistan as nation or state requires an understanding of that country in our post-9/11 era. At this moment in time, Pakistan seems to have "become the contemporary pivot of history," in Lawrence Ziring's phrase (*Pakistan* 368). Yet, just as these fictions' absences stretch back before the events of September 11, so too do the historical contexts that inform present-day perceptions of Pakistan. Ziring's characterization of General Pervez Musharraf's initially heralded ascension to power better captures this long view: "Another military coup and another wild celebration in the streets of Pakistan. Another unpopular albeit elected government had succumbed to its own excesses, and another army commander had seized the reins of power" (*Pakistan* 259). Repetition, both rhetorical and historical, emphasizes the ongoing nature of the many issues, including the army's role in political life and the persistence of corruption, that continue to resonate in post-9/11 Pakistan. But, specifics matter, too. As much as Musharraf's coup mirrors Zia's—both generals deposed elected governments—details differentiate the two periods, separated by a decade defined by the political seesawing of Nawaz Sharif and Benazir Bhutto. According to Farzana Shaikh, "remarkable parallels" do exist between the moments of these two coups: the crisis in 1979, sparked by the Soviet invasion of Afghanistan, finds its partner in the crisis of September 2001, sparked by the attacks on the US (198). In both instances, Pakistan found itself caught between Islamists, on the one hand, and a superpower, on the other. The recurrence of this triangulated relationship puts paid to Ziring's claim that "Pakistan was born into the cold war" (*Pakistan* 260), and the nation's relation to its regional neighbors and the US continues to be informed by its natal day. At the same time, Shaikh differentiates the last two periods of military rule in Pakistan by pointing out that whilst General Zia was able to improve his domestic political standing by pursuing a policy that enjoyed the support of Pakistan's Islamic radicals, General Musharraf was forced to confront them at a time when militant Islam was becoming an ever-stronger force.

(199)

One reason historians give for the increase in militant Islam's power in Pakistan finds its roots in the ways Zia's regime, funded by the CIA, used Inter-Services Intelligence to cultivate these militants to fight the Soviets in Afghanistan and, later, to fight the Indians in Kashmir, yet another crisis that has dogged Pakistan since its inception.

Now that India's in the mix, Pakistan's struggle to attain parity with its mammoth neighbor proves germane to the discussion. In Aparna Pande's view, Pakistan's quest to achieve this parity informed the nation's pursuit, initiated under ZA Bhutto, of the "Islamic bomb" (50–2). Pakistan's successful testing of its nuclear bomb in the summer of 1998 introduces the phenomenon of "nuclear nationalism," a unique permutation of Pakistani nationalism fueled largely by the confidence gained from equaling India's capability, as that nation also tested the same summer. These shows of nuclear power might have contributed to the high tensions between the long-standing rivals in the summer of 2002 after the terrorist bombing of the Indian Parliament. The US's presence in Afghanistan and its plans to invade Iraq only compounded the friction. At the same time, any mention of Pakistan's nuclear status brings to the fore AQ Khan's role, divulged in 2004, in sharing information and materials with the likes of Libya and Iran. This brief overview already complicates the portrait of post-9/11 Pakistan, as this picture needs a wide-angle lens to capture all the other nations and players, including, in addition, China and Bangladesh, that also shape the nation's standing.

More decidedly internal historical developments also inform perceptions of post-9/11 Pakistan. As I allude to above, General Musharraf's overthrow of Sharif's government in 1999 was initially greeted warmly by even the more liberal elements of Pakistani society, as Sharif's power grabs and his government's appearance of corruption soured public perception. Like Benazir Bhutto before him, Sharif sought exile outside of Pakistan's borders. The exilic status of Pakistan's previous two Prime Ministers bears noting, because the US and the UK became involved in brokering deals for both Bhutto's and Sharif's returns in 2007. In particular, the international media, as well as the crowds who greeted Bhutto in Pakistan in the fall of 2007, indicated the hope that Bhutto's return to Pakistan also signaled a return to democracy. By 2007, of course, Musharraf's rule had itself taken a turn for the worse. The General-cum-President's battles with the judiciary, to name just one example, and his closing of madrassas at the behest of the Bush administration, to take another, compromised Musharraf's standing and the population's trust in him. Benazir Bhutto's assassination and the government's botched investigation of it further diminished the public's confidence in Musharraf. Once elections were held in 2008, Bhutto's widower,

Asif Ali Zardari became President, and Sharif briefly shared power. This return to elected government has not lessened Pakistan's domestic turmoil, as the 2011 US raid on Osama Bin Laden's Abbotabad compound illustrates. This signal moment encapsulates many of the issues, including questions of national sovereignty and of the government's inclination toward Islamist sympathies, currently influencing Pakistan's internal and international relations.

By locating my discussion of these four post-9/11 Pakistani novels in this specific historical context—that is, one focused most intently on how Pakistan straddles the purported divide between the pre- and post-9/11 designations—I address other scholars' calls to de-center the US in examinations of representations of that event and its aftermath. The critical buffer provided by the decade that has elapsed since the September 11 attacks allows for the identification of major trends and as yet unexplored areas in 9/11-related literary and cultural production. In broad strokes, critics now recognize the predominance of trauma-themed representations, especially by American artists.[2] In Anna Hartnell's view, for instance, "[T]he subject of most prominent 9/11 representations have overwhelmingly—and in many ways understandably—been the traumatized western subject whose aim is to recover, as opposed to transform, the confidence of a pre-9/11 order" ("Specter" 477). Hartnell's juxtaposition of the infinitives "to recover" and "to transform" hints at how US-centric these representations are, since the desire for recovery gestures toward a return to a period that, in hindsight, appears more whole or safe. Aaron DeRosa keys in on this operant nostalgia in his assessment of "9/11 fiction," which, in his view, frames the attacks as "a violent irruption in an otherwise pristine world" (608). Yet, despite the singularity of the 9/11 attacks, their representation as a traumatic loss, a violent fall, perpetuates, in Richard Gray's estimation, a long-running thematic pattern in American letters. Calling it "an old story, at least as old as the American nation" (3), Gray tracks the "recurrent tendency in American writing, and in the observation of American history, to identify crisis as a descent from innocence to experience" (2). The perennial thematization of this transition from pre- to post-lapsarian worlds within American discourses functions to reinforce exceptionalist convictions and establishes a curious ahistoricism in that the theme itself obscures the ways in which US foreign and domestic policies shape public and private lives for Americans and for people the world over. Framed in terms of a fall, representations of 9/11, especially those generated from within the US, actually prove more "continuous than disruptive," in Rachel Smith's view, despite widespread contention that 9/11 ruptured the world irrevocably (155).

The thematization of 9/11 in terms of a traumatic transition from innocence to experience also strikes at the heart of a primary critical divide. Kristiaan Versluys's "poethical" approach emblematizes this one-sided critical tendency. Versluys stakes his critical claim in 9/11 literature that enacts a "'poethical turn,'" that is, "works [that] testify to the shattering of certainties and the laborious recovery of balance" (13). This approach's US-centered affinities become more apparent when Versluys claims that "9/11 is a rupture for everybody" and that, in its wake, "there is a globalized need to comprehend, to explain, and to restore" (4). In conjunction with its restorative impulse that so closely echoes the pre-/post-lapsarian tendencies Gray has identified, Versluys's critical perspective also bears a universalizing tendency as it diagnoses the "globalized need" for recovery after the rupture felt by "everybody." Such sweeping gestures imply a binary logic, as any position outside the universal norm becomes deviant. Thus, to the exceptionalism and ahistoricism that accompany the pre-/post-lapsarian thematization in 9/11 representations, this critical disposition adds the sense that other perspectives are aberrant at their most neutral. With specific reference to how these attitudes inflect the ability to understand the Other, Richard Crownshaw claims that they "revea[l] the dependence of 'us' on the figuration and objectification of 'them' in the West's, and particularly the US's, construction of the terrorist" ("Perpetrator" 82). Moreover, to frame this point in the language of my analyses' own key terms, these discursive and critical tendencies that reinforce universalizing, ahistorical, and exceptionalist visions of US-centered views occlude—in the sense of rendering absent— alternative narratives through an abstraction premised upon a conventional notion of the Western subject and its political ideals.[3]

A return to Hartnell's juxtaposed infinitives—"to recover" and "to transform"—also points toward alternative critical avenues that can broaden the somewhat shuttered approaches I've been discussing. Over and again, critics view the perpetuation of the trauma- and fall-based approach as a failure because of its self-referentiality.[4] In Richard Crownshaw's terms, "[T]he experience of the temporality of traumatic time...often precludes the critical consideration of American territory" ("Deterritorializing" 758). As a corrective, these critics advocate analyses that locate US concerns in broader historical, ideological, and political contexts. Such contexts, especially when they concentrate on territory, help fill in the absences and concretize the abstractions. Leerom Medovoi's "'world-system literature'" framework takes a step in this direction as it "maps the dynamics of the system as an interplay of subject and object—power and desire, force and affect—as they are propelled by the spatial dialectics of territory and capital" (657). As Medovoi deploys this framework, other nations "orbit" the US (645), thus emphasizing representations of relations between the US and other nations. Relatedly, Gray advocates a critical approach concerned with both synchrony and diachrony, as these two dynamics enact "a demonstration of both the structural continuities between the past and present and the processes by which those continuities are challenged, dissolved, and reconstituted" (19). In action, the long historical view cross-hatched with a focus on the immediate present manifest, for Gray, as a hybridity that "reimagine[s] disaster by presenting us with an America situated between cultures" (17). Like Medovoi, Gray keeps the US squarely in the frame by his interest in seeing post-9/11 America represented as "a transcultural space in which different cultures reflect and refract, confront and bleed into one another" (55). Other critics place value in moving outside a specifically American frame of reference, no matter how hybridized. Alex Houen, for example, advocates an aesthetic "deterritorialization," as he argues for the "potentialist novel" whose imaginative universe constitutes an "other world of possibility [and] presents an effective engagement with the world, at the same time as being experientially affective" (430). Michael Rothberg is perhaps more literal in his move outside the US as he argues for a critical approach offering a "complementary centrifugal mapping that charts the outward movement of American power" (153). Pointedly, Rothberg differentiates this outward movement from the immigrant fictions Gray prefers; for Rothberg, the hybridity wrought through the immigrant experience "recast[s] the domestic space" of the US and, thus, "would risk reproducing the American exceptionalism and ignoring the context out of which the terror attacks emerged in the first place" (157). As this spectrum of critical attitudes reveals, historical, political, ideological, and even geographical contextualization concretizes the abstract and fills in absences by highlighting prior involvements and unresolved issues and tensions.

The migrancy trope as these four novels construct it operationalizes the significance of this contextualization. Just as in S. Khan's *Five Queen's Road*, the idea of migrancy as it operates in these post-9/11 novels gains significance only in relation to belonging. And, similar to how S. Khan's novel frames belonging as state-enabled, the fictions featured in this chapter also invoke and reject the state in their efforts to find a more suitable anchor for identity. Before laying out the specific manner in which my analyses deploy the idea of migrancy in relation to the post-9/11 Pakistani novels, I want to highlight how my use of the term stands in relation to its postcolonial conceptual heritage. Elleke Boehmer's schematization of the "postcolonial migrant" has proven influential to the field. Conceding the term's elitism, Boehmer also emphasizes how migrant writing "foregrounds and celebrates a national or historical rootlessness...sometimes accentuated by political cynicism" (*Migrant* 240). These traits emerge, according to Boehmer, at a particular historical moment: after both decolonization and the struggles with new nationhood many postcolonial states have faced. In Andrew Smith's view, migrancy and its attendant narrative production allows "people to escape the control of states and national boundaries," but its oftentimes elite status "can involve forms of domination as well as liberation" (*Migrant* 245–6). Although the ways in which the postcolonial migrant has been formulated often risks cooptation and collusion—that is, a blunting of postcolonialism's "long tradition of self-consciously political writing"—the concept does challenge purist notions of identity (Boehmer, *Migrant* 240).[5] The migrant's "impurity" facilitates the theorization of the position's or condition's hybridity. Literary migration involves, for Boehmer, "transplantation and cross-fertilization" (*Migrant* 233). Similarly, Carine Mardorossian contends that "migrant art offers a transnational, cosmopolitan, multilingual and hybrid map of the world" (17). Largely positive in their connotations, these pictures of hybridity encourage the view that migrancy smoothes exchange, aids in mutual understanding. It's also worth underscoring that these formulations often figure migrancy as unidirectional from Third to First Worlds, South to North. Yet, according to Revathi Krishnaswamy, such positive framings of the encounters brought about through movement contribute to the "mythologies of migrancy" (125) as they overlook political, ideological, and/or cultural affiliations or prejudices.

With the tightening of borders for some travelers and the increase of migrants and refugees due to the "war on terror," many of the same critics who were instrumental in defining the migrancy trope pre-9/11 have revised the concept so as to establish an analytical category more germane to current geopolitical and cultural circumstances. Ahmed Gamal, for example, recasts the "post-migrant" as decidedly oppositional rather than collusive ("Post-Migratory" 3). Further, Boehmer, in the 2005 revision of her influential 1995 *Colonial and Postcolonial Literature: Migrant Metaphors*, proclaims her suspicion of "anything resembling a universal or transnational category of post-colonial writing [that entails] the homogenization of hybridity and migrancy as trans-cultural, universally form-giving conditions" ("Afterword" 250). One reason for Boehmer's emergent skepticism resides in the ways universalization, post-9/11, reinforces the "completely non-specific" implications of "war on terror" rhetoric, which diffuses itself so that "terror is everywhere" (Boehmer, "Postcolonial Writing" 144, 145). New articulations of migrancy can, thus, address the abstractions inherent to dominant 9/11 narratives. At the same time, revisions of "migrancy" also promote the restoration of "temporal depth, a sense of deep layering or thickness of history" (Boehmer, "Postcolonial Writing" 149). These attempts to assert historical perspectives otherwise precluded in dominant narratives work to fill in those broader absences that extend backward and forward in time from September 11, 2001, along alternative trajectories. As for the optimism of hybridity's nearly undammed fluidity, Boehmer recognizes such a view as "no more than a declaration of postcolonial good faith, or a convenient rhetoric," both of which rely on "an impossibly equal exchange between the different cultural players" ("Afterword" 252). Sheering the optimism from the migrancy trope allows for the identification of the brutalities that can accompany cross-cultural encounters, which isn't to say that migrancy now resigns itself to the inevitability of clashes or conflicts. Rather, to identify brutality is, in part, to underscore the urgent need to find more constructive methods of communication and understanding across difference.

The analyses I undertake in this chapter draw from and develop further these recently revised formulations of migrancy. As it functions here, migrancy provides a thematic through which to approach how these Pakistani fictions treat absence and abstraction. Each migrant figure harbors an absence pre-dating but ultimately not unconnected to 9/11. With the extension of absences to points before September 11, 2001, all of these narratives shift emphasis away from the immediacy of the attacks, thereby suggesting that other signal moments can inform the relations between and interpretations of historical events. Further, as victims and/or perpetrators of violence, the migrant figures in these novels vivify the abstractions associated with the "war on terror," giving material form to bodies inhabiting those "elsewheres", and shaped by nationalist and civilizationalist discourses. Thus, these fictions' conception of migrancy both builds upon the alternative critical avenues into 9/11 literature outlined by Medovoi and

Gray, for example, while they also challenge some of these critics' points. Medovoi's "world-system literature," for instance, positions Pakistan so that it "orbits around the US in a larger global system of wealth, culture, and power" (645). Although the expansion of critical terms, including what constitutes "Pakistani" and what "American" (645), helps Medovoi break out of the national circumscriptions beleaguering other 9/11 discourses, his framework still privileges the US by centering it, even if in indisputable terms of greater wealth or power. My analyses indicate that national borders still exert considerable power, demarcating who belongs and who doesn't, which prompts an examination of what happens when these fictions center Pakistan as they also recognize the US's dominance. Like Medovoi, Gray theorizes a post-9/11 critical paradigm also sensitive to migrancy. I certainly share Gray's interest in promoting the "ability and willingness imaginatively to act on [the] recognition" of difference. Yet, Gray's privileging of hybridity as an "enactment of difference" risks overlooking or diminishing the brutality that can accompany migrancy (30). Once again, Gray characterizes "deterritorialization" as the creation of a space "in which different cultures reflect and refract, confront and bleed into one another" (55). As a phrase, "confront and bleed" clearly acknowledges the possibility of conflict, but its presentation in a context that advocates for an optimistic, if indeterminate, pluralism suggests that cultures' bleeding into each other will create an intermingling, yet another hybridity. I want to explore the alternative: the results of confrontation and bloodletting that don't necessarily result in a constructed consanguinity.

HM Naqvi's 2009 novel *Home Boy* is the only novel of the four I analyze in this chapter that remains, with the exception of some digressions, entirely in the US. Focused on three friends—Chuck, AC, and Jimbo—with varying claims to a Pakistani identity, who weather the transition from pre- to post-9/11 in New York City, Naqvi's novel presents a gradation of the migrant condition: Jimbo, whose name is actually Jamshed, is a "bonafide American," "born and bred in Jersey" (3); AC, short for Ali Chaudhry, seeks a green card and is the "only immigrant" among the three friends (2); Chuck or Shehzad, the narrator, is a Pakistani expatriate who travels to the US for college (4). Hard partying and drug taking characterize the three friends' pre-9/11 lives in New York City, where they style themselves "Metrostanis" on the city's club scene (14). Post-9/11, Chuck, AC, and Jimbo embark on a quest to Connecticut to find a fourth friend, the Shaman, another Pakistani migrant, from whom they haven't heard since the attacks on September 11. Punctuated by warning signs from the start, the trip to Connecticut devolves rapidly: with the Shaman not at home, the three friends break into his house and raise the neighbors' alarm. The FBI soon arrives, arrests all three young men on suspicion of terrorist activity, and incarcerates them separately at the Metropolitan Detention Center in New York. Chuck and Jimbo eventually get released, but AC faces charges—not on terrorism but on drug possession. With his former club-hopping world irretrievably lost and his visa set to expire, Chuck returns to Pakistan but only after learning, by chance, that the Shaman was one of the victims killed in the World Trade Center. As this brief summary suggests, the Shaman serves as one of the narrative's absences, and the revelation of his death well after the three friends stand falsely accused of terrorism highlights the insufficiencies of post-9/11 domestic discourses that racially profile brown-skinned, apparently Muslim men. The novel's other absence involves Chuck's father, whose death in 1985 (242), when Chuck was only around five years old, establishes a parallel between that historical moment and the novel's post-9/11 present. This subtle comparison introduces the novel's treatment of affective attachments to both the US and Pakistan through Chuck's conflicted emotions about "home" born of his uncertainty over how and why his father died. Thus, *Home Boy* deploys migrancy and absence to explore the challenges of belonging and to ironize the domestic—i.e. the US—concretization of "war on terror" discourses.

As first person narrator, Chuck primarily presents 9/11 in terms of how US responses to it affect migrant identities. The novel's opening lines indicate how attitudes toward the likes of Chuck change: "We'd become Japs, Jews, Niggers. We weren't before. We fancied ourselves boulevardiers, raconteurs, renaissance men, AC, Jimbo, and me" (1). Chuck's litany of Others sets up an historical trajectory right from the start, insisting on a pattern in American domestic relations that pre-dates 9/11. At the same time, "fancied" suggests a measure of naïveté and agency, in equal doses, on the friends' parts. That is, the friends project their self-perceptions outward, believing that they can actively construct their own identities in America. Notably, these pre-9/11 identities included the characters' Pakistani roots while also inserting a new take on what that background means. Before the attacks, Chuck, AC, and Jimbo enjoy some measure of celebrity as "Metrostanis" on the city's club scene (14). "Metrostani," a term AC coins, signifies the friends' hard-partying, somewhat glamorous lifestyle, and contrasts their hyphenated identities to that of "Puppies": "Pakistani Urban Professionals" (170). This latter group resembles more closely the early waves of subcontinental immigrants to the US whose primary motivation was economic security (35). "Metrostanis" differ in that the social scene the three friends frequent, at least pre-9/11, is significantly more cosmopolitan and illicit, with its de rigueur drug use and its apparent disregard for the "coveted careers for able young Pakistani men" (35). The distance between Metrostanis and Puppies matters, pre-9/11, because it shows how Chuck and his friends outgrow the more traditional migrant Pakistani community established in large measure by AC's older sister, Mini, whom Chuck meets before both AC and Jimbo. Upon first coming to the US in the late 1990s, for instance, Chuck leans on Mini, a "pillar of the city's expatriate Pakistani community" and, more personally, "a foster mother" who stabilizes Chuck after his initial expatriate disorientation (22). Yet, as the friendships between the three young men strengthen, their affective center shifts to the community dominated by Jimbo's girlfriend Dora (22). Dora, a high society blue blood, represents for the three friends an entrée into the party scene wherein they take on their Metrostani identities. From within this self-propelled identity, New York City, pre-9/11, appears to Chuck as a place where "you felt you were no different from anyone else; you were your own man;

you were free" (20). The elision of difference derived from the city's pluralism, along with the "premise of the nation, the bit about 'your bruised and battered'" (19), makes the US seem to Chuck more welcoming than the UK, which is "habitable if not always hospitable" (19). As Chuck presents it, a migrant identity in pre-9/11 America resembles the optimistic pluralism common to much postcolonial discourse, wherein difference can be the basis for solidarity.

Migrant identities undergo a sharp change, post-9/11, as they morph into the latest entry on the list of maligned Others with which Chuck opens the novel. Certainly, the three friends' experiences with the FBI represent the most extreme example of the change in their abilities to claim belonging to the US. During his interrogation, Chuck realizes just how far outside the US national fold he is when the federal agent responds to Chuck's rights-based demand to make a phone call: "'You aren't American!...You got no fucking rights'" (135). Even their presence in New York City itself is different. One night after September 11, Chuck, AC, and Jimbo congregate at one of their usual haunts, only to be confronted by two other patrons, who, in their drunken state, refer to the three friends as "'A-*rabs*'" (30). Chuck registers the taunt as "the first time anything like this had happened to us at all," as the encounter is of a different kind all together from their usual barroom scuffles (30). The city changes, too, from Chuck's perspective. Roosevelt Avenue, or Little Pakistan, formerly a bustling neighborhood, is now, post-9/11, a place where "[e]very other shop seemed shuttered, and the sidewalks were mostly abandoned by the aunty patrols" (229). This section of the city itself becomes a kind of absence as, due to the "sweeps following 9/11, many had fled across the border" (229). Migrants of Pakistani descent can no longer inhabit their roles or their locales in the same way, for regular reminders barrage them with the message that they do not belong. This rejection manifests itself violently, as Chuck's, AC's, and Jimbo's incarcerations attest, and more subtly, as the three friends rejoin the Pakistani community they once left behind in favor of the club scene. Chuck describes the increased saliency of these communal ties:

> After 9/11 we heard not only from family and friends but from distant relatives, colleagues, ex-colleagues, one-night stands, neighbors, childhood friends, acquaintances, and in turn we made our own inquiries, phone calls, dispatched e-mails.
>
> (27–8)

This insular turn re-marks migrant identities as outside a collective US national identity and, in turn, seems to reinforce a Pakistani one by default. Gone are both the appearance of self-definition and the naïveté of believing in such self-determination.

For all the influence 9/11 exerts on migrant identities in the novel, Chuck makes only oblique references to the events of that day, figuring them as a kind of narrative absence. 9/11 occurs early in the novel's chronology. After a brief sketch of the friends' good, pre-9/11 times, Chuck simply states, "Two, maybe three weeks later we assembled at Tja! because we were anxious and low and getting cabin fever watching CNN 24–7" (7–8). This sentence's appearance after the atmospheric presentation of the club scene makes the "two, maybe three weeks later" designation seem as though it refers merely to some social downtime. But the reference to CNN later in the sentence signals that, at some point during those two to three weeks, 9/11 happened. On this same night, the friends get into the fight with the other bar patrons who call them "'A-*rabs*,'" though this confrontation occurs more than twenty pages later. Chuck once again omits any direct narration of the events of 9/11 when he describes where he was on that very morning. Arriving nearly late for a job interview in midtown, Chuck enters the office lobby and finds "no palpable signs of life on the fifty-sixth floor" (120). Moments later, he hears a "wheezy sob," which leads him to discover "ten, fifteen people gathered before a window facing south" (120). Chuck approaches the window and

> stood there for a long time, dazed and a little dizzy. I would have remained there for longer had the building not been evacuated, and though I found myself on the street afterward, safe and sound, in brilliant sunshine, I remained in a daze for weeks.
>
> (121)

Nowhere in his narration does Chuck describe what he or the office workers actually see. Because this scene would furnish an eyewitness account, the omission is even more striking than the earlier one wherein the mere mention of the passage of time is meant to convey the transition from the pre- to post-9/11 eras. Chuck's narratorial deflections regarding any direct engagement with 9/11 could be read as a reticence over representing or spectacularizing the violence. Or, these deflections may indicate another kind of representational insufficiency, one that foils expectations and, in doing so, acknowledges the need to include other perspectives by deliberately leaving them out. In other words, while Chuck does include instances of trauma—his own dazed condition—and of lashing out—the bar brawl—his narratorial absences, along with the plot-oriented ones involving the Shaman and Chuck's father, function to illustrate the material violence of the abstract "war on terror" and to expand the historical scope through the parallels established by Chuck's father's death.

The friends' inability to account for the Shaman after 9/11 serves as one of the novel's absences. In addition to highlighting how Chuck, AC, and Jimbo come to rely once again on the transplanted Pakistani community, their quest to find the Shaman also illustrates how the abstract "war on terror" bears material consequences for those it targets: namely, brown-skinned men who look as though they're Muslims. Chuck doesn't read the Shaman's obituary, which recounts his death in the World Trade Center on September 11, until long after he and his friends stand falsely accused of terrorist activities. Thus, as it unfolds in the novel's present, mystery enshrouds their quest to find the Shaman. Upon illegally gaining entry into the Shaman's Connecticut home, for instance, Chuck comments on the strange condition in which they find the house: Chinese takeout cartons are left on the counter, the air conditioning is set just "shy of fifty degrees," and then, "something weirder[:] Instead of cereal boxes and mineral water, the shelves were stocked with rows of cigarette cartons" (105–6). Coupled with the house's half-furnished state, these conditions give Chuck the impression that the Shaman's life is somehow off. The friends spend their time at the Shaman's house watching television, and Chuck describes two programs in detail. The first is a news story about a Pakistani immigrant who was arrested under suspicion of terrorism after he asked "*a passerby to photograph him against the Hudson*" (115; emphasis in original). A portent of the circumstances soon to befall the three friends, the news story prompts both anger and panic. The second program features an address given by then President George Bush. Chuck reacts viscerally, sobbing "unexpectedly and ridiculously" as he listens to Bush enjoin, "*Our grief has turned to anger, and anger to resolution. Whether we bring our enemies to justice, or bring justice to our enemies, justice will be done*'" (118; emphasis in original). Yet, what Chuck's weeping signifies remains unclear. While listening to Bush's speech, Chuck admits to being "stirred by the words," but, at the same time, he confesses, "My sense of grief, however, had not quite turned to anger, and anger had certainly not turned to the stuff of resolution" (118). And, as he cries, he recites a Koranic verse: "'We come from God and return to God'" (121). Chuck's emotional ambivalence and his recourse to the Koran signal a critical distance between his own and the President's attitudes toward the US response to the attacks. This scene occurs before Chuck's detention, before a federal agent reminds him that he has no rights because he's not American. Effectively, then, Chuck's conflicted state places him in the "against" camp of Bush's "with us or against us" dichotomy. Further, the strangeness Chuck notes throughout his time at the Shaman's house primes the reader to wonder, if not suspect, what motivates AC's drive to find the Shaman and why the Shaman lives as he does.

The novel tweaks the uncertainties raised by the mysterious circumstances of the Shaman's absence to illustrate how the three friends' post-9/11 identities place them not just outside of national belonging but also make them vulnerable to state-sponsored brutalities. When the FBI shows up at the Shaman's front door, motivated by "'an anonymous tip…that there's been some…suspicious activity in this house,'" AC challenges the agents' authority, asking them for a search warrant and refusing to answer their question about the three friends' national identities (127). The situation rapidly deteriorates, though, and, as with his eye-witnessing of the events of September 11, Chuck elects not to narrate the scene in detail:

> The sequence of discrete incidents that led to our arrest remains somewhat fuzzy, partly because it all happened so fast, partly because the adrenaline coursing through my head blinded me, but whatever happened, happened with the momentum of inevitability…I think [Holt, one of the agents] was the first to draw…Instead of raising my arms, however, I instinctively cowered,

holding my head between my hands. I remember praying, *Allah bachao*, God save us. I remember Trig [the other agent] instructed us to *sit-the-fuck-down* and *shut-the fuck-up*.

(128; emphasis in original).

In this scene, the representatives of the state use the threat of violence to stifle rights-based procedures and protocols. To Chuck, such a course of action takes on "the momentum of inevitability," suggesting pre-determination: the agents' predisposition to convict the three friends irrespective of the circumstance's particulars. Given Chuck's admission that the whole scene remains "fuzzy," that he remembers praying in Urdu gains much significance, as the language— and the recognizable "Allah"—emphasizes his foreignness and likely prompts Trig's profane directive to stop talking. Similar to the absence of any direct or immediate representation of the violence at the World Trade Center, Chuck's omission of the exact details of the friends' arrest points toward the need for an alternative perspective by leaving it unspoken. Separated from his friends and hooded for his transport to the Metropolitan Detention Center, or "'America's Own Abu Ghraib,'" Chuck suffers many indignities, including being told to "'Take off everything, sand nigger'" (137) and being locked up, alone, in a cell with a backed up, overflowing toilet (138). As he loses track of days, Chuck resigns himself to the realization that his treatment "seemed routine, the invective, the casual violence, the way things are, the way things are going to be: doors would open, doors would close, and I would be smacked around, molested, hauled back and forth between cells and interrogation sessions" (138). And the authorities mete out this treatment based on an "anonymous tip." For all he endures, Chuck later learns that Jimbo and AC had even worse experiences. Jimbo reveals to Chuck the "pink welts on his rounded shoulders" (227), for example. To Chuck, this evidence of the violence Jimbo endured is a "jarring display. Tracing the outline of a lash just above the shoulder blade, it occurred to me that if Jimbo had been beaten, AC would have been left for dead" (227). The coincidence of AC's drug possession provides the government with an escape route: they drop the false terrorism charges and, instead, prosecute him for possession, which carries a sentence of fifteen years to life (245). With a deus ex machina operating in its favor, the government does not have to account for the insufficiencies of its reasoning, the discrimination of its profiling, and the violence that results. The novel itself, however, draws attention precisely to these issues by making AC yet another absence and, as it turns out, a sacrifice to a national rabidity that should, instead, have mourned with AC, Chuck, and Jimbo over the loss of the Shaman in the World Trade Center.

Similarly, the absence of Chuck's father gestures toward a story that still needs telling by establishing a parallel between two signal moments in US–Pakistani relations: the 1980s and post-9/11. Late in the novel, Chuck reveals that his father died in 1985 (242). At that time, historically-speaking, the CIA's covert war against the Soviet Union was raging, and the US funneled untold millions and munitions through Pakistan to support the mujahideen, many of whom came from other parts of the Muslim world. Chuck makes no overt connection between his father's death and the Afghan conflict. Instead, Chuck's references to his father often entail a sense of not knowing. The first time the novel mentions the father, Chuck reveals,

> I am not even sure how he "passed away." According to family lore, he slipped in the bathtub, but I had a persistent suspicion, substantiated only by aborted conversations and skittish expressions on faces of aunts and uncles, that he committed suicide.

(36)

His father's death thus becomes a compounded absence, as Chuck is literally without a father and he remains uncertain over how or why his father died. This uncertainty itself becomes persistent in Chuck's life, evidenced, for instance, in his ambivalent reaction to Bush's speech that I discuss above. The father's absence also becomes a metaphor in the novel via a suitcase Chuck's mother gifts him for his trip to the US. Tying together migrancy and absence, the suitcase represents for Chuck missing narratives: "There was some story [in the suitcase] but I didn't know it. I didn't know anything about anything" (160). This admission of not knowing, this acknowledgment of insufficient narratives, matches a confession Chuck makes in hindsight regarding his own and his friends' efforts to define themselves as Metrostanis: "Later we...realized that we hadn't been putting on some sort of show for others, for somebody else. No, we were protagonists in a narrative that required coherence for our own selfish motivations and exigencies" (7). This statement lays the groundwork for the parallels between the two historical moments in that it conveys Chuck's understanding that the possibility of self-definition eluded him even before 9/11 and certainly after. Nonetheless, his concession suggests that belief in this possibility of self-definition may well be a pre-condition for claiming a sense of belonging to place, be it New York City or Pakistan. The purpose of the parallels between historical moments that the father's absence establishes is to show how missing narratives obstruct the articulation of such claims in both instances.

While Chuck doesn't explicitly connect his father's death with the Afghan conflict, the novel does include historical and political commentary, provided by AC, which quietly makes that link. Early in the novel, AC offers a disquisition on the US's cultivation of the mujahideen, recalling that the Reagan administration "'invited them to Washington and, ah, compared them to the Founding Fathers...Osama B. was one of them'" (12). As he continues with the history lesson, AC points out that, after the Soviets left Afghanistan, members of the US government washed their hands of the region, referring to the last "great" conflict of the Cold War as "'the obscure Afghan civil war'" (13). No long view narrative of the US's involvement in the Afghan war would be complete, in AC's telling, without mention of the Taliban, who, despite their genesis in the Soviet conflict, found themselves, post-9/11, "'on the wrong side of history'" (14). AC's narrative distinctly engraves connections between the two historical moments—the

1980s and post-9/11—and recasts the significance of Chuck's ambivalences and uncertainties, especially with respect to his affective attachments to the US and Pakistan.

The connections constructed between historical moments by the absence of Chuck's father expand the idea of being "on the wrong side of history," wherein neither the US nor Pakistan emerge as suitable objects of affective attachment. Even before his experience at the Metropolitan Detention Center, Chuck's reaction to Bush's speech—his ambivalence and his tears—re-emphasizes the alienation he feels from New York and, by extension, the US as he recognizes his Metrostani identity as a self-willed construct. Chuck's attitudes toward Pakistan are similarly wary. Just as the "bruised and battered" line from the Statue of Liberty draws Chuck into the narrative of US idealism, he is also invested in the idea of Pakistan. For example, though sparsely furnished, his "second-story walkup" apartment in New York does have a framed picture of "M. A. Jinnah, the founder of Pakistan, playing billiards, biting a cigar" (32–3). Part of Jinnah's appeal for Chuck is the politician's own migrant experiences; at the same time, by hanging a framed photo of Jinnah in his apartment, Chuck also signals his affective investment in what the idea of Pakistan represents. And, once again obliquely, the novel suggests a more complex attitude toward Pakistan as a nation and a state develops. While holed up at the Shaman's, for instance, Chuck comes upon AC watching pornography. Chuck suggests a change of channel, hoping "'there'll be something about Musharraf's speech'" (113). AC refuses obstinately, declaring, "'Nobody knows what's going on, but everybody's busy parceling myths and prejudice as analysis and reportage...All I want to know is why I can't get off on garden-variety porn these days'" (113–14). Hitting again upon the idea of uncertainty, which indicates a narrative insufficiency, AC's refusal serves once more as political commentary. The juxtaposition of Musharraf's speech with pornography suggests the obscenity of the former. Musharraf's position as military dictator or, more specifically, the demands of the US to which he accedes come off in this implicit comparison as exploitative, violent, even immoral.

Another scene to which Chuck is a witness and not a participant similarly critiques Musharraf's power. While at Mini's house, Chuck hears two Pakistanis debating Musharraf's legitimacy. One, a minister in Musharraf's government, declaims, "'Many on the left and right...have been maintaining that we should have held out, bargained [with the US], what have you, but Musharraf joined the coalition at considerable personal and national risk'" (166). In response, his skeptical interlocutor presses, "'But how can you defend a dictator?...That's the problem with you Pakistanis—'" (166). "Musharraf" could be swapped out for "Zia" in the minister's comments, as the ascendance of the two military dictators share many commonalities, as I discussed earlier. And the other man's objection might similarly have been launched at those who supported Zia some twenty years earlier. Additionally, the second man distances himself from a collective designated "Pakistanis" even though he is also one. The distinction this man makes—and which the minister, who chides, "'And what are you, my friend?'"

(166), won't allow—shows a splintering, a detachment from a national identity prompted by the actions of the state. This interaction compounds AC's critique even as it subtly extends the historical connections established by the absence of Chuck's father. Both instances begin the work of narrativizing absence, of addressing the insufficiencies noted by the characters' migrant positions. And, significantly, these attempts at narration don't invoke a hybrid or pluralistic ideal; rather, they bring forward the violence inflicted by the otherwise abstract "war on terror."

Changez, the protagonist of Mohsin Hamid's 2007 novel, *The Reluctant Fundamentalist,* undergoes many of the same experiences as Naqvi's protagonist. Like Chuck, Changez integrates almost effortlessly into pre-9/11 New York City, remarking, for instance, that moving to New York "felt—so unexpectedly—like coming home" (32). Post-9/11, Changez also sees the city change: "I ignored as best I could the rumors I overheard at the Pak-Punjab Deli: Pakistani cabdrivers were being beaten within an inch of their lives; the FBI raided mosques, shops, and even people's houses; Muslim men were disappearing, perhaps into shadowy detention centers for questioning or worse" (94). The rumors Changez tries to ignore reflect rather accurately the very experiences Chuck, AC, and Jimbo have in *Home Boy.* Both novels emphasize how their protagonists live in "marked" bodies that become all the more vulnerable or threatening, post-9/11. Where Chuck was a hit on the party scene, pre-9/11, Changez was an exotic favorite among the elite of Princeton and New York society (11, 42, 48). Post-9/11, Chuck suffers as the abstract "war on terror" inflicts physical pain and humiliation upon him. In response to the humiliation he suffers, Changez opts to maximize the stereotype of the threatening Muslim male by growing a beard, a physical provocation that manifests his anger over the brutalities visited upon brown men and his home nation. Another parallel between the two protagonists emerges in their realizations, made in hindsight, that what they took for acceptance actually was a powerful narrative desire at work. For Chuck, that narrative desire was his and his friends' self-propelled Metrostani identities. Changez's realization similarly involves a recognition of the constructed nature of his identity. Whereas Chuck's hindsight allows him to see through the myth of America as a migrant's haven, Changez's cuts through the related myth of the self-made man. That is, initially, Changez buys into the idea that the US is a meritocracy. Gradually, however, he identifies the power dynamics that link the selection of the meritorious with the maintenance of a system of superiority built more on economic than personal worth.

Hamid's novel also adds new elements to an analysis of Pakistani fictive representations of 9/11 and its aftermath. Migrancy and absence collaborate to refocus the fiction's affective energies onto Pakistan rather than the US. Their combined seismic thrust gains momentum from a notable reversal of the migrancy trope. Although Changez (once again like Chuck) is a Pakistani expatriate in New York City, Hamid's novel offers its most provocative contributions to the critical saliency of migrancy in a post-9/11 era by positioning the American, Changez's unnamed interlocutor, as the migrant. Like the conventional migrant, this American experiences disorientation, confusion, and even fear in Lahore. More significantly, by focusing on the American's migrant displacement in Pakistan, the novel draws to the surface the power dynamics inherent in the migrant experience, allowing Changez, as native, to exert control over the situation, which he does narratorially and, perhaps, violently. As Matthew Hart and Jim Hansen contend, "Hamid holds no brief for painless cultural translation or hybridization..." (508). Depending on how one reads the novel's conclusion, Changez may have torqued the power dynamics inherent in the migrant experience to the extent that he replaces the abstract—because anonymous—violence inflicted by global capitalism with the real brutalism of a violent assault. Alternatively, if the American does indeed kill Changez, then the novel's conclusion exposes the actual brutalities behind the putative objectivity of capitalist fundamentalism.[6] Further, this laying bare of the power dynamics attendant to the migrant experience permits an examination of Changez's affective attachments to Pakistan. While at first dazzled by the allure of success in the US, Changez reverses his gaze after 9/11, much as the novel reverses the migrancy trope, and discovers that to value the identity the US offers him is to render his own background an absence. To forestall this outcome, Changez returns home and takes an active role in the promotion of democracy in Pakistan. This move represents a carefully negotiated national identity, one premised on a valuing of cultural heritage and the power of pluralism rather than on a chest-thumping nuclear nationalism.

A quick examination of Changez's own migrant experiences contextualizes the implications of the novel's reversal of the migrancy trope. Changez borrows many of the conventions of the American immigrant narrative as he tells his American listener about his life at Princeton and, later, as a fledgling consultant at Underwood Samson.[7] While a thousand of the smartest Americans enrolled in Changez's class at Princeton, he makes his listener aware that he was one of only two Pakistanis to have that honor. As Changez puts it, "the Americans faced much less daunting odds" (*Reluctant* 3). The math, then, supports Changez's claim that students like him—i.e. international students—were "the best and the brightest" (*Reluctant* 4). Changez's computations, made in retrospect as he's relaying this story more than four years after he entered Princeton, already reveal his jadedness. He recognizes, for instance, that "[s]tudents like [him] were given visas and scholarships, complete financial aid, mind you, and invited into the ranks of the meritocracy" (*Reluctant* 4). For all these benefits, students like Changez are expected to "contribute our talents to your [the US's] society...And for the most part, we were happy to do so" (*Reluctant* 4). The clause "and for the most part" signals Changez's skepticism, and his follow up sentence—"I certainly was, at least at first" (*Reluctant* 4)—leaves no doubt in either his listener's nor the reader's mind that Changez has rethought the benefits afforded him through the US's supposedly meritocratic system. One of the cracks in the shell of the US's meritocracy becomes visible through Changez's experiences at that other US, Underwood Samson, the prestigious consulting company at which he gets a job straight out of Princeton. A vice president at the company proclaims to

Changez and the new recruits that Underwood Samson is "'a meritocracy... We believe in being the best...If you do well, you'll be rewarded. If you don't, you'll be out the door'" (*Reluctant* 35). This speech articulates the premise behind the myth of the self-made man, the one who lifts himself up by his own boot straps.

And, as Changez admits while talking to the American in Lahore, at first, he swallowed this line whole. When on assignment in the Philippines, for instance, Changez "attempted to act and speak, as much as [his] dignity would permit, more like an *American*" (*Reluctant* 65; emphasis in original). In New York, Changez entertains the idea that his "Pakistaniness was invisible, cloaked by [his] suit, by [his] expense account, and—most of all—by [his] companions" (*Reluctant* 71). Gradually, however, Changez peppers the narrative he spins for the American with enough hints to suggest his growing awareness of the cost of this Americanness. When engaging with his colleagues, those companions who Changez thinks reinforce his Americanness, Changez realizes that "shorn of hair and dressed in battle fatigues, we would have been virtually indistinguish- able" (*Reluctant* 38). The militarized vision Changez entertains links the recruits' consulting labor with war, suggesting that their concern for economic fundamen- tals amounts to violence. At another point in the novel, Changez voices his reser- vations about the work Underwood Samson does only to be told by one of his colleagues, "'You're working for the *man*, buddy. Didn't anyone tell you that at orientation?'" (*Reluctant* 98). Cumulatively, these insights amount to a revelation of the power dynamics operating behind a putatively objective meritocracy, one that promotes the idea that the individual controls his own rise or fall rather than positioning that individual in a larger system that runs on perpetuating privilege at the expense of those who are systematically disenfranchised. Changez realizes as much by the time his career implodes, an event precipitated in part by the US's reaction to 9/11:

> [Y]our country's [the US's] constant interference in the affairs of others was insufferable. Vietnam, Korea, the straits of Taiwan, the Middle East, and now Afghanistan...Moreover, I knew from my experience as a Pakistani—of alternating periods of American aid and sanctions—that finance was a primary means by which the American empire exercised its power. It was right for me to refuse to participate any longer in facilitating this project of domination...
>
> (*Reluctant* 156)

This explicit connection between military power and money defines, in large measure, for Changez what it means to be an American. The suffering and devas- tation visited upon the locations he lists amount to the price exacted for the privilege of claiming that national identity. Changez's migrant experiences school him in the arithmetic of this exchange.

Changez's presentation of the life he lived in the US highlights that what appeared to be an idea of subjectivity, one characterized by an autonomous self-determination based on effort and skill, turns out to be a product of a larger system that maintains itself through a concealed but no less systematic violence. These insights inform how the novel then frames its reversal of the migrancy trope. The unnamed American who serves as Changez's immediate audience as they sit together at a café in Lahore's Anarkali Bazaar consistently signals his discomfort, at least from Changez's perspective. Upon their first meeting, for example, Changez remarks that his approach appears to have "alarmed" the American (*Reluctant* 1). At other instances, this man seems "worried" (*Reluctant* 5), "suspicious" (*Reluctant* 11), "uncomfortable" (*Reluctant* 102), "puzzled" (*Reluctant* 53), "ill at ease" (*Reluctant* 108), and so forth. Such emotions and behaviors describe any migrant's disorientation. Indeed, many of these descriptors could modify Changez in New York after 9/11. With respect to the American, this destabilization comes off as even more striking due to his admission, mediated through Changez's response, that he is "well-traveled for an American" (*Reluctant* 64). Peter Morey comments that the novel's presentation of the American as "having strayed outside his element" "translates into lack of power as the American is baited about his exposed and lonely position" ("Rules" 141). Indeed, a discrepancy emerges between the American's imposing physical presence—Changez remarks repeatedly on his "expansive chest" and his "*bearing*" (*Reluctant* 2; emphasis in original)—on the one hand, and the vulnerability Changez ascribes to him throughout their conversation, on the other.

Yet, given the first person narrative structure, one can't help calling into question the ingenuousness of Changez's descriptions. Anticipating such an objection, Changez informs his interlocutor, in a move clearly meant to similarly enlighten the novel's reader,

> But surely it is the *gist* that matters; I am, after all, telling you a history, and in history, as I suspect you—an American—will agree, it is the thrust of one's narrative that counts, not the accuracy of one's details.
>
> (*Reluctant* 118; emphasis in original)

The narrative stress Changez puts on the American's demeanor connects to a narrative desire: to tell a specific history. In other words, by setting the American off balance, both in the context of the action of the novel (imagine a conversation in which one's partner repeatedly insists that one appears unsettled) and as part of the fiction the reader encounters, Changez imposes a history lesson upon his listener. Further, given the monologic nature of the narrative voice, this imposition is forcible. Although Changez "responds" to the American throughout the novel, not once does the narrative voice cede any space for the direct incorporation of the American's words, or anyone else's for that matter, as Changez ventriloquizes the other characters' speech as well. And, the conclusion's ambiguity reinforces the violence underwriting any encounter when narratives vie for dominance. The recurring predator/prey references support this claim (*Reluctant* 31, 60–1, 63, 77, 101, 123). Whether Changez turns out to be an actual threat to the American or a victim of the US's insecurity, his hospitality bears with it a recognizable brutality as he torques the American's very foreignness to impress upon him and the novel's audience an otherwise occluded historical perspective.

The reversal of the migrancy trope conducted by *The Reluctant Fundamentalist* situates Changez in the pole position, a powerful discursive location that facilitates Changez's re-evaluation of his repressed ties to Pakistan. As I note above, pre-9/11, Changez took advantage of his exoticism, reaping the benefits of being an intriguing Other as this role allowed him entrée into the social circles to which he aspired. Yet, by the time he starts working for Underwood Samson, Changez deliberately apes the behaviors of his American colleagues—he "learned to tell executives [his] father's age, 'I need it *now*'; [and he] learned to cut to the front of lines with an extraterritorial smile" (*Reluctant* 65), for instance—believing that doing so made his Pakistani identity invisible (*Reluctant* 71). With an indeterminate sincerity, in the telling of his story, Changez reveals his misgivings. At times, he claims he felt "ashamed" (*Reluctant* 65), or, when his love interest's father diagnoses Pakistan's pre-9/11 ills, Changez "felt himself bridle" not because of any inaccuracy in the other man's assessment, but because of "his tone—with, if you will forgive me, its typically *American* undercurrent of condescension..." (*Reluctant* 55; emphasis in original). The father's condescension results, the novel suggests, from the clipped and abbreviated understanding the US has of the larger world, including its relations with and impact upon nations such as Pakistan. Indeed, Changez doesn't fault the father's facts, for "his was a summary with some knowledge, much like the short news items on the front page of *The Wall Street Journal*" (*Reluctant* 55). Changez's analogy highlights the insufficiencies that rankle him: Americans like this father—a powerful, successful man who lives on New York's Upper East Side—glean their understanding from "short news items" in newspapers explicitly connected to the US's economic dominance. Complicated contexts and deep histories are absent from such perspectives.

Changez fills in these absences by highlighting a host of comparisons between the US and Pakistan.[8] These comparisons allow Changez to identify what he values about Pakistan, thus initiating a shift in his own affective attachments. For example, Changez describes a reversal in his attitude toward Princeton: "When I first arrived, I looked around me at the Gothic buildings—much younger, I later learned, than many of the mosques of this city [Lahore], but made through acid treatment and ingenious stone-masonry to look older—and thought, *This is a dream come true*" (*Reluctant* 3; emphasis in original). The retrospective insertion deflates the allure of the meritocratic illusions to which Changez initially subscribed. Moreover, by noting the artificiality of the campus's appearance, Changez implies the comparative historical shallowness of this bastion of the American elite. Inversely, Lahore's mosques possess a deep history, one that, again in comparison, appears to strike Changez as more authentic because not achieved "through acid treatment and ingenious stone-masonry." The value Changez places on Lahore's long history, which, notably, isn't necessarily Pakistan's, inspires an increasingly urgent sense of resistance. When Jim, his boss at Underwood Samson who grew up poor in New Jersey, claims a connection between them because the places of their respective childhoods "'were wasting away'" (*Reluctant* 97), Changez reflects upon his discomfort with the "idea that the place I came from was condemned to atrophy" (*Reluctant* 97). The passive voice verb form—"was condemned"—begs the question of by whom? Jim's disquisition provides a partial answer: "'Power comes from *becoming* change'" (*Reluctant* 97). A neat instantiation of a developmentalist mindset, Jim's conclusion about the necessity of dynamism appropriates in some measure the fluidity associated with theories of hybridity and transnationalism. Thus, Changez's misgivings about how Jim's perspective relegates Pakistan to the rubbish bin signals a qualified vigilance with respect to his home. That is, not only is Changez rejecting the (paradoxical) telos of Jim's narrative, but he is also implicitly pledging allegiance to his place in terms outside of those Jim advocates. Changez describes the moment at which he became aware of his shifting loyalties and values as an "exorcism [of] the unwelcome sensibility by which I had become possessed" (*Reluctant* 124). Where, upon returning to Pakistan in December of 2001, Changez, with "the Americanness of [his] own gaze," saw "how shabby [his family's] house appeared, with cracks running through its ceilings and dry bubbles of paint flaking off where dampness had entered its wall" (*Reluctant* 124), he comes to recognize, post-exorcism, the house's "enduring grandeur" and the richness of its history (*Reluctant* 125). Once again hitting upon the depth of the place's authenticity, Changez anchors himself in Lahore.

Hamid's novel makes a concerted effort to distinguish the types of identities that exert an affective pull on Changez. His attempts to fill in the absences overlooked by a valorization of Americanness demonstrate that Changez's affective attachments are to Lahore's deep history. This attachment is regionally oriented, as Changez stresses: "I am not poor; far from it: my great-grandfather, for example, was a barrister with the means to endow a school for Muslims of the Punjab" (*Reluctant* 9). As he casts back four generations, Changez subtly points out that his family has belonged to the northwest of India even before Pakistan's birth. Pointedly, the great-grandfather's endowment was for Punjabi Muslims, not Pakistani Muslims. This distinction between a regional identity (rather than a provincial one, if we focus on pre-partition India) and a national one matters, because it creates a space in which Changez negotiates between a dominant Pakistani nationalism and a new formulation of collective belonging that avoids the trap of us-versus-them nationalisms.[9] Pluralism is one of the hallmarks of the nationalism Changez promotes. In his account of his political activities in Pakistan, for instance, Changez points out that he protests alongside people of "all affiliations—communists, capitalists, feminists, religious literalists" (*Reluctant* 179). This sort of political solidarity across the ideological spectrum stands in stark contrast to the top-down enforced unity conventionally associated with dominant Pakistani nationalism.

Further, Changez insists that this coalition's political aims include advocacy for "greater independence in Pakistan's domestic and international affairs," a rather wide-ranging set of concerns (*Reluctant* 179). One international concern that fits under this heading involves Pakistan's long-standing tensions with India. Right alongside Changez's growing resentment of the US, for instance, are his misgivings over the dangerous friction mounting between the two subcontinental neighbors immediately after 9/11. In the novel's chronology, this friction approaches incendiary potential in late 2001 and early 2002, a period that matches extra-fictional reality. Upon his return to Pakistan in December 2001, Changez learns from his brother that "'there is an artillery battery dug in at the country house of a friend of [Changez's brother], half an hour from here, and a colonel billeted in his spare bedroom'" (*Reluctant* 125–6). Conversations about the possibility of war with India punctuate Changez's interactions with his family during this visit, leaving him with the impression that "there was unanimity in the belief that India would do all it could to harm us, and that despite the assistance we had given America in Afghanistan, America would not fight at our side" (*Reluctant* 126–7). As Changez has it, America only gets pulled into Pakistani anxieties through the conflict with India; that is, to position Changez's Pakistani loyalties as necessarily or automatically or wholly anti-American misses the more nuanced point of his concerns, as well as the longer history of conflict Pakistan shares with India.

Even as the novel injects these South Asian concerns, it still presents Changez's political position as unconventional. As the residents of Lahore go about their daily lives, they "hear the sounds of military helicopters flying low overhead; a rumor circulated that soon traffic would be halted on the motorway so that our fighter planes could practice landing on it, in case all of our airfields were destroyed in a nuclear exchange" (*Reluctant* 127). Unphased: that's how Changez characterizes his urban neighbors even in this heightened militaristic context that, once again, centers on Pakistani–Indian relations rather than on Pakistani–American ones (*Reluctant* 127). Changez checks his own incredulity over his compatriots' fortitude by ascribing it to the fact that "Lahore was the last major city in a contiguous swath of Muslim lands stretching west as far as Morocco and had therefore that quality of understated bravado characteristic of frontier towns" (*Reluctant* 127). In other words, despite what seems an imminent threat on the nearby border with India, these Pakistanis have an anti-Indian swagger, one that's been part and parcel of Pakistani nationalism from the start. Changez, however, doesn't join their ranks. Instead, he confesses, "But I worried. I felt powerless; I was angry at our weakness, at our vulnerability to intimidation of this sort from our—admittedly much larger—neighbor to the east" (*Reluctant* 128). Given the political activities in which he engages when he returns to Pakistan permanently a few months later, Changez apparently channels these anxieties into more recognizably proactive and democratic attitudes and actions. Perhaps Changez offers this self-representation as a democratic stalwart in order to manipulate the American listener and the reader. Maybe his claim that the "anti-American" label affixed to his activities misconstrues his real intent intentionally misleads. There's a chance that he really did engage in many protests long before the "first [one] to receive much attention" so decidedly painted him as threatening (*Reluctant* 179). The point is: the novel's overarching ambiguity, achieved through its narratorial technique, doesn't fully discount Changez's attempts to outline an alternative political position, one that facilitates his valuing of place outside the terms set by dominant nationalisms. Changez's migrant experiences schooled him in how power works through appealing narratives in order to perpetuate itself. His extended conversation with his American interlocutor provides Changez with the opportunity to reverse those dynamics and to fill the void they create through the crafting of his own narratives. Whether the novel ends with Changez's death or the American's, *The Reluctant Fundamentalist* connects the migrant condition with a brutality that may be punishment for challenging the system or a small victory in fighting it.

The last two novels I discuss in this chapter—Nadeem Aslam's 2008 *The Wasted Vigil* and Kamila Shamsie's 2009 *Burnt Shadows*—bear as many parallels as do Naqvi's and Hamid's novels. Aslam's and Shamsie's fictions go the farthest geographically and historically in their contextualizations of 9/11, thus initiating the imaginative work many critics have looked for in 9/11 representations. These contexts overlap partially, both foregrounding the importance of Afghanistan in any discussion of Pakistan and the US's relations over the past 30+ years. At the same time, this pair of novels shares much with the earlier pair: all four novels, for instance, feature a US federal agent—either from the FBI or the CIA—and, thus, deliberately insert state-centered considerations alongside powerful myths about the US; and, similar to *The Reluctant Fundamentalist*, Aslam's and Shamsie's novels also recast the migrancy trope by placing American characters in that role. The most significant contributions to the critical discussion that these last two fictions make involve their use of absence as the motivation for migrancy. So, unlike Naqvi's Chuck or Hamid's Changez who both become migrants out of a "personal" decision to seek education in the US and largely through their migrant experiences come to recognize what was absent, many of the characters in Aslam's and Shamsie's novels must move because of historically-related (rather than solely personal) loss or trauma, or they undertake a quest to fill in the absences born of historical brutalities. Thus, whereas in the first two novels absence becomes a force of separation always tinged with violence, in *The Wasted Vigil* and *Burnt Shadows*, absence brings the characters together. Yet, despite its centripetal pull, absence challenges the usual terms of collective belonging, especially the concept of the nation and its myths and ideologies. Given both novels' multinational mixes, the challenges apparently apply to any national formation, thereby implicating Pakistan, Afghanistan, the US, and so on.

The Wasted Vigil, which features a third person narrative voice that often merges with specific characters' perspectives, is set in post-9/11 Afghanistan in a house located in the shadow of Tora Bora. Absence precipitates the co-habitation of the four major characters in this house. And, although the plot does involve some changes in these characters' circumstances, none of them fill their absences or satisfy the quests that motivated their migrancies in the first place. Rather, their co-habitation creates a microcosm of divergent historical and ideological perspectives. As they diverge, these perspectives call into question the conditions and mindsets that link the novel's two primary chronological planes—the 1980s and the naughts of the twenty-first century—thus examining the possibility of incommensurable differences.

Marcus, an elderly, transplanted Englishman, owns the house at the center of the novel, which he shared with his Afghan wife Qatrina and their daughter Zameen. Although this house serves as the novel's setting and thus establishes a common ground, it also signifies the long duration of Marcus's own migrancy. Despite his forty-year long residency in Afghanistan, for instance, the narrator comments that Marcus looks "almost like a native" (*Wasted* 43). This use of "almost" qualifies Marcus's belonging or, put another way, prolongs his disorientation in a setting that evades claiming. Marcus's protracted migrant state derives in part from his national identity, which locates him in a specific historical relation to Afghanistan. Similarly, his absences result from history, too. Through a series of flashbacks, the narrative relays Zameen's abduction by Soviet soldiers in the 1980s and Qatrina's death by stoning under the Taliban in the spring of 2001. Marcus's doubled absences attract the other characters to his house.

Lara, a Russian woman, seeks out Marcus as part of her own quest to discover what happened to her brother Benedikt, a Soviet soldier who disappeared while fighting in Afghanistan nearly twenty years before the novel's present; Lara believes Benedikt may have known Zameen. The narrator describes Lara's migrancy as a persistent struggle in the sense that she puts herself at great danger, both with the Russian authorities and those Afghans sympathetic to the Taliban. Facing nothing but resistance and obfuscation from the Soviet and then Russian governments, Lara recognizes that "they continued to tell lies or sen[d] her from person to person to exhaust or frustrate her" even years after the end of the conflict (*Wasted* 23). Gaining motivation from a line from Tolstoy—"*Princess Marya, learning of her brother's wound only from the newspapers and having no definite information, was getting ready to go in search of him...*" (*Wasted* 67)—Lara must rededicate herself to her quest before each trip to Afghanistan. On her way to Marcus's during this most recent journey, Lara sustains a severe beating from an Afghan man who sympathizes with the Taliban, because, traveling in what she thought would be the safety of a burqa, Lara inadvertently pointed her feet "towards the west, toward the adored city of Mecca...a disrespect she was unaware of" (*Wasted* 7). Born of a brutal conflict that makes Benedikt's fate a cipher, Lara's migrant experience is similarly violent. And, Lara's unfamiliarity with the contexts into which she inserts herself compounds her suffering by indicating that she may never understand or know the how's and why's of Benedikt's life and death.

Another migrant, David, who worked for the CIA throughout that agency's involvement in the Afghan conflict, was romantically involved with Zameen after she escaped her abductors, but he only meets Marcus after Zameen disappears for a second time. David's connection to the CIA and to Zameen provides him with the knowledge that both Marcus and Lara desire. He knows, for instance, about the connection between Zameen and Benedikt—the soldier repeatedly raped the young woman while she was being held captive by his superior officer—though he doesn't share this information with either Lara or Marcus. Also, David knows the real circumstances of Zameen's death, but he doesn't share those details either. Both David's migrancy and his absences derive from two interconnected sources: his professional interests and his personal ties. The novel represents this blurring of the distinction between David's two commitments as complicating the "purity" of his attachment to the US. For instance, in one of David's first interactions with Lara at Marcus's house, he walks down a hallway, away from her room, an action the narrator describes as an act of contrition: "The soles of his shoes are worn the way the edges of erasers become rounded with use. As though he walks around correcting his mistakes" (*Wasted* 65). Despite David's later claim that his feelings regarding the "'mayhem [he] helped unleash'" as a CIA agent are a "separate matter" from his anti-Soviet convictions, this description of his shoes, of their ability to correct his mistakes, makes it difficult to discern for what David should be held accountable: only his "personal" actions or also his internalization of US Cold War ideologies? Later, for instance, the narrator reveals David's insight that, while "following the trail of [Zameen's] murderers, [he] would realize, he had been stepping on his own footprints" (*Wasted* 138). Again, for what is David to blame, for what responsible? Further, through these metaphors premised upon the ground David covers, the novel casts his migrancy as resulting in violence and as a cause for the very absence that continues to drive his wandering. David is drawn to Marcus's house through the two men's shared quest to locate Zameen's son, Bihzad, who himself disappeared in the sea of refugees and orphans overwhelming Pakistan as a result of the violence between the Soviets and the Afghan "rebels."

Casa, an accidental late-comer to Marcus's house, is both migrant and absence in one. The novel walks a curious line in its portrayal of these two fundamental aspects of Casa's identity:

> He doesn't even know his own name, doesn't even know how he ended up in the orphanages and madrassas. A nameless child becomes a ghost, he had been told once, because no one without a name can get a firm enough foothold in the next world. It roams the world, making itself visible to the living in order to be addressed in some way…
>
> (*Wasted* 246)

By casting Casa as such a complete cipher, the novel suggests, on the one hand, that his radicalism derives from a persistent existentialist trauma; the repetition of "even" highlights the baseness of his existence. On the other hand, given the novel's long historical view that connects the circumstances of 1980s Afghanistan to those of the post-9/11 era and the references to "orphanages and madrassas," Casa's profound disorientation also derives from the accident of his birth at that specific time—the mid-1980s—and in that specific place—somewhere between Afghanistan and Pakistan. This tension between being an existential cipher and a product of history anticipates how he struggles to maintain a critical distance from the house's other inhabitants. Blank slate that he is, at least according to the novel's foundational representation of his identity, Casa comes to sympathize with the Taliban and actively works to achieve that group's goals through the use of violence. And, yet, the narrative complicates Casa's convictions by, first, hinting that he may unwittingly be Bihzad and, second, by forcing him to acknowledge the other characters' perspectives on any number of topics, including Islam. As it is shaped by migrancy and absence, Casa's character thus introduces an unresolved interplay between the inherent and the historically-produced, an indeterminacy that specifies the novel's broader investigation of the (in)commensurability of difference.

Each of these four major characters thus manifests a unique type, a singularity, united—perhaps solely—through their residence in the house. The novel seems to equivocate on the possibility that the singularities the characters represent can recognize a common point in what any of the others bring to the scene, thus offering a way to connect through difference. Several instances in the narrative point toward the possibility of constructive historical parallels. At one moment early in the novel, for instance, Lara wonders about the significance of "American soldiers…ceremonially bur[ying] a piece of the debris taken from the ruins of the World Trade Center, after the terrorists up there [in the mountains around Tora Bora] had either been slaughtered or been made to flee" (*Wasted* 27). One could read it, Lara supposes, as an act of victorious aggression, a reminder to sympathizers that they would meet a similar fate. But then Lara

> thinks of the Church of the Resurrection on the banks of Griboyedov Canal in St. Petersburg. It is known as the Saviour of the Spilled Blood, built as it was on the spot where a bomb thrown by a member of the People's Will revolutionary movement had mortally wounded Alexander II in 1881.
>
> (*Wasted* 27)

Purportedly, the Russians built the church on the site of this violent occurrence to mark it as "sacred," which allows Lara to consider the American soldiers' actions as an effort "meant to grow [something sacred] out of the fragment of rubble" (*Wasted* 27). Lara's historical equivalencies frame both actions as morally good if not also morally just. Further, the equivalencies conjoin pre-Soviet Russia with the twenty-first century US, obliquely suggesting a negative judgment of Russia's violent transformation into the Soviet Union in the early twentieth century. The troubles Lara suffers at the hands of, first, the Soviet government and, later, the post-Soviet Russian government seem to support this conclusion; that is, Lara manifests ambivalence toward belonging to post-Soviet Russia, and pro-American sympathies could well influence that uncertainty. This suggestion also aligns with American attitudes, such as the ones David espouses, about the righteousness of US Cold War policy, including supporting the Afghan "rebels" against the Soviets and, perhaps, of US post-9/11 policy as well.

The novel appears to endorse other possible equivalencies, too, even though they end up calling each other into question. Thinking now of the Cold War nuclear posturing conducted by both the Soviet Union and the US, Lara recalls how the "U.S. Air Force had asked scientists to plan a nuclear explosion on the moon" (*Wasted* 28). Lara also knows, thanks to her cosmonaut father, that the Soviets wanted to stage the same spectacle. And, Lara thinks, "who wouldn't cower beneath a nuclear-armed Soviet moon, a nuclear-armed American moon?" (*Wasted* 28). The concurrence of the idea now renders the Soviets and the Americans equivalent, whereas the previous example leaned toward American righteousness. Lara's considerations go one step farther: nuclear explosions on the moon "never happened but [Lara] wonders if the terrorists didn't come close to something like it in 2001, an enormous spectacle seen by the entire world, planting awe and shock in every heart" (*Wasted* 28). The perpetrators of the 9/11 attacks act out of the same braggadocio, rendering all three parties similar. As unpalatable as these links are, they do force a careful consideration of the reasons motivating action or foreign policy. Unlike the previous example, whose invocation of the sacred also introduced the metaphysical, this connective series asserts the relevance of specific historical conditions at the same time as it also traces a longer historical trajectory. The point here is not to valorize or demonize the US, for example, but, rather, to illustrate how the formulation of a variety of links between events can make sameness or difference (in)visible.

The representations of Casa's interactions with the house's other inhabitants highlight this alternation between the visible and the invisible on a personal level. Casa initially travels with other militants to Usha, the town nearest to Marcus's house, to deliver a "Night Letter" warning the townspeople against cooperating with the Americans. The letter reads: *"We and others like us will never stop until we have covered ourselves in glory by reaching Jerusalem and blowing up the White House..."* (*Wasted* 106). Wounded during the mission and found in the perfume factory on Marcus's property, Casa accepts Marcus and David's ministrations and eventually finds himself unable to rejoin the other militants. Of the kindness the Englishman and American show him, Casa thinks, "Allah—in His wisdom—has planted these compassionate impulses in the hearts of non-believers, for Muslims to exploit and benefit from" (*Wasted* 158). This conviction allows Casa to justify his dissembling, for his housemates never suspect him of nefarious motives even after some American contractors voice their suspicions. The narrative voice makes visible the difference between Casa and the others, while Casa as a character renders this difference invisible to his housemates. But, at the same time, the novel identifies Casa's doubts. When Marcus explains the house's paintings to Casa, for example, the narrator observes that Marcus's words "confus[e Casa,] making him feel at times that he doesn't know much about Islam let alone other religions, that he knows little about Afghanistan let alone the world" (*Wasted* 188). And, in a series of encounters with Dunia, a young woman from Usha who also temporarily seeks the safety of Marcus's house, Casa goes so far as to reveal to her that, while he hates America, "'Sometimes nothing makes sense and [he] become[s] afraid'" (*Wasted* 235). Dunia accepts this confession without judgment and offers, "'What we have to make sure is that Muslims don't fall in love with the ways of the fundamentalists—then we'd be in trouble'" (*Wasted* 235). Dunia's use of the first person plural pronoun encompasses Casa in a collective called "Muslims" that she distinguishes from "fundamentalists." This pronoun recognizes Casa as this type of "Muslim" and, thus, makes explicit the possibility of Casa's belonging. In reply, the narrator reveals that Casa "flinches now and steps away…" (*Wasted* 235), but, when recollecting this interaction, Casa acknowledges to himself that Dunia "has shown him who he is [i.e. a fundamentalist]. He doesn't want to be that" (*Wasted* 279). Casa's doubts, invisible to all the characters but apparent to the reader, admit the possibility of sameness, of sharing a collective identity with those whom he previously categorized as incommensurably different.

The Wasted Vigil does check these possibilities, however, no matter the equivalencies they draw, suggesting that the entire comparative enterprise may actually obstruct connection or understanding. In addition to highlighting the ambivalence of Lara's attachment to Russia, for instance, the narrator also reveals that, at times, she's unwilling to consider comparisons between nations or ideologies as legitimate. When Lara confesses her guilt over having married her now dead husband because of his military and government connections, David responds, "'Your country made you feel guilty…They put so much unreasonable pressure on you, so many unreasonable demands. Of course you couldn't cope and looked for a way out'" (*Wasted* 230). In response, Lara offers, "'I wonder how much of it is to do with my country. Maybe it's who I am'" (*Wasted* 230), but, as the scene closes, the narrator reveals her inner thoughts:

> But whatever any of them [Lara's Russian friends] thought, one thing was always certain: even though they suffered, and had to struggle at times to bring meaning and even the most basic dignity into their existence, and even though in their search for justice and truthfulness they were beaten down and met with disappointment again and again—their lives were not available for use as an illustration. Theirs were not stories that could be read as an affirmation of another system.
>
> (*Wasted* 232)

Lara's unexpressed convictions disallow the framing of the US as righteous and cast David's efforts to assuage her guilt as patronizing and even self-serving. This formulation renders her experiences under Communism and David's under US democracy as incommensurate. Further, Lara's viewpoint begs the question of how one can productively and meaningfully encounter difference on its own terms. To believe otherwise, the novel later suggests, is to subscribe to myths. Lara makes just this point to David when he admits he had prior knowledge, years ago, of a raid the Soviets planned to conduct on an Afghan refugee camp outside Peshawar. David could have saved lives, but instead did nothing so that the world media would show Soviet brutality. As for his reason, David claims, "'We were saving the future generations of Afghanistan and the world from Communism'" (*Wasted* 290). Unmoved, Lara levels David's naïveté: "'You have spent your whole life believing such untrue things. Don't you know how alone you are, David? We are most alone when we are with the myths'" (*Wasted* 290). Not only does Lara's indictment of David's beliefs cut through the post-WWII idea of the US as the benevolent superpower, her charge also rests on the claim that assuming common cause—i.e. that Afghanistan and the world despises Communism as much as the US does—amounts to an investment in an illusion. Rather than surmounting differences, creating unity, such assumptions isolate, exacerbating difference.

Casa's willingness at the novel's end to go through with the suicide mission he embarked upon when he first travels to Usha to post the Night Letter settles the doubts plaguing him during his interactions with the others at Marcus's house. That Casa kills David, who comes upon the younger man and the other suicide bombers as they pray before they conduct their mission, also dispels, for the reader at least, the myths to which David has subscribed. That is, as David attempts to extend his hero's narrative by saving Casa, who David believes may be Bihzad, he signals his refusal to reckon with those "separate matters," including Zameen's death, in which he has been involved as a CIA operative. If Casa retreats into his defensiveness through his decision to rejoin the militants, David remains uncritical, or, as he's earlier characterized, "a believer" in his ability to discern what's right (*Wasted* 112). Casa's and David's twinned deaths illustrate the perils of such devoutness and bring a violent end to their absence-motivated wanderings. Lara returns to Russia with a fragment from a mural painted on the wall in one of the rooms in Marcus's house. This piece bears the image of "the faces of the two lovers [as they] made contact" (*Wasted* 318). By having Lara take this specific piece of the mural, the novel suggests her indulgence in a romantic framing of her time in Afghanistan, one that memorializes David, who was her lover for a brief time, and is of a piece with her tendency to wax nostalgic over Russia, "[h]er dear Russia" (*Wasted* 232). She bears this affective contradiction and compounds her own absences. As for Marcus, the novel closes with him still in search of the missing Bihzad, ever hopeful that he'll find his grandson and, perhaps, strengthen his ties to this place (*Wasted* 320). Collectively, the characters' ends, all of which refuse to settle the characters' migrancy in a positive fashion or to fill the voids they've carried, trouble any "pure" attachment to nation or collective. Indeed, purity appears impossible given the novel's indeterminate treatment of difference.

Kamila Shamsie's 2009 novel *Burnt Shadows* overlaps, as I note above, with Aslam's *The Wasted Vigil* in many ways. Both novels feature expansive historical and geographical contexts. *Burnt Shadows* reaches back to WWII and draws in characters from Germany, Japan, India, and Pakistan, adding to *The Wasted Vigil*'s cast of nationalities. This doubled expansion situates 9/11 as yet another marker in a long series of violent interactions between people and nations. Through this decentering, Shamsie's novel, like Aslam's, provides the type of global vantage point commentators see as necessary to formulate a less provincial understanding of our post-9/11 era. While setting, i.e. Marcus's house, illustrates how absence in *The Wasted Vigil* fuels migrancy and brings the characters together, multi-generational relationships between two families, the Weiss-Burtons and the Tanaka-Ashrafs, exert the same centripetal pull in *Burnt Shadows*.

The new contributions Shamsie's novel makes to the present discussion involve how the narrative distinguishes between privileged and unprivileged migrancies, which involve absence and brutality on a sliding scale from most to least privileged. The ability or desire to claim a national identity conditions the differences between migrant experiences: if a character can belong, then s/he experiences a neutral, even positive, migrancy. And, the novel suggests, less fraught migrant experiences come at the expense of those who struggle to belong. Having laid bare this inverse relationship, *Burnt Shadows* effectively dismisses the violence associated with national belonging, going beyond the ambivalence of *The Wasted Vigil*, to explore the possibility of a nationless belonging. Save for its emphasis on the brutalities that relate and hierarchize migrancy, Shamsie's novel reverts almost completely to a conventional migrancy trope premised on the possibility of cosmopolitanism. But only "almost completely," for, although Shamsie's novel posits as an ideal a deeply humanist subjectivity, it is one produced through historical relations rather than outside of them. Thus, *Burnt Shadows* offers an object lesson applicable to any national formation, including Pakistan's.

Punctuated by large jumps in time, the novel's chronology moves linearly from 1945 to 2002, a plotting that allows the third person narrator to locate "history's winners" in the most privileged migrant category. The novel opens in Nagasaki, Japan, on 9 August 1945, as Konrad Weiss, a transplanted German man, crosses town to meet with his erstwhile Japanese tutor and new love, Hiroko Tanaka. Konrad, resident in Japan for nearly eight years, has gone from privileged to less privileged status as both Germany's and Japan's fortunes have turned in their conflict against the Allies. Originally drawn to Nagasaki's cosmopolitan culture, Konrad wants to know more about how "Europeans and Japanese mix[ed] uncomplicatedly" (*Burnt* 6). This "promise" offers hope to Konrad, who seeks escape from both his "once-beloved country [that] he long ago gave up on trying to fight for or against" (*Burnt* 18) and the stifling environment of his half-sister Ilse's life in colonial New Delhi with her British husband James Burton (*Burnt* 6). Germany's surrender earlier in 1945 "shifted [Konrad's] status in Nagasaki from that of ally into some more ambiguous state which requires the military police to watch him closely..." (*Burnt* 9). Konrad is aware of how this turn of events affects those around him, making him very careful around Hiroko, for instance, so that she, too, doesn't become an object of scorn. Before Konrad can suffer any further humiliation or harm as a transplanted German in Japan, he dies when the US drops an atomic bomb on Nagasaki. During the short time Konrad is alive in the novel, his migrant identity undergoes a categorical slide from privileged, given his Europeanness, to ostracized due to his Germanness. Perhaps just as significant, Konrad's presence in Nagasaki introduces a traditional idea of cosmopolitanism by positively valuing an image of "*Nagasaki filled with foreigners*" and by having Konrad write about such a Nagasaki "*longingly*" (*Burnt* 9; emphasis in original). In killing Konrad and Hiroko's father, whose burns are so severe he looks more reptilian than human (*Burnt* 28), the bomb brutalizes Hiroko, searing the design of the kimono she was wearing into the flesh of her back. These traumatic experiences create Hiroko's absences and motivate her migrancy, as "Nagasaki itself became more unknown than Delhi," one of her most important destinations (*Burnt* 227). The novel's Nagasaki episode forges the first set of links between the Weiss-Burtons and Tanaka-Ashrafs. It also establishes Hiroko's experiences and perspectives as the central measure of human decency from which the other characters diverge. The degrees of divergence create a hierarchy of privilege.

The hierarchy's apex represents the most privileged characters for whom migrancy is a choice rather than a condition predicated upon absence or trauma. And this agency belongs to those on the winning side of history. After the Nagasaki episode, the novel jumps two years and much of Asia to land in New Delhi in 1947, where the only group to emerge as winners on partition's eve is the British. Recognizing that she can no longer remain in Japan, Hiroko travels to India with the thought of finding Konrad's half-sister Ilse, who has thoroughly anglicized herself by becoming Elizabeth Burton, wife of British colonial barrister, James Burton. Ilse's ability to slough off her shameful "'German connections'" by changing her name, which resignifies her national belonging, marks her migrancy to India from Europe as a privileged one (*Burnt* 20). James bests his wife as the pinnacle of this hierarchy, however. Before meeting the man in person, for instance, Hiroko sees the Burton family portrait hanging in their entry hall; Hiroko "saw immediately what the painter had captured so perfectly: the complacency of James Burton," a man, Hiroko thinks, who is "at ease with ease" (*Burnt* 43–4). James inhabits colonial India self-importantly. For example, in a conversation about Ahmed Ali's *Twilight in Delhi* with Sajjad, a young Indian Muslim who is James's employee and will become Hiroko's husband, James reveals his bloated self-regard with no compunction:

> "Do you think an Englishman will ever write a masterpiece in Urdu?" [Sajjad asks.]
> "No." James shook his head. "If there ever was a time we were interested in entering your world in that way, it's long past, and you wouldn't know what to do with us if we tried."
>
> (*Burnt* 40)

Appropriating the right to speak for the British throughout their centuries' long involvement in India, James dismisses even the possibility with his conditional statement. Further, he suggests that the Indians would be incapable of dealing with any British incursion into their literary traditions, perhaps implying an inherent British cultural superiority. James and Elizabeth's investment in their own cosseted existence extends to their son Henry, who was born in India. Recently shipped to an English boarding school, young Henry thinks of India as home (*Burnt* 58), an affective attachment of which his parents want to disabuse him (*Burnt* 84). As yet another signifier of privilege, Elizabeth's only concern surrounding partition is whether she'll find Sajjad still in Delhi when she and her husband return briefly from Mussoorie in October 1947 (*Burnt* 98). To

Hiroko, such considerations seem shallow, a sign of "the most extraordinary privilege—to have forewarning of a swerve in history, to prepare for how your life would curve around that bend" (*Burnt* 59). These examples illustrate the degree to which privilege insulates James's and Elizabeth's migrant status. As Sajjad boldly queries just before their shared time in Delhi expires,

> "Why have the English remained so English? Throughout India's history conquerors have come from elsewhere, and all of them...have become Indian. If—when—this Pakistan happens, those Muslims who leave Delhi and Lucknow and Hyderabad to go there, they will be leaving their homes. But when the English leave, they'll be going home"
>
> (*Burnt* 83–4)

The Burtons' shared Britishness protects them from the historical brutalities that radically alter the other characters' lives.

Some characters who experience migrancy in less privileged circumstances manage, nonetheless, to reattach themselves to a national identity. Sajjad Ashraf, for instance, becomes Pakistani against his convictions, as the quote above hints.[10] Unlike the Burtons, Sajjad has no warning of how history will impact his life. The new Indian government denies him re-entry into the country, because he was in Turkey for his honeymoon when partition happened. Incredulous, Sajjad tells Hiroko, "'They [the Indian government] said I'm one of the Muslims who chose to leave India. It can't be unchosen'" (*Burnt* 127). The fallacious use of choice in these circumstances casts Sajjad's forced exile from India and equally forced migration to Pakistan as if they were actions of a full agent. But, Sajjad's inability to "unchoose" marks his migrancy as less privileged than the Burtons. And, this migration bears an absence. Despite Sajjad's deep attachment to his moholla in Dilli, the politics and violence surrounding partition, coinciding as they do with his mother's death, mean that Sajjad's Dilli-centered "world itself was departing" (*Burnt* 107). In its place, Sajjad takes on a muhajir identity, remarking internally that "[h]e would not ever have believed that he would come to think of Karachi as home..." (*Burnt* 136). Raza, Sajjad and Hiroko's son, categorizes his father as a muhajir when Sajjad pressures the boy to do well academically: "Every father in this neighbourhood of migrants, each with stories of all they had lost and all they had started to rebuild after Partition, made a similar speech to his son" (*Burnt* 138). Muhajir, a term that means "migrant" and, in Islam, refers to the first Muslims who fled with the Prophet from persecution in Mecca, bears a particular resonance in Pakistani nationalist mythologies. Just as Raza's categorization highlights, muhajirs are those Muslims who crossed the newly created borders between India and Pakistan and, thus, often consider themselves the truest Pakistanis, as they sacrificed the most to become Pakistani and have no provincial identity—i.e. Punjabi, Sindhi, Bengali (pre-1971), etc.— to interfere with their claims to national belonging. Hardly unscathed by history given that, in addition to being barred from returning to Dilli, some of his relatives are killed in partition violence, Sajjad rebounds. Indeed, Sajjad's muhajir

identity ensconces him rather securely in one of Pakistan's most powerful founding myths.

As migrant experiences become less privileged, the novel presents characters'
attachments to national identities as more problematic. Like Sajjad, Henry Burton
proves flexible. Henry, who goes by the name of Harry as an adult, harbors his
affective attachment to the subcontinent but also readily adopts an American
identity. As a boy, Henry's self-identification as an Indian alarms his parents,
solidifying their decision to send him to England for school. Even as an adult,
Henry/Harry still recognizes the subcontinent as home. Through another narrative jump that lands Harry in Karachi in 1982, he thinks, "This is more like it…"
(*Burnt* 150). In contrast to Islamabad, where Harry conducts most of his CIA
business, Karachi speaks to what he desires: "Harry wanted chaos of his cities
and nothing less than beauty of his hill towns" (*Burnt* 150). The use of the third
person singular possessive pronoun "his" before subcontinental cities and hill
towns denotes an appropriation of place that could be characterized as imperialist. Henry's transition from British child of the colonial experience to American
man working for the CIA in 1980s Pakistan thus seems all the smoother. Harry's
ability to belong to the US is similarly effortless for him. In Harry's telling,
"America allowed—no, insisted on—migrants as part of its national fabric in a
way no other country had ever done. All you had to do was show yourself willing
to be American—and in 1949, what else in the world would you want to be?"
(*Burnt* 174). Although he claims to recognize the US's imperfections when his
father questions him about racism (*Burnt* 174), Harry holds on to the "idea of
[power] concentrated in a nation of migrants. Dreamers and poets could not come
up with a wiser system of world politics: a single democratic country in power,
whose citizens were connected to every nation in the world" (*Burnt* 175). Such a
portrayal of the migrant condition in America rehearses a favorite national myth
of the immigrant narrative, much like the one that appeals to Chuck and his
friends in Naqvi's *Home Boy*. From Harry's perspective, this uniquely American
political system resembles his uncle Konrad's own cosmopolitan vision of pre-
WWII Nagasaki.

And just as the narrative disallows Konrad's vision by highlighting his
ostracism as WWII comes to an end and sacrificing him in the US's bombing
of Nagasaki, it also complicates Harry's convictions, his easy appropriation of
an American identity. Without an explicit explanation as to why, Harry acknowledges that his identification as an American—via his work for the CIA—has
"become about excitement rather than idealism" (*Burnt* 175). Harry's reflections
also reveal that "it had been a long time since he'd thought about [his work]
in relation to justice, let alone dreamers or poets" (*Burnt* 175–6). Some unidentified force or experience dispels Harry's romantic tendencies, shifting the tenor
of his affective attachment to the US: no longer the unwavering patriot, Harry
is now, in the novel's final narrative jump to 2001–2, an American thrill seeker,
an avocation that easily extends into his work as a military contractor in the
novel's present. Post-9/11, Harry offers a qualified recognition of how his actions
contribute to others' suffering when, as he surveys a wasted Afghanistan, he

quotes Tacitus: "'We make a desolation and call it peace'" (*Burnt* 284). This moment seems like a breakthrough, because it directly connects what the Americans and their military contractors are doing in Afghanistan to the suffering it causes. Yet, later in the same post-9/11 episode, Harry refuses to take responsibility for what he's been a part of, dismissing the idea of responsibility as politics: "Sometimes I listen to these liberals in America and marvel at their ability to trace back all the world's ills to something America did, or something America didn't do" (*Burnt* 291). Harry's equivocations characterize his Americanness as reckless rather than heroic, but they show, nonetheless, how privilege inverts into and comes about through brutality.

The most extreme example of unprivileged migrancy the novel explores derives from Raza's experiences. In many ways, Raza represents a cosmopolitan ideal: his parents come from two different national backgrounds; he's multilingual; and his physical appearance defies easy categorization. Raza is hybridity and translation embodied. Ironically, in yet another instance when the novel disallows Konrad's cosmopolitanism, this fluidity and adaptability contributes to Raza's existential unsettledness and, later, to his own wanderings. As a boy in 1980s Pakistan, Raza grasps at a secure national identity, insisting volubly that his Japanese mother dress more like Pakistani mothers so that she integrates better into their Karachi neighborhood. Hiroko and Sajjad "hadn't known whether to howl with laughter or with tears to think that their son's teenage rebellion was asserting itself through nationalism" (*Burnt* 132). Later, Hiroko concedes that "[s]he had never really understood her son's need for belonging" (*Burnt* 226). The timing of Raza's adolescence is particularly telling, for it is to Zia's Pakistan he yearns to belong. But, rather than take on piety, Raza exploits his unplace-able looks to gain acceptance among the Afghan refugees in Karachi who work to support the mujahideen across the border. Allowing the refugees to take him as a Hazara, Raza embarks on a boy's adventure, playing with AK-47s and basking in the glow that comes from respectful acceptance (*Burnt* 167, 202). Markedly, Harry, too, mistakes Raza for a Hazara on their first meeting (*Burnt* 153), and the narrator reveals that Harry immediately recognizes an opportunity:

> Harry looked across at the dreamy-eyed young man with a gift for language, an ache for something to believe in, and features that would go unnoticed in many Central Asian states and parts of Afghanistan, too, and a thought flickered across his mind.
>
> (*Burnt* 189)

Raza's yearnings and Harry's idea to exploit the younger man's cosmopolitanism spur Raza's migrancy, first, inadvertently, to a mujahideen camp in 1983 and, next, as Harry's protégé at a military contracting outfit after 9/11.[11]

Both situations open Raza's eyes to the relationality between the privileged and the unprivileged. On the road to the training camp, for example, Raza "learnt, through absence, the luxuries he'd taken for granted" (*Burnt* 216). And once he realizes the literal geographical inescapability of the camp, "[h]is vision grew white at the edges and only the quickness of his breath kept him from throwing up. He had never known anything like this heat, this terror" (*Burnt* 231). Raza's recognition bears metaphorical import, too, as he witnesses for the first time the militancy and the violence that undergird the quest for national security. As Harry's protégé nearly twenty years later, Raza also learns how his cosmopolitanism makes him vulnerable. Harry's American colleagues call Raza's "allegiance" into question after Harry's gunned down by an Afghan who infiltrates the military contractors' base camp (*Burnt* 310). A significant departure from Harry's initial conviction that America welcomes all migrants equally, "allegiance" invokes a feudal system wherein the American military contractors are lord and Raza, a vassal. Further, such a relationship reduces Raza's dreams of belonging to a reality of submission and obedience. With little recourse left, Raza flees, feeling "the terror of unbecoming" (*Burnt* 314). Without any "documents that make him legal" (*Burnt* 314), that is, without citizenship to a nation, Raza has no identity. His cosmopolitan qualities do not make him a model for the globalized world; rather, they assist his transformation into a trafficked migrant.[12] Raza relies on his cosmopolitan qualities to journey illegally to Canada in the hope of seeing his mother. The horrors Raza experiences during this passage—including being buried in a truck bed filled with cabbages (*Burnt* 339) and squeezing into the hull of a boat already overpacked with other migrants (*Burnt* 342)—makes him wonder "[w]hat kind of world made men have to endure this?" (*Burnt* 343). In light of the base circumstances in which Raza finds himself near the novel's close, his adolescent disquiet over not belonging comes off as tragically naïve. Contextualized as part of the novel's broader presentation of migrant conditions and the absences that spark or result from these wanderings, Raza's experiences in the world of human trafficking reveal the underside of the stability born of national belonging that the Burtons claim so unreflectively, that Sajjad recovers, and that Harry no longer believes in but still enjoys.

Against this sliding scale of privilege, the novel presents an alternative type of belonging that seeks to rise above the nation. Hiroko, who James Burton sees, appropriately, as "disrupting all hierarchies" (*Burnt* 84), serves as the conduit for the articulation of this alternative. The only belonging Hiroko seeks after losing Konrad and Nagasaki is one characterized by foreignness (*Burnt* 143). With respect to Pakistan, for instance, a place in which she built a very conventional "home," Hiroko reflects, "It didn't bother her in the least to know she would always be a foreigner in Pakistan—she had no interest in belonging to anything as contradictorily insubstantial and damaging as a nation" (*Burnt* 207). This perspective on finding alternative identity formations outside the nation differs from the cosmopolitan vision Konrad's character introduces. In mixing "uncomplicatedly," the Europeans and Japanese who populate Konrad's idealized Nagasaki are still recognizable as Europeans and Japanese, just as the city features "Euro-Japanese buildings" (*Burnt* 6). Hiroko champions a foreignness that is not so easily recognized in national terms. As she continues her migrant odyssey through the entire chronology of the novel, Hiroko encounters many counter examples to the alternative she's trying to identify. After the

Nagasaki bombing, for instance, Hiroko relocates to Tokyo, where she works as a translator for the American military. While relaying her history to Sajjad, Hiroko anticipates his surprise that she would agree to work for the Americans: "'Working for the Americans! After the bomb, you might wonder how I could agree to such a thing...It was impossible, really, to hold anyone responsible—the bomb was so...it seemed beyond anything human'" (*Burnt* 63). Hiroko's time in Tokyo comes to an abrupt end, however, when an American GI tells her that dropping the bomb saved "American lives" (*Burnt* 63). The motivation behind the violence was clearly nationalist in intent, which reframes Hiroko's characterization of the bomb as "beyond anything human." That is, by making clear that dropping the bomb was about safeguarding people who count because of their national identities, the novel—through Hiroko—also suggests that to be human is to be recognizable in terms outside of national identities.

The novel continues to outline what "human" might mean through omission. When Harry's daughter Kim offers Hiroko sympathy over Nagasaki because the older woman "'lived it...[H]er father died in it. [Her] fiancé died in it. There's no shame in putting all the weight in the world on that'" (*Burnt* 299), Hiroko snaps: "'Is that why? That's why Nagasaki was such a monstrous crime? Because it happened to me?'" (*Burnt* 300). This response makes clear that personal experiences do not define a "human" identity either. The closest Hiroko comes to encountering the "human" she seeks is in New York City just before and after 9/11. Much like the characters from the other novels I've discussed in this chapter, Hiroko senses immediate belonging in the city because of the many languages and because there was "[n]othing foreign about foreignness in this city" (*Burnt* 295). In the immediate aftermath of the terrorist attacks, Hiroko "found herself caught up in a feeling of solidarity quite unfamiliar, utterly overwhelming" (*Burnt* 295). Perhaps it was the widespread recognition of suffering or vulnerability or life's transience that granted Hiroko this "overwhelming" feeling, "[b]ut then, things shifted" (*Burnt* 295). The sabre rattling and hyper-jingoism of post-9/11 America reassert, in Hiroko's estimation, the "shrunken" views accompanying national identities (*Burnt* 295). At the novel's end, with Raza finally apprehended by the American authorities under suspicion for Harry's death, Hiroko identifies how a person or a nation dehumanizes others: by "'put[ting] them in a little corner of the big picture,'" by making their deaths "[a]cceptable,'" by deeming them "'[e]xpendable'" (*Burnt* 370). For each of these actions, Hiroko identifies its historical provenance: Nazi Germany for the Jews, Hiroshima, Nagasaki, and Afghanistan (*Burnt* 369–70). These concrete references point out precise moments when the privileged determine their own and others' "human" worth. In doing so, these references insist on a recognition of (in)humanness in history. Rather than positing individuals as unproblematized incarnations of national identities, as Konrad's cosmopolitanism does, Hiroko's idea of the "human" demands historical contextualization and accountability. This formulation, then, disregards and, perhaps, even values the absences migrants, especially "illegal" ones, bear when they don't have the privilege of citizenship.

Notes

Introduction

1 Shaikh provides a thorough overview of Sir Sayyid's, Iqbal's, Mawdudi's, and Jinnah's political philosophies, paying particular attention to how Islam inflects each man's views on territorialized nationhood.

2 A "homeland" signified liberation from Hindu economic and political dominance. As a "safe haven," Pakistan offers refuge for "Islam in danger" (Shaikh 34).

3 Abrams does not present the "state-idea" so neutrally. As do many others, Abrams views that state as an oppressive force; thus, the representations referred to by the term "state-idea" are, from his perspective, necessarily *mis*representations that naturalize state dominance and individual subjection (75).

4 Arguments for the cultural legitimacy of literature premised on English's long history in the subcontinent differ from charges that English—or any language—bears ideology trappings. As Alastair Pennycook asserts, "Many now claim that English is no longer tied to any culture since it is now the 'property of the world' rather than the possession of the English-dominant nations. But such a proposition misses the point that English is deeply embedded in a set of social, cultural, political and economic relations" (158). Pennycook and his interlocutor, Sohail Karmani, focus particularly on the missionary history of ESL teaching in non-English speaking countries, a historical pattern they saw being replicated in post-9/11 calls from the US for educational reforms in Muslim countries that would incorporate more heavily the teaching of English (157–58). English's historical grounding in South Asia mitigates some of the pitfalls Pennycook identifies, as the language has been indigenized over the centuries. Amin Malak's *Muslim Narratives and the Discourse of English* also speaks to the relation between English and Muslim cultures and points out that, in these cultures, a "muslimization" of English—a "spontaneous, structureless cultural process"—occurs (8). Malak takes care to distinguish "muslimization" from "Islamization," characterizing the latter as demanding "disciplining, theological agency, or guardian institutions" (8). Ahmar Mahboob extends Malak's analysis into Pakistan in "English as an Islamic Language." On the indigenization of English in Pakistan from a linguistic perspective, see John Baumgardner's "The Indigenization of English."

5 Notably, AA Khan advocates for Urdu in Pakistan's fraught context of linguistic diversity.

1: 1947

1 See my *National Identities in Pakistan*, especially pages 29–31, for a discussion of this historiographical tendency to reinscribe the inevitability of Pakistan.

2 Jason Francisco presents a thorough critical overview of this historiographical shift in his review article, "In the Heat of Fratricide," even while indulging the familiar familial metaphor.

3 Singh was born in 1915 in Hadali, a Punjabi village now located in Pakistan. While widely considered an Indian writer, Singh's connection to this geographical region makes his novel a provocative case study in the nationalization of partition literature: is it an Indian novel or a Pakistani one? I include Singh's work here not to come down definitively on that question but to consider what's at stake if one did.

4 Gillian Dooley, DK Pabby, and Hadyn Moore Williams all read Jugga as heroic. In a different vein, both KC Belliapia and CN Srinath find Singh's portrayal of "human experience" lacking in *Train to Pakistan*. Priyamvada Gopal, like Kavita Daiya, remarks upon the prevalence of the romantic love narrative, calling it "sentimental" (71).

5 Morey's essay features a useful discussion of the train as an indicator of the indigenization of colonial technology in the specific historical context of Gandhi's "anti-technological vision" (169). I think such a context proves rich, especially given the novel's other subtle hints of a critique of Gandhism, such as when the subinspector unleashes his own impatience with Congress corruption: "'Ask anyone coming from Delhi and he will tell you that all these Gandhi disciples are minting money. They are as good saints as the crane. They shut their eyes piously and stand on one leg like a yogi doing penance; as soon as a fish comes near—hurrup'" (Singh 20). See also Ian Kerr's essay for an extensive discussion of how both Britons and Indians/South Asians represented the railways throughout the nineteenth and twentieth centuries. Kerr identifies Gandhi as one of the only Indian voices to object to the railways outright (313–14).

6 Oldenburg goes on to argue that Pakistan's and India's civil services proceeded to develop along much different courses, with the Civil Service of Pakistan becoming much more powerful in comparison to the Indian Civil Service (45).

7 Most commentators note the novel's autobiographical aspects. Mumtaz Shah Nawaz was extremely politically active in many of the same ways that her two characters, Zohra and Sughra, are; see, for example, Ahmed Shah Nawaz's introduction to the 2003 Penguin edition (vii-xi) and Tariq Rahman (*History* 23). That, before her untimely death, Shah Nawaz was also aware of the communal violence of partition and the creation of Kashmir as an immediate flashpoint between the two new nations indicates some deliberateness on her part to leave these realities out of her fiction.

8 Zohra's reticence is evident on two occasions. First, when attending an event during the 1940 League meeting in Lahore, Zohra feels "sick at heart" as she sees her dream of Hindu–Muslim unity die (Shah Nawaz 390). Second, when Zohra finally receives her father's blessing on her engagement to Ahmad, she declares her decision to join the League, in response to which Ahmad counsels her to avoid being "'carried away by false slogans'" (Shah Nawaz 449). I return to Zohra's ambivalence later.

9 This tension between direct and indirect political participation finds its corollary in the subcontinent's nationalist histories. David Willmer cites Muslim women's indirect political participation as an influential—and, for the British, worrisome—force in the 1910s, for example. These women called upon their abilities to influence the public actions of fathers, husbands, and sons from within the domestic sphere (577). In the same decade, Indian women of various religions also participated in political issues directly, according to Siobhan Lambert-Hurley, and in ways that went beyond communal identities (43, 45). By the 1930s, purdah was up for debate, according to Willmer, and, thus, so was the question of how Muslim women could engage with political issues (578).

10 Willmer cites Jinnah's speech at the 1940 Lahore session of the All-India Muslim League as the explicit articulation of the linkage between the League's demand for Pakistan and Muslim women's political activity (574). Shah Nawaz's fiction allows for the imaginative gestation of this link.

11 Sughra's direct participation in election canvassing occurs before elections set to be held in 1937 (Shah Nawaz 231). According to the novel, this election is significant because a segment of the female population has the franchise for the first time, thanks to the Government of India Act of 1935 (Shah Nawaz 230). Of course, historically, the League did not fare well in the 1937 elections, especially in Muslim majority areas like the Punjab (Kazimi 130–2). Sughra, however, remains unflagging in her new political devotion, telling her uncle, who ran unsuccessfully as the League candidate in Lahore, "'But there's always next time'" (Shah Nawaz 273).

12 Worried over Zohra's headstrong nature, her mother, sister, and sister-in-law discuss Rajindar's influence, and Sughra offers this view of Rajindar: "'But she's a bit too radical and independent'" (Shah Nawaz 289). Other than Surayya, who's only present in the novel's early chapters and is portrayed as "liberal" for being out of purdah, the other progressive females in the novel are Hindu.

13 MR Kazimi points out that the League performed respectably in the UP, a Muslim minority area, winning 27 out of 66 seats (130).

14 Two points: as is already well known, Sidhwa published her novel as *Ice-Candy-Man* in Britain in 1988 and then, when it was published in the US in 1991, changed the title to *Cracking India* on the advice of her publisher (P. Singh 293). As for Partition Studies, George also characterizes it as having a particular focus on gender (137).

15 Instead, Singh's and Shah Nawaz's novels are laden with decades of received interpretations about their meanings and their places in the larger field of partition literature. On this reception point, it's worth noting that Sidhwa's novel, of the three, is the focus of the most critical commentary.

16 According to the novel, Ayah's abduction happens in February 1948.

17 Sangeeta Ray emphasizes the need to attend to such specificities in her analysis of the novel (128–9). Jill Didur, Rosemary Marangoly George, and Harveen Mann view the novel's treatment of women's and gender issues as progressive to a degree (keeping in mind the silences about gender that pervade traditional histories of the partition). Ambreen Hai and Asha Sen take a significantly more critical stance, arguing that class and religious bias hinder whatever gender critique the novel may launch. I follow the novel's spelling of Lenny's religious identity; "Parsee" can also be spelled "Parsi."

18 This point is one that aligns Sidhwa's novel with Salman Rushdie's *Midnight's Children* (another is that Lenny's birthday falls on the day of Pakistani independence, 14 August). Many critics point out the debt *Cracking India* has to Rushdie's novel. Tariq Rahman notes Sidhwa's use of "surrealistic techniques, somewhat like Salman Rushdie," though he doesn't specify what those techniques are (*History* 131). Asha Sen views Lenny to be as unreliable a narrator as Saleem Sinai (70). Ananya Kabir places Sidhwa herself in the *Midnight's Children* generation, literarily and historically (177). None of these critics explicitly locate the connection between the two novels in their shared penchant for metafiction, however.

19 Colonel Bharucha tells the founding myth of the Parsees' arrival in the subcontinent in this scene as well (Sidhwa 47).

20 In addition to the critical point I raise about this passage's significance, Sidhwa voices two historical inaccuracies. First, Gandhi did not lead the "partition movement." No political activities or strategies of that era had such a name. Further, Jinnah was not a founder of the All-India Congress Party. That party was founded in 1885 when Jinnah was nine years old.

21 Hai's analysis is probably the most thorough in its argument of the novel's feminist shortcomings.

22 There is a lot of sex in this novel, including between a stepmother and stepson, and a lot of plotting to remedy its effects. It should come as no surprise, then, that there are subplots involving children who don't know their parentage or spouses grievously wronged. From these stories arise the motives for several revenge plots. Many of the

novel's villains operate according to what a reader would see as a personal wrong. There are a few instances, however, wherein villainous characters operate politically, too, and their politics are generally of a fundamentalist nature.

23 This early image of anglophilia is, as I note, just one manifestation of syncretism in the novel. Others involve the merging of Muslim, especially Sufi, and Hindu cultural elements. Such mergings do not, in the novel's construction of identities, compromise righteous political claims, such as those made by the Muslim League; rather, they serve to ground identity in place, i.e. in Pakistan.

24 The characters in Shah Nawaz's *The Heart Divided* certainly view this movement as an example of inter-communal unity. Ironically, many historians point out that the Lucknow Pact was unpopular with many Indian Muslims, especially in Muslim majority areas (Kazimi 99; Jalal, *Sole* 9).

25 During the last years of the Raj and before either the British or the Congress conceded even the concept of "Pakistan," Jinnah looked upon the presence of minorities in Muslim majority areas, such as the Punjab, as the safety valve that would insure the proper treatment of Muslims in Muslim minority areas (Jalal, "Inheriting" 30; Raja xxiv). According to Ayesha Jalal, Jinnah staked his "vague" demand for Pakistan, with "its territories undefined," against an undivided Punjab and Bengal ("Inheriting" 31). Jinnah was not to have both Pakistan and an undivided Punjab and Bengal, and, thus arguably, the insurance policy underwritten by the non-Muslim minorities within Pakistan was significantly devalued. The overdevelopment of Pakistan's bureaucracy compounded Jinnah's "failure" to implement his vision (Raja xxiv), foreclosing on the possibility of a robust democracy—and, hence, equal political participation and representation—in Pakistan. Both Jalal and Philip Oldenberg identify Jinnah's self-appointment as Governor-General as a factor that may well have inhibited the development of a participatory democracy from the start. Oldenberg sees Jinnah's occupation of the role of Governor-General as instituting a "'viceregal system,'" for instance (10). Likewise, Jalal argues that Jinnah negotiated for the role of Governor-General to possess enough power so that he could "consolidate the government of Pakistan's hold over its provinces" ("Inheriting" 49). As a result, Jinnah did not risk failing to construct a legitimate Constituent Assembly and, thus, prevented Pakistan itself from failing as a new nation.

26 Vazira Fazila-Yacoobali Zamindar advocates strongly for the use of terms such as "displacement" and "refugee" for the people who crossed the newly created borders between India and Pakistan. Her reasoning includes the initial expectation these displaced people had of returning to the homes they left behind (7). Indeed, much partition fiction includes such details: a departing family asks the neighbors to safeguard their house and belongings until their return, which, of course, never happens.

27 Clearly, Pakistan's and India's bureaucratic measures taken in the aftermath of Partition, especially each nation's Recovery and Restoration Bill, were also staked on some notion of communal "honor."

28 Rosemary Marangoly George reads partition literature as a type of diasporic literature in "(Extra)Ordinary Violence: National Literatures, Diasporic Aesthetics, and the Politics of Gender in South Asian Partition Fiction."

29 Kavita Daiya sees the "fetishization of the 'return home'" as a convention of much migrant literature (185).

30 Dina Lal actually inherited considerable wealth from his father, most of it via real estate holdings (S. Khan 52).

31 In her ethnographic work on partition refugees, Vazira Fazila-Yacoobali Zamindar writes that the administration of evacuee property in Pakistan is "remembered as the first site of the nation-state's corruption. The comment that 'evacuee property corruption *ki jar hai*,' evacuee property was at the root of corruption in Pakistan, was repeated several times, and stories of usurpation by a few people of such a limited and essential

resource as housing were commonplace" (150; emphasis in original). Amir Shah's machinations lend credence to these extra-fictional perceptions.

32 Many historians point out that, just before and immediately after partition, neither Britain nor India put much stock in Pakistan's viability as a nation. In a similar vein, much current discourse about Pakistan as a "failed state" arranges this nation's history so as to arrive "inevitably" at its current geopolitical and domestic difficulties. See both Naveeda Khan's *Beyond Crisis* and Maleeha Lodhi's *Pakistan: Beyond the 'Crisis State'* for a problematization of this pervasive view.

33 Wenzel explicitly models her concept of anti-imperialist nostalgia in relation to Renato Rosaldo's "imperialist nostalgia," which Wenzel understands to be a "regret for change of which one has been an agent" (7).

34 For more on how the British appropriation of the existing postal system helped consolidate colonial power, in part, through surveillance and the control of information, see also Bayly's *Empire and Information*, especially pages 58–60.

2: 1971

1 "Muhajir" is the term used to refer to the Muslim migrants who left India for Pakistan in 1947. The term has historical specificity in that, while meaning "migrant" generically, it has come to refer to Urdu speakers who largely settled in Sindh. The term also has religious connotations in that "muhajirs" were those early Islamic believers who went into exile from Mecca to Medina with the Prophet Muhammad. See my "'Freeing the Outlook of Man from Its Geographical Limitations': Nationalism, History, and Literature in Pakistan" in *National Identities in Pakistan: The 1971 War in Contemporary Pakistani Fiction* for an elaboration of the argument about the mythologizing of muhajir identity.

2 Bhutto lost much of this positive support by 1977, of course.

3 Notably, Benazir Bhutto referred to these "Stranded Pakistanis" as "Bangladeshi Biharis," which pulls together a reference to the group's pre-1947 roots in northeast India with B. Bhutto's interest in denying them Pakistani citizenship, post-1971 (Ghosh 24).

4 See my *National Identities in Pakistan*, especially Chapter 2, for a full analysis of the *Report* and its *Supplement*.

5 The mother's reliance on her sons to protect her daughters is the only intimation of the gendered aspects of the twins' "safety." Whatever anxiety the mother feels over the "'Bengali-speaking boys'" may or may not have an undercurrent of sexual violence. There is no proof anywhere in the text of anxiety over sexual violence. In fact, when the twins' Murtaza Uncle finally arrives in Lahore after managing to escape the outbreak of violence in East Pakistan, he's the only one in his immediate family who appears at all altered: "his wife and five-year-old daughter were looking just the same" (Soomro and Hameed 138). The absence of any sustained gendered anxiety over the violence of 1971 marks *Bengal Raag* as singular in the context of other English-language fictive representations of the 1971 war. Please see my *National Identities in Pakistan*, especially Chapters four and eight, for a discussion of this gendered anxiety.

6 According to Christophe Jaffrelot and his co-authors, the relocation of the capital from Karachi first to Rawalpindi and then to Islamabad functioned to consolidate Punjabi dominance, especially in relation to other ethnic groups in the west, to say nothing of the Bengalis: "The Muhajir's loss of influence was reinforced in 1960 when the capital was transferred from Karachi to Rawalpindi, a Punjabi garrison town. At the end of the 1960s it was again moved a short distance to the purpose-built capital city of Islamabad" (*History* 20).

7 Farzana Shaikh reinforces the notion that Ayub Khan's economic policies through the 1960s amounted to "'functional inequality,'" prompting East Pakistanis to "accus[e] Ayub's regime of reducing the east to an internal colony" (125).

8 For Jussawalla, this track has as signposts encounters with English, Christianity, and other Western hallmarks; a journey that brings the protagonist in touch with his/her "authentic" culture; and, ultimately, a turn away from Westernization (31).

9 Bilgrami's novel resonates with Asif Farrukhi's short story, "Expelled" (translated 2008), especially in their common portrayal of a man's memories of school as a site of nationalist normativity. Please see my *National Identities in Pakistan*, especially pages 67–83, for a discussion of Farrukhi's story.

10 Donald Tuck argues that Tagore's play is a critique of "dehumanizing" religious practices that perpetuated Brahman dominance (3).

11 Laila, who is eight in 1971, inadvertently tells Mashooq of Rani's love relationship, although she doesn't know that Rani is pregnant.

12 Few of the characters willingly view the hostilities between East and West Pakistan as a war. Whenever that word is used, most characters assume the reference is to the possible conflict between India and Pakistan, as in this scene where Sardar Begum asks Tariq, "'Talking of peaceful, is there going to be a war?'" To which Tariq responds, "'We're already at war'" (Mohsin 122). The characters' resistance to recognizing the violence occurring between the East and West Pakistanis as a war reinforces the novel's metaphorization of the conflict as "domestic violence," a euphemism that itself seeks to contain and control a phenomenon that has broader public and social dynamics.

13 Clearly, sex before marriage in this novel is a "stain"; an unmarried woman, whether she's having sex or not, is, according to Sardar Begum, an "'abomination'" (Mohsin 182).

14 I have pursued this idea of national amnesia in relation to the 1971 war in my book, *National Identities in Pakistan*. My argument there as here is that literature presents one way, albeit outside the auspices of official nationalist history, to imagine and represent experiences of the war and its aftermath.

15 Tariq expresses his dislike for the Army—he thinks to himself, "This bloody army's sucked the country dry"—after he sees the "well-ordered affluence" of the "playing fields, parade grounds and residential bungalows, behind the spacious gardens" (Mohsin 287).

16 Laila is in Sabzbagh for the duration of the fall of 1971 because she was sick and, thus, pulled out of school in Lahore.

17 When the narrative voice initially presents Fareeda's biography, it is at pains to establish that Fareeda desires a settled life in stark contrast to the cosmopolitan one she lived as her parents' daughter: Fareeda "nursed deep within her the longing to belong, to settle, to matter" (Mohsin 52). Tariq's generations-old family in Sabzbagh presents her with precisely the opportunity she has been looking for: "She had settled in that village with the contentment of a mother hen settling on her eggs" (Mohsin 53). Fareeda's desire to belong unequivocally separates her from what her mother represents, that is, an investment in the idea of Pakistan.

3: Islam before Pakistan

1 See Ayesha Jalal's "Conjuring Pakistan" for a discussion of the power of this idea, even without any claim to territory.

2 Jaffrelot further comments that the two-nation theory "did not endow Pakistan with the sociological qualities of a nation" (*Nationalism* 8).

3 Pakistan's commitment to secularity, which Jinnah outlined in his speech on the occasion of being elected President of the Constituent Assembly in 1947, changed by

1949 with the adoption by the Constituent Assembly of the Objectives Resolution, a commitment to frame Pakistani nationhood according to Islamic ideals. The nation's first constitution, passed in 1956, further inscribed this Islamic framework. Of course, what precisely that Islamic framework meant/means has been a contentious issue ever since. See S. Sayyid and ID Tyrer's "Ancestor Worship" for an overview of the battle to claim Jinnah as either a secularist or a "true" believer.

4 Divergent perspectives on the value of "composite" cultures and nationalist causes certainly punctuated debates in late colonial India. With respect to the role of Islam or, more precisely, the role of the 'umma (community of believers) in nationalist politics, the debate between Mawlana Mawdudi and Mawlana Madani, in part over the latter's *Islam and Composite Nationalism*, crystallizes the issues at stake, including the individual Muslim's relation to Islam and the place of the Muslim community in larger societies. See Vali Nasr's *International Relations of an Islamist Movement: The Case of the Jama'at-i-Islami of Pakistan*.

5 Metcalf identifies Francis Robinson and Imtiaz Ahmad as the two primary figures in the debate (xxii), with Robinson arguing for a more cohesive, top-down idea of Islamic leaders providing guidance on a "pattern of perfection" (Robinson 191) and Ahmad advocating for a more localized and, hence, plural conceptualization of Islamic practice.

6 Mahmood makes this claim regarding cultural conformity and Islam in a specifically post-9/11 American context. I do think, though, that his critique of the essentializing tendencies of "Culture Talk" correspond to the analyses Das and Metcalf offer of the syncretism debate in Pakistan and South Asia. All of these assessments share a concern for the consequences of representations that strip people of their historical agency and uniqueness.

7 This dual impulse—the destructive and the constructive—prompts Ahmed Gamal to label Ali's work as postcolonial metafiction ("Rewriting" 5).

8 I return to this depiction of the masses in the first panel of Plato's triptych below.

9 Gamal makes much the same point about untold stories with reference to Zahra, Hind and Zuhayr's great aunt, who burns her diaries thinking that no one would see value in them ("Rewriting" 8).

4: Zia's Islamization

1 See S. Sayyid and ID Tyrer's "Ancestor Worship" for an analysis of how histories of Pakistan have variously deployed Jinnah as a dedicated secularist and/or as a "Saladin" figure who saved Islam.

2 Notoriously, Zia promulgated Amendment Eight, which endowed the position of President with inordinate power. And, as is well known, despite finally calling for democratic elections in 1985, Zia effectively only agreed to "share" power rather than relinquish it outright to the people's elected representatives.

3 In the context of Pakistani Urdu language literature, see Kamran Asdar Ali's "Progressives and Perverts: Partition Stories and Pakistan's Futures," as it queers Manto's stories "to offer a critique of Pakistan's normative national history and to suggest a different path to understanding the country's past and possibly its future" (5).

4 Ziring is, of course, aware that, in Pakistan, the word "secularism" takes on a meaning somewhat different from its use in Western contexts.

5 Cohen and Weinbaum acknowledge that certain segments of Pakistan's population were pleased, if impatient, with Zia's Islamization; the religious groups, for example, "complained about the slow pace of reforms" (137). Similarly, Malik reports that "Zia enjoyed support equally from those in the middle class who had prospered under a 'stable' regime, and especially after Bhutto's nationalization, small businesses across

the country felt at ease" ("National Security" 1081). Ideologically and economically, Zia scored points in some powerful sectors.

6   Charles H. Kennedy's "Islamization in Pakistan: Implementation of the Hudood Ordinances" goes into great detail about these laws' evidentiary requirements and punishments. Kennedy also quantitatively traces how frequently punishments were actually meted out. See also Anita Weiss's "The Historical Debate of Islam and the State in South Asia," which situates the Hudood Ordinances in an historical long view of Islamic jurisprudence in a broader South Asian context.

7   Weiss concedes that this requirement proved so difficult to fulfill that the harshest penalties were rarely, if ever, inflicted (15).

8   Several historians—Nikki Keddie et al.'s "Pakistan's Movement Against Islamization," Iftikhar Malik's "The State and Civil Society in Pakistan," and William Richter's "The Political Dynamics of Islamic Resurgence in Pakistan"—note that ZA Bhutto actually initiated an Islamizing process by banning alcohol, making Friday the national day of rest, and deeming the Ahmadiya sect non-Muslims.

9   Benazir Bhutto devotes much of her posthumously published *Reconciliation: Islam, Democracy, and the West* to asserting the compatibility of democracy and Islam.

10 Marvin Weinbaum echoes the broader critical consensus that democracy was anathema to Zia's regime. Weinbaum also postulates that Zia's legacy can be seen in the present day by "low voter participation and factional politics aimed at delegitimizing those in power" (644).

11 Pakistan's first military dictator, Ayub Khan, abrogated the 1956 Constitution in 1958.

12 Volker Heins makes a similar point, viewing the alienation that results from conspiratorial thinking as coinciding with a broader sense of "powerlessness vis-à-vis society" (795). See also Ayesha Jalal's discussion of paranoia in Pakistani politics in her essay "The Past as Present." The use of paranoia and conspiracy theories in literature, however, doesn't necessarily lead to the same ends that Weinbaum, Heins, and Jalal identify. Literarily, conspiracy theories can signal agency and attempts to create solidarity.

13 Indeed, as many critics observe, conspiracy theorists often use the absence of information as a sign of the accuracy of their theories. See, for example, Brian L. Keeley's "Of Conspiracy Theories."

14 See Birchall for a discussion of the romanticization of the conspiracy theorist (46).

15 Birchall argues that conspiracy theories ironically mirror the structure of the very dominant histories and explanations they call into question. I take her point when it comes to the reliance on causality in these narrative structures, but I think her point about the "non-depletable opening" signals conspiracy theories' departure from standard historiographical structures insofar as this opening doesn't necessarily strive for a culminating telos.

16 Similar to Weinbaum's assessment of how conspiracy thinking works in the context of political discourse, Bruno Latour and Peter Knight express vexation over the interpretative tendencies of conspiratorial thinking in literary and cultural contexts. Latour, for example, views conspiracy theories as the "most gullible sort of critique" (230) insofar as they constitute "*instant revisionism*": "The smoke of the event has not yet finished settling before dozens of conspiracy theories begin revising the official account, adding even more ruins to the ruins, adding more smoke to the smoke" (228). In Latour's estimation, conspiracy theories as a form of reading or interpretation get us farther and farther from the "matters of concern" that should be the focus of scholarly energy (231). Knight also posits claims about conspiracy theories' relation to knowledge or the real, asserting that they "cas[t] satiric suspicion on everything, even [their] own pronouncements" (2). Both Latour and Knight suggest that conspiracy theories as forms of reading enact a breakdown of the signification process, hobbling the possibility of a collective, sustained meaning that spans ideological chasms.

17 John C. Hawley's collection *Postcolonial, Queer: Theoretical Intersections* was one of the first efforts to examine and compare insights from these two methodologies. As a basic starting point, Hawley observes that one obvious commonality between the two fields is an interest in where boundaries lie (8).

18 Hawley identifies the anti-essentialism of queer theory as one of the ways it distinguishes itself from gay and lesbian studies (3).

19 A "symptomatic" reading seeks to reveal what a text cannot say rather than what it does say. This stake in the unsaid and unsayable prompts Heather Love to characterize "symptomatic" reading as "depth hermeneutics" (383). Love and many others, including Bruno Latour in "Why Has Critique Run Out of Steam?" and Eve Kosofsky Sedgwick in "Paranoid Reading," also argue that the dominance of the "depth hermeneutics" or "paranoid reading" positions the critic so that s/he is the only one who can see through ideological subterfuge.

20 Latour worries about the appropriation by the political right of the critical methodologies that rely on "symptomatic" readings. The ability to call into question the "facts" of global climate change, for instance, illustrates to Latour the bankruptcy of this methodology (226–7).

21 Safia Bibi's conviction was eventually overturned. See Charles H. Kennedy's "Islamic Legal Reform and the Status of Women in Pakistan" for a detailed discussion.

22 I develop the connections between heteronormative masculinity and power below in my discussion of Ali's dual roles as conspirator and conspiracy theorist.

23 Major Kiyani, the ISI agent responsible for interrogating Ali, kills the Secretary-General right before Ali's eyes (225). His death can be read in two ways: either Major Kiyani wanted to demonstrate to Ali how much power he has, or the Major needed to kill the Secretary-General because he was a plant, a part of the larger conspiracy, which I discuss below, in which Ali finds himself enmeshed.

24 In some instances, Zaki makes explicit that he's retelling a story he's heard, as when he relays the story of his great aunt, Chhoti: "Daadi told the story of Chhoti's life one afternoon…" (46). At other times, he reasserts his narratorial voice jarringly. A third person narrator relays the bulk of the fourth chapter, which presents Zakia's biography up to the point when she gives birth to Zaki. After ninety-five per cent of the chapter unspools in this way, Zaki abruptly re-establishes his narratorial control: "Two months later, in the curtained ward of a Karachi hospital she gave birth to me: I was born into a world of prior absences that became lacks in my childhood" (135). Zaki's explicit re-insertion of his first person perspective in the narrative begs questions about how he knows what has already been relayed under the cover of a putatively distanced third person narrator. Similar questions arise late in the novel after much of the sixteenth unfolds through a third person perspective only to have Zaki once again—though more subtly—show from where the flashback comes (371).

25 Noman eventually confesses to Zahoor that he's responsible for the warnings (142), but the assassination plot is already in motion by that point.

26 At Amal's wedding, which takes place after this scene, Noman works through ways to describe how Junayd attends to Zahoor: "Junayd hovers, smoothly blending into the crowd while keeping an eye on Zahoor. I'll never have any one that devoted to me. At least ten years younger and always reverent, tonight Junayd assumes an authority over Zahoor that's almost fatherly. No, daughterly. No, wifely" (337). This short adverbial catalogue crystallizes how Junayd and Zahoor's relationship blurs boundaries, while also highlighting Sedgwick's point regarding the continuum between male homosocial and male homosexual bonds ("Between" 588).

27 Amal ponders her grandfather's attachment to Noman. She wonders, for instance, if the younger man "[i]s the grandson Nana never had?" (143). Alternatively, Amal thinks, Noman's appeal may be simply in Zahoor's desire to "spite his foes by welcoming one of their offspring" (143). Without any access to Zahoor's thoughts, these questions remain unanswered.

5: Karachi

1 "Muhajir," a term meaning "migrant," has a specific Islamic resonance, as it is used in reference to the first Muslims who accompanied the Prophet on his journey from Mecca to Medina. Spelling of the term varies: either "muhajir" or "mohajir."

2 For discussions of Karachi's lack of preparedness, see A. Khan, "Pakistan's Sindhi Ethnic Nationalism," Sayantan Dasgupta's "A Class Apart," and Moonis Ahmar's "Ethnicity and State Power in Pakistan."

3 Nichola Khan identifies a similar set of considerations as intermittently encompassed by the dominant interpretive frameworks used to analyze Karachi (226). Her own work, however, challenges any overly structural interpretive impulses, which, in N. Khan's view, "collapse political rhetoric into an extemporalization of *conditions* that may equal neither motivation nor intention" (226).

4 These four texts represent a selection of a broader field of Karachi novels, which challenges Hamida Khuhro and Anwer Mooraj's claim that the city "has inspired very little in that quarter" (viii).

5 I see Soja's "megacity" and Steve Inskeep's conceptualization of Karachi as an "instant city," which I cite later, as apt characterizations of the changes that are continuously producing Karachi. While there's no arguing that the city's infrastructure has kept up with the rate of change nor that the state itself has provided the necessary support for the city's growth, I do, nonetheless, see a distinction between the types of change "megacity" and "instant city" call to mind and that which Patricia Yeager refers to with her term "overurbanization." For Yeager, "overurbanization" is "urbanization without industrialization," or, put another way, "grow[th] without the benefit of a supporting economy and without the jobs and services the West associates with the metropolis" (14). The crucial difference in terms resides in economic activity; as I discuss later, Karachi, despite all its troubles, is economically vibrant, providing a mean standard of living well above that of the rest of Pakistan.

6 According to Ahmar, the MQM—later the Muttahida Quami Movement—was formed in 1984 (1033). In Ahmar's view, this group's recourse to an "ethnic" identity ran counter to their own proclivities, which leaned toward an overarching Pakistani nationalism. But, as Ahmar contends, "circumstances forced them to seek their identity on ethnic lines" (1033). Sarah Ansari substantiates Ahmar's claim when she observes that the use of an ethnic identity narrative by the MQM "suggests that Pakistan has fallen considerably short of its original aim of providing a homeland for the subcontinent's Muslims irrespective of their origins" (91). Put in the terms of my overarching focus, Ansari's argument identifies the wedge that comes between the idea of Pakistan and the collective identities that emerge in Karachi.

7 In "The Indigenization of English," Robert Baumgardner locates the coining of the phrase "kalashikov culture" in the 1980s (65).

8 Ahmar points out that Karachi "generates about 60% of Pakistan's total revenues" (1039), thus elevating the average standard of living significantly above that of other urban and rural dwelling Pakistanis.

9 This Karachi is surely the "mythological origin" to which Verkaaik refers (68–9), as I cite above.

10 Tim Creswell makes a similar point: "Some mobilities *are* acts of freedom, transgression and resistance in the face of state power which seeks to limit movement, police boundaries and inscribe order in space. It would be a mistake however to think of mobilities as in anyway essentially transgressive" (21).

11 According the Khalid B. Sayeed, The Defense of Pakistan Rules were formulated by Ayub after the 1965 war with India. These rules placed "restrictions on the holding of meetings or processions, and on carrying firearms and other weapons, for periods up to two months. Under the Defense of Pakistan Rules, Rule 32 was used to detain

persons who were deemed likely through their activities to threaten the security of the country, and Rule 47 to detain those who had committed 'prejudicial acts' (speeches or publications, etc.)" (100). This type of historical specificity characterizes the narrator's diatribes and stands in contrast to the undifferentiated stuckness Zahid experiences as part of the novel's larger allegory.

12 See Sayantan Dasgupta's "A Class Apart" for, as the title suggests, a reading of Shamsie's novel sensitive to class concerns, including how language factors into such divisions. Both Caroline Herbert and Bruce King focus more heavily on ethnic issues in the novel.

13 Elsewhere, I've similarly attempted to bring both class and ethnicity to bear on my reading of *Kartography*. See *National Identities in Pakistan*, Chapter six. In that chapter, I also explore the novel's preoccupation with 1971, arguing that the war's resonance in the novel's present highlights complicity. For my present purposes, I'm altering the terms of my analysis to point out how the novel questions the very validity of paralleling different moments in Pakistan's history.

14 See pages 241, 242, 248–9 for variations on this theme. Maheen, Karim's mother, also speaks to the question of historical parallels (273).

6: The Zamindari System

1 The zamindar's intermediary function changes, I argue, as the landowner comes to wield authority alongside if not above the state, as I discuss below.

2 Often cited as one of the most important early scholars concerned with gossip, Max Gluckman indentifies the discourse as a way to gauge social relations (315).

3 Social scientists and literary critics alike argue both sides of gossip's moral standing. Gluckman, an anthropologist, values gossip for its ability to secure group cohesion. Feminists from across disciplines see gossip as the disempowered's way of undercutting authority. Patricia Meyer Spacks's volume, *Gossip*, takes this stance and is probably the most important examination of gossip in women's literature. For more on gossip's moral status, see Hazel Smith and Susan E. Phillips.

4 My reading of the extension of the zamindari class's privilege and authority to include the likes of Ozi and his father, arguably representatives of a new Pakistani elite that benefits from contemporary globalization, counters Paul Jay's argument, which finds the novel "problematic for its failure to draw a link between colonialism in South Asia, Western capitalism, and contemporary forms of globalization" (56). Ozi's induction into the zamindari realm creates this link, since, as I discuss above, the zamindari system was a cornerstone of British colonial rule.

5 Daru cries a lot but never actually names what he's doing. After he gets fired from the bank, for instance, Daru describes his shock, but it's his boss who tells him to "'stop crying'" (*Moth* 23). Similarly oblique, Daru describes his reaction to Mumtaz's ending their affair: "I go inside and sit down and wipe my face, but no matter how much I wipe, it seems to stay wet" (*Moth* 229). All of these examples suggest Daru's emotional instability.

6 The other stories mostly favor the dependents' perspectives.

7 As the volume progresses, the stories cover several decades from the late 1970s to the early twenty-first century.

8 On this point, see Forest Pyle's "Raymond Williams and the Inhuman Limits of Culture," especially page 261.

9 March-Russell prefers "cycle" to "sequence," seeing the latter as restricting openness more than the former. "Cycle" allows March-Russell to invoke frame narratives, such as *A Thousand and One Nights*, which permits a reading of "cycle" as "concentric" rather than "cyclical" (107).

7: 9/11

1 Shaila Abdullah's 2009 novel, *Saffron Dreams*, stands as the counter example to the other Pakistani novels I'm discussing in this chapter. While Abdullah's story features the migrancy trope and an absence that pre-dates 9/11, it incorporates both in a much more conventional manner. The protagonist herself is the migrant figure, and her primary goal is to assimilate into American culture. Her husband, a waiter at Windows on the World, dies in the attack, thus allowing the novel to present the experience of 9/11 as a trauma not unlike the type present in much post-9/11 American fiction. In Abdullah's fiction, a good and proper mother offers a way through trauma.

2 See, for example, Anne Keniston and Jeanne Follansbee Quinn's "Introduction" and Peter Morey's "'The Rules of the Game Have Changed.'"

3 Similarly, John N. Duvall and Robert P. Marzee argue that myopic approaches "occlud[e] connections to, and knowledge of, transnational political affiliations, not to mention the long and continuing history of planetary terrorism" (394).

4 David Simpson's "Telling It Like It Isn't," Robert Eaglestone's "'The Age of Reason Was Over...'," and Richard Gray's *After the Fall* all argue this point.

5 Jopi Nyman also makes this point about the "impurity" of the migrant (10).

6 In "Migrating from Terror," Margaret Scanlon argues that, through Changez's migrant experience, Hamid's novel "revise[s] the West's vision of itself as a haven for the oppressed, a fortress of secular reason besieged by a fanatical Orient, whose latest representatives are migrants bearing bombs and contagion" (267). My argument certainly aligns with Scanlon's insofar as it reads the migrancy trope as upending convention. Our discussions part ways, though, when my analysis shifts its focus to Pakistan as Changez's affective center.

7 Leerom Medovoi goes a step farther, arguing that *The Reluctant Fundamentalist* "invert[s] the immigrant narrative by having the protagonist explain why he *left* the US" (645; emphasis in original).

8 In addition to the examples I discuss in this paragraph, Changez also compares the impressiveness of Underwood Samson's headquarters in a fancy Manhatten skyscraper to the majesty of the Himalayas (*Reluctant* 33-34). He notes, too, that "while the ancestors of those who would invade and colonize America were illiterate barbarians," his own civilizational forebears "had cities that were laid out on grids and boasted underground sewers" (*Reluctant* 34). Although "ashamed" at the present disparities between the two nations, Changez's long historical comparison also suggests the need for a history that would help contextualize each location's transitions.

9 This part of my argument connects to Rajini Srikanth's in that, like her, I refocus the affective impulses on Pakistan in relation to its South Asian neighbors as much as in relation to the US. Given our shared interests in considering how Hamid's novel engages with competing South Asian nationalisms, Srikanth and I both extend Hart and Hansen's assertion that the Pakistani nationalism operating in the narrative relates exclusively to that of the US (509-10).

10 Sajjad's mother refers to Pakistan as "'Muslim League nonsense,'" something Sajjad teases her about but doesn't explicitly disagree with (*Burnt* 52).

11 See Ahmed Gamal's "The Global and the Postcolonial in Post-Migratory Literature" for a comparative discussion of *The Reluctant Fundamentalist* and *Burnt Shadows*. One particularly striking parallel Gamal identifies between the two novels involves how both Changez and Raza function as janissaries for the American Empire (9).

12 Pascal Zinck also makes the point about Raza's being trafficked.

Bibliography

Abrams, Philip. "Notes on the Difficulty of Studying the State." *Journal of Historical Sociology* 1.1 (1988): 58–89.

Abdullah, Shaila. *Saffron Dreams*. Ann Arbor, MI: Modern History Press, 2009.

Adey, Peter. "If Mobility is Everything then It is Nothing: Towards a Relational Politics of (Im)mobilities." *Mobilities* 1.1 (2006): 75–94.

Aguiar, Mariam. "Making Modernity: Inside the Technological Space of the Railway." *Cultural Critique* 68 (2008): 66–85.

Ahmar, Moonis. "Ethnicity and State Power in Pakistan: The Karachi Crisis." *Asian Survey* 36.10 (1996): 1031–48.

Alam, Javed. "The Composite Culture and its Historiography." *South Asia* 22 (1999): 29–37.

Ali, Kamran Asdar. "Communists in a Muslim Land: Cultural Debates in Pakistan's Early Years." *Modern Asian Studies* 45.3 (2011): 501–34.

——. "Progressives and Perverts: Partition Stories and Pakistan's Future." *Social Text* 108 (2011): 1–29.

Ali, Tariq. *The Book of Saladin*. London: Verso, 2008.

——. *Night of the Golden Butterfly*. London: Verso, 2010.

——. *Shadows of the Pomegranate Tree*. London: Verso, 1992.

——. *The Stone Woman*. London: Verso, 2000.

——. *A Sultan in Palermo*. London: Verso, 2005.

Ansari, Sarah. "Partition, Migration, and Refugees: Responses to the Arrival of *Muhajirs* in Sind during 1947–48." *Freedom, Trauma, Continuities: Northern India and Independence*. Eds. DA Low and Howard V. Brasted. New Delhi: Sage, 1998. 91–103.

Ashraf, Saad. *The Postmaster*. New Delhi: Penguin, 2004.

Aslam, Nadeem. *Season of the Rainbirds*. London: Faber and Faber, 1993.

——. *The Wasted Vigil*. Canada: Bond Street Books, 2008.

Aydemir, Murat. "Introduction: Indiscretions at the Sex/Culture Divide." *Indiscretions: At the Intersection of Queer and Postcolonial Theory*. Ed. Murat Aydemir. Amsterdam: Rodopi, 2011. 9–30.

Bakhtin, Mikhail. *Speech Genres and Other Late Essays*. Trans. Vern W. McGee. Austin: University of Texas Press, 1986.

Balibar, Etienne. "The Nation Form: History and Ideology." *Review* 13.3 (1990): 329–61.

Baumann, Michael. "Rational Fundamentalism? An Explanatory Model of Fundamentalist Beliefs." *Episteme: A Journal of Social Epistemology* 4.2 (2007): 150–66.

Baumgardner, Robert J. "The Indigenization of English in Pakistan." *English Today* 6.1 (1990): 59–69.

Bayly, CA. *Empire and Information: Intelligence Gathering and Social Communication in India, 1780–1870.* Cambridge: Cambridge University Press, 2000.

——. "Knowing the Country: Empire and Information in India." *Modern Asian Studies* 27.1 (1993): 3–43.

Beachler, Donald. "The Politics of Genocide Scholarship: The Case of Bangladesh." *Patterns of Prejudice* 41.5 (2007): 467–92.

Belliapia, KC. "The Elusive Classic: Khushwant Singh's *Train to Pakistan* and Chaman Nahal's *Azadi.*" *The Literary Criterion* 15.2 (1980): 62–73.

Birchall, Claire. *Knowledge Goes Pop: From Conspiracy Theory to Gossip.* Oxford: Berg, 2006.

Bhalla, Alok. "Moral Action in Times of Duragraha: The Representation of the Sikhs in Partition Fiction." *Social Scientist* 34.5–6 (2006): 104–31.

Bhutto, Benazir. *Reconciliation: Islam, Democracy, and the West.* New York: Harper Perennial, 2009.

Bilgrami, Shahbano. *Without Dreams.* New Delhi: HarperCollins, 2007.

Boehmer, Elleke. "Afterword: Belated Reading." *Colonial and Postcolonial Literature: Migrant Metaphors.* 2nd edn. Oxford: Oxford University Press, 2005.

——. *Colonial and Postcolonial Literature: Migrant Metaphors.* 1st edn. Oxford: Oxford University Press, 1995.

——. "Postcolonial Writing and Terror." *Postcolonial Writing and Terror: A Concise Companion.* Eds. Elleke Boehmer and Stephen Morton. Hoboken, NY: Wiley-Blackwell, 2009. 141–50.

Boes, Tobias. "Modernist Studies and the *Bildungsroman*: A Historical Survey of Critical Trends." *Literature Compass* 3.2 (2006): 230–43.

Brooks, Peter. *The Melodramatic Imagination: Balzac, Henry James, Melodrama, and the Mode of Excess.* New Haven, CT: Yale University Press, 1976.

Castle, Gregory. "Coming of Age in the Age of Empire: Joyce's Modernist Bildungsroman." *James Joyce Quarterly* 40.4 (2003): 665–90.

Chambers, Claire. "A Comparative Approach to Pakistani Fiction in English." *Journal of Postcolonial Writing* 47.2 (2011): 122–34.

Cilano, Cara. *National Identities in Pakistan: The 1971 War in Contemporary Pakistani Fiction.* London: Routledge, 2011.

Coady, David. "Are Conspiracy Theorists Irrational?" *Episteme: A Journal of Social Epistemology* 4.2 (2007): 193–204.

——. "Conspiracy Theories." *Episteme: A Journal of Social Epistemology* 4.2 (2007): 131–4.

Cohen, Stephen, and Marvin G. Weinbaum. "Pakistan in 1981: Staying On." *Asian Survey* 22.2 (1982): 136–46.

Cole, Sarah. "Dynamite Violence and Literary Culture." *Modernism/Modernity* 16.2 (2009): 301–28.

Crane, Ralph J. "Inscribing a Sikh India: An Alternative Reading of Khushwant Singh's *Train to Pakistan.*" *Alternative Indias: Writing, Nation and Communalism.* Eds. Peter Morey and Alex Tickell. Amsterdam: Rodopi, 2005. 181–96.

Cresswell, Tim. "The Production of Mobilities." *New Formations* 4.3 (2001): 11–25.

Crownshaw, Richard. "Deterritorializing the 'Homeland' in American Studies and American Fiction after 9/11." *Journal of American Studies* 45.4 (2011): 757–76.

——. "Perpetrator Fictions and Trans-Cultural Memory." *Parallax* 17.4 (2011): 75–89.

Daiya, Kavita. *Violent Belongings: Partition, Gender, and National Culture in Postcolonial India*. Philadelphia, PA: Temple University Press, 2008.

Das, Veena. "For a Folk-Theology and a Theological Anthropology of India." *Contributions to Indian Sociology* 18.2 (1984): 293–9.

Dasenbrock, Reed Way. "Tariq Ali's *Islam Quintet*." *British Asian Fiction: Framing the Contemporary*. Eds. Neil Murphy and Wai-chew Sim. Amherst, NY: Cambria, 2008. 11–32.

Dasgupta, Sayantan. "A Class Apart: A Reading of Two 'Karachi' Novels by Kamila Shamsie." *Journal of the Department of English* 32.1–2 (2005): 299–313.

DeRosa, Aaron. "Analyzing Literature after 9/11." *Modern Fiction Studies* 57.3 (2011): 607–18.

Didur, Jill. "Fragments of Imagination: Re-thinking the Literary in Historiography through Narratives of India's Partition." *Jouvert* 1.2 (1997): 27 pars. 5 December 2009. <http://english.chass.ncsu.edu/jourvert/vli2/DIDUR.HTM>.

——. *Unsettling Partition: Literature, Gender, Memory*. Toronto: University of Toronto Press, 2006.

Dhulipala, Venkat. "Rallying the *Qaum*: The Muslim League in the United Provinces, 1937–1939." *Modern Asian Studies* 44.3 (2010): 603–40.

Dooley, Gillian. "Attitudes Toward Political Commitment in Three Indian Novels: *Kanthapura*, *Train to Pakistan*, and *Rich Like Us*." *Littcrit* 20.2 (1994): 30–9.

Duvall, John N., and Robert P. Marzee. "Narrating 9/11." *Modern Fiction Studies* 57.3 (2011): 381–400.

Eaglestone, Robert. "'The Age of Reason was Over…an Age of Fury was Dawning': Contemporary Fiction and Terror." *Terror and the Postcolonial: A Concise Companion*. Eds. Elleke Boehmer and Stephen Morton. Hoboken, NJ: Wiley-Blackwell, 2009. 307–28.

Edelman, Lee. *No Future: Queer Theory and the Death Drive*. Durham, NC: Duke University Press, 2004.

Felski, Rita. "After Suspicion." *Profession* 8 (2009): 28–35.

Francisco, Jason. "In the Heat of Fratricide: The Literature of India's Partition, Burning Freshly." *The Annual of Urdu Studies* 11 (1996): 227–50.

Gamal, Ahmed. "The Global and the Postcolonial in Post-Migratory Literature." *Journal of Postcolonial Writing* 14 June 2012 <http://www.tandfonline.com/doi/abs/10.1080/17 449855.2012.698638> 3 July 2012.

——. "Rewriting Strategies in Tariq Ali's Postcolonial Metafiction." *Postcolonial Text* 6.4 (2011): 1–19.

George, Rosemary Marangoly. "(Extra)Ordinary Violence: National Literatures, Diasporic Aesthetics, and the Politics of Gender in South Asian Partition Fiction." *Signs* 33.1 (2007): 135–58.

Ghosh, Papiya. "Reinvoking the Pakistan of the 1940s: Bihar's 'Stranded Pakistanis'." *Studies in Humanities and Social Sciences* 2.1 (1995): 131–46.

Gilmartin, David. *Empire and Islam: Punjab and the Making of Pakistan*. Berkeley, CA: University of California Press, 1988.

——. "Living the Tensions of the State, the Nation and Everyday Life." *Beyond Crisis: Re-Evaluating Pakistan*. Ed. Naveeda Khan. London: Routledge, 2010. 521–30.

Girdhari, VT. "Historical Text, Human Context: A Study of *Train to Pakistan*." *Khushwant Singh: The Man and the Writer*. Ed. RK Dhawan. New Delhi: Prestige, 2001. 82–7.

Gluckman, Max. "Gossip and Scandal." *Current Anthropology* 4.3 (1963): 307–16.

Gray, Richard. *After the Fall: American Literature since 9/11*. Malden, MA: Wiley-Blackwell, 2011.

Gopal, Priyamvada. *The Indian English Novel: Nation, History, and Narration*. Oxford: Oxford University Press, 2009.

Hai, Ambreen. "Border Work, Border Trouble: Postcolonial Feminism and the Ayah in Bapsi Sidhwa's *Cracking India*." *Modern Fiction Studies* 46.2 (2000): 379–426.

Hamid, Mohsin. *Moth Smoke*. New York: Picador, 2000.

——. *The Reluctant Fundamentalist*. Canada: Anchor, 2007.

Hanif, Mohammed. *A Case of Exploding Mangoes*. New York: Vintage, 2008.

Hansen, Thomas Blom. "Melancholia of Freedom: Humor and Nostalgia among Indians in South Africa." *Modern Drama* 48.2 (2005): 297–315.

Harrington, Louise. "'The Train Nation': The Railway as a Leitmotif in South Asian Literature." *Transport(s) in the British Empire and the Commonwealth*. Eds. Michèle Lurdos and Judith Misrahi-Barak. Montpellier: Université Paul-Valéry, 2007. 289–307.

Hart, Matthew. "The Politics of the State in Contemporary Literary Studies." *Literature Compass* 6.5 (2009): 1060–70.

——, and Jim Hansen. "Introduction: Contemporary Literature and the State." *Contemporary Literature* 49.4 (2008): 491–513.

Hartnell, Anna. "In Post-9/11 America: Updike's *Terrorist*, Islam, and the Specter of Exceptionalism." *Modern Fiction Studies* 57.3 (2011): 477–502.

Hasan, Arif. "The Growth of a Metropolis." *Karachi: Megacity of Our Times*. Eds. Hameeda Khuhro and Anwer Mooraj. Oxford: Oxford University Press, 1997. 171–95.

Hashmi, Alamgir. "Pakistani Literature in English 1993 & 1994: A Critical Survey." *Revista Allicantura de Studios Ingleses* 13 (2000): 223–8.

——. "Pakistani Literature in English: Past, Present, and Future." *South Asia Bulletin* 10.2 (1990): 48–53.

Hawley, John C. "Introduction." *Postcolonial, Queer: Theoretical Intersections*. Ed. John C. Hawley. Albany, NY: SUNY University Press, 2001. 1–18.

Heins, Volker. "Critical Theory and the Traps of Conspiracy Thinking." *Philosophy and Social Criticism* 33.7 (2007): 787–801.

Herbert, Caroline. "Lyric Maps and the Legacies of 1971 in Kamila Shamsie's *Kartography*." *Journal of Postcolonial Writing* 47.2 (2011): 159–72.

Hilti, Gabriela. "'That Dangerous Supplement,' Intertextuality: Gossip as History in Michael Ondaatje's *Running in the Family*." *Henry Street* 7.2 (1998): 36–52.

Houen, Alex. "Novel Spaces and Taking Place(s) in the Wake of September 11." *Studies in the Novel* 36.3 (2004): 419–37.

Huyssen, Andreas. "Nostalgia for Ruins." *Grey Room* 23 (2006): 6–21.

Hyder, Syed Akbar. "Towards a Composite Reading of South Asian Religious Cultures: The Case of Islam." *Perspectives on Modern South Asia: A Reader in Culture, History, and Representation*. Ed. Kamala Visweswaram. Chichester, UK: Blackwell, 2011. 23–32.

Inskeep, Steve. *Instant City: Life and Death in Karachi*. London: Penguin, 2011.

Jaffrelot, Christophe. *A History of Pakistan and Its Origins*. Trans. Gillian Beaumont. London: Anthem, 2004.

——. "Introduction: Nationalism without a Nation: Pakistan Searching for Its Identity." *Pakistan: Nationalism without a Nation?* Ed. Christophe Jaffrelot. London: Zed, 2002. 7–48.

Jalal, Ayesha. "Conjuring Pakistan: History as Official Imagining." *International Journal of Middle East Studies* 27.1 (1995): 73–89.

——. "Inheriting the Raj: Jinnah and the Governor-Generalship Issue." *Modern Asian Studies* 19.1 (1985): 29–53.

——. "The Past as Present." *Pakistan: Beyond the Crisis State.* Ed. Maleeha Lodhi. NY: Columbia University Press, 2011. 7–20.

——. *The Sole Spokesman: Jinnah, The Muslim League and the Demand for Pakistan.* Cambridge: Cambridge University Press, 1994.

Jay, Paul. "The Post-Post Colonial Condition: Globalization and Historical Allegory in Mohsin Hamid's *Moth Smoke.*" *ARIEL* 36.1–2 (2005): 51–71.

Jinnah, Muhammad Ali. "On His Election as the First President of the Constituent Assembly of Pakistan." *Jinnah Speeches as Governor-General of Pakistan, 1947–1948.* Lahore: Sang-E-Meel, 2004. 17.

Johnson, Brian. "Language, Power, and Responsibility in *The Handmaid's Tale*: Toward a Discourse of Literary Gossip." *Canadian Literature/Littérature canadienne* 148 (1996): 39–56.

Jussawalla, Feroza. "Kim, Huck and Naipaul: Using the Postcolonial Bildungsroman to (Re)define Postcoloniality." *Links and Letters* 4 (1997): 25–38.

Kabir, Ananya Jahanara. "Cartographic Irresolution and the Line of Control." *Social Text* 27.4 (2009): 45–66.

Karmani, Sohail, and Alastair Pennycook. "Islam, English, and 9/11." *Journal of Language, Identity, and Education* 4.2 (2005): 157–72.

Katz, Tamar. "City Memory, City History: Urban Nostalgia, *The Colossus of New York*, and Late-Twentieth-Century Historical Fiction." *Contemporary Literature* 51.4 (2010): 810–51.

Kazimi, MR. *A Concise History of Pakistan.* Oxford: Oxford University Press, 2008.

Keddie, Nikki, Joe Stork, and Eric Hooglund. "Pakistan's Movement Against Islamization." *Middle East Report* 149 (1987): 40–1.

Keeley, Brian L. "Of Conspiracy Theories." *The Journal of Philosophy* 96.3 (1999): 109–26.

Keniston, Ann, and Jeanne Follansbee Quinn. "Introduction: Representing 9/11: Literature and Resistance." *Literature after 9/11.* Eds. Ann Keniston and Jeanne Follansbee Quinn. New York: Routledge, 2009. 1–15.

Kennedy, Charles H. "Islamization in Pakistan: Implementation of the Hudood Ordinances." *Asian Survey* 28.3 (1988): 307–16.

Kerr, Ian. "Representation and Representations of the Railways of Colonial and Post-Colonial South Asia." *Modern Asian Studies* 37.2 (2003): 287–326.

Khan, Adeel. "Pakistan's Sindhi Ethnic Nationalism: Migration, Marginalization, and the Threat of 'Indianization'." *Asian Survey* 42.2 (2002): 213–29.

——. *Politics of Identity: Ethnic Nationalism and the State in Pakistan.* New Delhi: Sage, 2005.

Khan, Ashfaq Ali. "English in Pakistan." *Explorations* 1.1 (1969): 1–8.

Khan, Naveeda. "Introduction." *Beyond Crisis: Re-Evaluating Paksitan.* Ed. Naveeda Khan. London: Routledge, 2010. 1–28.

Khan, Nicola. "Violence, Anti-Convention and Desire for Transformation amongst Pakistan's Mohajirs in Karachi." *Cultural Dynamics* 22.3 (2010): 225–45.

Khan, Sorayya Y. *Five Queen's Road.* New Delhi: Penguin India, 2009.

Khan, Uzma Aslam. *The Geometry of God.* Northampton, MA: Clockroot Books, 2009.

Khuhro, Hamida, and Anwer Mooraj, eds. *Karachi: Megacity of Our Times.* Oxford: Oxford University Press, 1997.

King, Bruce. "Kamila Shamsie's Novels of History, Exile and Desire." *Journal of Postcolonial Writing* 47.2 (2011): 147–58.

Knight, Peter. *Conspiracy Culture: From Kennedy to the X Files.* London: Routledge, 2000.

Kramer, Beth. "The Double Nature of the Love Triangle: Sedgwick, Greene, Achebe." *Indiscretions: At the Intersection of Queer and Postcolonial Theory*. Ed. Murat Aydemir. Amsterdam: Rodopi, 2011. 115–28.

Krishnaswamy, Revathi. "Mythologies of Migrancy." *ARIEL* 26.1 (1995): 125–46.

Lambert-Hurley, Siobhan. "Fostering Sisterhood: Muslim Women and the All-India Ladies' Association." *Journal of Women's History* 16.2 (2004): 40–65.

Latour, Bruno. "Why Has Critique Run Out of Steam? From Matters of Fact to Matters of Concern." *Critical Inquiry* 30.2 (2004): 225–48.

Lodhi, Maleeha, ed. *Pakistan: Beyond the Crisis State*. New York: Columbia University Press, 2011.

Love, Heather. "Close but not Deep: Literary Ethics and the Descriptive Turn." *New Literary History* 41.2 (2010): 371–91.

Luscher, Robert M. "The Short Story Sequence: An Open Book." *Short Story Theory at a Crossroads*. Eds. Susan Lohafer and Jo Ellyn Clarey. Baton Rouge, LA, and London: Louisiana State University Press, 1989.

Mahboob, Ahmar. "English as an Islamic Language: A Case Study of Pakistani English." *World Englishes* 28.2 (2009): 175–89.

Mahmood, Safdar. *Pakistan: Political Roots and Development, 1947–1999*. Karachi: Oxford University Press, 2000.

Malak, Amin. *Muslim Narratives and the Discourse of English*. Albany, NY: SUNY University Press, 2004.

Malik, Iftikhar. "Pakistan's National Security and Regional Issues: Politics of Mutualities with the Muslim World." *Asian Survey* 34.12 (1994): 1077–92.

——. "The State and Civil Society in Pakistan: From Crisis to Crisis." *Asian Survey* 36.7 (1996): 673–90.

——. "What is Wrong in Karachi?" *Economic and Political Weekly* 33.33–34 (15–28 August 1998): 2219–21.

Mamdani, Mahmood. *Good Muslim, Bad Muslim: America, the Cold War, and the Roots of Terror*. New York: Pantheon, 2004.

Maniruzzaman, Talukder. "Group Interests in Pakistan Politics, 1947–1958." *Pacific Affairs* 39.1–2 (1966): 83–98.

Mann, Harveen Sachdera. "'Cracking India': Minority Women Writers and the Contentious Margins of Indian Nationalist Discourse." *The Journal of Commonwealth Literature* 24.2 (1994): 71–94.

March-Russell, Paul. *The Short Story: An Introduction*. Edinburgh: Edinburgh University Press, 2009.

Mardorossian, Carine M. "From Literature of Exile to Migrant Literature." *Modern Language Studies* 32.2 (2002): 15–33.

Margolis, Stacey. "The Rise and Fall of Public Opinion: Poe to James." *English Literary History* 76.3 (2009): 713–37.

Marsden, Magnus. "Mullahs, Migrants and Murids: New Developments in the Study of Pakistan: A Review Article." *Modern Asian Studies* 39.4 (2005): 981–1005.

Marx, John. "Failed-State Fiction." *Contemporary Literature* 49.4 (2008): 597–633.

Mason, Jeffrey. "The Face of Fear." *Melodrama*. Ed. James Redmond. Cambridge: Cambridge University Press, 1992. 213–21.

Masroor, Mehr Nigar. *Shadows of Time*. Delhi: Chanankya Publications, 1987.

Medovoi, Leerom. "'Terminal Crisis?' From the Worlding of American Literature to World-System Literature." *American Literary History* 23.3 (2011): 643–59.

Metcalfe, Barbara D. "Preface: Islam in South Asia in Practice." *Islam in South Asia in Practice*. Ed. Barbara D. Metcalfe. Princeton: Princeton University Press, 2009. xvii–xxv.

Mohsin, Moni. *The End of Innocence*. London: Penguin, 2006.

Morey, Peter. *Fictions of India: Narrative and Power*. Edinburgh: Edinburgh University Press, 2000.

——. "'The Rules of the Game have Changed': Mohsin Hamid's *The Reluctant Fundamentalist* and Post-9/11 Fiction." *Journal of Postcolonial Writing* 47.2 (2011): 135–46.

Moretti, Franco. "The Comfort of Civilization." *Representations* 12 (1985): 115–39.

Mueenuddin, Daniyal. *In Other Rooms, Other Wonders*. New York: Norton, 2009.

Mufti, Aamir R. "Orientalism and the Institution of World Literatures." *Critical Inquiry* 36.3 (2010): 458–93.

Mukherjee, Ankhi. "'Yes, Sir, I Was the One Who Got Away': Postcolonial Emergence and the Question of Global English." *Etudes Anglaises* 62.3 (2009): 280–91.

Nasr, Vali. *International Relations of an Islamist Movement: The Case of the Jama'at-i Islami of Pakistan*. New York: Council of Foreign Relations, 2000.

Naqvi, HM. *Home Boy*. New York: Shaye Areheart Books, 2009.

Naqvi, Maniza. *A Matter of Detail*. Karachi: SAMA, 2008.

Nawaz, Ahmed Shah. "Introduction." *The Heart Divided*. By Mumtaz Shah Nawaz. Lahore: ASR Publications, 1990. vii–xi.

Nawaz, Mumtaz Shah. *The Heart Divided*. Lahore: ASR Publications, 1990.

Nehru, Jawaharlal. "Tryst with Destiny." <http://www.svc.ac.in/files/TRYST%20WITH%20DESTINY.pdf> 2 August 2012.

——, and Liaquat Ali Khan. "Agreement between India and Pakistan on Minorities." *Middle East Journal* 4.3 (1950): 344–6.

Ngũgĩ wa Thiong'o. "The Language of African Literature." *Postcolonialisms: An Anthology of Cultural Theory and Criticism*. Eds. Gaurav Desai and Supriya Nair. New Brunswick, NJ: Rutgers University Press, 2005. 143–68.

Nyman, Jopi. *Home, Identity, and Mobility in Contemporary Diasporic Fiction*. Amsterdam: Rodopi, 2009.

Oldenburg, Philip. *India, Pakistan, and Democracy: Solving the Puzzle of Divergent Paths*. London: Routledge, 2010.

Pabby, DK. "Theme of Partition and Freedom in Khushwant Singh's *Train to Pakistan* and Amitav Ghosh's *The Shadow Lines*." *Khushwant Singh: The Man and the Writer*. Ed. RK Dhawan. New Delhi: Prestige, 2001. 42–52.

Pande, Aparna. *Explaining Pakistan's Foreign Policy: Escaping India*. London: Routledge, 2011.

Phillips, Susan E. "Gossip and (Un)Official Writing." *Middle English*. Ed. Paul Strohm. Oxford: Oxford University Press, 2007. 476–90.

Prakash, Gyan. "Science 'Gone Native' in Colonial India." *Representations* 40 (1992): 153–78.

Pye, Gillian. "Comedy Theory and the Postmodern." *Humor: International Journal of Humor Research* 19.1 (2006): 53–70.

Pyle, Forest. "Raymond Williams and the Inhuman Limits of Culture." *Views Beyond the Border Country*. Eds. Dennis L. Dworkin and Leslie G. Roman. New York: Routledge, 1993. 260–74.

Qasmi, Ali Usman. "God's Kingdom on Earth? Politics of Islam in Pakistan, 1947–1969." *Modern Asian Studies* 44.6 (2010): 1197–253.

Rahman, Tariq. *A History of Pakistani Literature in English.* Lahore: Vanguard, 1991.

———. "Review." *World Literature Today* 68.1 (1994): 218–19.

Raja, Masood Ashraf. *Constructing Pakistan: Foundational Texts and the Rise of Muslim National Identity, 1857–1947.* Oxford: Oxford University Press, 2010.

Rastegar, Kamran. "Trauma and Maturation in Women's War Narratives: *The Eye of the Mirror* and *Cracking India.*" *Journal of Middle East Women's Studies* 2.3 (2006): 22–47.

Ray, Sangeeta. *En-Gendering India: Women and Nation in Colonial and Postcolonial Narratives.* Durham, NC: Duke University Press, 2000.

Richter, William. "The Political Dynamics of Islamic Resurgence in Pakistan." *Asian Survey* 19.6 (1979): 547–57.

Rizvi, Hasan-Askari. "The Civilization of Military Rule in Pakistan." *Asian Survey* 26.10 (1986): 1067–81.

———. "The Paradox of Military Rule in Pakistan." *Asian Survey* 24.5 (1984): 534–55.

Robinson, Francis. "Islam and Muslim Society in South Asia." *Contributions to Indian Sociology* 17 (1983): 185–203.

Rose, Jacqueline. *The Case of Peter Pan, or, The Impossibility of Children's Fiction.* Philadelphia, PA: University of Pennsylvania Press, 1992.

Rothberg, Michael. "A Failure of the Imagination: Diagnosing the Post-9/11 Novel: A Response to Richard Gray." *American Literary History* 21.1 (2009): 152–8.

Rushdie, Salman. "Introduction." *Mirrorwork: 50 Years of Indian Writing, 1947–1997.* Eds. Salman Rushdie and Elizabeth West. New York: Holt, 1997. vii–xx.

Sayeed, Khalid Bin. "Pakistan in 1983: Internal Stresses more Serious than External Problems." *Asian Survey* 24.2 (1984): 219–28.

Sayyid, S., and ID. Tyrer. "Ancestor Worship and the Irony of the 'Islamic Republic of Pakistan.'" *Contemporary South Asia* 11.1 (2002): 57–75.

Scanlon, Margaret. "Migrating from Terror: The Postcolonial Novel after September 11." *Journal of Postcolonial Writing* 46.3–4 (2010): 266–78.

Schechtman, Joseph B. "Evacuee Property in India and Pakistan." *Pacific Affairs* 24.4 (1951): 406–13.

Scott, Nick. "Storied Infrastructure: Tracing Traffic, Place, and Power in Canada's Capital City." *English Studies in Canada* 36.1 (2010): 149–74.

Sedgwick, Eve Kosofsky. "Between Men: English Literature and Male Homosocial Desire." *The Novel: An Anthology of Criticism and Theory.* Ed. Dorothy Hale. Malden, MA: Blackwell, 2006. 586–604.

———. "Paranoid Reading and Reparative Reading, or, You're So Paranoid, You Probably Think this Intro is about You." University of Helsinki <https://helda.helsinkfi/bitstream/handle/10224/3628/2001-12> 29 May 2012.

Sen, Asha. "Re-Visioning Bapsi Sidhwa's *Cracking India* in a Post-National Age." *Kunapipi* 31.3 (2009): 66–82.

Sethi, Ali. *The Wish Maker.* New York: Riverhead, 2009.

Shah, Bina. *The 786 Cybercafé.* Karachi: Alhamra, 2004.

Shaikh, Farzana. *Making Sense of Pakistan.* New York: Columbia University Press, 2009.

Shamsie, Kamila. *Broken Verses.* Orlando, FL: Harvest Books, 2005.

———. *Burnt Shadows.* New York: Picador, 2009.

———. *Kartography.* Orlando, FL: Harvest Books, 2002.

Shamsie, Muneeza, ed. *And the World Changed: Contemporary Stories by Pakistani Women.* New Delhi: Women Unlimited, 2005.

Sherman, Taylor C., William Gould, and Sarah Ansari. "From Subjects to Citizens: Society and the Everyday State in India and Pakistan, 1947–1970." *Modern Asian Studies* 45.1 (2011): 1–6.

Sidhwa, Bapsi. *Cracking India*. Minneapolis, MN: Milkweed, 1991.

——, and David Montenegro. "Bapsi Sidhwa: An Interview." *The Massachusetts Review* 31.4 (1990): 513–33.

Siddiqui, Ayesha. *Military, Inc.: Inside Pakistan's Military Economy*. London: Pluto, 2007.

Simpson, David. "Telling It Like It Isn't." *Literature after 9/11*. Eds. Ann Keniston and Jeanne Follansbee Quinn. New York: Routledge, 2009. 209–23.

Singh, Jagdev. "'Shadows of Time': A Saga of the Changing Pattern of Communal Relations." *Journal of South Asian Literature* 26.1/2 (1991): 253–66.

Singh, Khushwant. *Train to Pakistan*. New York: Grove, 1956.

Singh, Preeti, and Bapsi Sidhwa. "My Place in the World." *Alif* 18 (1998): 290–8.

Slagle, R. Anthony. "Queer Criticism and Sexual Normativity: The Case of Pee-Wee Herman." *Journal of Homosexuality* 45.2–4 (2003): 129–46.

Smith, Andrea. "Queer Theory and Native Studies: The Heteronormativity of Settler Colonialism." *GLQ: A Journal of Lesbian and Gay Studies* 16.1–2 (2010): 42–68.

Smith, Andrew. "Migrancy, Hybridity, and Postcolonial Literary Studies." *The Cambridge Companion to Postcolonial Literary Studies*. Cambridge: Cambridge University Press, 2004. 241–61.

Smith, Hazel. "The Erotics of Gossip: Fictocriticism, Performativity, Technology." *Textual Practice* 23.6 (2009): 1001–12.

Smith, James L. *Melodrama*. London: Methuen, 1973.

Smith, Rachel Greenwald. "Organic Shrapnel: Affect and Aesthetics in September 11 Fiction." *American Literature* 83.1 (2011): 153–74.

Soja, Edward W. *Postmetropolis: Critical Studies of Cities and Regions*. Oxford: Blackwell, 2000.

Soomro, Durdana, and Ghazala Hameed. *Bengal Raag*. Dhaka: Writers.ink, 2006.

Spacks, Patricia Meyer. *Gossip*. New York: Knopf, 1985.

Srikanth, Rajini. "South Asia and the Challenge of Intimacy in the 'Global War on Terror'." *South Asian Review* 28.1 (2007): 68–86.

Srinath, CN. "The Writer as Historical Witness: Khushwant Singh's *Train to Pakistan* and Chamal Nahal's *Azadi*." *The Literary Criterion* 25.2 (1990): 58–66.

Stierstorfer, Klaus. "Tariq Ali and Recent Negotiations of Fundamentalism." *Fundamentalism and Literature*. Eds. Klaus Stierstorfer and Catherine Pesso-Miguel. New York: Palgrave, 2007. 143–60.

Talbot, Ian. *Pakistan: A Modern History*. New York: Palgrave, 2005.

Tovares, Alla V. "Public Medium, Private Talk: Gossip about a TV Show as 'Quotidian Hermeneutics'." *Text and Talk* 26.4 (2006): 463–91.

Tuck, Donald. "Tagore's Critique of Living Religious Traditions as Dramatized in *Sacrifice*." *The Journal of Indian Writing in English* 7.2 (1979): 1–15.

van der Veer, Peter. "Syncretism, Multiculturalism, and the Discourse of Tolerance." *Syncretism/Anti-Syncretism: The Politics of Religious Synthesis*. Eds. Charles Stewart and Rosalind Shaw. London: Routledge, 1994. 185–200.

Vazquez, Jose. "Subverting the Bildungsroman in Postcolonial Fiction." *World Literature Written in English* 36.1 (1997): 30–8.

Verkaaik, Oskar. "At Home in Karachi: Quasi-domesticity as a Way to Know the City." *Critique of Anthropology* 29.1 (2009): 65–80.

Vermeule, Blakey. "Gossip and Literary Narrative." *Philosophy and Literature* 30.1 (2006): 102–17.

Versluys, Kristiaan. *Out of the Blue: September 11 and the Novel*. New York: Columbia University Press, 2009.

Walton, Gary. "The Utopian Limits of Conspiracy Theory Journalism." *Reconstruction* 7.4 (2007) <http://reconstruction.eserver.org/074/Walton.shtml> 28 May 2012.

Weinbaum, Marvin G. "Civic Culture and Democracy in Pakistan." *Asian Survey* 36.7 (1996): 639–54.

Weiss, Anita M. "The Historical Debate on Islam and the State in South Asia." *Islamic Reassertion in Pakistan: The Application of Islamic Laws in a Modern State*. Ed. Anita M. Weiss. Syracuse, NY: Syracuse University Press, 1986. 1–20.

Wenzel, Jennifer. "Remembering the Past's Future: Anti-Imperialist Nostalgia and Some Versions of the Third World." *Cultural Critique* 62 (2006): 1–32.

Williams, Hadyn Moore. "The Doomed Hero in the Novels of Khushwant Singh and Manohar Malgonkar." *Khushwant Singh: The Man and the Writer*. Ed. RK Dhawan. New Delhi: Prestige, 2001. 53–64.

Willmer, David. "Women as Participants in the Pakistan Movement: Modernization and the Promise of a Moral State." *Modern Asian Studies* 30.3 (1996): 573–90.

Wood, James. *How Fiction Works*. New York: Farrar, Strauss, and Giroux. 2008.

Yaqin, Amina. "Variants of Cultural Nationalism in Pakistan: A Reading of Faiz Ahmad Faiz, Jamil Jalibi, and Fahmida Riaz." *Shared Idioms, Sacred Symbols, and the Articulation of Identities in South Asia*. Eds. Kelly Pemberton and Michael Nijhawan. London: Routledge, 2008. 115–39.

Yeager, Patricia. "Introduction: Dreaming of Infrastructure." *PMLA* 122.1 (2007): 9–26.

Zaidi, S. Akbar. "Karachi: Prospects for the Future." *Karachi: Megacity of Our Times*. Eds. Hameeda Khuhro and Anwer Mooraj. Oxford: Oxford University Press, 1997. 383–93.

Zameenzad, Adam. *The 13th House*. London: Fourth Estate, 1987.

Zamindar. Vazira Fazila-Yacoobali. *The Long Partition and the Making of Modern South Asia: Refugees, Boundaries, Histories*. New York: Columbia University Press, 2007.

Zinck, Pascal. "Eyeless in Guantanamo: Vanishing Horizons in Kamila Shamsie's *Burnt Shadows*." *Commonwealth* 33.1 (2010): 45–54.

Ziring, Lawrence. *Pakistan: At the Crosscurrent of History*. Oxford: Oneworld, 2003.

——. "Public Policy Dilemmas and Pakistan's Nationality Problem: The Legacy of Zia ul-Haq." *Asian Survey* 28.8 (1988): 795–812.

Index

Added to the page reference 'n' denotes a footnote.